To Grandma
Love Janet

Prince Philip

By the same author

Documents in British Economic and Social History

British History 1760–1914

The Industrial Revolution

A History of Post-War Britain

Our Future Monarch, Prince Charles

The Queen Mother

British Social History 1760–1978

Prince Philip

Peter Lane

ROBERT HALE · LONDON

First published in Great Britain 1980

ISBN 0 7091 8590 1

Robert Hale Limited
Clerkenwell House
Clerkenwell Green
London, EC1R 0HT

Photoset by Kelly Typesetting Limited
Bradford-on-Avon, Wiltshire
and printed and bound in Great Britain by
Redwood Burn Limited
Trowbridge and Esher

Contents

List of Illustrations

PICTURE CREDITS

BBC Hulton Picture Library: 1, 3, 4, 5, 12, 14, 19, 21, 23, 29, 33; The Illustrated London News Picture Library: 2; Paul Popper Ltd: 6, 9, 10, 11, 24, 25, 36; The Associated Press Ltd: 7, 22; The Press Association Ltd: 8, 34, 38, 58; The Central Press Photos Ltd: 13, 27, 32, 57; The Imperial War Museum: 15; Keystone Press Agency Ltd: 16, 45, 46, 49, 50; Camera Press Ltd: 17, 26, 28, 30, 31, 39, 40, 41, 43, 44, 47, 53, 55, 62, 63, 64, 65, 66, 67; Syndication International Ltd: 20, 35, 37, 42, 48, 51, 52, 54, 56, 59, 61; Eric Hosking: 60; Fox Photos: 18.

Acknowledgements

I WISH TO THANK the following for permission to quote from copyright materal: The Rt Hon. David Ogilvie, thirteenth Earl of Airlie, for the extracts from *Thatched with Gold* by Mabell the Countess of Airlie; George Allen & Unwin Ltd for the extracts from *The Monarchy and its Future*, edited by J. Murray-Brown; Jonathan Cape Ltd, for the letter by Cecil King taken from *The Cecil King Diary, 1965–1970*; Collins Ltd, for the extracts from *Diaries and Letters* by Harold Nicolson (copyright reserved), and *Asquith* by Roy Jenkins; Constable & Co. Ltd, for the extract from *King George V* by Harold Nicolson (copyright reserved); William Heinemann Ltd, for the extracts from *The Reality of Monarchy* by Andrew Duncan; David Higham Associates Ltd, for the extracts from *The Little Princesses* by Marion Crawford; Hutchinson Publishing Group Ltd, for the extracts from *Majesty* by Robert Lacey; The Institute of Economic Affairs for the extracts from *The Coming Confrontation*; Michael Joseph Ltd, for the extracts from *Out on a Wing* by Sir Miles Thomas, *Margaret, Princess Without a Cause* by Willi Frischauer and *Biography of Prince Albert* by Reginald Pound; Longman Group Ltd, for the extracts from *Prince Louis, Admiral of the Fleet* by M. Kerr and *Philip, An Informal Biography* by Basil Boothroyd; Macmillan Ltd, for the extracts from *King George VI* by Sir John Wheeler-Bennett (copyright reserved), *The Blast of War* and *The Tides of Fortune* both by Harold Macmillan, and *A Measure of Understanding* by Anna Frederica; John Murray for the extracts from *A Good Innings* by Viscount Lee of Fareham; Murray Pollinger, Literary Agent, for the extract from *The Environmental Revolution* by Jon Tinker which first appeared in the *New Scientist* in January 1979; Oxford University Press for the extracts from *Whitehall Diary, Vol. 1* by Thomas Jones; A. D. Peters & Co. Ltd, for the extract from *The Memoirs of Lord Chandos*; Routledge & Kegan Paul Ltd, for the extract from *When the Queen was Crowned* by B. Barker; Weidenfeld & Nicolson for the extracts from *Chips: The Diaries of Sir Henry Channon*, ed. R. R. James.

I am very grateful for the help I received from the officers of the following societies and institutions: The Council for National Academic Awards; The Concrete Society; The Duke of Edinburgh Award Scheme; The Law Society; The Incorporated Liverpool School of Tropical Medicine; The Medical Commission on Accident Prevention; The Institution of Public Health Engineers; The Variety Club of Great Britain.

I also wish to thank the many people who wrote with their personal memories of HRH and in particular wish to acknowledge the valuable contributions made by Eric Bailey, William Beattie, Lily Caldecatt, L. G. Coombes, Mrs P. M. Davies, C. Edwards, Jon Elliott, Mrs Audrey Firth, JP, G. A. Hancock, Irene Huggett, Michael Joyce, R. H. Lilley, George Lovell, Mrs A. M. MacLean, R. L. Mackie, W. A. Magill, Mrs R. M. Mennie, Mrs J. Miller, Mrs B. Mills, K. A. Moorish, Eric Oates, R. Palmer, Mrs C. M. Pegg, Mrs Dorothy Pilborough, Mrs Sagar, Graham F. Shirley, B. Smith, Ivor Spencer, M. R. M. Thompson, Mrs L. Woolford.

I regret that a number of people gave me of their time and recollections only on condition that their names were not mentioned anywhere, but my thanks to these is none the less sincere.

Finally, I wish to thank my wife and children for their great patience during the two years during which this work was in preparation. In particular, I want to thank our youngest child for waiting so long to have this book dedicated to him—Gerard Hugh Mostyn.

Introduction

EARLY IN 1947 there was speculation in the British Press about the possibility of an engagement between the heir-apparent, Princess Elizabeth, and a young officer in the Royal Navy, Lieutenant Philip Mountbatten. Few of those who read these reports knew much about the "dashing young Viking"[1] although after his engagement and marriage in 1947 and his wife's accession to the throne in 1952, many would claim to have known a good deal about him. But how well, if at all, do we really know him even now—or his background, or the varying and conflicting forces that shaped him so that he was ultimately judged to be a fitting husband for a future queen?

During the last thirty years Prince Philip has earned a widespread reputation as an outspoken commentator on many aspects of British life. This, in turn, has made him a target for a good deal of criticism, only some of which has been orchestrated by the Beaverbrook Press. In Chapters 40–42 we will examine some of the Prince's comments and those of his critics.

But opposition to Prince Philip did not originate with his unfavourable remarks on British industry, Press attitudes to the environment or whatever. In Chapters 16–20 I show that there was strong opposition to the proposed marriage, while in Chapters 25–29 I examine the evidence that there was a deliberate policy to downgrade the Queen's husband. This, I show, was more than the frightened reaction of a traditional Establishment at the thought of a young, vigorous, able and ambitious consort. It was part of a long-standing campaign against the Battenberg family. This had driven Prince Louis from public life in 1914. It had attacked the work and reputation of his son, the flamboyant 'Dickie' Mountbatten, who had, they asserted, "given India away" in 1947. Prince Philip, grandson to Prince Louis and nephew of the late Earl Mountbatten, was an almost natural target for the Battenberg-haters.

It is a measure of his ability that he has risen above this criticism. But it has left its mark and helps to explain the way in which he has interpreted his role as the Queen's husband. He was, as we shall see, the first royal consort to have had an unroyal education (Chapters 11–14) and to have been allowed to pursue a career which entitled him to entertain the laudable ambition that he might emulate both his grandfather and uncle by becoming a high-ranking naval officer. He had to abandon that ambition in 1952. But the drive and energy which might have been devoted to a naval career was turned into other channels. He became much more than a decorative partner to an active and popular Queen. He has been a lively and devoted father, one of whose main aims has been the supervision of his children's education. In particular he was deeply concerned with the education of Prince Charles, our future king (Chapter 31).

So it is that in 1981 we are able to look not only back—to 1947, 1952 and 1977—but also forward to the future and the time when his son succeeds to the throne. For the influence of Prince Philip will be felt during that reign almost as strongly as it has been felt during the present reign. In 1981 Prince Philip reaches the age of sixty—an age at which many of us are given to looking back on our own past and looking forward to the future which will be the present for our children. This volume is an attempt to do just this in the case of Prince Philip; it is also a tribute to the hard work of a successful consort.

Part I

1921–1930

1

A Royal Genealogy

EARLY IN 1921 Lord Louis Mountbatten, then a lieutenant in the Royal Navy, received a letter from his sister, Princess Alice, the wife of Prince Andrew of Greece. She was waiting for her fifth child to be born in her Corfu home and reminded Lord Louis:

> If the child will be a boy, he will be sixth in succession to the Greek throne. As things are today, with [King] Alex[ander] dead, Tino [King Constantine] threatened by [Prime Minister] Venizelos, and [Princes] George and Andrew unacceptable, my son, if God wills, could become one day the King if Monarchy prevails.[1]

On the 10th January 1921, Princess Alice gave birth to her fifth child and only son, His Royal Highness Prince Philip of Greece. In Chapters 2 and 5 we will unravel some of the complexities involving Alexander, Tino and the rest and we will see that his mother's fears were fully justified. We will also see that Venizelos played a major part in her husband Andrew's future and ensured that her hope that her son might become King of Greece was never realized. She could not be expected to know that "one day" this son would marry the future Queen of England or that she herself would die at Buckingham Palace.

With arrogant simplicity the anxious yet hopeful mother named her son Prince Philip of Greece. He was to find the absence of a surname a problem at various times in his life. When he went to school in Paris a teacher asked him his name. "Philip," he answered. "But Philip what?" "Just Philip," a little confused by the question. "But you must have another name." "Philip of Greece," he replied.[2] It is understandable that some boys took this as a sign of "foreign arrogance" and mocked him for being "of Greece". Much later in life, in Sydney, Australia, he had great difficulty in hiring a car from a garage which refused to accept his simple "Philip" on the hiring form and became even more annoyed and suspicious when he amended the signature to read "Philip of Greece".[3]

But in spite of the title the infant Prince did not have a drop of Greek blood in his veins. His ancestors included Russian, German, English and

Danish princesses but no Greeks. Indeed, the genealogy of his family is so complex as to merit a book to itself, *The Mountbatten Lineage* compiled by Philip's uncle when, as Viscount Mountbatten of Burma, he was Viceroy of India in 1947. In *Roots*, Alex Haley chose to use the novel as a vehicle for the purpose of tracing his own genealogy. Viscount Mountbatten stuck to facts, which showed that almost all his ancestors—and Prince Philip's—had been kings, queens, emperors, grand dukes and princes.

In compiling his "proud probe"[4] Viscount Mountbatten relied heavily on his mother's knowledge of family history. She was one of Queen Victoria's many grandchildren. It was she who helped draw up the family tree with all its many branches. Indeed, so complicated was this tree that Viscount Mountbatten devised a system of codes—in letters and numbers—to help him, at least, to understand it. Tables 1–3 are based on Lord Mountbatten's researches which show all the signs of the German race's uneasy passion for genealogy and family trees.[5]

The Mountbatten tables trace the family history back only to 1851 when Prince Alexander of Hesse eloped with Julie Theresa von Hauke, the daughter of a Russian general. Alexander had served in the Russian army but in 1851, on hearing of this "unworthy" marriage, Tsar Nicolas I cashiered the independent-minded German Prince. His father, the Grand Duke of Hesse, was equally furious at his son's marriage to a non-royal female. "You expect us to have a 'Fraulein Hauke' in the family," he demanded.[6] The Empress of Austria, one of Prince Alexander's relatives, invited him to serve under her flag. Later, in 1862, following the death of his father, he returned to Hesse, now ruled over by his brother, Grand Duke Louis III. By this time his sister Marie's husband had become Tsar Alexander II of Russia and had restored him to his rank and rights in Russia. This still left him with a problem arising from his morganatic marriage—none of his children was allowed a royal title. The new Grand Duke solved this problem by granting his 'commoner' sister-in-law the title of Princess of Battenberg. Her heirs and their descendants were thus entitled to call themselves Princes and Princesses of the House of Battenberg. Prince Alexander's children could now use the title of Serene Highness.

Prince Alexander and Julie, Princess of Battenberg, had five children. The second, and the eldest son, was Louis, Prince of Battenberg (Chapter 7), the father of Princess Alice (Philip's mother) and Louis, the late Earl Mountbatten of Burma. Prince Louis's wife was Princess Victoria of Hesse, the daughter of Princess Alice, Queen Victoria's favourite daughter (Table 1). So Princess Alice of Greece was a great-granddaughter of Queen Victoria and a great-niece to Edward VII, a cousin to King George V and an aunt to Prince Albert, later King George VI.

As a footnote to this brief survey of the history of the Battenberg family, it is worth noting that in 1862 the Austrian, French, Russian and British governments invited Prince Alexander to become a candidate for the vacant throne of Greece. Bismarck, Chancellor of Prussia, vetoed this proposal because he suspected Alexander of being too sympathetic to Austria and Russia, Prussia's main enemies. So Alexander's candidature did not proceed. If it had, the subsequent history of the Battenberg family would have taken a different course and, for example, there would have been no Philip of Greece, although as Table 3 shows, the late Earl Mountbatten of Burma might have become King of Greece.

It seems surprising that, in 1862, anyone should have wanted to be King of Greece, a country which had won its independence from the Turks in 1832. The revolutionaries who had led the struggle against the Turks had invited Prince Otto, son of King Ludwig of Bavaria, to take the throne of the newly-independent country. For thirty years the King had tried to reconcile the conflicting interests of his people—who, on the one hand, wanted peace so that their country could develop, but who, on the other hand, dreamt of winning even more land from the Turks and restoring the one-time Greater Greece. During the Crimean War Otto gave in to the demands of the more warlike Greeks. Taking advantage of Turkey's difficulties, he approved a Greek invasion of Epirus and Thessaly and encouraged his people to think that they were embarking on a victorious march to Constantinople. Russia, Britain, France and Austria had other thoughts and forced the Greeks to withdraw. Some of the more ardent Greek nationalists blamed the unfortunate Otto for this humiliation. They organized a revolt in Athens and in 1862 Otto was forced to abdicate.

The Greeks, having driven out one king, immediately set out to look for another. They first offered the throne of their restless country to Prince Alfred, the Duke of Edinburgh, Queen Victoria's second son. The Queen refused to allow her son to risk Otto's fate. Instead she and her Prime Minister, Palmerston, suggested that the Greeks should offer their throne to Prince William of Denmark whose sister, Alexandra, had recently married the Prince of Wales, the future Edward VII. The Danish royal family is known to genealogists as the house of Schleswig-Holstein-Sonderburg-Glucksberg. Through their Glucksberg connection the family was related to the Romanovs who ruled Russia, so Prince William's candidature was also supported by the Tsar Alexander II.

Britain helped Prince William's chances by agreeing that, on his accession, Britain would restore to the Greeks the Ionian Isles. These islands had been granted to Britain at the Congress of Vienna in 1815 and, in 1862, were administered by a British High Commissioner stationed in Corfu, where Prince Philip was born in 1921.

On the 30th October 1863 Prince William of Denmark ascended the throne of Greece as King George I—hoping that, by taking the name of the patron saint of the country, he might win the sympathy of its people. Horace Rumbold, then British Chargé d'Affaires in Athens, was present when the eighteen-year-old King took his oath in the Athenian Assembly and wrote: ". . . he looked so young and artless that the experiment seemed to all of us questionable and, indeed, highly hazardous."[7] His ministers were the very politicians who had plotted Otto's downfall and were, in Rumbold's words, "steeped to the lips in treason". It is little wonder that the new King reminded them that he had "a portmanteau ready packed." He appreciated that he might well need to return hurriedly to his native Denmark.

And if life in Greece was politically uncertain, it was also materially and physically very poor. His Old Palace had been looted by the mob after Otto's departure; there was little heating and, as the new King's son, Prince Christopher remembered:

> . . . there was only one bathroom in the whole place, and no one had ever been known to take a bath in it, for the simple reason that the taps would scarcely ever run. . . . The cold of the Palace was almost unbearable. The wind whistled down the corridors and curled like a lash in and out of the lofty salons.[8]

In 1867 King George I offended his original patrons—the British—by taking Princess Olga of Russia as his wife and, in British eyes, firmly linking his country's future with that of Britain's major enemy. Princess Olga was not sixteen when she married King George I. As her son was to write:

> The bride was such a child that she brought a whole family of dolls with her to her new country. For the entry into Athens she wore a little dress in the Greek colours of blue and white, and the crowds in the streets shouted themselves hoarse in welcome. Her shy youth and beauty conquered their impressionable hearts that day, and through all the vicissitudes of our house, she at least never lost their love.[9]

As Table 2 shows, King George I and Queen Olga had seven children, the youngest of whom, Prince Andrew, was to marry Princess Alice of Battenberg and to be Prince Philip's father. So there were even more royal strands to weave into the complicated pattern making up the genealogy of this Prince Philip of Greece.

The future Queen Alexandra of Yugoslavia was born within weeks of Prince Philip of Greece, but as Table 2 shows, she belonged to a later generation, being the great-granddaughter of King George I whereas Philip is a grandson. In 1959 she wrote *Prince Philip: A Family Portrait*, basing the earlier part of her book on the recollections of "my eldest relatives".[10] It is this royal author who tells us that Prince Andrew of Greece first met Princess Alice of Battenberg at the Battenberg home in Darmstadt when he was about twenty and she, "blonde and beautiful and scarcely seventeen".[11]

Prince Andrew had courted Princess Alice at Darmstadt and, by letter, after he returned to Greece. In 1902 the young couple met again at the coronation of King Edward VII and Queen Alexandra. Princess Alice was a maid-of-honour to Queen Alexandra whose husband, King Edward VII, was a "doting great-uncle" to the beautiful Princess. He, it seemed, liked to run "his hands through Alice's soft ringlets, [declaring] bluffly that no throne in Europe was too good for her."[12] Because of her ancestry Princess Alice was bound by the terms of the Royal Marriages Act of 1772. This decreed that ". . . no descendant of His late Majesty George II . . . shall be capable of contracting matrimony without the previous consent of His Majesty, his heirs and successors . . ."[13]

When King Edward VII was asked to approve the proposed marriage he "raised an eyebrow at an unpromising match to a younger son of the . . . new Royal House of the Hellenes."[14] However, the King gave his consent, stipulating that the marriage should take place "according to the rites of the Protestant Church".[15]

The engagement was officially announced on the 5th May 1903. The Prince of Wales and his wife (the future King George V and Queen Mary) gave a dinner party at Marlborough House in honour of the newly-betrothed. King Edward, Queen Alexandra and members of the Battenberg, Greek and Danish royal families drank toasts to the young couple. Various members of the many royal and noble families to whom the Prince and Princess were related rallied round to help them overcome the problem of the Prince's relative poverty. The Tsar of Russia, for example, gave them £100,000, which represented much more in 1903 than it does today.

The wedding took place on the 9th October 1903 at the Battenberg home in Darmstadt. There were three ceremonies, one civil, the second Protestant and the third being a wedding according to the rites of the Greek Orthodox Church. It was a chance for all the many royal families to get together and the guest list justifies Lord Mountbatten's "proud probe" into his family history. Queen Alexandra, as Prince Andrew's aunt, also represented King Edward VII, the bride's great-uncle. Tsar Nicolas II and Tsarina Alexandra were present as uncle and aunt of the bride. Prince Andrew's parents, the King and Queen of Greece, sat among dozens of Russian grand dukes, the brother of the Kaiser of Germany, most of the minor royalty from all over Germany, Austrian archdukes, Danish and French princes and a party of Battenbergs which included a three-year-old boy who was to become Earl Mountbatten of Burma. By hindsight we know that most of these rulers were swept away in the aftermath of the First World War. But in October 1903 they seemed secure in possession of their positions and determined to enjoy themselves at the Andrew-Alice marriage.

After the solemnities of the triple wedding ceremonies the guests sat down to dinner in the Old Palace at Darmstadt. As the time passed, even the servants were sent away to allow the guests that much more freedom; grand dukes and princes acted as waiters. It was, wrote one of the guests, "more like a Bank Holiday on Hampstead Heath than a royal ceremonial".[16] When the time came for the young couple to leave for their honeymoon there was a stampede of royals, led by the Tsar of Russia. Armed with bags of confetti and satin shoes the royals ". . . went straight for the backs of the people. [The Tsar] . . . putting his head down, rammed them and gradually pushed his way through . . . and reached the street . . . where Princess Alice [was] bowing her acknowledgements to the cheering crowd. At this moment she received the contents of the full bag of rice, which he [the Tsar] had carried, followed by the satin shoe. Casting dignity aside, she caught the shoe and, leaning over the back of the carriage, hit [him] on the head with it, at the same time telling him exactly what she thought of him."[17]

She is alleged to have called the Tsar "a stupid old donkey"[18] and to have "returned such a violent torrent of words that [he] was left standing in the cobbled roadway helpless with laughter."[19] The future was to hold few opportunities for the Tsar to be so happy, nor, as the next two chapters will show, did the marriage and history of Prince Andrew and Princess Alice live up to the gaiety and success of the wedding day. If Prince Philip's ancestry is ancient and proud, it is also, as we shall see, one which has been clouded by family tragedy.

2

The Father—Prince Andrew of Greece

IN HIS FAMOUS ANALYSIS OF President Woodrow Wilson, Sigmund Freud attributed the President's love for singing to his affection for his father, a leader in the local church choir. But the famous psycho-analyst went on to argue that Wilson's aversion for smoking was due to his reaction against his father's affection for his pipe. The more cynical may see this as a case of having one's cake and eating it, or one of having an each-way bet on the only two runners in a race. But what Freud sought to prove—as if it needed much proof—is that a father has an influence on his child. In the case of Prince Philip it is certainly true that one of the potent influences in his life has been his father, whom he "adored".[1]

In later chapters we will see that father and son met only rarely after Prince Philip was aged seven. However, we will also see that he remained loyal to his memory of the "tall, genial, smiling gentleman, a very lovable [man]"[2] who "would give him advice, whenever it was sought, with a gentle gravity."[3] We will see that he was proud of his father's military record and that he went out of his way to assert that his own choice of a naval career was due, in large part, to a wish to imitate his father.[4] As he has grown older, he has come to look very much like his father—the thinning hair, the spare frame, the prominent nose and enquiring eyes. He has also come to share at least one of his father's aversions—towards politicians and their advisers. Indeed, it could be that this aversion was imbibed at his father's feet in his early years. Certainly he must have learned to dislike and suspect politicians after hearing from his mother about the way in which his father was treated by the Greek governments between 1909 and 1923.

Prince Andrew was born in 1882, the fifth son and youngest child of King George I of Greece. He was brought up in the Old Palace in Athens "with its wood fires and awful plumbing",[5] where lighting came from smoky oil lamps. His brother, Christopher, has written about their father's attempts to alleviate the austerity of the Palace:

> My father, although he was habitually strict enough to keep us in awe of him, was the best of playfellows and could generally be persuaded to lead the processions (of bicycles or roller-skaters) winding in and out among the pillars, and after him would come the whole family in order of seniority . . . We would start off in stately fashion until, often as not, we smashed into one another and came to earth in a tangled heap, some of us shrieking with laughter, others with the pain of bruises.[6]

Prince Andrew, like the rest of the family, spent much of his childhood in an English Elizabethan-style mansion on an estate of pine-woods and heather-clad hills at Tatoi at the foot of Mount Parnes. His father had bought this estate in 1871 so that the family could escape not only the austerity of the Old Palace but also the constant reminders of the swirling morass of Greek politics. Both Prince Christopher and Prince Andrew had happy memories of the times spent at Tatoi where they walked over the hills, hunted for deer, stag, boar and wolf, and rode in carriages through the pine-trees.

Whatever might have been the austerity of life at the Old Palace there is little doubt that foreign royals also liked to go there. When the future King George V was a midshipman in the Royal Navy he was on a world cruise which started in September 1879 and did not end until August 1882. On 11th May 1882 the *Bacchante*, on which he was serving, reached Piraeus, the port which serves Athens. Here he and his brother, Eddie, were welcomed by their uncle and aunt, King George and Queen Olga of Greece. The two princes spent ten pleasant days at Tatoi. King George V's biographer writes:

> Fond as he was of his uncle, the King of the Hellenes, and of his Greek cousins, it was Queen Olga especially whom he loved. Uncle Willy, in after years would write him long and frequent letters . . . His cousins, Prince Nicholas and Prince George, were also frequent correspondents. But throughout his boyhood and early manhood it was Queen Olga—

humorous, gifted and affectionate—who became for him almost a second mother.[7]

When the time came to board the *Bacchante* and to sail for home the young Prince George wrote:

> May 20th 1882. The Palace, Athens. We dined at 7.0. All very sad at dinner. At 8.30 we had to say goodbye to darling Aunt Olga and cousins. We all cryed [sic] very much, we have spent such a delightful time here. We went with Uncle Will on board the *Bacchante* in his steam launch. We talked with him in the cabin until nearly 1.0; then we had to say goodbye to him. I was so sorry, I cryed [sic] again. We then went to bed.[8]

In January 1888 he was again in Athens, staying for a few days with his uncle and aunt. Apparently, Queen Victoria objected to his too-frequent visits to his Greek relations, for in a letter to his mother the young Prince George complained:

> Why on earth should I not? Why may I not go and see Uncle Willy if you and Papa wish me to? It is the greatest bosh I ever heard.

His natural fear of his grandmother, Queen Victoria, caused him to continue:

> Please don't leave this letter lying about . . . as there are some things perhaps that I ought not to have said . . .[9]

During this visit the future King of England met his six-year-old cousin, Andrew. We shall see that they were to meet in other and less happy circumstances in later years.

In 1889 Prince Andrew, then aged seven, was present at two family weddings. His eldest brother, Constantine (the 'Tino' mentioned on page 17), married Princess Sophie Dorothea of Hohenzollern, the granddaughter of Queen Victoria and, more significantly, the sister to Kaiser Wilhelm II of Germany. This German connection was to have a major impact on the lives of the whole family. Later that year his eldest sister, Alexandra, married the Grand Duke Paul of Russia. The inter-marriages between the various members of this and other European families was to prove of great value later on when the Greek family was exiled. Prince Andrew and his children, including Prince Philip, could always find some kind of home in one or other of the many castles or châteaux in which their relations were living. These inter-marriages also meant that everyone at the Greek Court had to learn to speak a number of languages. As Prince Christopher wrote:

> My parents spoke German to one another and English to us children, except to my brother, Andrew, who flatly refused to speak anything but Greek. We spoke Greek in the nursery and schoolroom.[10]

Prince Andrew's stubborn insistence on speaking only Greek may be seen as part of his total commitment to the country of his birth. He did not see himself as a Danish Prince of German extraction who happened to be born in Greece. While he could not, nor would not wish to, disown his ancestry, he did see himself, at least in his earlier years, as a Greek Prince. This childhood preference for things Greek was strengthened by his father's decision that Andrew should train for a career in the Greek Army. To prepare him for that career the King imposed on the young Prince a strict upbringing. Each morning at six o'clock there was a cold bath and a simple meal. Lessons lasted from seven until nine, to be followed by physical training under German instructors. After lunch there were more lessons before an evening meal and bed at seven o'clock. The young Prince proved to be a very able pupil, applying a quick intellect and an enquiring mind to whatever he had to study. When he was fourteen he left home to attend the military school in Athens to be drilled and taught by German officers. When he was seventeen he started on the final part of his course before being commissioned. His private tutor throughout this part of his training was a Greek major, Panayotis Danglis, the inventor of a new type of mountain gun and an officer with a high reputation among ballistics officers throughout the world. Under his guidance Prince Andrew studied fortifications and artillery, military history and technology, geography and topography. Other tutors were brought in for other, less military-centred studies—in languages, mathematics and the like. It was a long and arduous programme which, reported Danglis, showed that "the tall Prince was a man of quick intelligence". On 14th May 1901 the Prince began three days of examinations before the Board of Examiners. Following his success at these tests he was commissioned as a subaltern in the Greek cavalry.

As part of his training Prince Andrew had been sent to Hesse to serve with the 23rd Dragoon Guards. It was at Darmstadt, the traditional home of the Grand Dukes of Hesse, that he first met Princess Alice of Battenberg. Following their marriage in 1903 he and Princess Alice made their homes in Athens, Tatoi and at Mon Repos on the island of Corfu. This villa is now one of the tourist 'sights'. It is a villa which, originally, was built for the former British resident governors of the Ionian Isles. It was handed over to the Greeks as part of the settlement whereby Prince William of Denmark became King George I of Greece.

Today, as in 1903, the villa is approached via a road twisting up the hill to a small entrance drive with its magnolia tree. Inside there is a large sunny hall and a wide staircase winding up to the upper floor. On the ground floor there is a sitting-room with French windows leading to the garden, and a room which was formerly Prince Andrew's study and a dining-room. On the first floor there are three bedrooms and on a second floor there are, today, other bedrooms which have been added since Prince Andrew and Princess Alice lived in the house. Outside there is a path down which one can scramble the two hundred yards or so to the sea. The gardens contain a wide variety of trees—orange and eucalyptus, cypress and olive, magnolia and wisteria. Given the climate and the type of weather normal in this region, life must have been very pleasant in Mon Repos.

Princess Margarita was born in 1905; Princess Theodora in 1906 and Princess Cecilie in 1911. All three girls, as well as a fourth sister, Sophie (born 1914), were to marry German princes which, as we shall see, complicated life for their only brother, Philip, who was born at Mon Repos in 1921.

While Princess Alice was making a home for their children in the various houses in which they lived throughout the year, Prince Andrew was pursuing his military career.

Between 1903 and 1909 he, along with his brothers, had to watch while their father, King George I, tried to accommodate two diametrically opposed influences in Greek public life. On the one hand there was the Military League, led by revolutionary-minded men such as General Pangalos and Colonel Plastiras. They and their followers were anxious to create a military dictatorship in Greece—either with or without the connivance of the King. On the other hand there were the politicians, led by Prime Minister Venizelos, who wanted to set up a republican form of government which would have meant the deposition of the King. If the King moved to try to halt the progress being made by Venizelos and his republican followers he would have offended those Greeks who, while not being republicans, were still democratically minded. If, on the other hand, he stood idly by and allowed the republican, democratic movement to grow in strength, he ran the risk of offending the more right-wing and powerful elements in Greek society and above all in the Greek Army.

In 1909 the Military League used its influence in the Army and at Court to compel Prince Andrew and his brothers to resign their commissions. This lessening of royal influence was welcomed by Venizelos and the Republicans. But, like the leaders of the Military League, Venizelos and his supporters were prey to the 'Great Idea' or the Greek dream. This had been fostered throughout the nineteenth century by, among others, the British for whom the poet Lord Byron wrote:

> The isles of Greece, the isles of Greece,
> Where burning Sappho loved and sung,
> Where grew the arts of war and peace,
> Where Delos rose and Phœbus sprung.

For Byron and other Philhellenes, Greece was the birthplace of democracy which deserved to be restored to its former glory. It seemed fitting to many Greeks that once again a Greek government should hold Constantinople as once their Emperor Constantine had and that Asia Minor should again become part of a Greek Empire.

Prime Minister Venizelos had been born on the island of Crete but had become a victim to the 'Great Idea'. Between 1908 and 1912 Turkey was wracked by internal dissension and revolution. Turkey's difficulties became Greece's opportunities. In 1912 Venizelos formed the Balkan League consisting of Greece, Serbia, Montenegro and Bulgaria. While the Italians waged war against Turkey in Tripoli, the forces of the Balkan

League attacked "the unspeakable Turk". They captured Adrianople and forced the Turks to sue for peace.

In the autumn of 1912, Venizelos manoeuvred to get the countries in the Balkan League to declare war against Turkey. In September 1912 Prince Andrew stood on the balcony of the Old Palace holding the candle for his father to read the order for general mobilization to the milling crowds in the square below. The politicians and the officers of the Military League, faced with the prospect of sending an army against the Turks, immediately rescinded their previous decisions; Andrew, along with his other brothers, was restored to his rank in the officer corps. Indeed, when war was declared on the 8th October, the Crown Prince Constantine was Commander-in-Chief of the Greek Army, a strange reversal of fate dictated by military necessity. On the 10th November the Greek Army, led by Constantine, Prince Nicholas and Prince Andrew, marched into Salonica. In the previous month the royal princes had not only led their men to victory after victory over the demoralized Turks, they had also shared with their men the hardships of a war fought in mountain passes where communications were difficult and it was hard to maintain the supply lines. Along with their men they were often hungry and wet and found shelter as best they could in shepherds' huts and derelict churches.

On the 11th November King George entered Salonica in triumph. While not a ready prey to the disease of the 'Greek Idea' he shared his sons' pride at a job well done and at this evidence of their ability as military leaders. Unfortunately, there were many Greeks who did not believe that their King was an enthusiast for the cause of the Greek Dream. While he walked through the streets of Salonica he was shot by a Macedonian Greek.

Constantine succeeded to the throne, while the Greeks and their Allies in the Balkan League continued to make progress in the war against Turkey. The demoralized Turks, weakened by internal dissension and the war against Italy, were driven out of Macedonia and back towards Constantinople. The Turks sued for peace and at the Treaty of London in 1913 they ceded to the Balkan League almost all of what had been Turkey-in-Europe, retaining only a small strip of territory around Constantinople. But the members of the Balkan League fell out among themselves; the Bulgarians argued that they had played the largest part in the war and so deserved the largest share of the spoils. The Greeks claimed a historic right to Salonica, while the Serbs wanted an outlet into the Aegean Sea. Months of discussion were ended when the Bulgarians declared war on their erstwhile Allies. This gave the Turks a chance to recoup some of their losses for in the Treaty of Bucharest which ended this Second Balkan War, Turkey regained Adrianople, while Greece obtained Southern Macedonia, including Salonica. Part, at least, of the Greek dream—the 'Great Idea'—had been fulfilled.

3

Greek Politics, 1914–1922

BUT THE BALKANS continued to be the centre of international crises. Serbia wanted to extend her boundaries northwards to take in those Slavs who lived in Hungary, while the governments of the Austro-Hungarian Empire aimed at extending their boundaries southwards and at eliminating Serbia as a Power. Russia, itself a Slav state, felt obliged to support what it saw as the legitimate aims of Serbia, while Germany was allied to its neighbour, Austria, and promised to support her, 'as a knight in shining armour', should she move against Serbia.

On the day before Prince Philip's fourth sister was born, the Archduke Franz Ferdinand of Austria was shot and killed at Sarajevo in Bosnia. It is not part of this biography to examine the steps by which the various Powers reacted to this killing of the 28th June 1914. By the 4th August the forces of Germany and of Austria-Hungary were at war with those of Russia, France and Great Britain. The Turks, traditionally enemies to Russia, ultimately sided with the Central Powers and in November 1914 declared war on Russia and her allies.

King Constantine and his brothers were faced with a dilemma. On the one side there was Queen Sophie, formerly 'of Prussia', sister to the Kaiser who ruled in Germany. She was a strong-willed woman who, not unnaturally, urged her husband to side with the Germans. On the other hand the King's sister, Alexandra, had married a Grand Duke of Russia and exerted what influence she had with her brother to get him to side with her adopted country and its Allies in their fight against Germany. Constantine himself seemed to have been inclined to favour a declaration of support for the Germans, particularly after early German victories in Russia. His government, however, led by Prime Minister Venizelos, saw in yet another 'difficulty for Turkey', yet another 'opportunity for Greece' to extend its boundaries even further. A declaration of war against Turkey—and Germany—would, they argued, enable the Greek forces to continue that advance which had been halted by the Treaty of London in 1913. As if to provide support for this argument, the British Government, along with its Allies, let the Greek Government know that after the war there would be a division of Turkish spoils from which Greece would benefit, provided that she supported the Western and not the Central Powers.

Indeed, in August 1914 and again in March 1915, Venizelos offered to place Greek armies at the disposal of the Allies. His first offer was turned down because the British Foreign Secretary, Sir Edward Grey, was hoping to create a *bloc* of allies from among the Balkan countries and did not want to be seen to be picking up one or the other as separate allies. The second offer was rejected because Russia was unwilling to agree that Greek troops should be allowed to share in the expected triumphal entry into Constantinople. If the Greeks had their dreams, the Russians had theirs, which also centred on the occupation and annexation of parts of Turkey.

In March 1915 the Allied statesmen decided, reluctantly and half-heartedly, to try to force their way through the Dardanelles to open up a supply line to Russia and also to attempt to capture Constantinople. They hoped that this would bring the Balkan countries to join the Allies. Unfortunately, the Dardanelles campaign was a disaster as the Turks, led by Mustapha Kemal, proved an able enemy. Kemal's "inspired leadership"[1] proved as disastrous for Britain in 1915 as it was to be for Greece in 1922. Not only did the Allies fail to get through, but their defeat and withdrawal led Bulgaria to decide to join Germany in the hope that being on the winning side would help her make those gains which she had been denied in 1913. In September 1915 Bulgarian troops attacked Serbia. This brought into operation the Graeco-Serbian Treaty of Alliance. Venizelos immediately ordered the mobilization of the Greek Army, preparatory to a declaration of war in support of Serbia. King Constantine thereupon dismissed his Prime Minister and ordered a general election. Venizelos and his Liberal Party refused to take part in this election and the King was free to appoint a more sympathetic politician as Prime Minister.

Meanwhile the Allies, having lost their battle for the Dardanelles, used some of their forces to land in Salonica. They hoped to be able to go to the aid of the Serbians in their campaign against the German-supported Bulgarians. General Sarrail, the French Commander-in-Chief of Allied Forces, was anxious to protect his left flank from the possibilities of attack from Greece. Claiming rights under an International Convention of 1832 the Allies demanded that the Greek Army should be demobilized. The King refused to accede to this request.

This led to serious disturbances in Athens and other Greek cities. Venizelos and his Liberal-Republican supporters tried to prove that the King, under the influence of his wife and military advisers, was sympathetic to the Germans whereas the best interests of Greece lay in making war against Germany's ally, Turkey. The Government's secret police vied with Venizelos's henchmen in attacking politicians, journalists and other people in public life. Pitched battles were common and the streets of

Athens were frequently littered with dead bodies and the debris of the civil war.

In July 1916 Prince Andrew and his brother Nicholas were sent to London to explain their country's predicament and policy. While in England, Andrew met his wife's brothers—Prince George (later the second Marquess of Milford Haven) and Prince Louis (the late Earl Mountbatten of Burma) both of whom were serving in the Royal Navy. Neither Andrew nor his wife had any German sympathies. But while the two brothers were in Britain they were bitterly attacked by politicians and other spokesmen in the columns of the popular Press. The *Daily Mail* ran a hostile article under the headline "How Prince Andrew of Greece Repays our Hospitality". The article alleged that:

> Prince Andrew has been scheming with Colonel Metaxas, formerly of the Greek general staff and a prominent member of the Germanophile group, who had smuggled out information from Greece to Berlin, disclosing Allied troop movements . . . proof that the Greek princes have been intriguing behind the Allies' back is provided by letters intercepted by the British Secret Service.

One of Prince Andrew's last memories of wartime London was the newspaper placard with a headline "Tino's Treachery". During this visit the brothers went to see their cousin, King George V, and tried to assure him that the Greeks had no intention of helping the Germans. On his part the King insisted that on their return home they should "induce their brother, King Constantine, to 'see reason' ".[2]

On the 4th September 1916 King George V wrote a long letter to his Prime Minister about the Allies' conduct in Greece. In this he blamed the French for the way in which the Allies were interfering in Greece's internal affairs, exposing the King to the danger of appearing to be a puppet in their hands and so weakening his reputation among his people. He also wrote:

> Public opinion in Greece, as well as the opinion of the King, is evidently changing and if the Allies would treat her kindly and not, if I may say so, in a bullying spirit, she will in all probability join them.[3]

Unfortunately, the French seemed set on humiliating the King of Greece. At the end of December 1916 a Franco-British squadron commanded by a French Admiral arrived at the Piraeus and demanded that the King should, among other things, surrender to the Allies much of the Greek Army's equipment and material. On the 1st December a detachment of French and British marines landed to advance to Athens to collect this equipment. However, the Greeks resisted this interference with their country's internal freedom. There was a battle and the Allied forces had to withdraw. King Constantine sent a telegram to King George V arguing that the fighting had taken place because many Greeks believed that the Allies were acting as the spearhead for a projected landing by Venizelos's forces which would set up a republic. In reply

George V wrote of his "deep pain and concern" but also of "indubitable proof" of the Greek Government's pro-German actions and sympathies. The Greek King was told of the "deep and widespread indignation among my people" who continued to believe that King Constantine was, at best, an unsympathetic neutral or, at worst, an enemy.[4]

In August 1916 Venizelos and some of his followers had left Greece to set up a Provisional Government in Salonica under the aegis of the French-led Allied Forces. In return the King allowed his police to attack those Venizelists who had remained in Greece so stirring up unrest at home and confirming, in Allied eyes, his pro-German sympathies. By June 1917 Allied suspicions had turned to anger to the point that a powerful naval force was sent to the Piraeus and M. Jonnart, as High Commissioner, sent to demand the abdication of King Constantine. To give greater emphasis to this demand the Allied ships bombarded Athens, many of the shells falling around the Palace where Princess Alice and her daughters found shelter in the cellars.[5] On the 12th June 1917 Constantine abdicated and, with his wife and eldest son, left his country to live in Switzerland. Within a few weeks they were followed by other members of the Royal Family; Prince Andrew and Princess Alice and their children, Princes Christopher and Nicholas were all asked to leave. They, too, went into exile in Switzerland. Of these years of "hand to mouth existence"[6] Prince Christopher was to write:

> We lived in Switzerland for the next three years, spending our summers in Zurich and Lucerne and our winters at St Moritz . . . and existence with its daily worries over our ways and means. Our private incomes were stopped and we had to depend on borrowed money. As political exiles we were regarded as dangerous and suspicious characters and our friends could only visit us in the strictest secrecy for we were subject to a rigid espionage and had all our correspondence censored.[7]

This might have been the end of Greece for Prince Andrew and Princess Alice. If it had been, then Prince Philip would not have been born in Corfu and his life would have taken a different road. And there can be little doubt that the Allies were determined that this was to be the end of Greece for the ex-King Constantine and his family. On his abdication they had given the Crown not to his eldest son, Prince George—he was too closely associated with his father's policies—but to his second son, Alexander. Venizelos became Prime Minister and Greece declared war on Germany and Turkey just in time to reap the spoils of victory when the war ended in November 1918.

King Alexander was, for practical purposes, a mere puppet in the hands of the experienced Venizelos. Unfortunately, for the plans of that politician and his friends among Allied statesmen, Alexander died in 1920. He was on a visit to his vineyard keeper at Tatoi when his Alsatian dog was attacked by two pet monkeys. One of these bit the King as he went to help his dog. The bite proved fatal. Venizelos, already at war with Turkey in Anatolia, thought that the King's unexpected death provided him with the opportunity to bring the monarchy to an end and set up his Republic. He called a general election in which he offered the electorate the choice between him and his supporters—and a Republic—and the supporters of the former King Constantine, now exiled in Switzerland. Venizelos must have thought that he could not lose. But he did. And by a landslide. The new pro-monarchical government could hardly believe its own good fortune. Instead of immediately bringing the King back from exile, it allowed Venizelos another chance. It held a plebiscite in which the people were asked to vote for or against the restoration of Constantine. Venizelos received only ten thousand votes out of a poll of over a million.

Thus the King returned to a frenzied welcome from his people, in spite of Allied Notes which spoke of "great embarrassment" and his return as "a ratification by Greece of his hostile acts". And once again the other members of the family returned to their former homes in the Old Palace, Tatoi and Mon Repos. Prince Christopher, however, decided that there was no future for him in the uncertain world of Greek politics. He did not return to Greece. Having married Mrs Nancy Leeds, an American widow whose husband had made a fortune in the tin-plate industry, he decided to live in the USA and Europe. No one could have foreseen that Christopher's independence and wealth would be of great value to the family in the 1920s.

Writing about the death of King Alexander of Greece, Winston Churchill alleged: "A quarter of a million persons died of a monkey's bite."[8] If this claim is to be maintained it has to be proven that the subsequent war between Greece and Turkey, the defeats first of the Turks and then of the Greeks, each followed by murderous slaughter by the conquerors, were all due to a change of monarch. There is no evidence of this at all. In the short term the war between Greece and Turkey had its origins in the terms of the Treaty of Sèvres imposed on Turkey in 1920 by the Allied victors. During the discussions at Sèvres and elsewhere, Lloyd George had encouraged the Greeks to go to war against the defeated and demoralized Turks in order to gain part, at least, of that greater Greece which was the 'Great Idea'. Lloyd George, like a previous Liberal leader, Gladstone, had a deep contempt for the "unspeakable Turks" considering them an inferior race, unfitted to rule other people. Conservative members of Lloyd George's uneasy Coalition Government did not share this pro-Greek attitude. With India in mind they wanted a gentler treatment of the Muslim Turks in case the Muslims in India were roused against their British overlords.

But Lloyd George had his way. The Greeks received promises of British and French military aid. So it was that on the 15th May 1919 while Alexander still reigned, Venizelos ordered the Greek forces to move into war against Turkey, a decision later to be condemned by Prince Andrew as "always notable for the imbecility of its concept".[9] The initial stages of the Turko-Greek war seemed to support the optimism of Venizelos, Lloyd George and the French. Greek troops rushed to occupy Anatolia, including the ancient city of Smyrna, which was assigned to the Greeks by the Treaty of Sèvres on the 10th August 1920.

The restoration of King Constantine was taken by the French, in particular, but also by the British, as an unfriendly act. They used this restoration as an excuse to repudiate their obligations to Greece. The King and his government faced a double problem. On the one hand they were deprived of the economic and military assistance which they had been promised, and because of which Greece had felt able to embark on its Anatolian adventure. On the other hand, the King, still fresh to his throne, did not feel secure enough to order an end to the war which had been started to realize the 'Great Idea'.

While Lloyd George continued to try to provide at least diplomatic support for the Greeks, the French not only tore up their prior agreements with Greece but they actively turned to helping the Turks who, under the leadership of Mustapha Kemal, had begun to fight back.[10] The success of Mustapha Kemal's French-backed forces was as sudden as the advance of the Greeks had been in 1919 and 1920. By the middle of 1921 they had won several victories over Greek forces. At this point it was thought fitting that Prince Andrew should be restored to command one of these armies. He left Mon Repos a few days after the birth of Prince Philip.

In 1917 Venizelos had taken advantage of the abdication and departure of the Royal Family to dismiss over three thousand royalist officers from the Greek Army. To appoint these people to their old posts in 1920 and 1921 was not an easy business. There were the politically-appointed officers who now held high ranks. Were they to stand down? Or were the former officers to be appointed to some higher rank, over those who were now in charge? Prince Andrew had to face a good deal of opposition from some of his fellow officers when he went to the front to take command of an army.

In July, after only a month at the front, he wrote to the Commander-in-Chief, General Paulas, about a brigade which had been sent to join him:

> Its personnel was so ignorant that for days it was unable even to find the Division, in spite of my instructions. It was so untrained that in yesterday's action at Alpanos, in which the Division fought for six hours against a strongly entrenched force of 8,000 men, only four guns of one battery supported the attack. The brigade, during the whole of the action, was engaged in making endless reconnaissances, and when it did fire once, it fired at our own troops.[11]

By September 1921 Prince Andrew had become so sickened by the intrigues, slights, inept directions and incompetence that he faced from both senior and junior officers that he asked to be allowed to resign his command to return home to Mon Repos, his wife, daughters and infant son. In the final pages of his own book Prince Andrew recalled those three months in which he served with the army in Anatolia:

> For the first time after many centuries, since the time of the Byzantine rulers, a Greek King and a Greek Army trod the immense plains of Asia Minor. Full of eagerness, faith and self-sacrifice, the Greek soldier threw himself into the age-old struggle of his race—the struggle of civilization against Asiatic barbarism.
> The glitter of Greek bayonets was seen once more on the fields of Kiutahia and Eski-Shehr, on the Twin Mountains, on the shores of the Sakharia and in the Axylos desert. Gordium, Justianopolis, once more heard the shouts of Greek victory, the echoes reaching as far as Angora . . .
> Alas! the Greek soldier, who had strewn his bones during an entire decade in Macedonia and Epirus, in Thrace and in Russia, did not know that all his sacrifices were in vain; he did not know that there was a traitor in his ranks, who, jealous of the fame of his predecessor at Thermopylae, surpassed him in his efforts, and brought the Greek Army to the catastrophe of 1922 . . .
> Meanwhile our glorious dead lie by the side of their ancestors, the Hoplites of Alexander the Great and the Stratiotes of Heracles and Nicephorus Phocas, and the murmur of the waves of the Aegean bears to the Greek shores the re-echoing sounds of their message: 'O stranger, go, tell the Lacedemonians that here we lie, faithful to their orders.'[12]

On the 18th August 1922 Kemal's armies launched an offensive against the Greek armies in Asia Minor. The Greeks were heavily defeated. On the 9th September 1922 Prince Andrew's army was overrun and the Turks entered Smyrna in triumph. The Greek dream had turned into a nightmare. The Turkish forces drove on to the Dardanelles and to Chanak where a small British force under General Hartington stood between the Turks and the retreating Greeks. The British Government, under Lloyd George's influence, talked of declaring war on Turkey, but this idea received no support from Britain's former Allies, France and Italy. Nor did the British Dominions prove the submissive plants that they had once been. They all refused to support Britain if war broke out.

On the 27th September the unfortunate King Constantine once again packed his bags in the face of a revolution in Athens. He was replaced by his son as George II. The revolutionary government was led by Plastiras and Pangalos. It agreed that Prince Andrew should resign his commission and return to Corfu where he would be allowed to live, undisturbed, with his wife, daughters and infant son. Within a month, the British Coalition Government led by Lloyd George had fallen apart. Bonar Law, leader of the Conservative Party, wrote a letter to *The Times* in which he protested that "We cannot alone act as the policemen of the world", and argued that Britain ought to withdraw from Chanak, make a settlement with Mustapha Kemal and hope that the Greeks would be able to solve their own problems.[13]

Prince Andrew may have had a wry smile at the way in which British politicians came to grief over the Graeco-Turkish question. Certainly he was bitter about the way in which Greek politicians such as Venizelos and soldier-politicians such as Pangalos, had willed certain ends—the realization of the Greek dream—without being capable of providing the means needed to achieve those ends. He was even more bitter at the way in which, having failed, they tried to throw the blame for failure on one or other member of the Royal Family, exiling this one and that, calling Constantine back in 1920 only to throw him out again in 1922. Events of the next year or so were to make him even more bitter as the revolutionary government cynically broke the promises it had made him personally. This we will examine in Chapter 5. For the moment it is enough to see that if we want to find the causes of Prince Philip's jaundiced views of politicians, journalists and other fabricators of impossible dreams, then we might well start with the treatment meted out by such people to his father and, while he was still in a cot, to him personally. For Philip, as for Andrew, there is a crying need for people to apply their intelligence to any problem and to come up with a reasonable solution or set of solutions. Greek politicians between 1900 and 1922, like other politicians in other countries at other times, were well able to show their followers the 'Great Idea' but were unwilling to explain that this 'Idea' was incapable of realization without war, sacrifice and outside help. And the Greek Royal Family, pawns in the politicians' game, had to pay the major price for the latter's inability to deliver on their promises.

Chapter 4

The Mother—Princess Alice Battenberg of Greece

PRINCE ANDREW'S influence on Prince Philip was a mixed one. It was, to a great extent, a case of the son's loyalty to his father's memory and a determination on his part to show the royal world in which both of them moved that like his father the son, too, was able, courageous, intelligent and well-suited to be an officer in a fighting service. The father's influence was also a case of handing on some physical and intellectual traits—such as an impatience with people who cannot or will not carry out tasks for which they claim to be fitted. But at whatever level we look for the influence of the father on his son we have to conclude that it was one which was exercised, as it were, from afar. In later chapters we will follow the career of the father and see that Prince Andrew and Prince Philip rarely met after 1930, although, as we shall also see, Prince Philip often sought his father's advice and was anxious to prove himself to his absent father.

It is much easier to trace the influence of Princess Alice, his mother. She, after all, had the job of looking after him when his father was away at the Front during 1921 and 1922. It was she, more than the father, who organized their escape from Greece in 1922, as well as arranging for her brothers to care for Philip after 1930. She continued to be an influence throughout his life—during his naval career, his engagement, and his married life. It is perhaps symbolic of the difference between the influences of the two parents that Prince Andrew died, alone, in France in 1944 while his son was engaged in the war, whereas the mother died in Buckingham Palace in 1969 where she had lived for the last two years of her life with her son, daughter-in-law and grandchildren. And if Prince Philip has often seemed anxious to protect his father's memory, he has also always been assiduous in seeking to protect his mother from unsought publicity.[1]

Princess Alice Battenberg was born in Windsor Castle in 1885, the eldest child of Prince Louis of Battenberg who was serving in the Royal Navy. Her mother was Princess Victoria of Hesse, a granddaughter of Queen Victoria. Princess Alice spent most of her childhood in royal palaces—in Windsor, Kensington and Buckingham Palace. It is of some interest to historians that the Princess, with whom Queen Victoria often played, lived long enough to be the grandmother who, at Windsor and in Buckingham Palace, played with Prince Edward, the youngest of her own grandchildren.

She was born with a disease of the ear; thus she was almost deaf from birth and became increasingly deaf as she grew older. This meant that she had great difficulty with speech. For many years people thought that she was a deaf-mute and some biographers have described her as such. In fact, she taught herself to speak, albeit in an unnatural, deep voice. She also taught herself to lip-read so that she could communicate with the people around her. It is a reminder of the Tower of Babel in which she lived and moved that she had to learn to lip-read in French, German, and Greek as well as in her native English. It is for medical people to analyse the struggles which the Princess had to undergo in her continual attempts to come to terms with her difficulties. It is certain that these constant struggles gave her that drive which she handed on to her son. A friend is quoted as saying of their mutual stubbornness that she "was very much the mother of the son".[2] They also prepared her, from an early age, for the difficulties and hardships with which she was going to have to contend. It is perhaps not surprising that by the time Prince Philip was born in 1921 she was described by one writer as "somewhat eccentric".[3]

She was not always so. She had first attracted attention in 1893 when she was a bridesmaid at the wedding of the future King George V and Queen Mary. Her beauty had been a major reason why Prince Andrew courted her and finally won royal permission to marry her.[4] In 1908 a magazine reported: "The prettiest princess in Europe is said to be Princess Alice of Greece, the elder daughter of that popular naval officer, Prince Louis of Battenberg . . ."[5] And while a writer who never knew her felt entitled to describe her as "eccentric", those nearer to her spoke and wrote of her in a different vein. Queen Alexandra of Yugoslavia, a niece, wrote of "her warm sympathy and understanding . . . willing to give a mere child her full and undivided attention." She remembered her as a person who always seemed to be laughing, "profoundly religious", who had a fine sense of humour. The niece described her aunt as "forming phrases with a staccato emphasis that seemed to enrich them with a special significance." So much for the idea that she was a mute as well as deaf.[6]

Geoffrey Wakeford was a Court correspondent for a popular daily in the 1950s and 1960s. In his *Heir Apparent* he gives an account of the close relationship that existed between Princess Alice and her grandson, Prince Charles. In particular he gives an account of an Easter holiday which the Princess spent at Windsor in 1960 when Charles was home from Cheam School: ". . . she was nearly seventy-five but she was sympatico and Charles was devoted to her . . . From Greece she often sent him a stream of picture postcards bearing the latest Hellenic stamps . . . he . . . urged her to 'pretty well fill up the card with stamps and don't worry so much about the writing part'." Wakeford goes on to describe how she allowed him to play with her 'magic box' or hearing aid, and her handbag, "from which she could be relied upon to produce peppermint creams."[7] For Charles, at least, this was no eccentric, but a grandmother to be put on the same footing as those other grandparents of whom he was so fond—King George VI and Queen Elizabeth, now the Queen Mother.

From a very early age Princess Alice was "profoundly religious"[8]. It is possible that this was one way of seeking to sublimate her physical difficulties of hearing and speech. It is suggested by some writers that it was the result of the influence of her favourite Aunt, Ella, who had married Grand Duke Serge of Russia. After he had been assassinated, Princess Ella gave away all her money and property and founded a religious order for women who wanted to devote their lives to God and nursing the sick. Princess Alice, it is suggested, was so influenced by her aunt's example that she, too, was anxious to follow some sort of religious life. As the mother of four daughters, and, after 1921, a son, she was unable to do so. But when the older children had grown up and when Prince Philip had become very much the charge of her brothers, Princess Alice felt free to follow her own inclinations. She returned to Greece in the 1930s, mixed with the poor and helped to create a cottage industry specializing in Greek embroidery. She wore a religious-type garb of grey cloth with a nun-like headscarf. In 1949 after a Second World War which had seen her family once more torn as her sons-in-law fought on the German side while her brother, Lord Louis Mountbatten, and her son served in the Royal Navy, she finally 'gave up the world' to found a Christian Sisterhood of Martha and Mary.

But all that was far in the future. After her marriage to Prince Andrew she shared with him the pleasures and the discomforts of life at the Old Palace, Tatoi and, later, Mon Repos. While her husband followed his military career, at least until 1909, Princess Alice went to the School of Greek Embroidery, studying the complexities of this national folk-craft. The School had been founded by Lady Egerton, wife of the British Ambassador to Greece. Princess Alice became so proficient that in time she was able to help Lady Egerton and to become an instructress in her own right.

She also enjoyed the pleasures of visits to the many royal and noble families with which she was linked by that complex web of marriages which has been touched on in Chapter 1. There were visits to Germany, Russia, Rumania, and to her own native England where she visited her father whose naval career continued to blossom. He had a house in Spring Gardens, near Admiralty Arch, a suitable address for the man who was to become the most outstanding naval officer of his generation.

During the First World War, as we have seen, the Greek royal family was, at best, divided about the attitude which ought to be adopted towards the warring nations. King Constantine, her brother-in-law, was influenced by his German wife while Princess Alice, supported by her husband, took a pro-Allied line—not surprisingly in view of her nationality and the fact that her brothers were serving in the Royal Navy. Life in royal Athens must have been uncomfortable. Nor were things made any more pleasant by the reports she received from England of the accusation that the Greek King and his brothers—including her husband Andrew—were selling Allied secrets to the Germans. We have seen that she was at the Old Palace when the Allies shelled Athens in 1917 and that she went into exile with her husband in the same year. She shared the poverty described by Prince Christopher while the family lived in Switzerland. Nor were things much better when, with the others, she returned to Corfu and Mon Repos in 1920. She and Prince Andrew employed a Scottish housekeeper, Mrs Agnes Blower, whose husband was the gardener and odd-jobman. Mrs Blower told one author: "They did not live like royals" since everything in Mon Repos in 1920 was quite primitive. There was no electricity or gas, no supply of running hot water; when Princess Alice and her four daughters wanted a bath water had to be heated in buckets in the kitchen and carried upstairs.[9]

In September 1920, just after the family had returned from exile, Princess Alice surprised Prince Andrew with the news that she was pregnant. Her eldest daughter, Margarita, was now sixteen and her youngest, Sophie, was almost seven years old. We have seen that she wrote to her brother 'Dickie' of her hopes and fears for the future of her unborn child should it be a son. Her fears were hardly dimmed by the fact that her husband had to leave her with their daughters while he went to fight against the Turks. So he was not with her on the 10th June 1921 when Prince Philip was born.

Princess Alice recruited a British nanny, Miss Roose. Miss Roose had been nanny to the three daughters of Prince Nicholas of Greece, who later in life were better known as Marina, the Duchess of Kent, Olga, the wife of Prince Paul of Yugoslavia, and Elizabeth who became the Countess Torrington. Queen Alexandra wrote of "Roosie's" belief in things British—so that baby foods, woollen clothes and even soap were ordered out from England.[10] In his nursery Philip shared the austerity that was common in the house. There was little furniture, an old carpet and few toys.[11]

But from infancy Philip was 'trained' for travel. When he was only three months old his mother took him (and Nanny Roose) to London for the funeral of her father, Prince Louis, the first Marquess of Milford Haven. This gave the proud mother a chance to 'show off' her only son to her mother and to her brothers, George, the second Marquess of Milford Haven, and Louis, the late Lord Mountbatten, and to her sister, Louise, the wife of the future King of Sweden. During this visit Philip and his mother lived at Netley Abbey which is not far from Broadlands which later became Lord Louis's home and where Philip and Princess Elizabeth spent the first part of their honeymoon in 1947.

In July 1922 when her husband was still embroiled in the tangled web of the Graeco-Turkish war, Princess Alice took her son to London once again. This time she was a guest at the wedding of her brother, Louis, to the glamorous Edwina Ashley. Philip's four sisters acted as bridesmaids but the baby Philip was left in the nursery at Kensington Palace. He made no impact on the Mountbattens and the other members of the royal family, but his future and his relationship with his Mountbatten uncles was being determined by the events taking place in Asia Minor and Greece even while the marriage celebrations were taking place. Princess Alice, receiving reports of the defeat of the Army and the demands for the second abdication of King Constantine, hurried home to rejoin her husband. Little did anyone know that within weeks she, along with her husband and children, would once again be an exile.

5

The Escape from Greece—1922

THERE IS NOTHING UNIQUE in the claim that Prince Philip has inherited this or that physical or intellectual trait from his parents. This is true of all children. But the students and practitioners of the science of child-development assure us that heredity is not all, alleging that the events of the first few months and years of a child's life exert their own powerful influence over the way in which the child will develop. This belief was so strong in the 1950s, for example, and so many mothers read books by Dr Spock and other eminent child psychologists that cynics christened the generation of children born in that decade as the 'Spock-marked'. But there can have been few children whose first years were as disturbed as were Prince Philip's, and either he is the exception that proves the rule about the importance of those early years, or the child psychologists have got it all wrong.

Even while she was pregnant his mother had to suffer the anxiety of his father's recall to lead an army, the news that the war was going badly and the reports of political unrest which might affect her husband and the rest of the Greek royal family. When Prince Philip was about one year old, his father returned home, having refused, as we have seen, to be part of the débâcle. In September 1922 King Constantine was driven off the Greek throne by a Revolutionary Committee led by former generals. His son was appointed King George II. In October 1922 soldiers came to Mon Repos with a demand from the new Minister of War, Pangalos, that Prince Andrew should come immediately to Athens to give evidence at the trial for treason of three ex-Prime Ministers, two former Ministers of State and the ex-Commander-in-Chief of the Army, General Papulas. The Revolutionary Committee had previously told Andrew that he would not be disturbed in Corfu; no blame for the defeat was attributed to him. But now the summons came in terms so peremptory that the ineffectual Prince felt that he could do nothing but obey. Within a day or two of his departure, Mon Repos was placed under police surveillance.[1] Princess Alice, more of a realist than her husband, took this as the ominous proof that her husband had, in fact, been arrested and that she and the five children were being held under a form of house arrest as hostages—or future victims.

Prince Andrew had been taken from Corfu by destroyer to the mainland. Once in Athens he was, as Princess Alice feared, arrested on a charge of high treason and put into prison along with the other 'royal traitors'. His brother, Prince Christopher, was now a resident in the USA. In October 1922 the Greek Government had granted him a visa—for eight days—so that he could visit his family. It was quite fortuitous that this visit coincided with the fall of King Constantine and the rule of the Revolutionary Committee. He called on Princess Alice in Corfu, heard of her fears for Andrew's future and promised to do what he could. He went to Athens where Andrew was in prison. He wrote:

> No one was allowed to go near Andrew except his valet. Guards kept strictest watch and confiscated all letters and parcels. Finally I hit on the expedient of writing a letter on cigarette paper, rolling it tightly and putting it with cigarettes into his valet's case. Andrew answered with a short note, full of courage, but I knew that he had no hope of regaining his freedom.[2]

Christopher went to see King George II to ask him to use his influence to save his uncle. But the King, merely a puppet in the hands of the strong-minded leaders of the revolution, could do nothing. After the first trial on the 13th November six of the 'traitors' were shot by firing squads. The trial of Prince Andrew was fixed for the 2nd December. No one, least of all Prince Andrew, was in much doubt of the outcome of that trial. Indeed, as Christopher wrote:

> Andrew had just had a conversation with a former school-fellow, Pangalos, now Minister of War and instigator of his trial, that left him small grounds for optimism. "How many children have you?" Pangalos had asked suddenly, and when my brother told him, he shook his head: "Poor things, what a pity, they will soon be orphans."[3]

Andrew, it seemed, was to have only the semblance of a 'trial' before being shot.

But if Andrew seemed resigned to his fate and Christopher unable to persuade the King to intervene to save him, Princess Alice showed not only courage but that stubborn determination that was one of the characteristics she handed on to Prince Philip. She left the children in Corfu in the charge of their British nanny and went to Athens. She wrote letters to her brothers in London, to the Pope, to the King of Spain (who was married to one of her cousins) and to the President of France. All these rulers offered sympathy. Only in England was any action taken.

Princess Alice's youngest brother, Lord Louis, went to see King George V, a cousin with whom he had once served in the Royal Navy. He also went to see the Prime Minister, Bonar Law, who called in the Foreign Secretary, Lord Curzon. The upshot of this activity was a telegram sent by the Foreign Office to the British Legation in Athens:

> The King is most anxious concerning Prince Andrew. Please report on His Royal Highness's present position, and continue to keep us informed by telegram of any developments.[4]

Lord Curzon ordered Commander Gerald Talbot, a former Naval Attaché in Athens, to go to Greece to find out what was happening. If it were not for the fact that the issue was one of life or death, one might be inclined to treat the rest of the story as some sort of 1920s version of poor quality spy-fiction. Talbot wore a disguise and had false papers. He arrived in Athens on the morning of the 29th November. The British Legation in Athens sent a telegram to the Foreign Office:

> Private and secret. 29 November 1922. 8.30 p.m. There is no doubt that Prince Andrew's position has become much more dangerous since execution of Ministers and I hear his trial is to begin on November 30th. Mr G. Talbot, who arrived this morning after executions, is concentrating on saving Prince Andrew and I think he will have a better chance of succeeding than legation now that rupture of diplomatic relations has taken place . . .[5]

While Talbot was making his way to Athens, King George V, using his powers as Commander-in-Chief of Britain's Armed Forces, sent a message to the Admiralty asking that a cruiser be sent to Athens to help Talbot's mission of rescue. The cruiser, *Calypso,* was commanded by Captain H. A. Buchanan-Wollaston who piloted his ship into the Bay of Athens late on the night of the 29th November. At about the same time Talbot was in conference with Pangalos, whom he had known when he was working in Athens. In spite of all Talbot's pleas for clemency, Pangalos was insistent that Andrew had to die along with the rest of the 'royal traitors'. As he was making this point an assistant came into the room to tell him that a British warship was in the Bay, its guns pointing ominously skyward.[6] This news concentrated the mind wonderfully. Pangalos suddenly agreed that the Prince should be released. This allowed the Legation to send the following telegram:

> Private and most secret. 30 November 1922. 1.0 a.m. Most urgent.
> Mr Talbot has obtained this evening promise from Minister of War and also from Colonel Plastiras, the two leaders of government, that Prince Andrew will not be executed but allowed to leave the country in charge of Mr Talbot.
> Following is the arrangement agreed upon:
> Prince will be tried on Saturday and sentenced to penal servitude or possibly death. Plastiras will then grant pardon and hand him over to Mr Talbot for immediate removal with Princess by British warship to Brindisi or to any other port en route to England. British warship must be at Phaleron by midday December 3rd and captain should report immediately to Legation for orders, but in view of necessity for utmost secrecy, captain should be given no indication of reason for voyage. This promise has been obtained with greatest difficulty and Talbot is convinced that above arrangement be strictly adherred to so as to save Prince's life. As success of plan depends on absolute secrecy of existence of this arrangement even Prince and Princess cannot be given hint of coming. Talbot is convinced that he can rely on word given him and I see no other possibility of saving Prince's life.[7]

This was a strange reversal of the use of British naval power. In 1920 when

Constantine was sailing back from exile, the Admiralty had issued orders that the *Averoff*, in which he was travelling from Italy, should not be saluted on her passage by any ships of the Royal Navy. King George V had argued that this disregard for normal naval courtesy was unduly vindictive; at his request the Admiralty ordered that all British ships should be withdrawn from the route of the *Averoff* so that there was no need either for an acknowledgement or for commanders to follow the original order not to salute a sister ship.[8] Now, two years later, the British Navy was being used in what was to be one of the last examples of gunboat diplomacy. In 1850 Palmerston had used the might of the British Navy to compel the Greek Government to come to terms with Don Pacifico, a Spanish Jew, born in Gibraltar and therefore a British subject, who claimed that the Greek Government owed him compensation due for damages done to his property in Athens during an anti-Jewish riot. Many politicians, including Gladstone and Richard Cobden, had thought that Palmerston's action was immoral and high-handed. Defending himself from an attack in the House of Commons, Palmerston asked the House to decide:

> . . . whether, as the Roman in days of old, held himself free from indignity when he could say *Civis Romanus sum*; so also a British subject, in whatever land he may be, shall feel confident that the watchful eye and the strong arm of England will protect him against injustice and wrong.[9]

Andrew was unable to claim *Civis Brittanicus sum*; but Princess Alice was British and Andrew was a cousin of the King, George V, so perhaps the Palmerstonian belief in the need for protection extended to Andrew by proxy. In any event, George V was proud of the part he had played in the rescue of his cousin—and his family—from a violent end. In 1934 Prince Philip was at Buckingham Palace for the wedding of the Duke of Kent to Princess Marina of Greece. King George V came across the thirteen-year-old boy and remarked: "You're Andrew's boy."[10] No one could have foreseen in 1922 or in 1934 that the young Prince would have a closer relationship with the British Royal Family.

Pangalos was almost as good as his word to Talbot. The Prince was tried and sentenced to imprisonment, deprivation of rank and titles, banishment for life, and the loss of his Greek citizenship. The Court found him guilty of the ignominy of disobeying orders and abandoning his post. The sentence went on: "But consideration being given to extenuating circumstances of lack of experience in commanding a large unit, he has been degraded and condemned to perpetual banishment."[11] In 1970 documents on British foreign policy, 1919–1939, were being edited in preparation for publication. Among the documents involved were the telegrams concerning Talbot's venture and an account of the trial and sentencing of Prince Andrew. The editors sent copies of this material to the Queen's Private Secretary to ask whether there would be any royal objection to their publication. Prince Philip was consulted about this material. Loyal even at this late stage to his father's memory he jotted a comment asking that the Court's verdict should be deleted: "People might think it was true."[12]

After the Court had passed its vindictive sentence based on false accusations, Pangalos himself, with the *Calypso*'s guns in mind and occasionally in sight, personally took Andrew from prison during the night and drove him and Talbot to the ship where Princess Alice was waiting. The ship sailed to Corfu to pick up the five children and their Nanny, who carried Prince Philip in her arms.[13] On board the *Calypso* the officers gave up their cabins and the family crowded in. Prince Philip slept in an orange crate which the sailors had padded to save him from being hurt.

On the 6th December 1922 Captain Buchanan-Wollaston, commander of the *Calypso*, wrote to wish an aunt a happy birthday. In 1969 (by which time the former Captain was a retired Vice-Admiral, still alive at the age of ninety-one) this letter was sent to Prince Philip by a descendant of the aunt. In this letter he wrote:

> Little of interest has occurred to me since my last. The one thing interesting is our little voyage from which we are now returning. We were hurried off secretly to Phaleron Bay without an idea of the reason. We found on arrival we were to quietly slip off with Prince and Princess Andrew of Greece. He was possibly to be condemned to death as you will know, anyhow in danger of his life. Well, we slipped off all right and picked up their four daughters and baby son from Corfu next day . . . and disembarked them yesterday at Brindisi. Princess A. has two brothers in our Navy (she was a Battenberg). The Prince is delightful and so English, and I am quite in love with the youngest daughter aged 8. They were rather amusing about being exiled, for they so frequently are . . .[14]

The family travelled to London by easy stages, stopping off to pay a visit to the Pope. They went to stay at Kensington Palace, the home of Princess Alice's mother, the Dowager Marchioness of Milford Haven. She was the widow of Prince Louis of Battenberg and mother of Prince George and Lord Louis who were to play a large part in Prince Philip's future. But no one could have foreseen then, just how significant a part that was to be.

6

Life in Paris, 1923–1930

PRINCE PHILIP resents the common assumptions that "I'm a Mountbatten . . ." and that "I was brought up by Lord Mountbatten."[1] In later chapters we will see why these assumptions have become generally accepted. We will also examine some of the reasons for Prince Philip's wish to play down his link with the Mountbattens—other than that his mother was a Mountbatten. But a major reason for his objection to the erroneous belief that Earl Mountbatten ('Dickie') is his father is his continued wish to draw attention to his father's family. In part this is a normal filial piety. In part, however, it is due to the facts of the case. As he says, "I grew up much more with my father's family than I did with my mother's."

Prince Philip and his sisters spent the first few months of their exile in London while their parents went to America to visit Prince Christopher and his very wealthy American wife. On their return the family moved from London to make their home—they hoped a permanent one—in Paris. Here they relied on the help provided by another of Prince Andrew's brothers—Prince George. He had married Princess Marie Bonaparte, a great-granddaughter of Napoleon's brother, Lucien. She was very wealthy, her mother being Marie Blanc, the daughter of the founder of the Casino at Monte Carlo. It was Prince George and his wife, Marie, who provided Prince Andrew and his family with their Parisian home. At first they lived in a suite of rooms in a large mansion owned by Prince George. This mansion was on the rue Adolphe Ivan on the edge of the Bois de Boulogne. Like so many other royal homes it has been pulled down in the name of progress to make way for a huge apartment block. Their stay there was a brief one—either because the family found the quarters too cramped, or, more probably, because the cost of maintaining the suite was too much for the Prince who had no easy or regular source of income.

Prince George and Princess Marie lived in their own mansion on the rue de Mont Valerien, a very large property in extensive grounds at St Cloud. There was a lodge in the grounds, "a shoe-sized house causing no staff problems"[2] so that there was no need for a large staff of servants. Prince George offered his lodge to his brother and sister-in-law and it became their home for some years. Indeed, this is the house which Prince Philip recalls as his childhood home. Here he lived with his father, mother, sisters, Nanny Roose and a few faithful servants who had followed the family from Corfu and who worked for little more than their keep.

Prince Philip is therefore justified in calling attention to the part played by his father's family in his early years. Nor was it only a matter of a house. There were frequent visits to relatives in Germany and in particular to the Hesse family. There were holidays at Darmstadt where his parents had been married[3] and well-documented summers at their summer residence at Panka on the Baltic. His cousin, later Queen Alexandra of Yugoslavia, was only a few weeks older than Prince Philip. She has written almost lyrically about Panka with its trees and farm, its animals and the nearby sea where there was sand to be played with and pools to be fished with nets.[4]

And at Panka there was also the chance to meet more of those children and adults to whom he was related by the marriages of his uncles and aunts. It was at Panka that the five-year-old Philip learned how to escape from the bathroom while Nanny Roose was testing the water in the time-honoured way, with her elbow. The resulting chase of a near-naked Philip by an ageing Nanny, along the corridors of the mansion, in and out of dressing-rooms and bedrooms, seemed to have been enjoyed by everyone. Maybe it was the memory of this childhood fun which helped the father, Philip, to make bathtime a period of fun for his own children.[5]

Yet he had still not finished with his father's family. There were other periods of the summer to be spent at Cotrocene, the royal home near Bucharest, where his cousin, Michael of Rumania, was the same age as Prince Philip. And although he had become King of Rumania on the death of his grandfather, Ferdinand, it "made no difference to our play . . .".[6] At Cotrocene the three cousins—Philip, Michael and Alexandra—had their tricycles, climbed trees, swam in the lake which was near the house and learned to row small boats.

Sometimes while they were staying in Rumania the children would go to another of the royal houses on the Black Sea or to Sinaia, "high in the mountains . . . lovely!"[7] Here and at the Black Sea there were horses to be ridden. Michael was the more confident on horseback because he was "accustomed to it" whereas Prince Philip had had nothing to do with horses. However, it was Prince Philip who was the more at home with the sea which initially scared the King of the landlocked kingdom of Rumania.

And there were even visits to the birthplace of Corfu once Greece had settled its domestic affairs and once more restored the father's nationality and the family felt able to return 'home' again, if only for holidays. When they had first left Greece behind them they had been stateless. Prince

Andrew's cousin, King Christian X of Denmark, came to the family's rescue by issuing them with Danish passports. Prince Philip, although 'of Greece', had returned once again to his paternal ancestor's origin.

He would have known nothing of these diplomatic negotiations nor anything of their significance. He was too young to be concerned about the problems that his father faced with regards to money. For Prince Philip, and indeed, for his much older sisters, life in Paris, Darmstadt, Wolfsgarten, Langenburg, Salem, Sinaia, Bucharest, Corfu or at the Black Sea, as well as in London, was very pleasant. There were hundreds of relations to give the children care and attention, and, as the sisters explained, for the youngest child, Philip, there was the special care lavished on him by virtue of his being the youngest.[8] While there was not the vast retinue of servants that there might have been in Corfu or at the Old Palace, life was not "particularly unhappy . . . unsettled".[9]

But for the father there was the constant anxiety about money. King George V had been quite prepared to use his power to help rescue Andrew from danger of death. He was, however, quite unwilling to "pay for any extravagance Andrew might indulge in".[10] This was the statement of a man who was himself very thrifty and, perhaps, already aware of Andrew's penchant for high living. Andrew had lost whatever property he owned in Greece as well as his army pay. He received some help from Princess Alice's brothers—Prince George, the second Marquess of Milford Haven, and Lord Louis Mountbatten. But this help was only enough for the girls' education.[11] This was hardly surprising, for as we shall see, neither of these brothers were wealthy.

After some time Prince Andrew did manage to get some money from the rent of a farm in Greece of which he was part-owner. In January 1923 ex-King Constantine died and left his brother a small legacy. Prince George, enriched by the proceeds of the profits of the Casino at Monte Carlo, was a willing and welcome source of money, as was Prince Christopher. So there was enough money to pay for the children's schooling, for their travel to one or other of their relations for a holiday and for a modest establishment in the lodge at St Cloud. It was hardly a "hand-to-mouth existence" of which one author has written.[12] Nor was there any truth in the stories that Princess Alice opened a shop to try to make some money to help eke out the family's finances. She did, in truth, open a *boutique* which she named *Hellas*. Here she sold Greek embroideries, tapestries and antiques. Whatever small profit she made was devoted to the poor and needy, mostly Greek refugees who appealed to her for help.

But if there was enough money for essentials and for expensive schooling there was none of that "glory which had vanished" and, in relative terms, the family was poor. This did not prevent Philip's parents enrolling him in the MacJannet Country Day and Boarding School at St Cloud where the fees were very high—but paid by US-based Christopher. In a sense there was some justice in this—since the school was a progressive kindergarten founded by an American teacher, Donald MacJannet. He had gone to France to study the French language. While there he saw a need for an American school to cater for the needs of the sons and daughters of diplomats and others interested in giving their children an English education. MacJannet had previously taught at the National Cathedral School in Washington. He drew on this experience when he started his own school which quickly recruited the children of ambassadors and other prominent people.

In 1927 Princess Alice brought her son, Philip, to meet MacJannet. She explained that she wanted him to be educated in an Anglo-Saxon school because "I hope that my son will have his future in an English-speaking country."[13]

Most of the teachers were Americans and it is hardly surprising that Philip picked up an American accent. He had learned English from Princess Alice who had also taught him to read, although when he entered the MacJannet school he was "unable to write a word".[14] He was also proficient in German which he had learned from his father and which he practised on his frequent visits to his German relatives. Within a short time he had acquired a third language—French, the result of living in Paris for about seven years. While his proficiency in languages may have been of only marginal value to him as a naval officer, it has been of great value to him as the Queen's husband, making him that much more fit for the task of helping her in her contacts with overseas visitors.

From August 1929 Philip was taught by a young English teacher, Catherine Pegg, the Principal of the Lower School. Catherine Pegg had taught at Birkenhead before teaching in London, where she took a post as governess to a Finnish boy whose family lived most of the time in Berlin. Here she met Nicholas Levitsky, a Russian refugee whom she married. When the Levitskys went to live in Paris Catherine found employment at the MacJannet school.[15]

In November 1947 when Prince Philip's engagement was announced, Mrs Levitsky was living in the United States. She wrote a long article for the *Christian Science Monitor* recalling her experiences in the Paris school where she taught the young Prince Philip.[16]

> One sunny morning in April 1929 I found myself facing for the first time a class of small American boys. It was Grade III of a well-known American school for boys in St Cloud, the pretty suburb of Paris. The school was housed in three buildings, situated in a pleasant garden shaded by enormous old elm trees (which gave the school the name of The Elms). The house in which the faculty and boarders lived had been at one time the home of Jules Verne and was full of exciting associations for boys.
>
> Although I had had some six years of teaching in English schools, this was the first time I had met American children of whom I had heard rather startling tales . . . On this Monday morning therefore I found myself feeling somewhat nervous . . . I began by introducing myself and then proceeding to ask the twelve small, bright-eyed, intelligent-looking little boys to do the same thing. All went well with the first six—three Americans, one Chinese

> boy, a Norwegian boy and a French boy. The seventh boy, blond, blue-eyed, looking very much like an English pre-school boy in his grey flannels and striped tie, introduced himself with an angelic smile as simply "Philip."
>
> "Philip what?" I asked.
>
> "Just Philip," came the reply gently.
>
> "But you must have some other name," I answered.
>
> "Philip of Greece," he murmured in an embarrassed whisper, and I let the matter drop.

The new teacher quickly found that her royal pupil was really an ally . . .

> Dictation followed. I began in my most distinct, staccato manner. "There were . . ." (Thah wah). Not a pen moved; eleven bewildered pairs of eyes looked at me. I repeated my phrase. Still they remained immobile. Suddenly my blue-eyed Philip, looking very sympathetically towards the novice I seemed to be, turned to his comrades and explained, "She means *thurr wurr*," and all heads bent down and began to scratch. That crisis was over.
>
> Philip and I became good friends. He would sit on my right hand at the dining table, not as an honoured guest but because he was a particularly agile and careful carrier of hot dishes. He never would wait for the maid to carry in the different courses, for, as he explained to me, his mother had taught him that a gentleman does not allow women to wait on him . . . Often he would remain after school was over to chat with me as I corrected exercises. He instituted himself as a class monitor and without being asked, would straighten desks, collect waste paper, water the plants and think out different ways of making our school look more attractive . . .
>
> . . . I had a phone call from his sister. Could I possibly trace a small gold bibelot which Philip had traded with one of his school-fellows for a three-coloured lead pencil? She was sorry to bother me, but the bibelot was a present from the King of England and they thought that Philip should keep it. I was able to trace it and I remember how sad and downcast Philip was when I made him relinquish the pencil. He had felt that he had made the better bargain of the transaction.

Catherine Pegg Levitsky remembered how popular Philip had been, trying to play American football and baseball when he would "spurt across the sports ground, taking a tumble here and there, only looking rather disconsolate if he happened to tear his plus-four trousers, for his wardrobe was not extensive and he told me that his mother would remonstrate if he came home with torn clothes."

Mrs Levitsky concluded her article with the comment: "When the time came for him to go to his English school we were, teachers and school-fellows all, sorry to part with our tried and trusted democratic little friend whom we all had known as 'Just Philip'."

At The Elms Philip was a "rugged, boisterous boy . . . always remarkably polite . . . full of energy [who] got along with the other children."[17] Here he acquired a liking for art, something which he has handed on to Prince Charles. But above all, Prince Philip learned to enjoy competitive sports and games. He was already a good swimmer and diver and now he learned to box and to play baseball. The child, in this as in other cases, was father to the extrovert man who has always enjoyed physical activity and the challenge of polo and sailing, as well as the social activities that follow these male-dominated recreations.

But there was more to the young Prince than that. His head teacher had found him "remarkably polite". Others, too, recall that he had one of his mother's characteristics—to be concerned for and prepared to do something to help those less well-off than himself. Queen Alexandra wrote of the incident which occurred when the cousins were holidaying at Berck. One of the children in the group was a girl whose hip was diseased so that she had to lie in the garden or on the balcony of the villa while the other children played on the beach. Some friend bought beach toys for everyone—except the bed-ridden invalid. It was Philip who took the toys which he had just been given and gave them to the child in her cot.[18] This was another side to the boy who was better known for urging his cousins into competitions; he always wanted to swim further, run faster, ride better and dig deeper than anyone else. Maybe this particular drive was due to some Freudian-type wish to show that he had not inherited his father's latter-day ineffectiveness; perhaps it was due to a child's wish to show the rarely present father that the son, too, could achieve as both believed the father had. But this almost compulsive drive to succeed was balanced by that unusual trait of kindness, a trait which he has continued to show in later life.[19]

His formal education at The Elms was supported by that informal education which he received at home, particularly from his mother. It was she who told him about his family roots, about her life in Hesse, about the uncertain lives led by the Greek Royal Family since 1903 and about life in the Court of the almost legendary Queen Victoria. This insight into family history was reinforced by his cousin, Princess Marina, the daughter of Prince Andrew's brother, Prince Nicholas and Princess Helen. Marina was older than Prince Philip and while they were cousins he tended to look on her almost as an aunt. She frequently visited the house at St Cloud much to the younger cousin's delight and helped him further understand the complex ancestry of this exiled family. But, on this score at least, he is adamant: "If you want to know anything about the family, ask Mummy," he would say in later life.[20] As we have seen, there is evidence that she may have played a similar role as family history teacher to Prince Charles and the other royal children with whom she lived in her later years.[21]

But if his mother was resilient, able to think of others less fortunate than herself, and willing to take trouble to see to the future of her five children, Philip's father was a much less happy man. He carried the scars of the unjustified trial, the savage sentence and the memory that his own people would probably have condemned him to death if they had had their own way. It is, perhaps, not surprising that his family agreed that he "was intractable, his equanimity in tatters . . . unable to forgive the way in which, after long years of honest military service, he had been subject to public insult and indignity for the sins of others."[22]

Slowly he and Princess Alice drifted apart. Perhaps she devoted so much time to religious work and charities that she tended to ignore him.

Perhaps he, nursing his justified grievances, felt that she had too little sympathy for him. But there were other, deeper differences. When he threw off his depressions Prince Andrew was "a tall, genial, smiling gentleman . . . would take Mummy and myself to *Le Tout Paris* and other smart Parisian restaurants . . . a connoisseur of all the good things of life . . . a silver bucket of something on ice . . . the choicest dishes . . . a man of the world."[23] It is not surprising that the extrovert Prince Philip should have "adored his father"[24], who would tease him about his ability as an athlete yet would treat him "with a gentle gravity" whenever he looked for advice.[25]

But there was an increasing incompatibility between the gay extrovert with his taste for good living and the religiously-orientated mother with her taste for "good works". In two years, 1930–1931, all four daughters were married. Sophie, the youngest, was only sixteen when she married her cousin, Prince Christopher of Hesse, who died fighting for the Germans in 1944. Cecilie married her first cousin, the Grand Duke George Donatus of Hesse. This marriage was quickly followed by that of Margarita, the eldest daughter, to Prince Gottfried von Hohenlohe-Langenburg, a great-grandson of Queen Victoria while Theodora became the wife of Berthold, the Margrave of Baden and the son of Prince Max of Baden, the founder of the school at Salem to which Prince Philip would one day go as a reluctant pupil.[26] Although these marriages did not take place until 1930–1931, the engagements and the preparations for the marriages had taken a good deal of the family's attention throughout 1929 and 1930. Both parents seemed to have felt that having thus provided for their daughters they had done their parental duty—giving little thought to their only son still, in 1930, only nine years old. While there was no legal separation nor formal divorce, the two drifted apart. Princess Alice, as we have seen, became increasingly involved in religious affairs. She later went back to Athens to work among the poor. In the 1930s Prince Philip visited her when on holiday from his school. During one such visit he met Frederica, who had married his cousin, Paul, the Crown Prince of Greece. Princess Frederica was another of the German Princesses to marry into the Greek Royal Family and was destined to be Queen of Greece. In 1936 she met Philip and later wrote:

> Later I tried to learn [Greek] with Prince Philip of Greece, the present Duke of Edinburgh. When he was about fifteen he used to spend part of his holidays with us, and his Greek hardly existed as he had been brought up abroad. We decided to have Greek lessons together but they became so hilarious that we had to give them up, we laughed too much.[27]

Queen Frederica also confirms that Prince Philip, now fifteen, was still the competitive extrovert anxious to make his horse jump higher than anyone else's.

In 1939 Prince Philip's cousin, Alexandra, was staying with Princess Alice in her little house near Kolonaki Square in Athens. She wrote of her aunt's constant glancing at the clock on the day when Prince Philip was expected for one of those "comparatively infrequent occasions" when he visited his mother.[28] Then came the war during which Princess Alice remained in Greece throughout the German occupation, helping to alleviate the sufferings of the Greek people as best she could. In 1944 Harold Macmillan was Head of the British Mission to Greece which had now been liberated from German occupation. He visited various members of the Greek Royal Family. Later he wrote:

> Princess Andrew of Greece, whom I next saw, was living in humble, not to say somewhat squalid conditions. Her brother, Lord Louis Mountbatten, had been sending urgent telegrams . . . asking for news. Princess Andrew had stayed in Greece throughout the occupation . . . working hard . . . specially for children.
>
> [In his diary he wrote:] She made very little complaint . . . she admitted that she and her companion needed food . . . She went on to speak of her son. Apparently the boy is in our Navy—a Lieutenant or Sub-Lieutenant—and is doing very well. The Princess was hoping he might be in the Mediterranean; but he has gone to the Far East.[29]

And if, in 1930, Princess Alice had her sights fixed on the return to Athens after her daughters' weddings, Prince Andrew had his eyes turned to the South of France where his sister-in-law's family owned the Casino at Monte Carlo. Here he was to make his home. It was from here that he wrote to Prince Philip in reply to the schoolboy's letters from England. It was from here that he travelled to Greece in 1936 for the celebrations in Athens of the restoration of the monarchy, where, for a few days, father and son met up again. When war broke out in 1939 Prince Andrew stayed in the South of France. He died on the 3rd December 1944. The Royal Family of the Principality of Monaco organized his funeral at which a French Army escort walked by his bier to the Russian Orthodox Church in Nice. In 1946 a Greek cruiser, the *Averoff*, in which the ex-King Constantine had sailed back to Greece in 1920[30], was once again called into action to carry Prince Andrew's body back to Athens. He was reburied in the garden at Tatoi under a gravestone which says simply: "ANDREA VASILOPAIS, Prince of Greece, Prince of Denmark. 1882–1944." Here at last his countrymen recognized him for what he was, Vasilopais, son of a King. One of Prince Philip's first actions after the war was to go to Monte Carlo to wind up his dead father's estate—an indication that he died owing money.[31]

We have run ahead of the story. In 1930 there were signs of strain in the household at St Cloud. If the parents were agreed on anything it was that their only son must not be exposed to the sort of treatment that had been meted out to the father. He should be trained for a different career. Princess Alice's brothers, Lord George and Lord Louis, advised her to send the young boy to England where he could go to school and where they could supervise his upbringing, leaving her free to become involved in her religious activities. Prince Andrew's brothers and sisters-in-law were aware of the impending break up of the marriage and they agreed that England was a much safer place in which to bring up a royal exile than was Republican France or a bitterly divided Germany.

And so it was that in 1930 Prince Philip came under the wing of his mother's family, the Mountbattens. At first he lived at Kensington Palace with his ageing grandmother, but it soon became evident that the extrovert and lively boy found life too restricting at this Palace. So Lord George, who had been appointed his guardian, took him to live at Lynden Manor, his own home. Although he was to spend many holidays in Germany and Rumania, meet his mother occasionally in Athens and Corfu, from 1930 onwards Prince Philip, the Greek Prince of Danish extraction, became, for practical purposes an alien residing in England. From 1930 onwards his life became closely interwoven with that of the Mountbattens. In the next three chapters we will examine the careers of three of the leading figures in that family and see what impact their histories and careers had on Prince Philip's future.

Part II

THE BATTENBERG INFLUENCE

7

Prince Louis of Battenberg (1854–1921)

THERE ARE THREE REASONS why a biography of Prince Philip should contain a whole chapter devoted to a brief account of the career of his grandfather, Prince Louis of Battenberg. In the first place Prince Louis was, as we shall see, "the outstanding sailor of his generation"[1] who rose to become First Sea Lord. His career acted as a model for that of his own son, the late Earl Mountbatten of Burma, and for that of his grandson, Prince Philip. Like his grandfather and uncle, the young Prince had shown by 1952 the drive and ability, ambition and dedication that might have carried him, too, to the top post in the Royal Navy. But Prince Louis's career was cut short in 1914, as we shall see, in a hurtful and savage way. This insult to the Prince's career always rankled with his son, and since that son had a good deal of influence over the career and future of Prince Philip, it is worthwhile considering how the British people treated him in August 1914. Finally, it is evident that the attack on Prince Louis was merely the first stage in what may be seen as an almost continuous attack on the family, whether known as Battenberg or Mountbatten.

In 1953 the American magazine *Time* noted "a deep undertone of nervousness and grumbling in the starchy back benches of the Tory party." The magazine went on:

> Philip is not universally beloved by Britain's blue-bloods. They mistrust him; his politics are comparatively liberal; he plays fast and loose with some of the stuffier conventions of the Palace; he is a foreigner . . . Above all, he is a Battenberg.[2]

The family had not used that name since 1917 as we shall see in Chapter 8. But the observant commentator from *Time* had noticed how the British Establishment in its attempts to limit the power and influence of Prince Philip had stooped to its xenophobic depths, as it had done in 1914.

Clement Attlee, Britain's Labour Prime Minister from 1945 until 1951, had a well-earned reputation for tart, often monosyllabic, utterances. It is in this light that we have to view a statement of his:

> It's a funny thing, those Mountbattens are the only members of the Royal Family who have ever shown any great ability. All three of them—Prince Louis, a great sailor who was done in by the *Globe* in 1914; Dickie, Lord Mountbatten, who became Chief of the Defence Staff in spite of being royal, not because of it; and Philip, I think, if he had a chance.[3]

This relatively long statement from the normally taciturn Attlee has to be seen as a tribute to a genius which this family has displayed.

Prince Louis was born in 1854, the eldest son and second child of the love-match between Alexander, Prince of Hesse, and Julie, who was given the title of Princess of Battenberg. In 1866 Prince Alexander had taken Austria's side in the war against Bismarck's Prussia. The twelve-year-old Prince Louis had first seen his father ride out to war and then, six weeks later, return in defeat. Few of those who attacked Prince Louis's reputation in 1914 were aware of the fact that the first danger to his boyhood had come from Prussia, whose power the people of Hesse both feared and opposed. In 1862 his cousin, Prince Louis of Hesse, heir to the childless Grand Duke Louis III, married Queen Victoria's second daughter, Princess Alice of England. It was she who first gave Prince Louis of Battenberg an interest in England. Through her, he met Queen Victoria's second son, Alfred, the Duke of Edinburgh (1844–1900) who was making a career for himself in the Royal Navy. Prince Louis decided that he, too, would become a sailor. None of the German states had a navy so it was suggested to him that he might join the Austrian Navy; his cousin, Emperor Franz-Josef, was prepared to help organize things for him. But the twelve-year-old Louis told his father that if he were going to be a sailor he wanted to join the "greatest navy which belonged to England". His father explained that to do this would mean giving up his German citizenship to become a British subject. "That is what I intend to do, sir," said Louis—and did it.[4]

So it was that in 1868 Prince Louis left his home at Darmstadt to join the Royal Navy. On the 14th October 1868 he went before the public notary at Gosport and swore the solemn oath of allegiance to the Queen of Great Britain and Ireland, signed a paper and became a British subject. His Serene Highness Prince Louis of Battenberg then entered the Royal Navy as a cadet. This is not a biography of Prince Louis. Details of his career have been documented and analysed in well-written accounts by Alden Hatch and Richard Hough.[5] What emerges from a study of that career was that Prince Louis was a highly intelligent, able and efficient officer who climbed to the top of the career ladder on his own merits. He supported the energetic Fisher in attempting to reform the British Navy; he personally was responsible for the opening of the two naval colleges at Osborne and Dartmouth which ensured that midshipmen would receive four years' training and education before they went to sea and not two as in the past. He ensured that the Reserve Fleet was kept in a state of readiness rather than being left in moth-balls as had been the case[6], spent ten years from 1904 trying to persuade the rest of the Establishment that merchant shipping ought to be armed, and organized a course at the Naval College at Greenwich for staff officers. This 'planning staff' course later developed into the Imperial Defence College, the post-graduate school for future admirals.

All this desk-bound planning was based on a long career afloat which had seen him pass his first examination with the highest marks ever awarded, train his men so that they became the best gunners in the fleet,[8] and make each ship in which he held command "the smartest ship in the squadron, or fleet", so that by 1901 he was considered to be one of the two best officers in the British Navy.[9]

For the purposes of this story we have to omit a close study of this fascinating career and move to 1912 when Winston Churchill became First Lord of the Admiralty—the political head of the Royal Navy.

Churchill appreciated that the modernization of the British Navy had been due almost entirely to the energy and determination of Admiral Sir John Fisher. He had been First Sea Lord from 1904 until his retirement in 1910. Even after his retirement and elevation to the peerage, Fisher continued to be consulted by politicians and naval staff about naval matters. They were aware that Fisher was convinced that some time in 1914 or 1915 Britain would find herself at war with Germany and that in the ensuing struggle Britain's main weapon—offensive and defensive—would be the navy. It is not surprising that Churchill, on coming to the Admiralty, should have consulted the retired Fisher as to who ought to become First Sea Lord. Fisher wrote:

> I propose that he should take as his First Sea Lord Prince Louis of Battenberg. The very ablest Admiral that we possess both afloat and ashore . . . the most capable administrator in the Admirals List *by a long way* . . .[10]

But Prince Louis was only appointed Second Sea Lord and, in July 1912, Commander-in-Chief of the Blue Fleet in the annual naval manoeuvres. While in command of this fleet he had been appointed Admiral. Then on the 9th December Churchill brought him back to Whitehall as the First Sea Lord, having sacked Sir Francis Bridgeman. Prince Louis's friends and naval contemporaries were delighted. As one claimed: "He was born a royal prince but lived it down."[11]

In the summer of 1914 Churchill and Prince Louis agreed that it would save money if, for that year, the navy did not hold its annual manoeuvres. Instead they decided to plan a trial mobilization of the Third Fleet, the whole of the Royal Naval Fleet Reserve and all reserve officers. This was the first complete test mobilization in the history of the navy. It began on 15th July 1914—a date that had been fixed in 1913 and had nothing to do with the assassination of the Austrian Archduke at Sarajevo on the 28th June; 200,000 men reported to the various naval depots. The old ships of the Third Fleet sailed from Chatham to Spithead to join the ships of the First and Second Fleets in a grand review. This was the greatest assembly of naval power the world had ever seen. On the 19th July the ships put to sea for exercises following which the fleets returned to their various ports. The First Fleet was stationed at Portland; the ships of the Second Fleet went to their home ports still fully manned by their nucleus crews and men of the Intermediate Reserve; the older ships of the Third Fleet were back at Chatham, manned only by the barest of skeleton crews. All the regular reservists had been paid off.

Both the First and Second Fleets were ready for battle on Friday the 24th July, 1914, and were commanded to remain so until Monday the 27th July when the First Fleet was due to disperse in squadrons for various duties, while the Second Fleet was due to discharge the reservists among its crews.

It was the 24th July, 1914, that the Cabinet received a copy of the ultimatum which Austria had sent to Serbia. When Churchill showed Prince Louis a copy they agreed that there was a real danger of war. However, this did not prevent the Cabinet—including the percipient Churchill—from following their normal practice of going away for the weekend, crisis or no crisis. As Prince Louis noted: "Ministers with the weekend holidays are incorrigible."[12] So it was that Prince Louis, alone in his room at Whitehall, watched the reports come in on Saturday and Sunday which showed that Russia, Austria, Germany and Serbia were moving inexorably towards war. It was he who told Churchill this when his political superior telephoned at about noon on Sunday. His report sounded so ominous that Churchill declared: "I'll be with you by nine o'clock. Meanwhile I authorize you to do whatever is necessary."[13] By six o'clock that Sunday evening the Austrian ultimatum to Serbia ran out. Meanwhile, the British fleets were waiting for six a.m. on Monday morning before they dispersed and, in the case of the Second Fleet, began to discharge the reservists in their crews.

Prince Louis decided that he could not wait for Churchill's return. He sent a message to the Commander-in-Chief ordering the First and Second Fleets to remain mobilized, ready to fight. The message was signed: "Louis of Battenberg".[14] Churchill approved this message when he came in at nine p.m. and persuaded Sir Edward Grey, Foreign Secretary, to add his approval before hurrying back to the Admiralty where he and Prince Louis drafted the communiqué which was made public:

> ORDER TO THE FIRST AND SECOND FLEETS
>
> Orders have been given to the First Fleet, which is concentrated at Portland, not to disperse for manoeuvre leave for the present. All vessels of the Second Fleet are remaining at their home ports in proximity to their balance crews.[15]

On the 28th July Austria declared war on Serbia. Prince Louis issued the orders which sent the First Fleet to its war station at Scapa Flow and the Second Fleet to assemble at its place at Portland. As Churchill said: "The King's ships are at sea"[16]—thanks to the initiative of Prince Louis, the First Sea Lord. But they were not at war until eleven p.m. on the night of August 4th—the deadline given by the British Government for the withdrawal of German forces from Belgium. The Germans ignored the British demand, made no reply to the British message, so that when Big Ben sounded its eleven strokes a message was sent to all the ships in the Royal Navy: "COMMENCE HOSTILITIES AGAINST GERMANY. LOUIS BATTENBERG."[17]

On the 4th August 1914 crowds gathered outside Buckingham Palace to cheer the announcement that war had been declared. In his diary the King wrote:

> *Tuesday, August 4th.* I held a Council at 10.45 [p.m.] to declare war with Germany. It is a terrible catastrophe, but it is not our fault. An enormous crowd collected outside the Palace; we went on to the balcony before and after dinner. When they heard that war had been declared the excitement increased and May and I with David went on to the balcony; the cheering was terrific. Please God it may soon be over . . .[18]

There were those who assumed that it would all be over by Christmas, and others for whom Rupert Brooke spoke when he wrote: "Now, God be thanked Who has matched us with His hour . . ."[19]

Within a few weeks, however, it had become clear that it was indeed "a terrible catastrophe" and that it would not "soon be over". The German armies defeated the Russians in the East while in the West the Germans almost won the war within the first few weeks. Day after day the casualty lists filled the columns of the national papers which also reported that the Royal Navy was at anchor in Scapa Flow and not out fighting the enemy. Meanwhile, the propagandists got to work to show that the Germans were "the beastly Huns" who hacked the hands off Belgian babies with their bayonets. It was not long before the British people had been brainwashed into hating everything German—Wagner's music was banned and dachshunds hissed at in Hyde Park—and the hysteria was increased by the reports that the British Navy, commanded by a German-named prince, was incapable of halting the enemy. The German cruisers, *Goben* and *Breslau*, had escaped from the supervision of the Mediterranean Fleet with its three battle cruisers, four large armoured cruisers and several light cruisers. Admiral Milne had allowed the two German cruisers to slip from their coaling station at Messina and to make their way to the Dardanelles where, as it proved, they were welcomed by the Turks who became persuaded that the Germans would win the war and so came in on the German side.

On the night of 27th–28th August the British won the Battle of Heligoland Bight. But this good news was quickly forgotten when on the 22nd September a U-boat sank three British cruisers off the coast near Yarmouth. About 1,500 of the men on board died. The sinking of the *Aboukir*, *Hague* and *Cressey* drew public attention to the Prince. Newspapers alleged that these losses could not have taken place without some treachery at the top. Rumour followed rumour, none of them losing anything in the telling. On the 3rd October, Fisher wrote: "One of the queer canards that are flying around London is that Prince Louis of Battenberg, First Sea Lord of the Admiralty, is 'confined to the Tower of London . . .'."[20]

Officers and ex-officers who were jealous of the way in which Prince Louis had reached the top, and of his support for the reforms which Fisher had implemented before 1914, took advantage of this wave of unpopularity to add their fuel to the fire of rumour. Indeed, his former friend, Lord Charles Beresford, himself once an eminent naval officer, so attacked the reputation of Prince Louis that Churchill was driven to write a letter saying that if he did not stop spreading these rumours, Beresford would not attain his ambition of being made an Admiral of the Fleet (Retired). Nor did he.

One gets a good idea of the period from the memoirs of Lee of Fareham who, as Sir Arthur Lee, was Conservative spokesman on Naval Affairs in the House of Commons in August 1914. Writing of the Beresford affair Lee remembered:

> Whilst up in London I suddenly became involved in a squalid fracas with Lord Charles Beresford, whom I had heard one day, in the hall of the Carlton Club, holding forth to a group of MPs about the 'scandal' of retaining Prince Louis as First Sea Lord—seeing that he was "a German and a potential traitor who ought rather to be interned".
>
> This wanton and treacherous blow beneath the belt, delivered by a brother naval officer who had always professed to be his friend, was the culmination of a base intrigue against one of the ablest, most trusted and best loved sailors who had ever held that great office . . . the idea that Beresford should be deliberately instilling poison into the public mind—already infected with 'spy-mania'—seemed to me almost an act of treason . . . I went to see Winston and adjured him to take whatever steps would be effective to protect the honour of his own chief colleague and adviser . . .
>
> Winston went off the deep end . . . wrote a letter of censure to Beresford warning him that if his offence was repeated the Admiralty would take drastic and disciplinary action . . . the next day I was rung up by Beresford who proceeded to abuse me with great violence threatening legal proceedings for "foul and malicious libel".
>
> In addition . . . he . . . set on foot a movement to have me expelled from the Carlton Club for having committed a gross breach of the Rules in reporting to a non-member and "political opponent" a conversation which I had heard within the Club precincts.
>
> [Lee refused to make the "full and complete apology" demanded by the leaders of the Conservative Party and the officials of the Carlton Club. This led to his condemnation by the Club Committee.]
>
> Upon this I promptly tendered my resignation from the Club . . . It became evident that Prince Louis's position was now so undermined that his retirement seemed inevitable, unless Winston was prepared to risk all and to stake his own fortunes upon retaining him as First Sea Lord.[21]

During October, however, the situation worsened. The light cruiser *Hawke* was torpedoed; the German ships, *Emden* and *Karlsruhe*, were sinking British merchant shipping in the Indian Ocean and Admiral Von Spee's fleet was active in the Pacific Ocean. On the 3rd October Churchill's plan for the defence of Antwerp was shown to be the charade that Prince Louis had always thought it was. But it was he, as well as Churchill, who had to carry the burden of public blame for the loss of 2,500 men of the untrained Royal Naval Division who were lost either as casualties or interned in neutral Holland.[22] The newspapers, led by the *Globe*, carried their attacks on Prince Louis to new heights—or depths, according to one's point of view. They carried letters which ranged from suggestions that he should resign, to accusations of incompetence and even charges of treason. By the 26th October the campaign was having an effect. The Prince wrote:

> My responsibility and constant anxiety in this great office are very heavy, and being continuously attacked and yet quite helpless—although assured afresh of the Government's confidence—I feel sometimes that I cannot bear it much longer . . .[23]

On the same day the *Globe* carried an editorial which asserted that the newspaper was receiving hundreds of letters protesting against Prince Louis's position as First Sea Lord. While the editorial, in customary Heepish style, protested its own confidence in his ability and patriotism, it nevertheless "felt obliged" . . .

> . . . for the sake of the First Sea Lord himself, not less than for that of the nation . . . we ask that some authoritative statement shall be issued of a nature so emphatic and so unqualified as to remove once and for ever every cloud of doubt, and to silence every breath of rumour.[24]

But who was to issue such a statement? Prime Minister Asquith was preoccupied with preserving his own skin or in writing letters to Miss Violet Stanley.[25] In any event, he was not immune from racial prejudice as can be seen from one such letter written on the 3rd November 1914: "My dreams continue . . . there was another, of which I have only a dim memory, in which . . . I was supplanted by Herbert Samuel—as Prince Hal says, 'a Jew, an 'ebrew Jew'. Do you think that is going to be my fate?"[26]

Perhaps the rebuttal of the false charges should have come from Prince Louis's political overlord, Winston Churchill. But he too was struggling merely to survive against the onslaught of criticism from his former colleagues in the Tory Party and from the criticism of those who thought his leadership was inept. It was not for him to spend his energy defending another, for as Asquith noted of his Cabinet colleague, he had not much "endowment of the instinct of loyalty . . .".[27]

But in all probability, there could not have been any statement which would have satisfied the baying Press. In any event, on the day after that editorial in the *Globe*, the 27th October 1914, news came that one of the finest new dreadnoughts, the *Audacious*, had struck a German mine off Lough Swilly and although the crew had been saved the ship had been sunk. On the following morning the *Globe* printed a shoal of letters demanding the resignation of the First Sea Lord. During the day Prime Minister Asquith noted:

28th October. The sinking of the *Audacious* . . . is cruel luck for Winston, who has just been here pouring out his woes . . . Winston's real trouble, however, is about Prince Louis and the succession to his post. He must go, and Winston has had a most delicate and painful interview with him. Louis behaved with great dignity and public spirit, and will resign at once . . .[28]

So much for the allegation in *The World Crisis* in which Churchill wrote: "I was therefore not surprised when, towards the end of October, Prince Louis asked to be relieved of his burden."[29]

Nearly fifty years later, in July 1962, the then Prime Minister Harold Macmillan endeavoured to restore his own failing fortunes by sacking over half his Cabinet. Jeremy Thorpe, then leader of the Liberal Party, commented on the work of 'Mac the Knife' by paraphrasing the Gospel: "Greater love hath no man than that he lay down his friends for his life . . ."[30]. Prince Louis's life was to be laid down to try to save that of the politicians. But, as in 1962, the niceties were observed. Prince Louis wrote a letter of resignation:

28th October 1914
Dear Mr Churchill,
I have lately been driven to the painful conclusion that at this juncture my birth and parentage have the effect of impairing in some respects my usefulness on the Board of Admiralty. In these circumstances I feel it to be my duty, as a loyal subject of His Majesty, to resign the office of First Sea Lord, hoping thereby to facilitate the task of the administration of the great Service to which I have devoted my life, and to ease the burden laid on H.M. Ministers.
I am, Yours very truly,
Louis Battenberg
Admiral[31]

In his reply Churchill paid some tribute to the work which he had done:

29th October 1914
My dear Prince Louis,
. . . I cannot further oppose the wish you have during the last few weeks expressed to me, to be released from the burden of responsibility which you have borne thus far with so much honour and success . . .
The Navy of today, and still more the Navy of tomorrow, bears the imprint of your work . . . the result of the labours we have had in common, and in which the Board of Admiralty owes so much to your aid . . .[32]

In his diary King George V noted:

October 29th, 1914. Spent a most worrying and trying day . . . At 11.30 saw Winston Churchill who informed me that Louis of Battenberg had resigned his appt. as 1st Sea Lord . . . I feel deeply for him; there is no more loyal man in the Country.[33]

Lee of Fareham might be allowed the last word. Having hoped that Churchill would "risk all and . . . stake his own fortunes upon retaining" Prince Louis, Lee went on:

This he signally failed to do and when Prince Louis in a letter of immense dignity and stoical self-sacrifice, tendered his resignation the First Sea Lord

The founders of the Battenberg family; Prince Alexander of Hesse-Darmstadt and his bride, Countess Julie von Hauke, who was later created the Princess of Battenberg. They were Prince Philip's great-grandparents.

Prince Louis of Battenberg (eldest son of the family's founders) and his fiancée, Princess Victoria of Hesse-Darmstadt. She was the eldest child of Queen Victoria's most able daughter, Princess Alice, whose youngest daughter, Alix, was the unhappy wife of the last of the Russian Tsars, Nicholas II.

Left: King George I of Greece and Queen Olga with (back to the camera) Queen Alexandra, wife of Edward VII. The two Queens were daughters of King Christian IX of Denmark whose youngest daughter, Marie, was the wife of Tsar Alexander III of Russia and mother of Tsar Nicholas II, whose facial resemblance to King George V can be traced to this Danish background.

Below: Prince Andrew of Greece with (*from left to right*) Princess Alice (Prince Philip's mother) and their daughters Theodora and Margarita. This photograph was taken in London in December 1922 after the family had been rescued by the intervention of Prince Andrew's cousin, King George V.

Right: The one-year-old Prince Philip of Greece in London in 1922 for the wedding of his uncle, Lord Louis Mountbatten, his mother's younger brother.

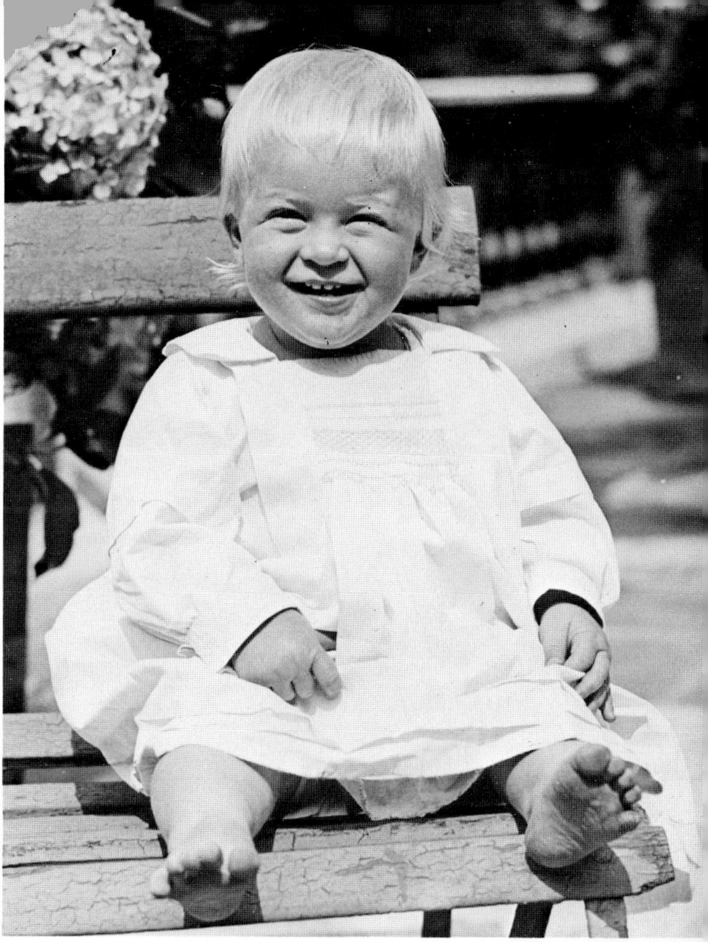

Below: At school in Paris – in a Robin Hood play. *Left to right:* Prince Jacques de Bourbon, Prince Philip, Theodore Culbert (son of a USA embassy official) and an English girl.

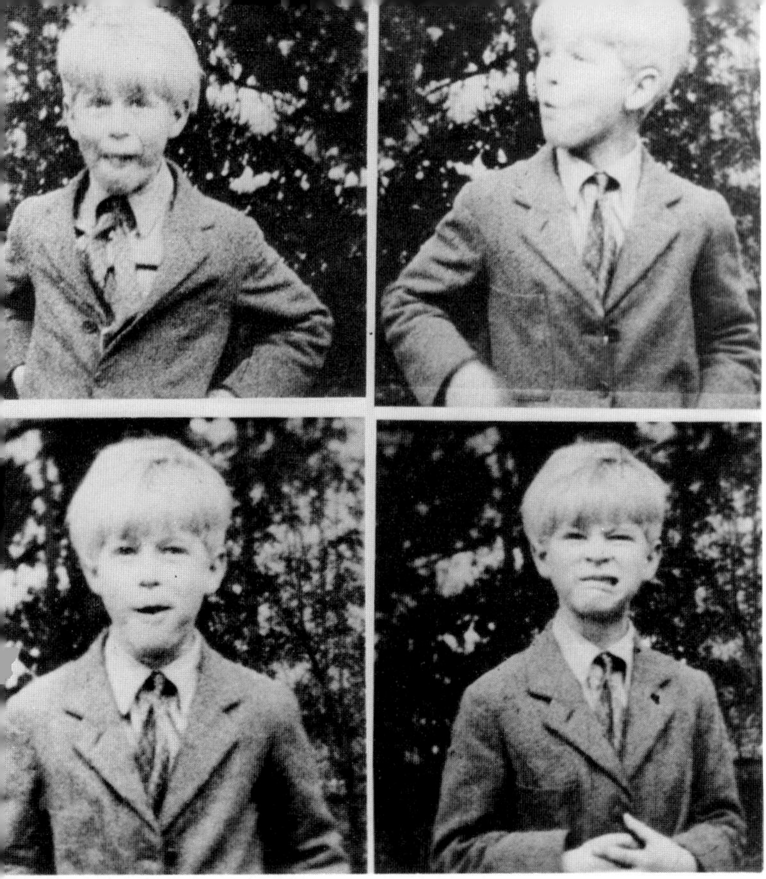

Determined to win a biscuit-eating race at school in Paris.

With his cousin Michael, King of Rumania, on the sands around the Black Sea near Constanza in 1928.

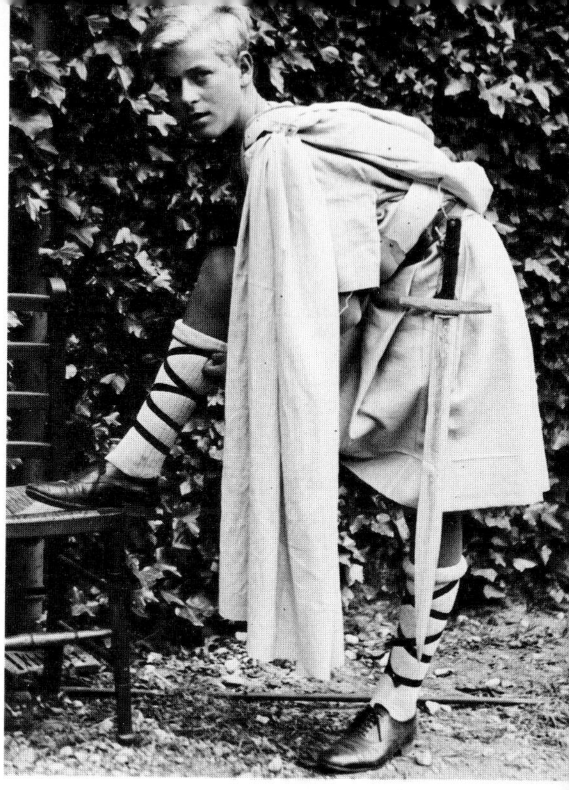

bove left: Prince Philip aged 15 in the little fishing harbour at Hopeman near Gordonstoun. *bove right:* August 1935 and Prince Philip as Donalbain in the Gordonstoun production of *acbeth* – in which Prince Charles, in his turn, played the lead. *Below:* Captain of the Gordon-oun cricket team (seated third from left) in the summer of 1939.

Above: Kurt Hahn, the German-born educationalist, who, as headmaster of Salem and Gordonstoun, had a major influence on Prince Philip. *Below left:* Lord Louis Mountbatten with the then Prince of Wales (later the Duke of Windsor), on board HMS *Renown* during a world cruise, 1919. *Below right:* Lady Edwina Mountbatten in 1925.

Captain Lord Louis Mountbatten's flotilla leader, HMS *Kelly*, on which the Duke of Windsor returned from France in 1939 and which was sunk during the Battle of Crete in May 1941.

Admiral Lord Louis Mountbatten, Supreme Allied Commander South-East Asia with Chinese Generalissimo Chiang Kai Shek (in dark glasses) and Madam Chiang when they visited Chinese troops at a training base at Ranchi. Chiang Kai Shek was on his way back from the Cairo Conference where he had met President Roosevelt and Winston Churchill.

A portrait by the famous photographer, Karsh of Ottawa, of the "glittering Mountbatten", whose tragic death at the hands of Irish assassins shocked the world in general and the Royal Family in particular.

accepted it with a pusillanimity which was ill-concealed by a turgid public valedictory.[34]

Later that day Prince Louis went to see King George V, who had once served under his command as a lieutenant. In 1892 they had been together when news came of the death of the Duke of Clarence, the oldest son of the Prince of Wales. On that occasion Prince Louis had had to comfort the young Prince who was now in direct line of succession to the throne. Prince Louis had told him: "You could have no better training for your new responsibilities than that of having been a naval officer . . ." Now, in 1914, it was the turn of King George to comfort the older Prince Louis. To show his trust in him the King made him a Member of the Privy Council which, he noted in his diary, "pleased him".[35]

Once the damage had been done, people very belatedly rushed to defend the Prince's reputation. From Jellicoe, the Commander-in-Chief of the Grand Fleet, came a telegram:

HAVE RECEIVED WITH THE MOST PROFOUND SORROW THE INFORMATION CONTAINED IN YOUR TELEGRAM. THE WHOLE FLEET WILL LEARN THE NEWS WHEN PUBLISHED WITH THE DEEPEST REGRET. WE LOOK TO YOU WITH THE GREATEST LOYALTY, RESPECT AND GRATITUDE FOR THE WORK YOU HAVE ACCOMPLISHED FOR THE NAVY.
JOHN JELLICOE.[36]

A former First Lord, Lord Selborne, described the resignation as "nothing less than a national humiliation". J. H. Thomas, a Labour MP and trade-union leader, wrote to *The Times* pointing out that if the Press were thus able to hound a good man from office on unsubstantiated rumour "it will be difficult for public men to endeavour to serve their country in the manner we have a right to expect." *The Times* praised Prince Louis in a long editorial; the *Daily Mail* described him as a "loyal and noble figure"; even the *Globe* sank to the level of praising his resignation as a "very noble act of self-abnegation".

It is little wonder that Lord Louis, his son, had, and Prince Philip, his grandson, also has an inbred suspicion of the Press, the politicians and the Establishment which could so maltreat a man. For Prince Louis the future seemed bleak. In 1917, as we shall see, he had to change his name. He also lost a fortune which he had invested in a mine in Russia—taken over by the Bolshevik Government after November 1917—as well as money he had invested in Germany, lost in the inflation which wrecked the German *mark* after 1919. But on the 21st July 1921 he was asked to take the chair at the annual dinner of the Royal Navy Club, normally attended by about fifty to eighty members. When it became known that Prince Louis was to take the chair about eight hundred members turned up, many from countries overseas. The First Lord of the Admiralty, Lee of Fareham, wrote:

I took the opportunity, which I had long desired, to express publicly my sympathy with [him] on the stroke of Fate which had befallen him, and my belief that the trust and affection with which he was regarded, by both

> officers and men, throughout the great service to which he had devoted nearly his whole life, had never wavered and were as strong as ever.[37]

When Prince Louis rose to answer the toast proposed to him by Lord Lee, the cheering lasted for five minutes. "Most remarkable and significant," wrote Lord Lee. He was so impressed with this evident support for the Prince that he wrote to the King proposing that Prince Louis be promoted by a special Order-in-Council to the rank of Admiral of the Fleet on the Retired List. The King's Private Secretary replied:

> The King has read your letter . . . with much satisfaction and is delighted to give his approval to your proposal to promote [him] to the rank of Admiral of the Fleet on the Retired List to date from the 4th August 1921.

It is ironic that this was the anniversary of the date of the outbreak of war in 1914. The letter goes on:

> His Majesty has always felt most keenly for [him] whose distinguished service terminated under circumstances which, as you say, can only be regarded as tragic.[38]

In August 1921 Prince Louis, a new Admiral of the Fleet, was invited to take a cruise on the battle cruiser *Repulse* on which his son, Lord Louis, was a lieutenant. He returned from the cruise on the 10th September and went to stay at the Naval and Military Club. His wife, Princess Victoria, and their daughter, Louise, were staying in a neighbouring hotel. Prince Louis told them that he wasn't feeling very well and on Sunday, 11th September, they sent for a doctor to visit him. On Sunday afternoon they left him in bed to go to collect some medicine. On their return they were met by the Club's housekeeper with the news that when she had gone to clear away Prince Louis's tea-tray she found him dead.

But even in death he has not always been left to rest. In 1960, when a Declaration in Council made public the Queen's decision that her children were to bear the name Mountbatten-Windsor, the *Daily Mail* reported: "Prince Louis of Battenberg, whose name did not then ring sweetly in British ears . . ."[39] in an attempt to smear the family name. As we shall see, the family had not used the name Battenberg since 1917—but that was no hindrance to the British Press in their campaign against the Mountbattens.

8

A New Name for an Old Family, 1917

THE RESIGNATION OF Prince Louis did nothing to halt the suspicions of the credulous people against things foreign. Newspapers raised a clamour over the presence in St George's Chapel at Windsor of the Garter banners of enemy emperors, kings and princes. King George V argued that these banners were symbols of past history and that they should remain where they were, "at all events, until after the war, when there may be other developments."[1] The more rabid among the anti-German writers suggested that the Chapel should be raided by 'patriots' and the banners torn down by force. King George decided to accept the advice of his Ministers. On the 13th May 1915 a notice was issued announcing that the names of the eight enemy Knights of the Garter had been struck from the Roll of the Order. The banners were quietly removed. However, King George insisted that the brass plates bearing the names and titles of these foreign rulers should remain affixed to their stalls. As Lord Stamfordham wrote to the Dean of Windsor:

> They are historical records and His Majesty does not intend to have any of them removed. The King was not inspired by a desire for any dramatic action and, had it not been for a somewhat hysterical clamour headed by Mr Bottomley in the columns of *John Bull* and by the *Daily Mail* for the instant removal of the banners, they would probably, by the King's orders, have been in due due course unostentatiously taken down.[2]

The level of the anti-foreign hysteria may be judged from the fact that its leaders were the *Mail* ("a paper written by office boys for office boys")[3] and Horatio Bottomley who enriched himself by getting well-paid as a salesman of government war bonds—and who ended up in jail in the 1920s.

But the appetite of the 'patriots' was only whetted by their success in this instance. They then persuaded MPs to ask questions in the House of Commons about those foreign princes who were still legally members of the British Royal Family. The King thought that such questions were "too petty and undignified" to be considered by a wartime Parliament.[4] Prime

Minister Asquith decided to try to draw off the critics by appointing a Committee of the House of Lords to examine the position of these foreign princes. Lord Bryce headed this Committee, which reported in 1917. Its report led to the introduction of the Titles Deprivation Act of 1917. The Dukes of Cumberland and of Brunswick as well as Viscount Taaffe (Lord Ballymore) had "adhered to the King's enemies"; they were deprived of their titles, but not until March 1919.

Later, in 1915, there was a public campaign which resulted in a prosecution being brought against Sir Ernest Cassel to show by what authority he claimed the title of Privy Councillor. Cassel had been born in Germany which was enough for some jingoists to condemn this friend of Edward VII and George V, and a major subscriber to government appeals for money in the first two years of the war. He was also a multi-millionaire, another thing held against him by the less successful among the 'patriots' who argued that his wealth must have been ill-gotten because he was a foreigner who had made his money in England. Finally, and maybe most significantly, Cassel was a Jew; anti-Semitism is never far below the surface in England, and easily breaks through in times of stress when the English look for a scapegoat, although never as brutally as the Russians or Germans.

The Courts decided that Cassel's appointment was perfectly valid. This did nothing to lessen the hurt felt by a man of whom Lady Oxford said: "No one was ever more loyal and generous to the country of his adoption."[5] This episode is relevant to a study of the Mountbattens, since in 1922 Cassel's granddaughter, Edwina, was to marry Prince Louis's second son and to become famous in her own right as Edwina, the Countess Mountbatten of Burma. She had a well-earned reputation , of which she was proud, of being a liberal—especially in racial matters.[6] Her friendship with Gandhi and other 'native' leaders did nothing to soften the hostility felt by the Establishment towards the Mountbatten family in 1947—when Prince Philip was in the process of becoming naturalized before his engagement to Princess Elizabeth.

The xenophobia reached new depths in 1917 as the U-boat campaign threatened to starve Britain into submission. At the same time there was a wave of Republicanism following the overthrow of the Tsar in Russia's February Revolution. Riding on the crest of this latest wave, the novelist, H. G. Wells, wrote a letter to *The Times* in which he wrote that the time was ripe to throw off "the ancient trappings of throne and sceptre". He also attacked what he described as "an alien and uninspiring Court". This remark angered the King who told Lord Carnock (Harold Nicolson's father), "I may be uninspiring, but I'll be damned if I'm alien."[7]

During May 1917 there was a further twist to the Germanophobia from which the British suffered. There was a whispering campaign, it seemed, to the effect that Britain's inability to win the long-expected victory and the danger that she might indeed be starved out by the U-boat campaign, were due to the fact that the King and many of his relatives still living in

England had German-sounding names. Lady Mary Warrender said that when someone repeated this tale to the King, "he started and grew pale".[8]

It is a sign of the uncertainty that gripped the country during the dark months of 1917 that the King sent for his secretary and asked him whether there was any truth in the reports of these rumours. When told that there was, the King asked what he should do. Stamfordham, himself a victim of the fever and fear, told the King that his best answer was to change his name—in itself a victory for the rumour-mongers.

And now there took place a short period of hectic activity at Court which, in other circumstances, might have deserved the description 'bizarre'. For when the King asked the College of Heralds what was, in fact, the name of his family, the learned Heralds replied that they were "not quite positive". The Heralds were only confident of one thing; the King's name was assuredly not Stuart. Perhaps it was Guelph, the name by which William IV had been known before his accession in 1830?[9] Or was it Wettin, which was the 'family' name of Prince Albert? Or perhaps Saxe-Coburg-Gotha, which was the 'house' name of the Prince Consort's family? Certainly it was agreed that the King's father, Edward VII, had been the first King of the House of Saxe-Coburg-Gotha.

Only one thing was certain from this jumble of information that poured out from the College of Heralds. No matter which name the King might finally agree was his, it was bound to be a German name. Equally, it was certain that almost all his closest relatives were similarly blessed (or cursed) with German-sounding names. Queen Mary, for example, was of the House of Teck. Others of his cousins at the British Court were named Gleichen, Schleswig-Holstein—and, as we have seen, Battenberg.

The bewildered King decided that some English name be found by which his family should be known. There now followed the second act of the 'Comedy of the Heralds'. Some proposed that he call himself Stuart, others Tudor, still more York, or alternatively, Lancaster. Oldcastle, Fitzroy (too French), D'Este (too Italian) and Plantagenet were all considered and rejected. It was Stamfordham, the hard-working Private Secretary, who discovered in his researches that, at one time, Edward III had been known as 'Edward of Windsor'. Here was a fine English name, the name too, of one of the family's favourite homes. On the 26th June Lord Rosebery, a former Prime Minister, wrote to congratulate Stamfordham for having "christened a dynasty . . . few people in the world . . . have done this . . .".[10] The news was made public in an announcement in the Press on the 18th July 1917:

> We, of Our Royal Will and Authority, do hereby declare . . . that as from the date of this . . . Proclamation Our House and Family shall be styled and known as the House and Family of Windsor, and that all the male descendants in the male line of . . . Queen Victoria who are subjects of these realms, other than female descendants who may marry or have married, shall bear the said Name of Windsor. And we hereby further declare . . .

> that We for Ourselves and . . . Our descendants and all other descendants of . . . Queen Victoria relinquish the degrees, styles . . . titles . . . of Dukes and Duchesses of Saxony and Princes and Princesses of Saxe-Coburg and Gotha, and all other German degrees, styles . . . titles and appellations to Us or to them heretofore belonging or appertaining.

The Kaiser gave the lie to the report that he had little sense of humour by commenting: "Fine. Next time we play Shakespeare we'll call it 'The Merry Wives of Saxe-Coburg-Gotha'."[11]

The Queen's family name was changed from Teck to Cambridge; her brothers, the Duke of Teck and Prince Alexander of Teck, became, respectively, Marquess of Cambridge and Earl of Athlone. The King's two cousins, Princes Louis and Alexander of Battenberg became respectively, Marquess of Milford Haven and Marquess of Carisbrooke, with the family name of Mountbatten—a literal translation of their German name but also the name of a fort on Plymouth Sound. Indeed, Prince Louis ensured that all his titles were associated with the sea; Milford Haven is the fine harbour on the Welsh coast; his second title, which his eldest son might wear by courtesy, was Earl of Medina, after the river near Kent House.

Lord Stamfordham went to inform the Party leaders at Westminster about the list of the King's new titles and the proposals for the other members of the Royal Family. He is alleged to have been nervous about the possibility of an unfavourable reaction from Labour Party leaders at the proposal to make Prince Louis a marquess. He kept this information to the last. While he was hesitating before making this final announcement, J. H. Thomas, a Labour leader, asked, "What about Prince Louis?" When Stamfordham explained his new titles Thomas replied, "Well, I don't think that's half enough, and neither does the Labour Party. What that man has done for our Navy . . . Intelligence and many other things, is beyond belief, and the way he was kicked out at the beginning of the war was a scandal. I wrote him about it at the time and he wrote back a fine manly letter with never a word of complaint. I shall keep that letter all my life."[12]

These changes of family names were followed by new definitions and restrictions of the use of the titles 'Royal Highness', 'Prince' and 'Princess'. The *London Gazette* carried the terms of the Letters Patent on the 11th December 1917.

> The children of any Sovereign of the United Kingdom, and the children of any sons of such Sovereign, and the eldest living son of the eldest son of the Prince of Wales, shall have at all times, hold and enjoy the style, title or attribute of Royal Highness, with their titular dignity of Prince or Princess prefixed to their respective Christian names, or with their other titles of honour. That, save as aforesaid, the titles of Royal Highness, Highness or Serene Highness and the titular dignity of Prince or Princess shall cease, except those titles already granted and remaining unrevoked.[13]

So, while Prince Louis became a Marquess, his sons, Prince George and

Prince Louis, lost their right to their princely prefixes as well as their right to use the title of Serene Highness. From the 11th December 1917 they were to be known as the Earl of Medina and Lord Louis Mountbatten respectively. Princess Alice also acquired a new family name—that of Mountbatten, and when Philip of Greece was looking for a surname in 1947 it was hardly surprising that he decided to use her surname. So the events of the First World War had their influence on the future of the yet unborn Price.

9

Prince George of Battenberg, Second Marquess of Milford Haven

WHEN ATTLEE DREW ATTENTION to the ability of three of the Mountbatten family it was noticeable that he passed from mentioning the father, Prince Louis, on to his second son, then the Earl Mountbatten of Burma and so on to Prince Philip.[1] There was no mention of Prince Louis's eldest son, Prince George of Battenberg. Born in 1892, the third child in the family, he grew up as did his sisters in the period when his father was climbing the Admiralty ladder.

Prince Louis, who knew his sons better than did Prime Minister Attlee, "had more respect for George, who was far more brilliant as a boy and seemed more stable."[2] To some readers this may come as a shock for we became accustomed to think of Lord Louis as the outstanding Mountbatten. It is true that even in the 1930s Lord Louis outshone his elder brother, who was of a more modest and quiet disposition and who "left little imprint on his time".[3] But once again we have to face the fact that George "was a naval officer of remarkable abilities who was generally accepted as the inheritor of his father's brilliance,"[4] while Lord Louis "developed more slowly than his distinguished father and his brilliant brother, George,"[5] partly because Lord Louis "was no scholar; George had been a great deal more interested in his lessons."[6]

If Prince George had his father's brilliance, he certainly did not inherit his obsessive drive to succeed. Writing of Prince Louis, the naval historian Arthur J. Marder alleges that "he was inordinately ambitious and made no bones about it."[7] Those who try to explain this ambition—so rare among royalty—suggest that it was Prince Louis's way of compensating for the morganatic marriage of his parents, which he may have considered had cast some slur on his true royalty. Others suggest, quite to the contrary, that it was the plebeian blood of his mother which drove him on the self-advancement. Whatever the cause, there can be no doubt that he had that ambition and did manage to prove himself as a sailor and as a public servant.

In his turn, Lord Louis, the younger son, was badly affected by his father's humiliation in October 1914. Whereas he had been only an average student and a far from outstanding midshipman, it seems as if the events of October 1914 and of December 1917 awoke in him that determination that perhaps had been latent until then, and "a blazing ambition to vindicate his father in his own person . . .".[8]

Prince George was eight years older than Prince Louis. In July 1914 he was in charge of the gun turret of the new battle cruiser *New Zealand* on station at that gigantic review of the British Fleet (p. 77) while the younger brother, Louis, was only a cadet, assigned for that review to a lowly post on the old pre-dreadnought ship also called *New Zealand*.

Prince George was still a lieutenant on the *New Zealand* in November 1915. The ship was stationed at Rosyth and his father, although no longer First Lord, was staying on board as the guest of the Rear-Admiral Gordon Milne. On the 23rd November a telegram came from the Admiralty:

> FOUR GERMAN BATTLE CRUISERS, SIX LIGHT CRUISERS, AND TWENTY-TWO DESTROYERS WILL SAIL THIS EVENING TO SCOUT ON DOGGER BANK . . . ALL AVAILABLE BATTLE CRUISERS, LIGHT CRUISERS AND DESTROYERS FROM ROSYTH SHOULD PROCEED TO A RENDEZVOUS AT 55°13'' N, 3°12'' E, ARRIVING AT 7.00 A.M. TOMORROW . . .[9]

Prince Louis tactfully refused the Rear-Admiral's kind invitation to sail with him into action. So, unlike his son, he missed the Battle of the Dogger Bank in which Beatty commanded the British Fleet which sank the German cruiser *Blucher*, and mauled the battle cruisers, *Seydlitz*, *Moltke* and *Derfflinger*. Unfortunately, Beatty's flagship was hit; he ordered Admiral Moore to take command of the fleet and to "keep closer to the enemy". Unfortunately Moore failed to see this signal and continued on his pre-ordained course so that the rest of the German Fleet escaped. Nonetheless, Prince George had seen action. He was also at the Battle of Jutland a year later, again commanding the two forward twelve-inch guns which became overheated through constant firing. Most biographies of the Mountbattens tell us that during the Battles of Dogger Bank, Heligoland Bight and Jutland, the turret commanded by Prince George fired more shells than were fired by any other turret during the First and the Second World Wars.[10] Prince George often recalled the exploits of the war in conversation with Prince Philip after he had become a sort of step-father to the young Prince.

Unlike his younger brother, Prince George seems to have taken his father's humiliation more philosophically. Maybe this was because he was that much older and less impressionable. Maybe it was because he had seen at least a little of the world and was aware that fortune is, indeed, "a fickle jade". Perhaps their very close relationship could not be affected by anything that the yellow Press and a people made nervy by war wrote or said. He knew his father and could ignore the opinions of those who did not.

In 1921 he was serving in *HMS Cardiff* when he received the news of his father's death. As the elder son he inherited his titles and became the second Marquess of Milford Haven while continuing to serve in the Navy. His younger brother and his sisters now regarded him as the head of the family. In 1930 his sister, Princess Alice, agreed with him that Prince Philip was in danger of being spoilt or 'cissified' in an all-female household. She agreed to allow Prince Philip to go to school in England where the Marquess promised to provide that male discipline which the growing youngster needed and would not get from an increasingly absent father.

The Marquess had already provided some of the money that the exiled family needed while living in Paris. Indeed, Queen Alexandra describes him as one of the "chief benefactors" during this period.[11] When Prince Philip came to live at Lynden Manor he had the companionship of George's son, David, who was about two years older than him but with whom he struck up a close friendship which lasted until after Prince Philip's marriage at which David was best man.

David was already a boarder at Cheam School, so it was hardly surprising that the Marquess found the money to send Prince Philip to the school as well. He also played the part of proxy father—going to sports days, speech days and other events so that Prince Philip would not feel that he was that much different from the other boys. And while Prince Philip spent part of his holidays with his European relatives, most of his time was spent in the Marquess's home where the Countess of Milford Haven made him very welcome. Here, indeed, he knew the warm atmosphere of a stable family.

The Countess was the daughter of Grand Duke Michael of Russia. It is alleged that she retained the tastes of one who had known the opulence of pre-Revolutionary Russia. We have seen that Prince Louis had left little money to his children, and one result of this was that the second Marquess, whose only income came from his naval pay, was unable to continue to meet the expenses of an extravagant wife plus the cost of bringing up two boys. In 1932 he resigned from the Royal Navy. He became the British representative of the Sperry Gyroscope Company of America and a director of a number of public companies, including Marks & Spencer, which were anxious to make use of his many talents.

So he had the money to maintain his wife in the 'station to which her childhood had accustomed her' and still afford to keep the two boys at

Cheam. It is not surprising that Prince Philip felt a debt of gratitude towards this uncle for whom he had a deep affection. In part this was based on the realization of what was being done for him, not only at Cheam but also in providing him with a home at Lynden. But in part it was the affection of an energetic and ambitious youth for a man of ability who had seen action during the First World War. Some people have suggested that Prince Philip's choice of a naval career was due to the influence of this favourite uncle. Indeed, the British Information Service prepared a brief biography in preparation for the marriage in 1947. This said:

> In choosing a naval career he was following the tradition of the Mountbatten side of his family. Prince Louis of Battenberg was an Admiral of the Fleet and First Sea Lord; his son, the second Marquess, served in the Royal Navy, like Prince Philip's cousin [David] the third Marquess, and his uncle, Admiral Lord Mountbatten of Burma.

Philip resented the way in which the insular British had chosen once again to ignore his father and his family. He amended the copy to read:

> In choosing a career in one of the services he was following the tradition of both sides of his family. Both his grandfathers served at sea. His father was a career officer in the Greek Army and both his father's and mother's brothers served in the Navy.[12]

In the summer of 1938 Prince Philip and David Milford Haven spent part of their holidays in Venice with Princess Alexandra and her mother. Alexandra wrote:

> Mummy and I knew that [David's] father was not well but little knew how seriously ill he was. Almost before the summer ended, Uncle George died of cancer. He was only forty-six . . . at a crucial stage of his career, Philip had lost the uncle who had so long been closer and more encouraging than any foster father.[13]

Thus it was at this relatively late stage in his life that Prince Philip became the responsibility of Lord Louis.

It seems fitting to end this brief examination of the career of the second Marquess of Milford Haven with something said by Earl Mountbatten during a television film on his life and times. Writing of his brother's death, Earl Mountbatten said:

> 1938 was not only a bad year politically, it was especially sad for our family, because in April my brother, the Second Marquess of Milford Haven died at the age of forty-six.
>
> Georgie was seven years older than me [*sic*]—just enough to be a real hero to me. To see him taken away in the prime of life by cancer was an agonizing experience. I adored him. He must have been one of the cleverest men I have ever known—I think his brain was twice the size of mine. But then, he was quite different from me. Everybody loved him; I don't think he had an enemy in the world. He was the sort of person who, instead of reading detective stories, would sit down and read problems of higher calcalus and solve them in his head. When he was a squadron gunnery officer, he would take a chair and compose complicated orders for a squadron concentration

shoot in his head, and then he would dash them off on a typewriter on a wax master and have them duplicated without any revision. He was a brilliant man.[14]

10

Lord Louis, Earl Mountbatten of Burma

Author's note: I had written this chapter before Lord Louis's death in August, 1979. In view of all that was written at the time and in the light of his own book which appeared just after his death, it may seem superfluous, even presumptuous, to allow this chapter to stand. But the story of Prince Philip cannot be told without some reference to the late Earl, and this brief account of his career may serve to remind older readers of the once-great man and introduce him to younger readers.

WHEN HE AMENDED the brief survey of his career, Prince Philip was anxious at one and the same time to pay tribute to his father's memory, and, more significantly, for the purposes of this chapter, to try to show that the Battenberg influence was not as strong as people generally assumed. There was no mention in his amended version of the summary of the family by name and therefore no mention of "his uncle, Admiral Lord Mountbatten of Burma".[1] But in spite of this princely attempt to put the record straight, it remains true that there is a general assumption that Lord Mountbatten played a major role in Prince Philip's upbringing. Many people believe that he continued to be an important influence on the life of Prince Philip after his marriage to the Princess Elizabeth, which helps to explain why the Establishment, major figures in the Conservative Party and some Press lords combined in an unholy alliance to denigrate him.

If we link this hostility towards Lord Mountbatten with the general belief that he had a great influence over Prince Philip we may be able to begin to explain the hostility towards the Prince which has been shown, fairly consistently, by the same forces which were hostile towards his uncle. And it will be part of this story, in later chapters, to show how Prince Philip has reacted towards these waves of criticism at different points in his career.

The late Earl Mountbatten of Burma was born at Frogmore in 1900, the youngest child of Prince Louis, then aged forty-six, and Princess Victoria who was thirty-seven. He was eight years younger than his "brilliant brother" George and, as often happens with the youngest child, was somewhat spoilt by his middle-aged parents and in particular by his mother who had more time to devote to him than she had been able to spend on the three older children. His father was away for a great deal of time, but when at home, he too enjoyed the pleasure of spoiling the infant Louis. In return for this affection the youngest child not unnaturally learned to love both his parents in a way which was not always typical of children born into royal households. One only has to examine the childhood of the children of King George V and Queen Mary to see how traumatic an experience a royal upbringing could be.

Like his brother and sister he quickly became accustomed to following his father as he moved from one station to another, and to visiting the family's many ruling royal relatives, from Austria through Rumania and on to Corfu where he stayed with his sister, Princess Alice, and Prince Andrew, before going on to Russia to stay with his Tsarist cousins before making his way back through the homes of the German relations and so to Spain where his cousin, Ena, was married to King Alfonso.

It was during these travels that he became known in the widespread family as 'Dickie' Battenberg. At first he had been called Nicky, since Nicholas was one of his five names. But when the Battenbergs stayed with the family of the Tsar there were too many 'Nickies' and the Battenberg girls changed their brother's diminutive to 'Dickie'—and so it remained.

During his early years he was educated, in between travelling, by his mother. But she and Prince Louis soon learned to accept the fact that this younger brother was not as clever, as interested or as able as Prince George, who was not only brilliant and hard-working but much better at other things such as sports. When he was ten he followed his brother's footsteps and went to Lockhurst Park Preparatory School. But here again he failed to live up to the records which his brother had set so that the parents decided not to expose him to further humiliating comparisons. They did not send him to Cheam School where Prince George had been a leader in both games and studies. Instead, when he was thirteen, 'Dickie' was sent to Osborne on the Isle of Wight to begin his training for a naval career. Here he was treated as just another naval cadet, followed the course in mathematics, seamanship, signalling, rowing, sailing and engineering as well as instruction in English language and French. In 1914 he passed out of Osborne as thirty-fifth in a class of eighty and went on to Dartmouth to complete his training.

While he was at Osborne his father, then First Sea Lord, visited the

College to review the naval cadets. The father remembered the humour with which he passed by his younger son, his eyes gleaming with pride. The son remembered the pride he felt for his father. Later, in July 1914, he and the other Osborne cadets were sent to help man the Third Fleet for that Grand Review which Prince Louis organized so fortuitously. He was stationed on an old ship, the *New Zealand*, and watched with pride as his father, along with King George V, steamed through the Fleet arranged in its lines of column all dressed out in their bright flags, their four-inch guns cracking out the Royal Salute. Maybe it was here, for the first time, that the young Battenberg felt that patriotism, that pride in his King and country and in the Royal Navy that were to be the hallmarks of his later career. Certainly it was here that he fully appreciated the true magnificence of his father who was in charge of these massive fleets and who stood with his King to make the review.

It was in October 1914, as a new cadet at Dartmouth, that he had to cope with the reports that his father had been publicly humiliated and forced to resign from his post of First Sea Lord. Alden Hatch tells of another cadet, Stephen Fry, seeing Lord Louis standing to attention by the flagpole in the College grounds, the tears running down his cheeks.[2] In 1968 Lord Louis wrote:

> The news of my father's resignation came as a terrible shock to me . . . I remember having to go away and think about it alone. The other cadets were kind and decent about it . . . but I didn't want to see them. I just wanted to be by myself.[3]

This was a most decisive day in the career of the young cadet and because of the influence he had, or was supposed to have had, on the career of Prince Philip, it was also a decisive day for the unborn Prince. It was the day that the youngest Battenberg decided that he would remake, in his own career, the shattered career of his father and prove to the world that the Battenbergs earned and deserved their successes. It is worth noting that when Prince Andrew's career was shattered in 1922 he proved to be bitter but ineffective.[4] Perhaps it was that he had suffered too much earlier in his career of exile and recall: maybe he had run out of resilience. But in the Battenberg family there seemed to be a will to succeed which was unusual in royal families—where success is achieved, if at all, with effortless ease. For the Battenbergs—father and son—it had to be worked for.

Early in 1916 Lord Louis passed out from Dartmouth, now eighteenth in his class of eighty. He took a final three-month course at the College at Keyham in Plymouth where he passed out top of the class—he was on his way. He was sent to serve on Admiral Beatty's flagship, the *Lion*, which had been damaged at the Battle of Jutland in which Prince George had seen action. But the *Lion* saw no further action because the German Fleet remained bottled up in harbour and never again challenged the Royal Navy.

One interesting foretaste of things to come was provided by the young midshipman when he reported to *Lion*. On the breast of his simple uniform he wore a ribbon given to commemorate his attendance at the coronation of King George V. Many officers had served for two years of war and had yet received no medals or decorations. Some considered that young Battenberg's ribbon was a flamboyant piece of ostentation on the part of the young midshipman. This was to be a feature of the later man and of his critics: he could never have been accused of being the shrinking violet, earning deservedly the sobriquet 'the magnificent Mountbatten' in the 1920s. Indeed, his critics would always latch on to this facet of his character, sometimes in envy, sometimes in anger.

His love for decoration and for the perquisites of rank help to explain why he resented so bitterly the Declaration on Titles which was published in the *London Gazette* on 11th December 1917; because of the King's decision he lost his right to use the title of Serene Highness which the Battenbergs had formerly been allowed. Later he wrote:

> It was all rather ludicrous. I'd been born in England, and I'd always felt completely English. Having an English name didn't make me any more English. But such was the mood of the country . . . Anyhow, now I was Midshipman Lord Louis Mountbatten . . .[5]

But this further attack on the family was one of the reasons for Lord Louis's continuing interest in its history and in the ramifications which have linked it with so many ruling families and former ruling families.

Lord Louis saw no action during the last years of the war and when 'peace broke out' he was a sub-lieutenant on a submarine. Many ships were laid up, many officers dismissed from the service. Lord Louis was sent to Christ's College, Cambridge, where his cousins, Prince Albert (later George VI) and Prince Henry (later the Duke of Gloucester) were also undergraduates. During this year he also had a chance to enjoy the social life of upper-class London, then able and willing to enjoy the end of wartime austerity. There were still the great mansions such as Crewe House, Wimborne House, Chesterfield House and Londonderry House where dinner was served on gold plate by footmen wearing knee breeches and powdered wigs. Lord Louis and his bachelor cousins, including the Prince of Wales, were welcome guests at such functions and at the forty or so embassies where they met the rich and powerful.

In 1920 he served as an ADC to the Prince of Wales during his tour of the West Indies, Australia and New Zealand and received an invitation to fill the same post during the tour of India planned for 1921. Before that, however, he had met Edwina Ashley, a granddaughter of Sir Ernest Cassel who had been attacked by the Press in 1915 as a foreign-born Jew who was yet a Privy Councillor.[6] Neither she nor Lord Louis knew that Sir Ernest had made her the heir to his fabulous millions. They were two young people, one a dominating extrovert, the other a quiet yet witty introvert. He took her to meet Prince Louis who welcomed the granddaughter of a man who had suffered—as he had—unjustly. In September she and Lord Louis were on holiday with the Duke and Duchess of

Sutherland in Dunrobin in Scotland when news came of Prince Louis's sudden death. Lord Louis left for London, to be followed, four days later, by Edwina Ashley. On her arrival in London she was met by her grandfather's secretary with the news that Sir Ernest had died on that very afternoon in his study at Brooke House, where Edwina had acted as hostess for her grandfather for many years.[7]

The two young people were shattered by the deaths of men whom they had loved. In October 1921 Lord Louis sailed with the Prince of Wales to India. Edwina went back to her home at Broadlands which she had left because she was unable to get on with her stepmother. Having borrowed a hundred pounds from an aunt she decided to travel out to India to be with Lord Louis. In Bombay she horrified the clerk at the railway office by asking for a third class ticket to Delhi. This would have meant travelling with Indians. Not for the first time she failed to see what was so very wrong about Europeans mixing with Indians.[8] In the event Lord Louis was contacted and insisted that she travel first class and that he would make the financial arrangements later. In Delhi the young couple met up again and within a few weeks they had become engaged. Because of his relationship with the Royal Family, Lord Louis, like his sister Princess Alice, had to obtain the King's permission before the engagement could be announced publicly.[9] They were married on the 22nd July 1922 at St Margaret's, Westminster, their guest list reading like a royal *Who's Who*. Public interest was roused by the presence of the King and Queen, Queen Alexandra, the royal princes and members of the royal families and ex-royal families from all over Europe. There was also a great deal of interest in the bride since she was the heiress to Sir Ernest Cassel's fortune. He had died leaving about £6,000,000 at a time when miners were being paid about £1.50 a week and schoolteachers about £300 a year. The estate was divided into shares: one-eighth went to his niece and a quarter to his nephew; the remaining five-eighths was left in trust, two-eighths of the income from this going to Mary Ashley and three-eighths to Edwina, the remainder to their children. He left his sister £30,000 a year together with Moulton Paddocks and Brooke House; after her death these too would pass to Edwina. This meant that initially her share of the estate was about £750,000 and her income was about £60,000 a year, or about £45,000 after taxation. But none of this was to come to her until she married or reached the age of twenty-one.

It is hardly surprising that while, as we shall see, Lord Louis pursued his naval career, the young Mountbattens were able to afford to join what today might be termed the 'jet set'. They travelled extensively while on honeymoon and later when he was on leave. They met and became friendly with the stars of stage, screen and sports—Douglas Fairbanks, Jerome Kern and Will Rogers as well as the legendary baseball star, Babe Ruth. Newspaper accounts of their doings may have satisfied the taste of that wide public which enjoys reading about members of the Royal

Family, but they served only to stoke up that upper-class antagonism towards the latest of the Battenbergs.

In 1914 the young Battenberg had been placed eighteenth out of the class of eighty cadets entering Dartmouth. By the time he had completed his training he was top of that class. When he returned to pick up "the threads of my naval career in January 1923 . . . it was time to get down to hard work again, because I was determined to make a success of my profession, as my father had done."[10] He joined the *Revenge* at Constantinople a month before Prince Philip was rescued from Corfu by the *Calypso*.[11] At the end of 1924 the young sub-lieutenant Lord Louis Mountbatten went to the Signal School at Portsmouth and in 1925 he attended the Higher Wireless Course at Greenwich. After this he was sent to Malta to serve as Wireless Officer in the *Queen Elizabeth*, flagship of Admiral Sir Roger Keyes, Commander-in-Chief, Mediterranean. Later he wrote: "This was the most sought-after appointment for a newly fledged Signal Officer—but I had earned it by coming out top in the Signal Course."[12] A report on him from the Signal School noted that he was "thoroughly recommended for promotion as likely to do well in the higher ranks of the Service." After his service in Malta a confidential report described him as "a natural leader, who exerts a strong influence and constantly inspires success . . . Quite unspoilt by success."[13] In 1927 he had been promoted to the rank of Lieutenant-Commander and in 1932, "I had reached the rank of Commander, and was due to get what every naval officer wants—command of a ship."[14]

His first command was HMS *Daring*, one of the newest destroyers. But he and his crew had to exchange ships after only a few months. *Daring* went to the China Destroyer Flotilla while Mountbatten was given command of an old First World War destroyer, *Wishart*. He organized a band, started a ship's newspaper and led his men to sweeping victories in the Flotilla Regatta in September 1935, so that the *Wishart* became 'Cock of the Flotilla'.

In 1936 he was promoted to the Naval Air Division—a branch of the service which had been started by his father and which he worked to bring back—as the Fleet Air Arm—under control of the Navy.

In June 1939 he was appointed Captain commanding the Fifth Destroyer Flotilla. All the ships in the command were brand new of the 'J' and 'K' class—which was still being developed. Mountbatten took command of his own ship, the flotilla leader, on the 23rd August 1939—ten days before war broke out. The story of his ship, HMS *Kelly*, was told by Mountbatten's friend, Noël Coward, in the film *In Which We Serve*, in which Coward (playing the Mountbatten role) wore Mountbatten's cap.

The ship was torpedoed during the Norwegian campaign of 1940 and was brought back under tow to the Tyne for a refit. Mountbatten had other ships as a command vessel while *Kelly* was being repaired; he took part in the bombardment of Cherbourg and undertook the normal war work of a destroyer commander. In November 1940 *Kelly* returned to service and the Fifth Flotilla was sent to the Mediterranean where German dive bombers were making continual attacks on Malta. The destroyer flotilla was used to prevent supplies reaching Rommel in North Africa and in May was sent to support the Army's defence of Crete. *Kelly* was sunk by German dive bombers and Mountbatten and the other surviving members of his crew were taken aboard a sister ship, *Kashmir*, and taken to Alexandria. Mountbatten wrote:

> I went ashore in the first boat and when I reached the landing stage almost the first person I saw was a cheery young midshipman, grinning all over his face. It was my nephew, Philip. "What are you grinning at?" I asked him. "You've no idea how funny you look," he replied. "Your face is absolutely brown and your eyes are bright red." "What's so funny about that? You chaps who fight battles in big ships never get dirty." But I was very glad to see him.[15]

In August 1941 Mountbatten was given command of the aircraft-carrier, *Illustrious*, which had been damaged while stationed in Malta and was being repaired in the US Navy Yard at Norfolk, Virginia. While he was in the USA supervising the repairs, he received a telegram from Prime Minister Churchill ordering him "home here at once for something which you will find of the highest interest."[16]

When he met Churchill at Chequers, the Prime Minister offered him the post of Adviser on Combined Operations in succession to Admiral of the Fleet, Lord Keyes. "I said I'd rather be back at sea in the *Illustrious*. That really made him snort. 'Have you no sense of glory? Here I give you a chance to take a part in the higher leadership of the war, and all you want to do is go back to sea . . .' So that was that; no further argument: On October 27th 1941 I became Adviser on Combined Operations."[17]

Mountbatten's job, according to Churchill, was to "turn the south coast of England from a bastion of defence into a springboard of attack."[18] Commandos were trained to use specially-designed landing craft for attacks on the German-held French coast, and on other coasts of German occupied Europe.

In December 1941 Mountbatten's first raiding venture took place. A cruiser and four destroyers of the Navy, some six hundred commandos and a few RAF squadrons combined in an attack on the islands of Vaasgo and Maalow in south Norway and on the Lofoten Islands in the north. Fish-oil factories, a power station, wireless stations and coastal defences were destroyed; 150 Germans were killed and 98 captured; some 15,000 tons of shipping was sunk, while British casualties were 'light'. This was the first time that all three Services had combined in this way.

In February 1942 paratroops and commandos from landing craft attacked the German radar base at Bruneval, about twelve miles north of Le Havre. The station was demolished, and several pieces of equipment captured and brought back "with the loss of only one man killed and seven missing".[19] But the biggest raid took place on the 28th March when the object of the exercise was to put out of action the dry dock in St

Nazaire Harbour—the only dock on the Atlantic coast big enough to take the giant German battleship *Tirpitz*. From one point of view the raid was a success; the dock was destroyed and *Tirpitz* was never able to come into the Atlantic. On the other hand, "casualties were heavy, as we had to expect".[20]

Ten days before this raid Mountbatten had been named 'Commander of Combined Operations'. He had felt embarrassed when in October 1941 he took over, "a mere Captain", from the famous Admiral Keyes.[21] Now in March 1942 he became the fourth member of the Chiefs of Staffs Committee, "the body which directed British strategy in every theatre of war".[22] He was moved up the Navy List to Acting Vice-Admiral at the age of forty-one (two years younger than Nelson had been when promoted to Vice-Admiral). He also became an Honorary Lieutenant-General and an Honorary Air-Marshal—the first time that anyone except the King had held rank in all three Services.

Henry 'Chips' Channon met Lord Louis about this time. In his diary he wrote:

> *30th April. 1942*: Lunch with Mrs Greville in her suite at the Dorchester. It was a pleasant party. The Kents, she, lovely and amber-coloured, he in an Air Force uniform . . . Both Mountbattens. What a dazzling couple they are. I sat between them and found Dickie much grown in stature since he took up his highly important, indeed vital, command. But he remains simple and unaffected, and only when I talked of his nephew, Prince Philip of Greece, did his sleepy eyes light up with an affectionate, almost paternal, light.

But the new Commander of Combined Operations faced bitter hostility from "the Service Ministries—the Admiralty, the War Office and the Air Ministry—each of which had its own way of doing business, and bitterly resented a new organization cutting through its cherished red tape."[23] The Navy thought that it ought to be left free to fight the battle of the Atlantic; some Army chiefs were jealous of the way in which Mountbatten was able to "see Winston by myself".[24]

During the summer of 1942 Mountbatten was in Washington discussing, on Churchill's behalf, the question of the proposed invasion of Europe. He impressed Roosevelt and his advisers with reports of the success of the Combined Operations—and in doing so laid the seed which flowered in the shape of the integrated Allied Headquarters later in the war. He also persuaded them that it was not feasible to think of invading Europe without large numbers of landing craft and the speedy capture of a deep-water port.

In August the Americans delivered enough landing craft for the lifting of one whole division. Mountbatten and his colleagues decided to take the port of Dieppe. On the 19th August the Dieppe raid took place. Most of the troops involved were Canadians; the German defences proved to be much stronger than had been thought; the attackers had insufficient long-range guns to subdue them so that they met "a murderous fire". The losses were enormous: 3,363 of the 5,000 officers and men were killed or captured. The Royal Regiment of Canada lost 24 of its 26 officers and 464 of the 528 men to had taken part in the raid—which Mountbatten admitted deserved the description of "a catastrophe".[25]

But out of that bitter lesson Mountbatten learned the need for plenty of air cover, for a long period of heavy bombardment preceding any landings, and above all "that you cannot capture a port without so damaging its facilities as to make it useless."[26] From this last point developed the idea of PLUTO (the pipeline under the sea which carried petrol to the Normandy beaches in 1944) and of the Mulberry Harbour. By the time of the Allied invasion of Europe, Mountbatten was far away in Burma. About a week after D-Day the army leaders visited the Normandy beachhead. They sent a telegram to Mountbatten:

> Today we visited the British and American armies on the soil of France. We sailed through vast fleets of ships with landing craft of many types pouring out more men, vehicles and stores ashore. We saw closely the manoeuvre in process of rapid development. We have shared our secrets in common and helped each other all we could. We wish to tell you at this moment in your arduous campaign that we realize that much of this remarkable technique, and therefore the success of the venture, has its origins in developments affected by you and your staff of Combined Operations. Signed; Arnold, Marshall, King, Brooke, Smuts, Churchill.[27]

Lord Beaverbrook, owner of the *Daily Express*, was proudly Canadian. He blamed Mountbatten personally for the slaughter of 'his' Canadians at Dieppe. Beaverbrook ignored the opposition which Mountbatten had faced from Navy and Air Chiefs who refused to give him the massive support he thought such a raid needed. Beaverbrook preferred to personalize the disaster and his newspapers maintained a life-long hostility towards Mountbatten—and towards Prince Philip, the inheritor of the Mountbatten name in 1947.

By the time Mountbatten had received the congratulatory telegram from Churchill and the organizers of the invasion of France, he was Supreme Commander of Allied Forces in the South-East Asia Command. On the 22nd August 1943 Churchill met President Roosevelt at Quebec. From here he wrote to Deputy Prime Minister Attlee:

> The President and General Marshall are very keen on Mountbatten's appointment. There is no doubt of the need of a young and vigorous mind in this lethargic and stagnant Indian scene . . .[28]

His appointment was announced on the 25th August 1943. He had his doubts about taking up this post because, he said, "I wanted to go back in command of a ship."[29] However, when he was told that Roosevelt, Churchill, Marshall and the others wanted him to take up the post and that he had the support of the British and American Chiefs of Staff, he accepted.

On the 7th October 1943 the new Supreme Allied Commander set up his headquarters at New Delhi. He found that the Navy was still waiting for reinforcements, that the soldiers in his command had not received much training in jungle warfare and were dispirited after so many defeats at the hands of the Japanese, so that only the Air Force seemed to be continuing the offensive against the Japanese who, from their stronghold in Burma, were hammering on the gateways to British India.

He set out to raise the morale of the troops under his command. He toured continuously so that he was seen by most of the men of the 'Forgotten Army'. Some former soldiers remember the informal way in which, on arrival, he would order them to break ranks and gather round his jeep to listen to his plans for their future. Others remember that, having discovered that they rarely received mail from home, he organized things so that within a week or so there began a regular delivery of mail. Still others remember his newspaper which reached every man and which ensured that everyone was aware of what was going on. But no matter which particular incident or development these ex-soldiers remember, they all agree that Lord Louis brought a new spirit to the beleaguered forces under his command.[30]

Mountbatten organized a new type of training for soldiers, set up a Combined Operations team and supported General Slim's attempts to make his Fourteenth Army a successful fighting force. In February 1944 the Japanese launched an offensive in Arakan; this time the British did not retreat and by the 22nd February the Japanese had called off the battle. "This was a nasty shock for the Japanese," wrote Mountbatten.[31] On the 5th March 1944 Orde Wingate's brigade of 'Chindits' were flown in to launch the attack on Japanese-held Burma; on the 8th March the Japanese launched their own attack on Imphal which was to lead to "our definite victory in India . . .".[32] Imphal and Kohima were surrounded. Mountbatten ordered that the Fifth Indian Division be flown from Arakan—the first time a large armed formation had been transported from one battlefield to another by air. British strength was built up at Imphal so that they were able to launch a counter-offensive. After seventy-four days the Japanese retreated, having lost 53,000 men while the Fourteenth Army had lost 17,000 men. Mountbatten now ordered the British to take the offensive, fighting even through the monsoon season of 1943–1944 so that by January 1945 the British had crossed the Irrawaddy and attacked Mandalay which was captured on the 20th March. The Japanese Army was now in full retreat; the British pressed on throughout April and entered Rangoon on the 4th May.

After a Fourteenth Army victory parade in Rangoon on the 14th June, Mountbatten and his staff sat down to plan the attack on Malaya and Singapore. At the same time he had to learn to cope with the political results both of the Japanese victories of 1942–1943 and of the British victory in Burma in 1944–1945. Was he to hand over power to the Burma National Army which had supported the Japanese or was he to try to hold Burma down with the Burma Army hindering his progress? On the 1st June he issued a directive:

> The guiding principle which I am determined shall be observed is that no person shall suffer on account of political opinions honestly held, whether now or in the past, even if these may have been anti-British, but only on account of proven crimes against the criminal law, or actions repugnant to humanity. This principle is no more than an elementary point of British justice.[33]

This annoyed the old Government of Burma whose officials were released from prison camps as the British advanced through Burma. Some of his own political advisers did not support his attitude, while leaders of the Burma National Army thought they would do better for themselves if Mountbatten ended the period of Military Government and allowed the British to set up again a Civil Government. He agreed to do this and in October 1945 the pre-war officials took charge again. Mountbatten wrote:

> I now think this was a mistake because I knew this Civil Government didn't share my views; I should have tried harder to convince the Burmese or at least to have delayed matters. And then, according to my Burmese friends, there would have been a good chance of Burma remaining inside this Commonwealth. But what's done is done.[34]

By October 1945 the world had moved on. Mountbatten had met the US Commander MacArthur in July 1945 to plan the invasion of Malaya and Singapore. Later in July he was called back to Europe; Churchill wanted the SEAC Supremo to attend the Potsdam Conference where he met the new President of the United States, Harry S. Truman, and the Russian dictator, Stalin, the heir to the powers once exercised by Mountbatten's uncle, the last Tsar of Russia. He was in London on the 26th July when the results of the general election were announced and the Labour Government took charge. Mountbatten, a life-long Labour sympathizer, knew, respected and liked the new Prime Minister, Clement Attlee—which did not endear him to the majority of Conservative and Establishment figures. He wrote:

> Already my job was becoming more political than military. When I reported to Mr Attlee I explained to him the line I proposed to take with the liberated territories when we had driven the Japanese out of South-East Asia—now an imminent prospect. I was delighted to find that I had his full backing—I had a feeling that I was going to need it.[35]

On the 5th September Mountbatten's forces re-occupied Singapore where on the 12th September Mountbatten took the surrender of the 680,000 Japanese in South-East Asia. Now, at the age of only forty-five, Mountbatten found himself ruling over Burma, Malaya, the Dutch East Indies, Borneo and French Indo-China. His 'kingdoms' contained about 128 million people with still about 750,000 Japanese at large. He and Lady Mountbatten turned their attention first to liberating the prisoners of war. Lady Mountbatten was Superintendent-in-Chief of the St John Ambulance Brigade. She had had a grisly experience with the recovery of Allied prisoners of war from Germany and Lord Mountbatten was glad to have her help in South-East Asia. Together they visited most of the camps where men had been kept in terrible conditions; they organized supplies of food and medicine to try to save the lives of men who were near death.

The most important part of Mountbatten's work, however, involved negotiations with the leaders of the nationalist movements throughout the vast area under his control. He was glad to hand French Indo-China over to the Free French forces commanded by General Le Clerc; the tragedy of modern Vietnam then began to unfold as the French failed to appreciate the situation—that the days of Empire were over. In Indonesia Mountbatten clashed with the returning Dutch who, like the French in Vietnam, hoped to turn back the clock. He was glad to hand this territory over to the Dutch Government in July 1946—but saddened by the subsequent history of their attempt to ignore the strength of Indonesian nationalism.

When 'Pandit' Nehru came to visit the Indian community in Singapore, Mountbatten and his wife went out of their way to befriend him—much to the annoyance of the British civil administrators. This was to be important for Mountbatten's future—but was one of the causes of the anger which the stuffier Establishment felt towards him and his unconventional wife.

In May 1946 Mountbatten handed the problems of Malaya and Singapore to Malcolm MacDonald who had been appointed Governor-General by the Attlee Government. He himself went back to London to take part in the victory parade through London in June 1946. During the second half of 1946 he received a plethora of honours and decorations—from the City of London, various universities, Allied governments—and a new title, Mountbatten of Burma. The King conferred on him "the most coveted award of all" when, in an ancient ceremony, Mountbatten became a Knight of the Most Noble Order of the Garter, his banner hanging alongside those of his fellow-knights in St George's Chapel, Windsor.

The Navy also honoured him by promotion from the substantive rank of Captain to that of Rear-Admiral. Now, he felt, he could once more concentrate on furthering his naval career. "I very badly wanted to get back to sea."[36] But, as we know, it was not to be. In March 1947 he was back in India as Viceroy charged with the task of organizing the Independence of the vast sub-continent.

> When Mr Attlee asked me to take on this job he rather took my breath away. This was not something that could be settled straight off, and in fact we had several meetings about it. I asked to see the King; as King-Emperor he kept very close touch with Indian affairs. I pointed out to him that the chance of complete failure was very great indeed; and it would be bad for him to have a member of his family fail. He replies; "But think how good it will be for the monarchy if you succeed." And he then asked me formally to accept the appointment.[37]

It is no part of this biography of Prince Philip to trace the tortuous steps by which Mountbatten drove the Indian nationalists to agree on the method of granting India its independence, nor to go into the reasons why the sub-continent was divided into a Hindu-dominated India and a Muslim-dominated Pakistan. On the 15th August 1947 India won her independence. Mountbatten, as the last Viceroy, handed over responsibility to 'Pandit' Nehru, the first Indian Prime Minister, and Rajendra Prasad, President of the Constituent Assembly. They in turn accorded him the signal honour of being the first Governor-General of Independent India, an office which he took up as he ceased to be Viceroy.

But it is part of this biography to note that Mountbatten's involvement with Indian affairs was resented by many in Britain. Churchill led the Conservative Party in its opposition to the granting of independence to the former "jewel in the Imperial Crown". He and his supporters blamed Mountbatten for having played a part in this "betrayal". They and others resented the obvious friendships which had developed between the Mountbattens and many of the nationalist leaders. In particular, there was an outcry against the photograph of Gandhi with his arm around Lady Mountbatten's shoulder. Beaverbrook, the imperialist-minded proprietor of the *Daily Express*, resentful of the part played by Mountbatten in the Dieppe tragedy, used his influence and that of his papers against the new Governor-General—and against his nephew, 'Phil the Greek'.

In June 1948 Mountbatten handed over the office of Governor-General of India to Rajagopalachari. He returned home to find that the Conservative Press, most members of the Conservative Party, old friends, and, "most hurtful of all", Winston Churchill had turned against him. His whole family, including the Duke of Edinburgh, were the subject of spiteful attacks. This atmosphere of ill-feeling was not the easiest in which to try to rebuild his naval career. As Rear-Admiral he was sent to command the First Cruiser Squadron in Malta where he was under the command of men who had served under him when he was Supremo in South-East Asia. In 1949 he was promoted to Vice-Admiral and appointed to be Fourth Sea Lord of the Admiralty. In May 1952 he returned to the Mediterranean as Commander-in-Chief and at the end of that year became Commander-in-Chief, Allied Forces, Mediterranean.

In 1953 he took part in the coronation celebrations. He recorded:

> Strangely enough, I felt even closer to our new Queen than to either her father or her uncle though both were my contemporaries and friends. She and her sister, Princess Margaret, were playmates of our daughters, Patricia and Pamela, and so we got to know them well as children. And then, after her marriage when my nephew was serving in the Mediterranean Fleet they shared house with us in Malta. I look back on that as one of the happiest times of my life.[38]

Others, eager to make their own interpretations of events, thought that they saw "Mountbatten muscling in on the monarchy" and became even more critical of him and of his nephew.

In 1955 he became First Sea Lord, the professional head of the Royal Navy. ". . . It was Winston Churchill who was responsible for the appointment, one of his last acts in high office. That made him the only man to have appointed a father and son to the post of First Sea Lord. It also meant that he had got over his hard feelings about what I had done in India. I was glad about that."[39]

During his time as First Sea Lord Mountbatten helped re-shape the Navy for its tasks in the modern world. In July 1958 he was appointed Chief of the Defence Staff and set about the most sweeping changes to take place in the Armed Forces, "the result of twenty years' experience in war and peace".[40] He used his experiences as Commander of Combined Operations and as Chief of SEAC to show that inter-Service organization and operations were not only possible but beneficial. He proposed that the Minister of Defence should have supreme power over the three Service departments. This aroused the hostility of his Service colleagues but won the support of Prime Minister Macmillan:

> I can think of no Service Chief other than Dickie who would have been prepared to upturn centuries of tradition and to take the decisive step of depriving the separate Services of their independence. That was Dickie's strength. He was ready to defy tradition in big things, in the same way as he upheld it in small matters. He was quick to take decisions, often too quick, and sometimes obstinate in upholding them. Having come to a view about what could reasonably be done, 'could' usually became 'should', and in due course, 'should' was the only possible solution.[41]

This trait did nothing to endear him to the more conventional-minded and tradition-bound. But by the time he retired, in 1965, the unified Command was a reality, one of the ways in which Mountbatten left his mark on history. In retirement, Admiral of the Fleet the Earl Mountbatten of Burma continued to play an active role in public affairs; the Government used him to head Commissions of Enquiry—notably into the problem of keeping long-term prisoners in safe custody. He continued to be an active President of many charities and associations and attended the many royal weddings, baptisms and funerals of the 1960s and 1970s.

His assassination at the hands of the IRA shocked the civilized world. But, as a television film revealed, he had prepared for his death—and the funeral would have pleased "a most accomplished showman . . . a very proud man at heart."[42]

Part III

AN ENGLISH EDUCATION, 1930–1940

11

Cheam School, 1930–1933

WE HAVE SEEN from the confused *mélange* of Prince Philip's ancestry that perhaps only one thing is clear, namely that he was not English. It was doubtful whether, by right of birth, he was a Greek even before the Revolutionary Government deprived him and the rest of the family of their nationality. It could be argued that he was a Dane by virtue of his grandfather's descent and the passport he held after 1923 by the kindness of the King of Denmark.[1] By virtue of his mother's ancestry it might have been argued that he was a German—and his sisters' marriages to a quartet of German Princes seems to support that argument.

In 1947, as we shall see, he became a naturalized Englishman,[2] just as his Battenberg grandfather had done in 1868. The first steps along the road towards that adoption of a new nationality were taken in 1930 when he was sent to live with his Uncle George in Lynden Manor. And as an important part of his introduction into the peculiarly English way of life there was the period which he spent at the boarding school in Cheam in Surrey.

The link between the Battenbergs and Cheam School was started by Prince Louis when he was First Sea Lord. He was impressed by the confident behaviour of two midshipmen and asked where they had gone to school. "We were friends at Cheam School," they told him.[3] It was, we are assured, because of the impression these two boys made on him that Prince Louis decided to send Prince George there, and in his turn Lord George Mountbatten sent his son, David, to the school. When Prince Philip came to live with his family Lord George thought it only natural that he should go to the boarding school with his elder cousin.

Cheam School is one of the oldest preparatory schools in England. Founded during the Civil War, it celebrated its tercentenary in 1947 when one of its most distinguished ex-pupils was going through the process of becoming naturalized, engaged, ennobled and married. Originally the school had been in London. During the Great Plague the headmaster moved out of London along with most of those who could afford to do so.

Thus, in 1665, the school was established in Cheam, then a small village near Sutton, Nonsuch Palace and other royal homes at Richmond, Ham and Kew. The school building was known as Whitehall, an attempt perhaps to recapture something of the flavour of its London origins.

The school's reputation grew and so did the number of pupils, so in 1719 it moved to a new thirteen-acre site, but still in Cheam. A sign of its high reputation is the list of eminent former pupils which included a future Prime Minister, Henry Addington, later Viscount Sidmouth; three sons of the nobility, Lords Donoughmore, Aberdeen and Randolph Churchill, father of Winston Churchill; and two future Viceroys of India, Lords Willingdon and Hardinge of Penshurst.[4] During a large part of the nineteenth century the position of headmaster was filled by a succession of Tabors—father and sons. This led to the school becoming known locally as Tabor's School, something which is remembered today in Tabor Court, a block of flats standing on the site of what had once been Cheam School. (David and Prince Philip were among the last pupils to go to the school in Cheam.) In 1934 the trustees considered that the former village had now become too busy a suburb of London. They sold the Cheam site and re-opened the school in Headley, about five miles from Newbury in Berkshire. It was to this school, still called Cheam School, that Prince Charles was to go in 1957.

For Prince Philip in 1930, as for Prince Charles in 1957, this was the first time away from home and relations. We know that Prince Charles found his first years very hard. His more extrovert father, however, revelled in life among boys of roughly his own age and enjoyed being taught by men—and in any event, there was always the company of an older cousin with whom, as another bonus, he spent pleasant holidays at Lynden Manor or with Lord Louis and Lady Edwina.

The boarding school in the Surrey village looked comfortable from the outside, but inside it was another matter. The headteacher and others, such as the matron, insisted on discipline. Boys had to tidy their dormitories in which they slept in ancient beds. Indeed, even in Headley little had changed when Queen Elizabeth II went to look over the school with Prince Charles. She is said to have tested one of the beds in a dormitory and to have told Prince Charles, "You won't be able to jump up and down on these beds," a reflection of her understanding of her children's behaviour in Buckingham Palace as well as of the relatively spartan conditions which are to be found in many independent schools.[5]

And, when needed, discipline was imposed with the aid of corporal punishment. During the tercentenary celebrations in 1947 Prince Philip introduced Princess Elizabeth to "my late headmaster who used to cane me". At which the Princess replied with a smile, "I hope you gave it to him good and proper."[6]

Each morning, having made his own bed to the satisfaction of the matron or one of her assistants, Prince Philip along with the other ninety or so boys went off to breakfast and then a normal school time-table. Like his Uncle Louis he was not at that time very interested in academic things and study was a bore. It is not surprising then that his reports were mediocre. He liked history and won a prize in French. When his cousin was told of this, "I am afraid that I laughed rudely. 'What was the handicap?' I demanded, and when he sheepishly confessed that there had been none, I asked him jolly well why not after all the years he had lived in Paris!"[7]

But he did lose the American accent he had acquired at St Cloud and learn to play English games—captaining the soccer team in his final year. He also continued to show that search for excellence and sense of competitiveness he had always shown in sport in general. He tied for first place in the high jump and won the diving championship—again not surprising in view of the amount of time he had previously spent in or near the water. He played hockey on roller-skates—and lost half a tooth because of a clash with his cousin, David. He and David were together on a Boy Scouts' camp in Dover to which they travelled by bicycle. Saddle-sore, they decided that they would hitch a ride back home after the camp. They went to the docks at Dover, where they found a Thames sailing barge which was loading with grain bound for London. The master agreed to take Philip, David and some others back around the coast. For two nights they slept on sacks of grain in the hold, reporting to their cousin that they were "thrilled".[8]

And so for three years Philip led the life of an English schoolboy from an upper-class family; school, holidays at home or abroad, and always the security of Uncle George's home at Lynden Manor. But in 1933 this came to an end. His sister, Theodora, had married Berthold, the Margrave of Baden, in whose castle the legendary Kurt Hahn had founded his new school. Although Hahn was no longer headmaster, the school continued to run on the lines he had laid down. Prince Philip's sister thought it would be a good idea if her young brother came to the school where she could keep an eye on him and from which he could go to visit their mother, now separated from their father and in need of some sort of stabilizing influence.[9] Philip would be able to visit her more often from Baden than from England and so maybe help provide the reassurance she seemed to require.

Reluctantly, therefore, he left Cheam.[10] It could not have been a bad introduction to the English way of life because when he came to choose a school for Prince Charles he chose his own old school, Cheam.

12

Kurt Hahn

THE FIRST WORLD WAR had its effects on the life of the unborn Prince Philip—grandson to the ill-treated Prince Louis and son of the unfortunate Prince Andrew, both of whose careers were affected by the war. In this chapter we will see how that war affected the type of education that the Prince received and examine the reasons why that education took place in Scotland and not, as his family had intended, in Germany.

In the autumn of 1918 the Kaiser of Germany appointed Prince Max of Baden as the Chancellor (or Prime Minister) of Imperial Germany. By this time the Kaiser and most of his leading advisers realized that the war had been lost. The submarine campaign had failed to starve the British people into submission; the USA had entered the war on the Allied sides in 1917 and during 1918 there was a steady build up of the number of fresh, vigorous, well-armed troops into the trenches. Meanwhile, there was increasing evidence of despondency in Germany, the result of the effects of the British naval blockade. The German commanders had made their own last effort in the spring of 1918. They brought back a million men and thousands of guns from the Russian front and, for the first time, were able to bring their whole army to fight on the one, albeit long, front.

Ludendorff, the German commander, started his offensive in March 1918. There was a series of German thrusts; the first was against the British who fought a number of battles around Arras and Amiens which slowed down the German advance; then in April the Germans attacked the British in the north, and the Flanders battlefields of Ypres were the scene of great slaughter. It was here that the British commander, Haig, issued an order: "With our backs to the wall and believing in the justice of our cause, each one must fight to the end."[1]

By the end of April the advance had been halted. Ludendorff then switched the attack to the Aisne valley where the Germans overran the French and, as in 1914, came to the Marne and the roads to Paris. The dispirited French received massive aid from the fresh American troops and held the line. Then on the 18th July the Allied Supreme Commander,

Foch, ordered a counter-attack. Tanks rolled, artillery blasted and aircraft bombed the German lines which broke—for the first time. In August the British-led Allied forces defeated the Germans around Amiens—"the black day of the German army," said Ludendorff, who had to listen to his retreating soldiers mocking the raw recruits coming to take their place at the front.[2]

"Nothing succeeds like success." The Allies, for so long on the defensive, now exploited their new-found position of being the attackers. By the end of September the whole of the Allied Front was advancing. On the 4th October the Germans asked for an armistice. The Allied reply consisted of Wilson's Fourteen Points—which the Germans rejected. At this stage Ludendorff resigned from his command, fearing that the politicians' stubbornness would lead to the complete defeat of his army. The Allies pressed on—and Prince Max, now Chancellor, intervened to save his country from the humiliation of invasion and occupation. The Kaiser urged Prince Max to seek "an armistice with honour" with Wilson, Lloyd George and the French Prime Minister, Clemenceau. In this way he hoped to save his throne as well as his army.

Prince Max was both a humanitarian and a realist. He appreciated that if Germany were to get the honourable peace which was essential, and if, more significantly, she were to become a democratic country deserving of an honourable place among the nations of the world, the Kaiser would have to give up his throne, and the Prussian clique which had dominated Germany since 1870 would have to be replaced. So, on the 9th November, without warning him, Prince Max announced his Emperor's abdication, declared his country a Republic and prepared to surrender to the Allies on the 11th November 1918.

Later, the German nationalists would claim that their army had not been defeated, and that the war had been ended only by politicians who had "stabbed them in the back".[3] Army leaders were willing supporters of this myth which was used by Hitler both in his climb to power and in the years after 1933 when he held supreme power in a new Germany.

After doing what he thought was best for his country, Prince Max gave up his post to make way for a Socialist Chancellor, Ebert, whose government met at the town of Weimar. Prince Max went back to his home at Schloss Salem, his estate on the shores of Lake Constance, where he decided to set up a new type of school. Lake Constance is, in a sense, an international lake, for its eastern waters are bounded by Austria, Switzerland and Bavaria. The Schloss, or Castle, at Salem was an impressive building, much larger than Buckingham Palace[4] but far less comfortable. Only the rooms are heated, even today, the passages and corridors being left unheated.[5]

Prince Max realized that the old Prussian élite had led Germany astray into military adventures which had ended in humiliating defeat. He wanted to educate a new élite, in new principles, at his new school which, in 1920, had only four pupils along with his own son, Berthold. He hoped that he would be able to produce new leaders for a new Germany, less rigid, less brutal and more humanitarian than the Prussian leaders had been. During the war Prince Max had learned to admire the way in which the British refused to accept what seemed the inevitable defeat. Rightly or wrongly, he attributed this stubborn determination to the way in which Britain's leaders had been educated at their public schools. At Schloss Salem he hoped to introduce the best elements of these schools into his own new venture.

When the school started Prince Max was its headmaster, but as it began to grow he turned to a former colleague, Kurt Hahn, and appointed him as head; it is with Hahn's name that the school is normally associated. Hahn had been a political adviser to Prince Max while he was Chancellor and had been a member of the German delegation at the negotiations which led to the Treaty of Versailles. He had been one of those who had been called in to write a constitution for the new democratic German Republic set up in 1918.

Kurt Hahn himself was already aware of the influence of the British public schools. Before the war he had been a Rhodes Scholar at Oxford where he came to admire the merits of the products of the British schools, claiming that they benefited from having been "taught to argue without quarrelling, to quarrel without suspecting, to suspect without slandering".[6] Given that both he and Prince Max had much the same ideas of what they wanted to do—and of the British model which they wished to imitate—it is not surprising that many people have seen Hahn's schools as a resuscitation of the principles of Dr Arnold.

Indeed, as one examines both Hahn's writings and the way in which his principles were put into practice the more he seems to have taken the best out of Arnold and allied it with the best out of Plato, enclosing both in a typical Teutonic system of rigid application.

He insisted that the nation, and school, should do "all it can to make the individual citizen discover his own powers; the individual citizen becomes a cripple from his own point of view if he is not qualified by education to serve the community."[7] Once the individual had been helped in this process of self-discovery he had then to be taught "to live as a member of a community, with all that that implies in learning to give and take and play a part in a common life."[8] For if Prince Max's pupils were to become the new leaders of a democratic Germany they would have to be men of a different character from the Prussian leaders of the past. Indeed, Hahn wrote, "Our [Prussian] educational system is chiefly concerned with the transmission of knowledge, and accepts no responsibility for the training of character."[9]

And there we have the main aims of the Salem School; self-discovery, the development of character, and the realization that leaders had to serve their communities.

Dr Arnold's reforms had led to the 'muscular Christian', the elevation of games to a dominating role in school life. Hahn insisted on the 'muscular' part but down-graded games.[10] Before breakfast "all boys ran slowly for 400 yards, preferably on their toes. All boys skipped in the morning and did physical drill at night. Many climbed a rope each day. Four times a week, all the year round, academic studies in the mornings had a 45-minute break for the practice of running, jumping and javelin throwing."[11] Almost every afternoon there was physical labour—the building of a running track or a new block of the school—as well as various forms of work performed for the benefit of the local community.

By 1930 the reputation of the school had grown to the extent that there were now over four hundred pupils. At first the fees had been such that only the very rich could afford to send their boys to Salem. It was Hahn who worked out a scheme whereby middle-class parents would be able to send their sons along, part of the fees being met from bursaries and other subsidies. However, there was a good deal of opposition to what was happening at Salem. There were the ultra-nationalists who remembered that Prince Max had, in their terms, "betrayed the Fatherland" in 1918 and had compounded his guilt by allowing a Socialist Government to be formed. Then there were those who believed that Prince Max and Salem were trying to 'anglicize' German youth and so weaken that peculiarly German character that they respected.

Even worse was to follow the advent of Hitler to power in January 1933. On the 1st April Hitler declared a boycott of all Jewish shops, business houses, lawyers and doctors. Lady Rumbold, wife of the British Ambassador in Berlin, wrote to her mother on the 2nd April 1933:

> In the morning we went out in the car . . . I said I fully intended to go into a shop to buy even if it was picketed by Nazis. We tried Wertheimer, a dense crowd was standing at each entrance and in front of the doors two or three Nazis aggressively blocking the way. We saw that it was impossible without making a scene to push past. We then went down the Kurfusterdam. Nearly every other shop is Jew there. We walked along with the crowds. The shops were mostly open, but in front of each Jew shop were two or three stalwart Nazis blocking the door . . . On every Jew shop was plastered a large notice warning the public not to buy . . . and often you saw caricatures of Jewish noses. It was utterly cruel and Hunnish the whole thing, just doing down a heap of defenceless people . . . Then on the address plates at the entrances of blocks of flats of Jewish doctors, lawyers, and business men were plastered the same kind of warning so the whole of Berlin was speckled with these placards.

On the 5th April Sir Horace Rumbold wrote to the British Foreign Secretary: "Large concentration camps are being established in various parts of the country, one camp near Munich being sufficiently large enough to hold 5,000 prisoners."[12]

It is not surprising that Hitler should have ordered the arrest of Kurt Hahn whom he defined as "the decadent Jewish corrupter of German youth."[13] Fortunately for Hahn, Hitler was still fresh to power and had not yet become as ruthlessly efficient as he would be. Protests from Prince Berthold, acting as headmaster in Hahn's enforced absence in jail, and from powerful friends on whom he and his family were able to call, helped to make Hitler hesitate. Britain's Prime Minister, Ramsay MacDonald, made a direct appeal to the ageing President Hindenberg of Germany, and it was he who stepped in to order Hahn's release. Not surprisingly Hahn decided that there was no future for him, or for his school at Salem. He left Germany to live in England; the school closed down soon after this—but re-opened, under Hahn, in Scotland.

Prince Philip had gone to the school in the winter of 1932–33 and had not known Hahn. But even though his relative, Berthold, was headmaster, Philip did not enjoy Salem. He had never wanted to leave England in the first place, nor did he appreciate the rigid nature of the Teutonic time-table and the emphasis on games and physical training. It is possible that his sister and her German relatives would have prevailed and forced him to remain at Salem, but during 1933, while Hahn was first in prison and then in England, Philip made his own position in Germany impossible. He found the rise of the Nazi menace more ludicrous than threatening. He mocked the doctrine of Aryan supremacy and openly laughed one day at the Nazi salute—the right arm outstretched. Indeed, in the market square of Uberlingen, not far from Salem, Philip not only imitated the goose-stepping and saluting, he even suggested that maybe all the soldiers wanted 'to be excused'. It became obvious to Berthold, Theodora and the other German relations that Philip did not appreciate the danger in which he was placing the whole family. They decided to send him back to England and Uncle George. "We thought it better for him, and also for us," said Theodora.[14]

Back home in England Prince Philip was to come under Hahn's influence again at Gordonstoun. It is worthwhile considering how strange are the twists of fate. His father had been brought out of Greece by King George V; he himself owed a great deal to a headmaster who was similarly rescued from Germany by a British Prime Minister. As we will see, his own ideas on education owe a good deal to Hahn as does his Duke of Edinburgh Award Scheme. If Hahn had not left Germany and if Salem had continued to operate after Hitler's accession, or if Philip had stayed in Germany even after Salem had closed, he might then have become a member of the German armed forces as did many of his cousins. As it was, he left Germany and returned to England to confirm, unknowingly, his Englishness; and if that had not happened, there would have been no meeting with Princess Elizabeth in the summer of 1939.

13

Gordonstoun, 1934–1938

SAFE IN ENGLAND, Kurt Hahn founded a school where he could put his ideas into practice. While an Oxford student he had often walked through the hills around the Moray Firth, where, in 1934, Gordonstoun House and estate was up for sale. The house is about one mile from the sea and the 300-acre estate backs on to the mountains. Here Hahn and his pupils would not only be remote and secure in their privacy, they would also have both the sea and the mountains in which to practise that physical component of Hahn's system of education.

The house, which was to play a part in the development of both Prince Philip and, in the 1950s and 1960s, of Prince Charles, had had royal links in the 1880s. The then owner, Sir William Gordon-Cummings, had been the major character in the notorious Tranby Croft affair which had led to Edward, the Prince of Wales (later King Edward VII), being revealed as a reckless gambler in country houses.[1] In 1934 Hahn bought the house and estate and started his school, not far from Lossiemouth, birthplace of Ramsay MacDonald who had helped Hahn escape from Germany.

He was fortunate in finding the support of a number of eminent people, a sign that he was well-known and respected. Among the governors of his new school were the Archbishop of York and Mr Claude Elliott, the headmaster of Eton—solid establishment figures. Then there was G. M. Trevelyan, the historian, who with Elliott gave the school an educational blessing. John Buchan, the Scottish novelist, and later Lord Tweedsmuir, Governor-General of Canada, provided the flavour of local support. Lord Allen of Hurtwood, friend of Ramsay MacDonald[2] and a conscientious objector during the First World War, was the governor whose presence indicated that Hahn's ideas were supported by people of radical views.

It has been claimed with some justification that Prince Philip helped to build the school.[3] A ruined mill on the estate was converted into a residence for the masters. The boys, including Prince Philip, had to convert former stables into dormitories and classrooms. As the number of pupils increased from 30 in 1934 to about 150 in 1938, so the boys helped to build extra classrooms, dormitories and dining-rooms in a set of huts glorified by the name Windmill Lodge. Since the school had to be as far as possible self-sufficient, the pupils also helped to build up a farm. As Prince Andrew reported with pride, his son even helped to build a pigsty,[4] a feat which was also recalled by one of his fellow-pupils who came to the school shortly after Philip and remembered:

> Having been told before my arrival at Gordonstoun that I would find "a Greek prince" there, I was keen to see in what way such a person differed from an ordinary schoolboy and found, not surprisingly, that there was little or no difference. Philip was a junior in 1935 and as such was entitled to five shillings [25p] per month pocket money. I can still recall the rueful expression on his face when, having broken a vase valued at four shillings and five pence he was handed seven old pennies [3p] to last him for a whole month.
>
> My mother, on a parental visit to Gordonstoun saw Philip in a 'fatigue party' engaged in clearing a dining table and remarked that he appeared to be the most energetic worker in the group. This, I think, exemplified his attitude to routine duties. He disliked domestic chores as much as anyone else but would perform them with alacrity in order to free himself for more congenial occupations.[5]

Prince Philip and the other boys had to help run and maintain their own quarters as well as the schoolrooms. There was plenty of manual work to be done in gardens and farm, in building and decorating as well as in the day-to-day cleaning of the place. In the 1950s the Press made a good deal out of reports that Prince Charles had to empty the dustbins at Gordonstoun. So, in turn, had every other pupil, for there was, from 1934 onwards, a roster of work at which each pupil took his turn. This was one of the ways in which Hahn taught his pupils to serve the community.

Hahn had not known Prince Philip at Salem where the latter had been unhappy and unco-operative. Writing of his first year at Gordonstoun his headmaster wrote:

> When Philip came to Gordonstoun his most marked trait was his undefeatable spirit. He felt the emotions of both joy and sadness deeply, and the way he looked and the way he moved indicated what he felt. That even applied to the minor disappointments inevitable in a schoolboy's life. His laughter was heard everywhere. He had inherited from his Danish family the capacity to derive great fun from small incidents. In his school work he showed a lively intelligence. In community life, once he had made a task his own, he showed meticulous attention to detail and pride of workmanship which was never content with mediocre results.[6]

Many of the characteristics noted in this first impression were amplified and illustrated during Philip's years at the school. "Often naughty, never nasty",[7] he developed in a marked way that trait for doing whatever he tackled in the best possible way. This was a maturing of that competitiveness which he had showed as a child[8] which made him "never content with mediocre results" in other people's efforts. Here, at Gordonstoun, he showed for the first time that impatience with others who, in his opinion, were not trying, and that anger with needless failure, both traits which have marked his adult life.

At Salem he had been a rebel against the system. At Gordonstoun he was little better. One of his contemporaries recalled:

> If Philip did not see the necessity for any type of work nothing could persuade him to put his heart into it, whether it was practical or scholastic. The Classics Master told him that he "of all people" ought to want to learn Greek. Philip said that he had got on without either ancient or modern Greek up till that time and did not see the point of learning either. The Classics Master's reply, drawled in an old Etonian accent redolent of Bertie Wooster, became a school catch-phrase: "The trouble with you, Philip, is that you're too-oo blinking blasé." Boys used to tease Philip by repeating this phrase which annoyed him because, on the whole, it was an unfair criticism.[9]

Hahn proposed that the boys take a hand in building a coastguard station, suggesting that when it was complete the boys might help to man it—thus providing a service to a wider community. Philip showed what Hahn described as "passive resistance"[10] until he was assured that this was a worthwhile project and not just some do-gooding venture. He became the leader of the building team during the autumn so that the station was ready for the winter season. Since that time the station has been manned by Gordonstoun boys whenever there has been a gale warning. This example bears out one of Hahn's main claims:

> There are three ways of trying to win the young. There is persuasion, there is compulsion and there is attraction. You can preach at them, that is a hook without a worm; you can say, "You must volunteer", that is of the devil; and you can tell them, "You are needed." That appeal hardly ever fails.[11]

Hahn had engaged Commander Lewty, a retired Royal Navy officer, as sailing instructor. Philip and the other boys had to help build and repair their own boats and to maintain the schooner in which they sailed in the Moray Firth. He was one of those who won his badge of seamanship which entitled him to sail out around the Shetlands, the Outer Hebrides and Norway. There were no reporters around to say whether, at any of their ports of call, he had a glass of cherry brandy as his son had in 1961.[12] Commander Lewty wrote of him:

> He is a cheerful shipmate, very conscientious in carrying out both major and minor duties, thoroughly trustworthy and unafraid of dirty and arduous work.[13]

A contemporary remembered Philip as one of those fortunate people who are immune from seasickness:

> This meant that on the school nautical expeditions he was given the job of cook. I was quite the opposite and only once ventured on one of these expeditions, spending the whole journey across the Moray Firth lying moaning in the hold of the ketch *Diligent*. Ignored by my callous companions who appeared to care not whether I lived or died, I was touched when, just as we reached the safety of Hopeman harbour, Philip and his

assistant cook appeared in the hold and said, "We have decided to give Bovril to everyone who has been sick. You were the sickest, so you shall have the first cup." Never was a cup of Bovril appreciated more.[14]

For Philip, Gordonstoun was entirely different from Salem. But for Hahn, both schools were the same—at least in their aims. That a boy should be helped to discover himself and to do better than he dreamt he could is reflected in the school motto: *Plus est en vous*. That the boys should be taught to serve the community—of the school and of the locality—maybe by building a coastguard station, maybe by helping the local blacksmith in his forge. Indeed, Prince Philip pestered his family in 1936, constantly asking, "What would you like made in iron? I'll make it for you. We do it ourselves in the smithy in the village."[15]

Along with other boys at the school, Philip was sometimes treated at the outpatients' department at the nearest hospital, Dr Gray's Hospital, Elgin. Here, "in the nurses' sitting-room, long before the newspapers got to speculating on the subject, it was decided that the ideal match for Princess Elizabeth would be 'our young Prince'." The nurses, blacksmith, local fishermen and others liked the 'no nonsense' character illustrated by a story given to me by someone who had a friend who, in 1936, was a maid at Gordonstoun.

> She was in the habit of bringing her aprons home for laundering and one day when she had been unable to come for them her mother saw some boys from the school passing. She went to the door and called to them: "Do any of you know Annie?" One boy stopped and asked: "Is that Annie, the dining-room maid?" The mother replied in the affirmative and asked if he would mind taking up a 'parcellie' to her.
>
> "Not at all," he said and took the parcel. Later a scandalized Annie came home and informed her mother that it was the young Prince she had asked to take up her aprons.
>
> "Ah weel," said her mother. "Prince or no he was guy pleased to get the jammy piece I geed him. He went off up the road munching into it just like any ither hungry loon!"[16]

Philip was reunited with his family in 1936, a year after the Greek monarchy had once again been restored. King George II, who had been bundled off the throne in 1924, was brought back as a result of a plebiscite. In 1936 it was decided to bring back for re-burial the bodies of King Constantine, Queen Sophie and Queen Olga, all of whom had died in exile. Philip's cousin, Alexandra, had not seen him since he had started at Gordonstoun—from which he was given leave to attend the celebrations linked with the re-burials. In 1936 she "gazed in amazement at my blond, handsome cousin. He had suddenly shot up; he was thin without being gangling . . . had sailed the North Sea in complete charge of a cutter . . . this was a new up-and-coming member of the family to please and interest some of his elders."[17]

During this family reunion Philip met his father who had kept in touch with him by the occasional letter and was always eager to tell other members of the family how well his absent son was doing in Gordonstoun.[18] But this meeting in Athens was the first face-to-face contact the father and son had had since 1933. It was also at this gathering that Philip realized for the first time that he held a certain position in the family. The older generation were obviously ageing—his father, Uncle George, Uncle Nicholas and Uncle Christopher.[19] In the line of succession to the Greek throne, now occupied by George II, there was the King's bachelor brother, Paul, Uncle George's son, Prince Peter, also a bachelor, and then there was Philip. Given the uncertain way in which the Greeks threw out some kings and restored others, it was not beyond the bounds of possibility that he might, one day, become King of that unhappy country.

In 1937 there was another family reunion when Prince Paul, then Crown Prince of Greece, married Princess Frederica of Brunswick. Prince Peter, King Michael and Prince Philip were the three best men, holding the crowns over the bride and groom during the Greek Orthodox ceremony. Once again Philip met his mother, who was living quietly in Athens, and his father. Some relatives suggested that Prince Andrew should come back to live in Mon Repos in Corfu; the Greek monarchy was, it seemed, firmly established and popular, and there was no reason why all the exiles should not return. Some also suggested that Prince Philip should become a student at the Greek Nautical College with a view to entering the Hellenic Navy where his promotions would be assured and rapid.

Prince Andrew knew from the reports sent by Lord George that Philip was doing well at school. He was showing "tenacity and drive" and "doing specially well in mathematics and geography, which Uncle George may have hinted were both of importance to a naval career. He was one of the school's best in modern languages."[20] Since it was by now fairly obvious that he was going to be a sailor, there was something to be said for using his family's influence and making a career in the Greek Navy.

But Prince Andrew was still bitter because of the humiliations of his trial and banishment. He did not wish to return to Greece. It is unlikely that he made any effort to persuade Philip to do so either. Like his grandfather, Prince Louis of Battenberg, Prince Philip had, it seems, decided that his future lay in the British Navy. Maybe he felt English because of the influence of Lord George with whom he spent part of each holiday at Lynden Manor and who acted the part of step-father at school functions. Maybe he was already under the influence of the dashing Lord Louis with whom he sometimes stayed in his fabulous thirty-roomed penthouse in Park Lane.

In 1938 Lord George died and Lord Louis took on the responsibility of looking after his nephew—in whom perhaps he and Lady Edwina saw the son they themselves had never had. For his part Philip saw in the brilliant, dynamic and restless Lord Louis that model on which to base his own career. If Lord George had been the one whom Philip had loved, Lord Louis was the one whom he admired and wanted to emulate.

Lord George died in the autumn of 1938 as Philip left Gordonstoun where he had been Guardian (or head boy), captain of the hockey and cricket teams and one of the few whose ability entitled them to sail single-handed in the Moray Firth. In his final assessment of the departing pupil Hahn wrote:

> Prince Philip is universally trusted, liked, and respected. He had the greatest sense of service of all the boys in the school. Prince Philip's leadership qualities are most noticeable, though marred at times by impatience and intolerance. He will need the exacting demands of a great service to do justice to himself. His best is outstanding; his second best is not good enough. Prince Philip will make his mark in any profession where he will have to prove himself in a full trial of strength . . .[21]

His home was now in Park Lane where Lord Louis served to quicken Prince Philip's natural ambition to enter the Royal Navy. During the winter of 1938–1939 he went to Cheltenham to be coached by a Mr Mercer for the examinations for applicants for entry to the Royal Naval College at Dartmouth. It was Lord Louis who arranged that Greek-born Danish Prince Philip be allowed to sit this examination meant for entrants coming from English public schools and naval cadet centres.

He sat the examinations in the spring of 1939 and was placed sixteenth out of the thirty-four candidates who qualified. On the 4th May 1939 he put on the uniform of a Royal Naval cadet at Dartmouth. During his time at Dartmouth, as throughout the rest of his career, he would show how valid were Hahn's comments on his qualities—good and bad. Hahn's influence on his development was a major one and Prince Philip's awareness of this was reflected in his decision to send Prince Charles to Gordonstoun.

14

Dartmouth, 1939–1940

ON THE 30TH SEPTEMBER 1938 Prime Minister Neville Chamberlain returned in triumph from his third meeting with Adolf Hitler, bringing, he claimed, "Peace in our Time".[1] King George VI and Queen Elizabeth appeared with him on the balcony of Buckingham Palace to receive the applause of the crowds which had gathered to greet the man who had achieved "Peace with Honour". Few people agreed with Winston Churchill when he spoke in the House of Commons during the debate on the Munich Agreement:

> We really must not waste time . . . upon the differences between the positions reached at [the two earlier meetings] and at Munich. They can be simply epitomized . . . £1 was demanded at the pistol's point. When it was given, £2 was demanded at the pistol's point. Finally the dictator consented to take £1 17s 6d and the rest in promises of goodwill for the future. The German dictator, instead of snatching the victuals from the table, has been content to have them served to him course by course . . . a disaster of the first magnitude has befallen Britain and France.[2]

Within weeks British attitudes had changed. On the 19th of October the King's Private Secretary noted that "the Prime Minister . . . was determined to get more aeroplanes, better ARP and some kind of National Register."[3] As Prince Philip began the final preparations for his examinations the failure of appeasement was made clear. In the first fortnight of March 1939 Hitler organized a revolt among the Germans living in Czechoslovakia, used this as an excuse to force the Czech Government to agree to the independence of Ruthenia and Slovakia, and then made them place the rest of the country under German protection. On the 15th March he was in Prague proclaiming that "Czechoslovakia has ceased to exist."

For Chamberlain all this came as a shock. On the 10th March he had declared publicly that "the outlook in international affairs is tranquil".[4] But on the 17th March he denounced Hitler as "a perjurer", adding that while being willing to give up a good deal in the search for peace "there is one thing I must except, and that is the liberty we have enjoyed for hundreds of years, and which we would never surrender."[5]

Following his success in Czechoslovakia, Hitler turned his attention to Poland. On the 31st March 1939, Chamberlain told the House of Commons that Britain and France "would feel themselves bound at once to lend the Polish Government all support in their power" if Hitler moved against them.[6] To give some backing to this promise, the British Government announced, on the 17th April, that they were to introduce compulsory national service. The King and Queen went on an important State Visit to the USA in June. On the 2nd July they were back in London to review twenty thousand representatives of the nation's Civil Defence Forces, which the King described as a sign of "the determination to make the country ready to meet any emergency whatever the sacrifices or inconveniences . . ."[7]

It was against this lowering international backcloth that Prince Philip entered Dartmouth on the 14th May 1939. From the very beginning he worked as hard as Hahn had suggested he could. Maybe he "felt an inner urge to justify himself, first to the father whom he so seldom saw, and second to the fine memory of the uncle now beyond reach."[8] Maybe, too, he wanted to live up to the reputation of the then Captain Louis Mountbatten who achieved the first place in his own final course before embarking on wartime service.[9] Nor was it lost on the cadets and their officers, that in all probability this class would be involved in war in the near future.

Within a few months he won the King's Dirk, awarded to the best cadet of each term. "I cannot help but be pleased," he wrote at the time.[10] This was a surprising result in view of his modest place in the entrance examinations, but it was in line with the high marks which he had gained in the tests and the oral examination—380 out of 400. These had shown that he was well endowed with self-reliance, intelligence and judgement, all of them qualities essential for the future leader and the basis for his quick success at Dartmouth. Kurt Hahn, now a naturalized Britisher, must have been pleased with the report of his former pupil's success, which he had prophesied.

Prince Philip was promoted to Cadet-Captain which gave him a chance to exercise those qualities of leadership over his juniors. He was, it seemed, in the mould of Lord Louis and people spoke of the brilliant future that was open to him. However, some of his classmates and juniors remember that he showed the "impatience and intolerance" of which Hahn had warned him.[11] They recall not only his hard work and ability, his energy and obvious ambition to succeed, but also an arrogance which tended to make him seem a bully, particularly to the less able and less eager.

He also played hard while at Dartmouth. He was a good squash player, played cricket for the College and won the javelin competition in the Devonport Athletic Championships so helping to put Dartmouth high on the list of competing clubs. These were to be the last peacetime championships to be held at Devonport until 1946.

King George VI, Queen Elizabeth and the two Princesses had started their summer holiday by taking a voyage in the Royal Yacht, *Victoria and Albert*, accompanied by the King's Naval ADC, Captain Lord Louis Mountbatten. Both men looked forward to the visit to the Royal Naval College at Dartmouth where they had both been cadets. For the King it would be a relaxation after the burden of the visit to the USA and the worry over the international situation. For Lord Louis it was a chance to return to the scenes of former triumphs before taking delivery of his first ship, HMS *Kelly*, then being fitted out in the Tyne.

The yacht put into the River Dart on the afternoon of Saturday, 22nd July, and the King enjoyed his two-day visit which brought back childhood memories.[12] Lord Louis was "a moving spirit in the background",[13] anxious to play an active role in affairs involving his nephew.

Prince Philip and Princess Elizabeth had already met on several occasions—not surprising since they were relatives and mixed in the same royal circles. In 1934 when she was eight and he thirteen, they had met at the marriage of Princess Marina of Greece to the King's younger brother, the Duke of Kent. They had also met in 1937 during the Coronation of King George VI—Philip's second cousin. But it is doubtful whether they paid much attention to each other, the difference in their ages being in itself enough to separate them from one another.

Philip was known to the Royal Family not only because he was Princess Alice's son and the little boy who had lived for a time in Kensington Palace; he was also a fairly frequent visitor, as Lady Airlie recounts:

> Even during the years when he was at his first school in Paris, Prince Philip came over to visit his grandmother and his uncles . . . On one of these visits he was taken to tea with Queen Mary at Buckingham Palace, but she told me long afterwards that she only remembered him vaguely as "a nice little boy with very blue eyes". Later, when he was at Gordonstoun and spending part of his holidays with the Duke and Duchess of Kent, he made much more impression on her. "He's very handsome," she told me. "He has inherited the good looks of both sides of the family. He seems intelligent too. I should say he had plenty of common sense."[14]

So it would not have been unusual if he had been invited to meet the King and Princess Elizabeth during this two-day visit to the College where he was already a leading cadet. The senior cadets were invited, along with their officers, to lunch on board *Victoria and Albert* on Monday, and a smaller number from the senior cadets were invited to dine aboard on the Sunday evening. Given Prince Philip's position as "best cadet" of his term he would in any event have been among those who were taken to the *Victoria and Albert* on both occasions.

But some commentators suggest that Lord Louis, "the moving spirit", was busily at work trying to forge a close relationship between his admiring nephew and the heir-apparent, Princess Elizabeth. If so, and there is no evidence to support the suggestion, then Lord Louis was helped by two unforeseeable twists of fate. On the Sunday Prince Philip was Captain's Messenger; for that day he was the senior cadet who had to be at the Captain's beck and call. In the second place, some of the cadets were down with mumps and a second batch were down with chickenpox. The Royal party was due to attend Divine Service in the College Chapel. The College doctor considered that the two Princesses might be in danger of infection if they went to the crowded chapel. So they were sent to the Captain's house while the rest of the party went to chapel.

At this point ". . . my Aunt Elizabeth (the present Queen Mother) and Uncle Dickie put their heads together and presently hauled Philip out of chapel to help squire the two little girls."[15]

Accounts of this meeting between the Prince and the two younger Princesses vary. There is the blow-by-blow account written by Marion Crawford, Princess Elizabeth's governess. Then there are the accounts based on hearsay, such as that written by Queen Alexandra, who acknowledges her position by her "I believe" in part of her story.[16] Many accounts can be dismissed as, at best, only partly true; some are incapable of getting the dates right, ignoring the fact that in 1939 Sunday (the day on which the College Chapel was full) was the 23rd July not 22nd July as sometimes suggested; others haven't even taken the trouble to get the geography right, putting the River Dart in Weymouth Bay which is about fifty miles away; still others write of the Royal party arriving aboard the Royal Yacht *Britannia*, which had not then been built.

Even Miss Crawford's eye-witness account has to be read with some suspicion. Could she really have recalled the actual words used by each of the players in the drama? Did they actually speak the stilted lines put in their mouths? How far was her account, written in 1950, coloured by her hindsight of the events of 1947? We may accept Miss Crawford's description of the "fair haired boy, rather like a Viking, with a sharp face and piercing blue eyes."[17] She was also probably correct in asserting that the thirteen-year-old Princess gazed at the eighteen-year-old cadet as if he were "a strange creature out of another world . . . a hero".[18]

Queen Alexandra claims that "Philip rather resented it, a youngster of eighteen called to help entertain a girl of thirteen and a child of nine [Princess Margaret]".[19] She bases this, it seems, on Miss Crawford's claim that he was "rather offhand in his manner. He said 'how do you do' to Lilibet, and for a while they knelt side by side playing with the trains. He soon got bored with that. We had ginger crackers and lemonade in which he joined, and then he said, 'Let's go to the tennis courts and have some fun jumping the nets.' "[20]

Queen Alexandra was with the Queen and Prince Philip "years later as they tried to recall the occasion, I heard him affectionately joking with Lilibet. 'You were so shy,' Philip said. 'I couldn't get a word out of you.' " But if we are to believe Miss Crawford, it was a case of hero-worship: "She never took her eyes off him the whole time. At the tennis courts I thought he showed off a good deal, but the little girls were much impressed. Lilibet said, 'How good he is Crawfie! How high he can jump!' He was quite polite with her, but did not pay her any special attention. He spent a lot of time teasing plump little Margaret."[21]

Hatch suggests that Lord Louis had been a "very conscious instrument of fate" in bringing his nephew into the royal orbit.[22] It was, it seems, at his suggestion that Philip lunched aboard *Victoria and Albert* as company for the two Princesses. But, if as a reminder of the difference in their ages, when Prince Philip and the other senior cadets came aboard for dinner that evening, Princess Elizabeth was already in bed, subject to the rigours of the nursery time-table.[23]

After that lunch on Monday the Royal Yacht weighed anchor and set sail down the River Dart. She was followed by half the College, the cadets using all sorts of craft from launches to sailing dinghies and rowing-boats. The King, while appreciating this pleasant sign of their loyalty, was afraid that there might be an accident. He told Captain Sir Dudley North, "This is quite unsafe. You must signal them to go back."[24] All the cadets obeyed the signal which fluttered from the masthead—except one; Prince Philip continued to row madly after the yacht. "At last, he alone was left, rowing away as hard as he could, well out into the open sea. Lilibet took the glasses to crane for a last glimpse of him, still rowing far behind."[25]

The King is supposed to have said, either, "The young fool" or, "The damned young fool."[26] At all events orders were shouted through a megaphone and the cadet-Prince lifted his oars in salute and then turned around.

How significant was this meeting between the two great-great-grandchildren of Queen Victoria? According to Hatch, Philip was attracted to his little third cousin while "Lord Louis's mind may have been working like a computer . . ."[27] seeing, one has to assume, the advantages to his family of a royal wedding. Another author writes of Lord Louis as having "manoeuvred to gain for his nephew his present exalted place . . ." going on to make the disclaimer that this imputation is baseless and unwarrantable",[28] which makes one wonder why it was repeated, or why the same author described Lord Louis as having an "opportunist mind".

When Prince Philip was asked when he had decided that he was going to marry Princess Elizabeth, he replied, "Well, certainly not at Dartmouth."[29] One may reasonably assume that few, if any, eighteen-year-olds consider marriage to a thirteen-year-old relative. But there is some evidence, apart from Miss Crawford's, that for Princess Elizabeth this meeting was of major importance. In 1958 Sir John Wheeler-Bennett completed his biography of King George VI, in the writing of which he "received much kindness and invaluable assistance from Her Majesty, Queen Elizabeth the Queen Mother."[30] Queen Elizabeth II also took a considerable interest in this biography of her father whom she had loved very deeply. Wheeler-Bennett, like any other author using material from the Royal Archives, had to submit his work to Her Majesty so that she could see the Royal material in its context of the biography. We may assume then that Wheeler-Bennett's biography has the stamp of royal approval. There is then a major significance to be attached to a sentence about Prince Philip: "This was the man with whom Princess Elizabeth had been in love from their first meeting."[31] In 1958, when this biography appeared, the Queen and Prince Philip had been married for eleven years; that she allowed this sentence to appear cannot be attributed to calf-love. We may assume that it expresses the truth as she and her mother remember it.

But for Prince Philip, the ambitious cadet, there were more immediate calls on his time and energy. During the summer it became increasingly evident that war was imminent. It came as no surprise when it eventually started with Hitler's invasion of Poland on the 1st September; Britain declared war on Germany on Sunday, 3rd September. For the cadets at Dartmouth this served to spur them on to even greater efforts and no one worked harder than Prince Philip. He won the coveted Eardley-Howard-

Crockett Prize as the best cadet in the College which was worth more in naval circles than was suggested by the £2 book-token that went with it. It is worth pointing out that most of the other cadets had been at the Royal Naval College since they were thirteen while Philip was a late entrant who did not start at the College until he was seventeen and a half. The others ought to have been indoctrinated into the spirit of Dartmouth and the Navy over their long years while he had to acquire his standing over a short period. This makes his success all the more creditable.

So, on the 1st January 1940, Prince Philip of Greece was commissioned as a midshipman. Unfortunately, he was only eligible for a temporary commission, since he was a Greek (since 1935 and the Restoration) and foreigners were, and are, only allowed to hold temporary commissions. Not even Lord Louis could change this regulation. If he was to follow a career in the Royal Navy Prince Philip would have to become a naturalized Britisher. "Lord Louis advised him to seek naturalization, only to learn that the necessary legal machinery had been suspended for the duration of the War."[32] The question of his naturalization was to prove more of a problem than he and Lord Louis had imagined, as we shall see.

Part IV

ON BECOMING A MARRIED ENGLISH PRINCE

15

Prince Philip's War, 1940–1945

PRINCE PHILIP'S PART IN the Second World War falls almost naturally into sections and is in its own way a micro-study of the British part in that war with its periods of inactivity followed by massive defeats which preceded the later and conclusive victories. But Prince Philip's life was also affected by the way in which the war affected his father and mother and by the part played by the Greeks in general. This period saw the maturing of the man himself, for he was eighteen in 1940 and going on for twenty-five when he arrived back in Britain in January 1946; he had been a mere midshipman when he first sailed from England to which he returned as the "best junior Commander Officer in the Fleet" in January 1946. Throughout this hectic period there also took place, almost imperceptibly, the deepening of his attachment to Princess Elizabeth. For him, as for countless others, this wartime period was a most significant part of his life.

There are many other people for whom merely meeting him at this time was significant and remains so today. One correspondent writes of meeting him "in the early days of the war when HMS *Kelly* was being built by Hawthorn Leslie at Hebburn-on-Tyne when I met both the Prince and his uncle, Lord Louis Mountbatten, as my cousin's husband was second-in-command of the *Kelly*." At dances at the Gordon Hotel "both Lord Louis and young Prince Philip were charmers . . . both really good-looking and perfectly groomed. I am old now, about the same age as Lord Louis, disabled and house-bound . . . but still have a vast amount of pleasure in remembering those good days and the great pleasure I had in having had quite a close friendship with two of the nicest men it has ever been my luck to know."[1]

The Lords of the Admiralty had the problem of what to do with this outstanding cadet. He was, after all, a citizen of Greece, which was still a neutral country. There might have been international complications if he had been killed in action, wearing a British naval uniform. In 1940 the least active areas of operations were the Indian and Pacific Oceans. So

Prince Philip was posted to the battleship *Ramillies* guarding convoys of troop-ships between Australia, New Zealand and Alexandria.

Prince Philip joined *Ramillies* on the 20th February 1940 armed with his midshipman's log issued to all 'middies' so that they may record their own language all matters of interest or importance in the work that is carried out on their stations, in their fleet, or in their ship. The objects of keeping the journal are to train midshipmen in (a) the power of observation, (b) the power of expression, (c) the habit of orderliness.[2]

Basil Boothroyd drew heavily on Prince Philip's journal to show that the young officer was very observant and well able to express himself in word and in drawing. As if to remind him—and us—of his lack of surname, the title-page of the journal carried the name "Philip, Prince of Greece".[3]

The *Ramillies* made two stops in Australia while Prince Philip was one of the crew. Perhaps it was his natural restlessness, or perhaps it was because it was his first shore leave that led him to "see as much of the country as possible, even getting as far as a cattle station in Queensland, where he spent three or four days working as a jackaroo."[1] Finally the *Ramillies* was sent to convoy Australian troops to Alexandria. This was too near the active theatre of war, so on the 12th April Prince Philip was quickly transferred to the East African station. He joined the cruiser *Kent*, once the flagship and crack gunnery-ship of the China Station but now assigned to convoy duty in the Indian Ocean. The ratings on board *Kent* had served in the China Station since the middle of 1937 and when war broke out were on their way home for long leave. Their homeward trip had been halted because of the outbreak of war which meant that the crew had not only to put up with having an admiral aboard his flagship—with the attendant calls for sentries, frequent changes of dress and parade-like drills—but also the boredom of repetitious convoy duties. Many of them felt that "to be lumbered with a prince of the Royal House of Greece" was almost "a last straw".[5] But those who recall their feelings also have the goodwill to remember that the young "snottie" became a popular member of the crew—partly because he was so eager to learn, partly because he too was seen to be subject to the orders of the "host of gold braid", and partly because he was always "smiling and cheerful to everyone . . .".[6] Of more significance to his naval future was the commendation of his Captain: ". . . my best midshipman . . .".

One of the crew remembered:

> In 1940 we had to investigate the Islands in the Indian Ocean and find out if the Governor of Chagos Island was pro- or anti-British. Lt-Commander Blundell was in charge, midshipman Philip was middy of the boat and we had a crew of seamen with guns hidden.
>
> Lt. Commander Blundell went ashore with some wireless ratings but everything was in order and the Governor was invited to take a trip with us just to see how we caught fish. We went out to sea a little way and the officer let off a small charge of dynamite and when it went off underwater the area was full of kicking, stunned fish. The question was who was going in for

them? Well, midshipman Philip had come prepared having had his bathing shorts under his clothes. He immediately stripped off and was soon in the water alongside of a few seamen throwing the fish into the boat. You may have seen him playing polo on ponies, but I know he can throw a very good water polo ball in the shape of a fish. I should know. I was twice almost knocked out of the boat by one of his throws.

We were very sorry when he left us . . .[7]

In September he transferred to the *Shropshire* at Durban. He wrote to various relatives about the shore leaves in South Africa which he "robustly enjoyed".[8] His wartime career took a decisive turn on the 28th October 1940 when the Italians invaded Greece. This meant that Philip was no longer a neutral. Lord Louis, now Captain of the *Kelly* and Commander of the Fifth Destroyer Flotilla, sent off telegrams to his colleagues in the Admiralty suggesting that his ambitious and able nephew be assigned to more active service. In December he was drafted to the battleship *Valiant*, then serving in the Mediterranean, and was put in command of a section of the searchlight control.

One of those who remembered him was a former sailor then serving on *Valiant*, who also had a brother among the crew. A third brother serving on *Diamond* came aboard *Valiant* on Christmas Day, 1940:

. . . with a view to us having a little family celebration on that day. Prince Philip spotted the three of us talking together while waiting for the liberty boat (he was midshipman of the watch). He called me on to the quarterdeck and said, "Not another Lovell, surely?" I said, "Yes, Sir." He immediately called a fast motor-boat alongside and said, "Off you three go and enjoy a good run ashore."[9]

On the 2nd January 1941 the *Valiant* took part in the bombardment of Bardia which preceded General Wavell's first advance into Cyrenaica. In his journal Prince Philip wrote:

That evening at dusk the Battlefleet put to sea and shortly afterwards we were told that we were going to bombard Bardia on the Libyan coast. We arrived off the coast on Thursday morning at dawn. In the dark the flashes of the guns could be seen a long way out to sea. We went to action stations at 07.30 and at 08.10 the bombardment commenced. The whole operation was a spectacular affair.

Then a few days later the *Valiant* was in action again, this time off the south of Sicily. He wrote:

At dawn action stations on Friday gunflashes were sighted on the starboard bow. We increased speed to investigate and by the time we were within five miles it was almost daylight. *Bonaventure* signalled that *Southampton* and herself were engaging two enemy destroyers. We could just see one of these destroyers blowing up in a cloud of smoke and spray. The other escaped. Shortly after this, the destroyer *Gallant* hit a mine and her bow was blown off and floated slowly away on the swell . . . At noon two torpedo bombers attacked us, but a quick alteration of course foiled their attempt, and their fish passed down the port side. Shortly after this, sixteen German dive-bombers attacked the *Illustrious.* She was hit aft and amidships and fires broke out. Then the bombers concentrated on us and five bombs dropped fairly close . . .[10]

But there were frequent reminders of the fact that he was, after all, Philip, Prince of Greece, and not a British naval officer. He had had three months' leave before joining the *Valiant* and had spent that time in Athens, in neutral Greece. Here he had some time with his mother and other members of the family whom 'Chips' Channon also met while working for the British Government on a mission to the Balkans. In his diary Channon wrote:

9 January [1941] *The Legation, Athens*
. . . The Royal set-up at Athens is complicated; there is the isolated King who sees no one; there are the Crown Prince and Princess [Frederica], who . . . remain aloof from the world . . . She is a touch unpopular, being German . . .; there is Princess Andrew, who is eccentric to say the least and lives in semi-retirement; there is Prince Andrew, who philanders on the Riviera whilst his son, Prince Philip, is serving in our Navy . . .

On 21st January 1941 Channon met Prince Philip at a cocktail party, noting in his diary that "He is to be our Prince Consort . . . He is charming but I deplore such a marriage; he and Princess Elizabeth are too interrelated."[11]

We will see that Channon's confidence about the future marriage was to be dimmed as the years went on, and we will also see that Prince Philip himself does not appear to have given any thought to marriage at this stage. His leave in Athens gave him a chance to discuss his mother's future and her attempts to start a new religious order in the face of opposition from the leaders of the Greek Orthodox Church. Indeed, rather than thinking of marriage, Prince Philip was worried about the way in which the war was affecting his mother. For if he had been transferred to *Valiant* and had been able to see action, this was only because Italy had invaded Greece and so brought him—the Greek Prince—into a position in which the Admiralty no longer had to shield him. But this invasion meant that his mother and other relatives were very much in the front line and this gave him a great deal of concern.

After the battle off Sicily, *Valiant* was sent to the Piraeus and Philip once again had some short leave with his family. He was with them during an air-raid.[11] In his journal he noted:

While in Greece I had ample opportunity for studying the campaign in Albania. Unfortunately I was unable to visit the front and watch the fighting on the spot. Considering the unequal balance of numbers and materials, the reason for the success of the Greeks is their magnificent morale, and the Italien's [sic] lack of it . . .[12]

But he realized that Hitler would be unable to allow his Italian ally to wallow in uncertainty in Greece or to suffer defeat in North Africa. We know that Rommel was sent to lead the North African campaign and, in May 1941, German forces were sent to Greece. By this time Philip was back on active service. But he must have known, in February 1941 while he was still in Athens, that the day of reckoning could not be far away. He tried to persuade his mother to leave Greece. She refused, preferring to stay with the orphan children whom she had gathered around her in a home provided by the Greek Government. She had seen how the family had been split because of the First World War. Now, in the Second War, the divisions affected her much more immediately. Her son and brother were fighting in the British Navy; her daughters, on the other hand, were married to Germans who, in 1941, were high-ranking German officers. Maybe one of her reasons for wishing to stay in Athens was the hope that she might be able to get in touch with her daughters again. Maybe, too, she hoped that her sons-in-law would be able to exert their authority to obtain for her some sort of protection in the event of a German occupation of Athens.

Late in February 1941 Philip was aboard *Valiant* when it sailed from the Piraeus to go back into active service in the Mediterranean, now the major theatre of war with the campaigns in North Africa, Greece and Albania reaching new heights.

Admiral Sir Andrew Cunningham commanded the British Mediterranean Fleet which was supported by Greece-based aircraft. On the 28th March the Italian Fleet were discovered off Cape Matapan and there took place what has been described as "the most sweeping British naval victory since Trafalgar".[13] The first sighting had been made by an RAF flying-boat which saw the fleet steaming south-eastwards across the Mediterranean. Its progress was both plotted and delayed by dive-bombing aircraft flying off aircraft-carriers and from Greek bases. This gave Cunningham's fleet a chance to catch up with the Italians late at night. *Valiant, Warspite* and *Bareham* were the battleships in the fleet and it was their guns which in twenty minutes blasted and sank three Italian cruisers and two destroyers, and seriously damaged many other warships, including the battleship *Vittorio Veneto. Valiant* was assigned the task of using its searchlights to illuminate the enemy targets, and Prince Philip commanded a section of a searchlight battery.

It is noticeable that all the people who wrote to me about their memories of Prince Philip's time on *Valiant* mentioned his part in this battle, "the first naval battle in the dark since the Battle of the Nile".[14] They also drew attention to the fact that he lived the life of the ordinary midshipman, "his hammock was his bed, his chest his wardrobe", and that "lower deck ratings regarded him as a pleasant, non-pompous and helpful young officer".[15]

He came in for a mention in Sir Andrew Cunningham's despatches. This was indeed a baptism of fire for the nineteen-year-old who described the action as "as near murder as anything could be in wartime. The cruisers just burst into tremendous sheets of flame."[16] While he was pleased by the "mention in despatches", he also welcomed the Greek Cross of Valour awarded him by the King of Greece.

Within the next few weeks, however, that King and most of his family had been driven from Greece by the invading Germans. On the 26th April the British evacuated the Greek Government and members of the Royal Family from besieged Athens and took them to Crete, where they hoped to set up a national government as a centre of resistance to the Germans. British troops were diverted from North Africa to try to hold Crete against German invasion, and so deprived Britain of that impetus which had been gained in North Africa—but all to no avail, for Crete was indefensible. On the 20th May it was invaded by German parachute forces supported by a vastly superior German airforce. On the 21st and 22nd May there took place the Battle of Crete in which Philip on *Valiant* and Lord Louis in command of *Kelly* both took part. *Valiant* was struck by dive-bombers. "One bomb exploded just abaft the quarterdeck screen on the port side . . . the other landed within twenty feet of it, just inboard of the guard rails, blowing a hole in the wardroom laundry . . . There were only four casualties . . ."[17]

Valiant had to return to Alexandria for repairs. During the first few days there Prince Philip and others watched the sorry stream of damaged ships making their way from Crete; some carried members of the Greek Government, others carried survivors from sunken ships. One such survivor was Lord Louis; HMS *Kelly* had been sunk by a direct hit from a 1,000-lb bomb which caused the ship to turn turtle. On the *Kandahar*, battle-scarred but safe, was David Milford Haven, nephew to Lord Louis and the boy who had introduced Philip to life at Lynden Manor and fellow-pupil at Cheam.

In Alexandria Philip had a chance to enjoy some leave with various relatives, including Princess Frederica[18] and Princess Alexandra,[19] both of whom have written accounts of the more pleasant days of this part of their enforced exile. He spent some time with Lord Louis who "gave him hell for not writing more often, for Philip was a lazy correspondent, while his uncle poured out letters literally by the thousands."[20] He also had a chance to reflect on the dangers now facing his mother in German-occupied Athens.

But he was, after all, a naval officer and in June 1941 he was ordered back to England to take the qualifying examinations he needed before he could be promoted to sub-lieutenant. With other midshipmen he sailed on an old liner, the *Duchess of Atholl*, then doing duty as a troop-ship. This old, coal-burning ship was routed around the Cape rather than through the more dangerous waters of the eastern Mediterranean. She put into Durban, where Philip met up again with members of the Greek Royal Family who were also making their way to England. After a short but pleasant interlude[21] Philip and four other midshipmen persuaded the authorities to take them off the *Duchess of Atholl* with its unreliable engines and slow speed and put them on an empty troop-ship bound for England, calling in at Halifax en route to pick up Canadian troops. This ship also stopped at Puerto Rico where the Chinese stokers deserted. The

Captain then ordered the five midshipmen to 'volunteer' as stokers until they reached Newport, Virginia. For this six days' arduous work Philip was awarded a certificate as a trimmer, which some think is "among his most treasured souvenirs".[22]

From September 1941 when he arrived in England until July 1943 Prince Philip was stationed in home stations which gave him a chance to spend some time with the Duke and Duchess of Kent, with David, the 3rd Marquess of Milford Haven, and others of his relatives. But the major reason for his home posting was to help him pass his qualifying examinations in which his ability, ambition and experience combined to enable him to gain four firsts and a second. This gave him nine months' seniority out of a possible ten on promotion to sub-lieutenant in February 1942.

One correspondent remembered him while he was at the shore station on Whale Island, HMS *Excellent*, on a gunnery course, and an exploit which involved him and another young officer 'borrowing' bicycles to get back after missing the last transport back from Southsea. They foiled the attempt of a policeman to stop them but on the complaint of the Chief Constable of Portsmouth they were confined to base by the Captain of the Base.[23]

In February 1942 he was then assigned to *Wallace*, the flotilla leader of the destroyers operating out of Rosyth. One of the W/T section on *Wallace* remembered that:

> It was during a southbound East Coast convoy trip that we received the signal announcing the appointment of Prince Philip to the ship, and I, in fact, was on watch and took the signal. It read, with typical naval simplicity:
>
> To: WALLACE
> From: C. in C. Nore
> Sub-Lt H.R.H. Prince Philip of Greece
> and Denmark, R.N., will join you on
> arrival at Sheerness.
>
> The news spread quickly around the ship but the royal title did not particularly impress the lower deck. The peacetime Navy was well-sprinkled with titles. Earls, Dukes, Baronets and Honourables were plentiful, and, at that time, nobody had ever heard of Prince Philip of Greece and Denmark.[24]

An ordinary seaman aboard remembered that "Prince Philip joined the *Wallace* about two weeks after I did . . . I remember it created a seven-day wonder, having a member of royalty aboard."[25]

The *Wallace* and the rest of the destroyers in the flotilla were on convoy duties, guarding ships sailing along the coast from Rosyth to Sheerness. This run was nicknamed 'E-boat alley' because of the constant attacks on the relatively slow-moving convoys by fast-moving German E-boats armed with bombs and torpedoes. As one member of the crew recalled in 1978:

> East coast convoys at that time were deadly—aircraft and E-boat attacks were commonplace and Prince Philip was spared none of these in common with the rest of the crew.[26]

Another member of the crew recalled:

> *Wallace* was based at Rosyth when Prince Philip joined . . . her duties were mainly convoy escort . . . Convoys ran like trains—one left Methil for the south every day and another from Sheerness for the north, throughout the whole of the war. Under normal conditions, the trip took two and a half days in each direction with about twelve hours at Sheerness and possibly twenty-four hours in Rosyth before another trip was made.
>
> In the narrow confines of the East Coast—bounded to seaward by our own mine barrier—there was no room for evasive action when enemy attacks occurred. In the early days, convoys could be made up to over 100 merchant vessels, and from the Wash southwards you were in single file which resulted in a convoy that could be over 20 miles in length from front to rear.
>
> Attacks by aircraft and E-boats were commonplace and when mines and the treacherous weather of the North Sea were added, the demands made on destroyers escorting convoys were high. It was commonplace in the earlier days of the war for convoys to have only two destroyers, with no radar, air support or other sea support. Things gradually improved as the war progressed and United States aid showed its effects, but nevertheless, those responsible for handling the destroyers needed to know their jobs at all times.[27]

And, it has to be remembered, one of those "responsible for handling" *Wallace* was Prince Philip of Greece and Denmark. In July he was promoted to Lieutenant and in the following October, at his Captain's request, he was promoted to First Lieutenant. At twenty-one he was the youngest officer in the Navy to hold the position of senior executive officer in a ship the size of the *Wallace*. His success in his examinations and his quick promotions had been earned by efficiency, acceptance of responsibility and evidence of initiative. Some gossips attributed his quick climb to the influence of his 'Uncle Dickie'.[28] Men who served with him knew that he had won his success by his own hard work. None of his fellow-officers or members of the lower deck begrudged him his success on board the "over-crowded and over-worked" destroyer.[29] One of the men who served on *Wallace* compared Philip with his uncle:

> Lord Louis was revered by all who served under him, and there is no doubt that much of the character of that man had rubbed off on Prince Philip. In so many ways the two men were alike— strict disciplinarians demanding utmost efficiency, and yet tempered with good humour and genuine concern for the men of the lower deck. Men would go anywhere and do anything for Lord Louis, and this loyalty and affection (without any sloppy sentimentality) was soon given to Prince Philip in *Wallace*.[30]

A member of the crew's memory of some incidents helps to explain why Philip was held in high regard:

> I think it was late February that some tankers broke out from Sweden and were making their way to England. The *Wallace* and other destroyers from Rosyth were sent over the the Skagerrak to bring them in. One ship I know was found and escorted to safety. Then we came across another one being attacked by German bombers. This one we had to sink after attempting to

> fight off the attackers.
>
> It was after quite a few such coast convoys . . . that the *Wallace* was in collision one day after leaving Sheerness in a thick fog while taking evasive action from a bomber flying low overhead. A merchant ship leading one line of the convoy cut right into the forward boiler room killing a leading stoker and badly scalding two others . . . Prince Philip went down into the flooded boiler room to try and free the trapped man. The *Wallace* was then unable to make steam and we had to wait a long time for a sea-going tug to tow us into Sheerness.

As this ex-sailor noted: "He was a good officer and well liked by the ship's company . . . officers . . . and lower deck who know too well that everyone on board a destroyer is definitely in the same boat."[31]

As senior executive officer Philip insisted that the *Wallace* should be the best ship in the flotilla. On board the sister ship, *Lauderdale*, was a young Australian lieutenant, Michael Parker, equally determined that his would be cock ship. The friendly rivalry between the two young officers blossomed into a friendship which was to last for many years, Parker becoming equerry to both Prince Philip and Princess Elizabeth after their marriage in 1947. But their rivalry involved their crews, who were set to achieve high ratings in service routine, discipline and physical fitness. There was nothing wrong in this; indeed, in wanting his ship to be the best in the squadron, Philip was following a path trodden by his grandfather, his uncle, and countless other ambitious officers in their own times. But both Prince Louis and Lord Louis had been able to combine their own ambition—for themselves and their ships—with a real regard for the well-being of their men. There is no evidence that Prince Philip was able to inspire the same affection in his crews, who gave him their respect because of his abilities but denied him that affectionate regard which they gave to the equally efficient but more popular officers.

In July 1943 *Wallace* left its home station to take part in the Allied invasion of Sicily. For Prince Philip this was a strange reversal of fate. When he had served in *Valiant* he had helped in the evacuation of British troops from Crete. Now, two years later, he was back in the Mediterranean helping the Allies to invade another island.

One of the *Wallace*'s crew recalled: ". . . we took part in covering the Canadian landing: on the second night we were subject to a prolonged dive-bombing by Stukas and were continually at action stations."[32] Another of the crew remembered: "On one occasion she was attacked by enemy aircraft for over two and a half hours without any help being given or expected, and Prince Philip coolly directed most of the operations from the bridge."[33] During the landings ". . . we went to Malta to fuel and take on ammunition and whilst there a destroyer came alongside with some captured Italian generals together with Lord Louis Mountbatten who came aboard to see Prince Philip."[34]

In September 1943 the old destroyer was sent back to England for a refit. It was during this period of home leave that Prince Philip stayed at Windsor Castle. In February 1944 he was appointed First Lieutenant on the *Whelp*, one of the new 'V and W' class of destroyer then being built. One of the gunners on board remembered meeting Prince Philip at the Hawthorn Leslie shipyard at Hebburn-on-Tyne where *Kelly* had also been built. "A few weeks later we set sail for Scapa Flow where she had her first and successful trials. We were then formed into a squadron comprising many types and sizes of ships, making our way to the Far East soon after . . ."[35]

Whelp formed part of the Twenty-seventh Flotilla of the Eastern Fleet stationed at Ceylon. In August 1944 the *Whelp* sailed from England, escorting *Ramillies* to Algiers and afterwards to the Straits of Boniface in readiness for the invasion of Southern France. Although he was on his way to the Far East Philip was, as he steamed along the Mediterranean, nearer his father than he had been for some time. His father was now living on the Riviera where "he still lives on board the yacht *Davida* at Cannes, and says he is not hungry as he is a small eater. Food conditions are near starving . . . he is now cut off from outside news . . . the port authorities have confiscated his radio."[36] He was not far from the headquarters of a German Panzer Division billeted in Monte Carlo.[37] He had been warned by his doctor that he had a serious heart condition but he took part in the celebrations that followed the liberation of Southern France—by which time Philip was out of the Mediterranean and on his way to Australia. On the 3rd December 1944 Prince Andrew "got out of bed and donned his dressing-gown, seated himself in his armchair and quietly died, meeting death itself like the great gentleman he always was. With the fullest honours that the little Principality of Monaco could render, and with detachments of the French Army honouring him in Nice, he was taken to rest in the Russian Orthodox Church in Nice . . . the Greek Consul-General paid the necessary expenses."[38] It was 1946 before Prince Philip had time to go to Monaco to wind up his father's small estate.

Meanwhile Prince Philip was 'Number 1' to fellow-officers on *Whelp* and 'Jimmy-the-one' to the crew. A Chief Petty Officer met him every day "as I prepared and discussed with him daily, prior to Request men and Defaulters which he dealt with before the Captain . . . As an officer he was very efficient and tried to know as much as he could about all the various departments' jobs and would take part with repairs, etc. Nothing took part without his participation. It was generally known aboard ship that he was 'courting' the Princess as their letters coming and going were as informal as our own. The Princess's envelopes bore no special mark and the Prince took no umbrage to the lads shouting out, 'There's Jimmy's party' when the Princess was seen on the makeshift cinema screen on which we saw the *Pathe News* on the occasions we were in harbour."[39]

Another member of the crew wrote of "Jimmy-the-one being a brave man who held the confidence of the men. The *Whelp* was a happy ship, even in the 'total war' in which it was so much and so many times subjected with 'the Jap' and saw much success actively against the enemy at Sakishima, Okinowa and lastly and victoriously in Sagami Bay off Tokyo . . . two 'epics' saw him take out one of the ship's whalers and rescue one Hellcat (an aircraft belonging to the accompanying carrier) pilot, shot down after an affray during a sortie with several hari-kari pilots . . . and just as meritorious, but in different circumstances, he rescued one of the crew clinging to a buoy by securing the *Whelp* to the buoy and recovering the drowning seaman . . .".[40]

The *Whelp* and the rest of the Twenty-seventh Flotilla was part of the Eastern Fleet commanded by Admiral Somerville which was part of the British Pacific Fleet based in Australia. This Fleet was one small part of the forces commanded by Lord Louis, now the Commander-in-Chief of the South-East Asia Command. After action against the Japanese, *Whelp* went to Australia for a refit before being sent to escort the *Duke of York*, flagship of Admiral Fraser, as it sailed into Tokyo Bay late in August to take part in the ceremony of surrender by the Japanese. Here the *Whelp* acted as host ship to a group of former prisoners of war. One remembered:

> After three years as a POW in Japan we were taken off by an American landing barge, and before being taken to an American hospital ship, we called in to the British destroyer, *Whelp*. While on board we mixed with the crew and had tea, sandwiches and rum. As we were leaving one of the crew said to me, "The Prince of Greece is on this ship." I'm afraid I replied, "Who the hell is he?" Little did I realize . . .[41]

On the 2nd September 1945 the Japanese signed the surrender document on board the American warship *Missouri* where General Douglas MacArthur took the surrender on behalf of the Allied Governments. Lord Louis used his influence to get Prince Philip on board the *Missouri* for the surrender. He then appointed him to serve for a short time on his personal staff which was then helping the "magnificent Mountbatten" to settle the affairs of South-East Asia.

Then *Whelp*, with Philip aboard, and other ships were commissioned to take former prisoners of war back home to England where they arrived in January 1946. *Whelp* returned to Portsmouth where, for the last two months of her commission, Philip was placed in command. This was a recognition of what his first Admiral called "the best junior commanding officer in the Fleet".[42] He seemed well set to imitate the success of Lord Louis and of his grandfather, Prince Louis, to whom he had a striking physical resemblance now that he wore a 'full set' of beard and moustache.[43] The twenty-five-year-old officer now moved into Lord Louis's house in Chesham Street and began again the battle over his naturalization, as well as his courtship of Princess Elizabeth.

16

The Problems of Naturalization

WHEN HE LEFT DARTMOUTH Prince Philip had been given a temporary commission in the Royal Navy. As a foreigner he was not eligible for a permanent commission. There was no long-term future for him in the British Navy unless he became a British citizen. So, in 1940 and acting on Lord Louis's advice, he decided to apply for British citizenship, just as his grandfather, Prince Louis of Battenberg, had done about seventy years before. He filled out and submitted Form S, "for aliens in the fighting services".[1] If he had been an ordinary alien there is little doubt that his application would have been processed and in due course he would have become a naturalized Britisher. This was what happened in thousands of other cases. But a royal prince was no ordinary applicant. We have seen that in 1940 the Foreign Office prevailed on the Lords of the Admiralty to keep Prince Philip as far away as possible from the danger of being killed in action. In the case of his Form S, it was the Home Office which had to grapple with the intricacies of allowing this Greek Prince to become a British citizen. This was the government department which, in 1940, was also handling the problems of evacuation, civil defence, the issue of air-raid shelters, the organization of a skeleton system of underground government which would have become effective if Britain had been invaded, as well as the problem of Press censorship, the future of Mosley and the British Union of Fascists, etc. Given all this, it is not surprising that nothing was done to further this initial and complicated application.

On his part, Prince Philip seemed to have given the question little thought during the next couple of years. He was, after all, very involved in many other things. We have seen that he was a successful and active naval officer and that from time to time he had leaves which he enjoyed to the full. Given his penchant for getting on with the job in hand and his preference for the concrete rather than the abstract, there seemed more sense in concentrating on becoming "the best junior officer in the Fleet" rather than involving himself in bureaucratic wranglings over citizenship. In any event, the issue would be solved in due course and meanwhile, he may have thought, he was in practice if not in law the very model of a modern naval officer.

In 1944 Lord Louis still found time in his busy SEAC Headquarters to write to his nephew reminding him, aboard *Whelp*, that he would get no further in his career until he had settled the issue of citizenship. Lord Louis showed his interest in his nephew's future by also writing to King George VI asking him to use his power with the Government to get things moving. The King, however, always conscious of the correct protocol that had to be followed, pointed out to Lord Louis that the British Government could do little and he himself would do nothing until the King of Greece allowed his cousin to give up his Greek citizenship. So Lord Louis turned to that monarch, in exile in Cairo.

King George II of Greece was, as we shall see, very involved in trying to safeguard his own uncertain future in the face of the growth of a Communist-led republican movement in Greece. At first he was unwilling to agree to Prince Philip ceding his Greek citizenship. He argued that, on his hoped for return to Athens, he would need all the support he could get including that of this active, intelligent and able younger relative. However, other members of the family used their influence to show King George that Philip had already made up his mind to seek a career in the British Navy, that he had inherited from his father a bitter dislike for Greek politicians which would make him a very uneasy helpmeet in post-war Athens, and that it would be spiteful as well as foolish to deny him the chance of acquiring British nationality.

So, late in 1944, the King of Greece gave the necessary consent. But by this time, *Whelp* and Prince Philip had left England and were on their way to Australia and the final scenes of the great struggle against Japan. There was no chance, therefore, to follow up the question of citizenship. Indeed, it was King George VI who took up the issue in the spring of 1945,[2] no doubt prompted by Lord Louis. The Home Office produced the files and the matter was discussed between the Home Secretary, Prime Minister Churchill and the Foreign Secretary, Anthony Eden. Once again the application was left to be caught in a 'catch 22' situation resulting from the peculiar nature of the Greek political situation, itself the result of the German invasion of that unhappy country and the subsequent flight of the King and his Government. Although the Germans occupied the country, the people had refused to settle down under the Nazi heel. Resistance movements sprang up and quickly fell into three major groups. The National Liberation Front (known from its Greek initials as EAM) formed its own band of partisans called ELAS. This was dominated by Communists. Another group, EDES, was loyal to the old-fashioned republican political leaders while a third, EKKA, proclaimed that it was fighting in the hope that a moderate socialist government would be formed after the war. There was no group which came out in support of the restoration of the monarchy after the war.

In *Homage to Catalonia* George Orwell showed that during the Spanish

Civil War the various anti-Franco forces spent almost as much time fighting each other as they spent combating Franco's forces. The same was true of Greece in 1942 and 1943 when ELAS in particular seemed intent on destroying the non-Communist partisans. The British had some hold over the partisans since they all relied on British supplies of technical assistance as well as food and money. So, in July 1943, the British Government forced the warring factions to send representatives to a meeting in Cairo where, on the 4th July 1943, the King of Greece broadcast to his people and declared "officially that the future of Greece and its constitution, whether monarchist or republican, should be settled after the war by free elections."[3]

Harold Macmillan was the British Minister deputed to deal with the question of the future of Greece and it was he who helped arrange the Cairo meeting and the agreement which led to the King's broadcast. But this agreement was itself merely the signal for more of that intrigue of which Macmillan wrote bitterly.[4] Was the King to return to liberated Greece before or after the elections to which he referred in his broadcast? ELAS wanted the King to postpone his return until after the elections; the King, Churchill and President Roosevelt wanted his return before the elections. As Macmillan wrote:

> It is difficult for those accustomed to the more orthodox methods of electioneering among Anglo-Saxon nations to realize the tremendous powers of any government on the spot in most other countries to win a plebiscite. Dictators always win them by overwhelming majorities, as Napoleon III and others have proved. The argument, therefore, about whether the King should be in Greece when the vital decision was taken was not academic, it was of vital importance.[5]

ELAS refused to accept the decision which the Allied leaders had made; there was an increase in the scale of the civil war among the partisans; the unrest spread to the soldiers and sailors in the Greek forces fighting on the Allied side in Italy and North Africa. They mutinied in favour of the ELAS solution to the "King's affair"—that he should not return until the first post-war election had been held and the people given a chance to show whether they wanted a republican, a communist or a monarchist government. The mutiny among the Greek soldiers was only solved after Churchill had ordered that British forces use force to squash it.[6]

The King was forced —by these events and by the obvious opposition from major forces in Greece—to agree not to return until the elections had been held. So, on the 18th October 1944, as the Germans retreated from Athens, a Greek government, led by M. Papandreou and supported by British forces, moved in. Harold Macmillan accompanied the government.

Macmillan's hopes that the Greeks might now move towards some sensible solution of their problem was ill-conceived. First the politicians quarrelled among themselves as the rival groups fought for power. Then on the 3rd December the ELAS communist-led forces rose in revolt against the government which had to call on British troops to help put down this rising, ordered by Stalin as part of his campaign to take control of the whole of the Balkan area. While Churchill shared Macmillan's belief that the rebellion had to be put down, their joint decision was heavily criticized in Britain, "by Aneurin Bevan and others from the Left [and] critics in other parts of the House . . . and a great part of British opinion is disturbed and hostile."[7]

It became evident that many ELAS supporters were fighting not to set up a communist government so much as to prevent the return of the King whom they suspected, not without some reason, of having willingly acquiesced in the cruel Metaxas dictatorship which had governed Greece after 1936. To try to split these people from the hard-liners among ELAS forces, the British forced the King to agree to the setting up of a regency with the popular Archbishop Damaskinos as Regent. He would be Head of State until the elections had been held. On Christmas Day 1944 Churchill and Eden went to Athens to give their support to proposals for a conference of leaders of the warring forces. This took place on the 27th December and on the following day an armistice was signed which led to a truce being arranged to start on the 12th January 1945. Damaskinos's government was recognized by ELAS as well as by the rest of the partisans. It was now hoped that, in peace, the Greeks could be allowed to get on with solving their constitutional problems.

It was against this confused backcloth that the British Government was asked in 1945 to give a decision on Prince Philip's application for naturalization. There was no certainty that the elections, due to be held in Greece in 1946, would lead to a restoration of the monarchy. If, in the spring of 1945, the British Government did not allow one of the royal family to give up his Greek citizenship to become a British citizen would that be taken by the suspicious Greeks as a sign that the British—who, in effect, controlled their country at the time—were pro-monarchist? Or, and here was the 'catch 22', if the Government gave that permission, was it indicating that, in its considered opinion, the monarchy would not be restored and that Philip was to be congratulated for having got out of Greece while there was still time? It is not surprising then that the British Government should have advised the King "to postpone the question of Prince Philip's naturalization until after March 1946 when the Greek general election and the plebiscite on the monarchy would have taken place, and this advice was adopted."[8]

The general public knew nothing about the young Greek Officer Prince or of his efforts to become a British citizen. Neither did all his relatives as Queen Alexandra showed when she recalled:

> An incident illustrating the complexity of Philip's problems occurred when Peter [exiled King of Yugoslavia] and I went to have tea with Uncle Georgie [King of Greece] in the royal suite at Claridge's. With his tea the King always insisted on having a little home-made jam which was specially made for him

> by a friend, but in order that the precious jam jar should not be removed by hotel servants Uncle Georgie invariably hid it away . . . and then forgot where he had hid it. We had to search high and low . . . "It's about as difficult as finding a way for Philip," the aide-de-camp remarked with an amused glance towards us. Peter returned his smile, but I confess I was singularly obtuse, for the remark sailed right over my head.[9]

In March 1946 the Greek people had their elections and their plebiscite. Sixty per cent of the voters wanted the King to return, which to ordinary eyes may appear to be a conclusive enough victory. But the politician-pessimists who were virtually in charge of Prince Philip's application looked at the size of the opposition vote. Forty per cent of the voters had shown that they were opposed to the restoration of the monarchy. This large minority was made up, in the main, of supporters of ELAS, the communist-front Stalin-controlled movement.

In the spring of 1945 the Prime Minister had been Winston Churchill. When Philip's application came up for consideration after the Greek plebiscite, the Labour Government was in power in Britain and it was Prime Minister Attlee and Foreign Minister Ernest Bevin who led the government team at the discussions. And the 'catch 22' situation had not disappeared, although it may have been somewhat altered, for now it was argued that for a member of the Greek royal Family to be seen to be ceding his citizenship so soon after the plebiscite might be taken as a sign that, in spite of their victory, the monarchists realized that they had only a tenuous hold on the throne. Those who thought in this way argued that Prince Philip would be portrayed as merely the first of the many who would be seeking to give up their connections with the Greek throne. On the other hand, in the 'catch 22' position, there were those in the Labour Government who argued that it might be deemed inadvisable for a Labour Government—with its reputation for being left-wing and radical—to be seen to be providing "aid and comfort" for one of the family to whom the Greek Left were so bitterly opposed. It is difficult to recall now that in the first heady days after the end of the war there was the hope that "Left will speak out with Left" and the British Labour Party, if not all members of the Labour Government, believed that it had a "special relationship" with Stalin and the Russian Government. To facilitate Philip's application might be taken as an affront by the Russian-controlled ELAS movement—and by Stalin himself.

By this time, too, there was an additional complicating factor. Prince Philip made his first application in 1940 in order that he might be able to gain a permanent commission in the Royal Navy and make his career in that service. This, after all, was what Prince Louis had done as long ago as 1868, and this was the motive behind his application for another consideration of his case in 1943–1944. But in 1946 this was not the only reason why he was so anxious to become a British citizen, because by now he and Princess Elizabeth were very much in love and intended to get married, in spite of King George VI's opposition to such a match. The

Above: The day of the meeting with Princess Elizabeth (seated third from left) during the first visit of the Royal Family to the Royal Naval College, Dartmouth. Prince Philip stands behind (in cap) with Lord Louis Mountbatten on his right. *Below left:* Princess Elizabeth at Windsor on her 13th birthday in 1939. *Below right:* Prince Philip with his 'full set' as the Australians saw him during his visits there while serving on HMS *Whelp*. This is the photograph which Princess Elizabeth kept on her desk.

Princess Elizabeth as Aladdi
and Princess Margaret as the
Princess in the pantomime a
Windsor, Christmas 1943.

Prince Philip leaving Crathi
Church with Colonel Micha
Bowes-Lyon on 8 Septembe
1946, during his Balmoral holiday. Rumours of an engagement had just been denied by 'a Palace spokes-man'.

Above: The bridegroom-to-be in the role of instructor at the Petty Officers' Training Centre, Corsham, Wiltshire, 1947. *Below*: Stag party, 19 November 1947. Prince Philip celebrated his last night as a bachelor with naval friends. On his left was 'Uncle Dickie', now Earl Mountbatten of Burma and the first Governor-General of the newly-independent India. Seated on the far right of the group was Prince Philip's cousin and best man, the Marquess of Milford Haven.

1947. Marriage solemnized at Westminster Abbey in the Close of St Peter, Westminster in the County of London

No.	When Married.	Name and Surname.	Age.	Condition.	Rank or Profession.	Residence at the time of Marriage.	Father's Name and Surname.	Rank or Profession of Father.
203	20th November 1947	Philip Mountbatten	26	Bachelor	H.R.H. The Duke of Edinburgh, K.G	Kensington Palace	Andrew Slesvig-Holstein-Sonderbourg-Glucksbourg (deceased)	H.R.H. Prince Andrew of Greece
		Elizabeth Alexandra Mary Windsor	21	Spinster	Princess of the United Kingdom of Great Britain & Ireland	Buckingham Palace	Albert Frederick Arthur George Windsor	H.M. King George VI of the United Kingdom of Great Britain & Ireland and of the British Dominions beyond the Seas: Defender of the Faith

Married in Westminster Abbey according to the Rites and Ceremonies of the Established Church by Special Licence by me,

Geoffrey Cantuar:
Alan C. Don D.D.

This Marriage was solemnized between us,
Philip
Elizabeth

in the presence of us:—

George R.
Elizabeth R
Mary R
Alice
Princess Andrew of Greece
Margaret
Henry
Alice

Marina
Patricia Ramsay
Alexander Ramsay
Alice Mary
Athlone
Victoria Milford Haven
Nada Milford Haven

Edwina Mountbatten of Burma
Mountbatten of Burma
Haakon R
Michael R
Frederika
Frederik R

The extended family at the Royal Wedding, 20 November 1947. (*See* Key, page 333).

Above: On honeymoon at Broadlands, the Hampshire home of the Earl and Countess Mountbatten of Burma. *Below left:* A study by the photographer Baron, Prince Philip's friend for many years, of the Prince with his infant son, Charles. *Below right:* One of many group photographs taken after the christening of Princess Anne in October 1950. This one shows Edwina, Countess Mountbatten of Burma, standing behind Princess Elizabeth with Lord Louis on her right.

.owing in a whaler race at
Ialta and determined to
ıake his ship the 'cock' ship.

e commander on his ship
ıgpie in Malta, 1951, during
last year at sea and during
first and last command.

Prince Philip partnered by Princess Elizabeth taking part in a Canadian square dance organized by the Governor-General, Lord Alexander, during the Royal Tour of Canada, 1951. The informality of their dress won the hearts of the Canadians.

19 April 1952 and the Royal worker on a visit to the Mosley Common Colliery during his tour of the Lancashire coalfields.

question of the engagement and marriage will be considered fully in Chapter 18, but it has to be mentioned here because it loomed large in the King's mind when he took part in the discussions on Prince Philip's proposed naturalization.

In June 1946 the issue was still unresolved. Lord Louis arrived home from the Far East, "wrapped in clouds of glory",[10] to take part in the Victory Parade through London. He had received a host of decorations from foreign governments and was to receive a host more, including a Sword of Honour and the Freedom of the City of London and a new title commemorating the great campaign which he had led—Mountbatten of Burma. The King was also to confer on him the Order of the Garter. It is little wonder that he wrote: "It was wonderful to be home again; it was wonderful to be honoured in all these ways."[11]

We have already seen that Lord Louis took a lively interest in the career of his nephew, even when he himself was engaged in the arduous task of running SEAC. Now that he was home and free of major responsibilities for a time, he took up Prince Philip's cause with renewed vigour, especially when he realized that it was now a question not only of Philip's career but of his marriage to the heir to the British throne. He urged his cousin, King George VI, to try to use his influence with the politicians so that the naturalization could take place. Lord Louis also spoke to the Labour leaders to the same effect.

But however willing Prime Minister Attlee and Foreign Minister Bevin might have been they were also political realists. In Athens the Greek monarchy was being supported by a British army of occupation but opposed by the guerillas of ELAS. Newspaper reports told of the cruel fighting of an urban guerilla war, of the cruelty with which the Greek Government treated prisoners and of international condemnation of the way in which that government, backed by Britain, was trying to maintain law and order. The Labour Government had to face the criticisms of many left-wing Labour MPs, eighty-six of whom signed a Commons' Motion condemning the Greek Royal Government for its "barbaric atrocities".

Lord Louis may have hoped to have had some influence with Attlee and Bevin. He was, after all, known to be a Labour voter and his wife to be "very left". Indeed, it was because of his liberal views he was to be called on, in March 1947, to be the last Viceroy of India, sent by Attlee to grant Indian independence. But, by the same token, all this meant that Lord Louis's support for his nephew's cause—whether for naturalization or for the proposed marriage—was bound to raise the hackles of those on the right of the British political spectrum who regarded him as "the grave-digger of the Empire".[12] Even in 1946 and before it was known that he would be the last Viceroy of India, Mountbatten had become well known for his opposition to colonialism—in former French Indo-China (Laos, Cambodia and Vietnam), in the former Dutch East Indies (later Indonesia) and in Burma, Malaya, Singapore, and India. He had affronted the 'sahib' mentality by the way in which he welcomed local ('native') leaders as 'Pandit' Nehru and Gandhi. In the ranks of the Conservative Opposition, led by Winston Churchill, and in the recesses of the London Clubs where politicians met the retired and disgruntled former Imperial Administrators, there was deep antagonism towards anything to do with Mountbatten—and that included his nephew.

Indeed, it appears as if the issue might have dragged on for ever. There seemed little prospect of the Greek situation ever becoming so favourable as to allow for Philip's naturalization while opposition inside both the Labour Party and, for different reasons, inside the Conservative Party, would have grown, if anything, stronger with the passing of the years. It was Princess Elizabeth who forced everyone's hand in the summer of 1946 when she told her father and mother that Prince Philip had proposed to her and that she had accepted his proposal. In Chapter 18 we shall see how the King reacted towards this news and how he put off the official announcement until he and his family had returned from a long tour of South Africa. But if the young Princess was as determined as she seemed to be, then the question of Philip's naturalization had to be settled quickly.

While the King and the rest of the Royal Family were in South Africa, Attlee and his Lord Chancellor, Lord Jowitt, pushed through Prince Philip's application. Attlee managed, as he always did, to win over the wild men of the Labour Left and ignored, as he always did, the equally wild men of the Tory Right. Lord Louis used his charm to win over the editors of the *Sunday* and *Daily Express*. These newspapers had been most vociferous in their anti-Mountbatten campaign and they were to become even more virulent in 1947 and 1948 when Mountbatten was in India. But in February 1947, while the Royal Family was still in South Africa and before the announcement of Mountbatten's appointment as Viceroy, Lord Louis invited the two editors to meet him in his home at Chester Street. Beaverbrook, owner of the *Express* newspapers which acted as outlets for his spleen, knew nothing of the meeting, at which Lord Louis asked what public feeling would be if it was announced that his nephew was becoming a British citizen. They said that it ought to go all right. They could hardly have said other, given that they were in Lord Louis's home, listening to the great man appeal to their judgement of the prospects for his nephew who was sitting quietly in the corner watching his uncle manipulate the opinion-formers. Once the *Express* chain had been won over, Lord Louis knew that there was little danger of criticism from any of the other Fleet Street editors.

Meanwhile, just before Christmas 1946 Prince Philip filled out the questionnaire in which he agreed that he was financially solvent, that he spoke English and that he continue to serve the Crown. He sent this to the Home Office and went off to spend Christmas with the Royal Family at Windsor. When they left for South Africa he returned to his naval duties and waited for the Home Office machine to churn out his papers. One other question had to be settled before the papers could be issued; what name was he going to use? If he became a British citizen he had to renounce all his foreign titles—and would no longer be able to sign himself Philip of Greece. But he had no surname—and the Home Office required him to have one before they could issue his papers. In Chapter 17 we shall see how this problem was solved and how he decided to use his mother's family name, Mountbatten.

The mills of the Home Office finally ground out their papers and on the 18th March 1947 it was announced in the *London Gazette* that British citizenship had been awarded to "Mountbatten, Philip; Greece; serving officer in His Majesty's forces; 16 Chester Street, London S.W.1." There was no public fanfare, for this was just one in a list of 817 such changes of nationality.

Princess Elizabeth was in South Africa when she received a letter from ex-Prince Philip telling her that his naturalization had come through. As she told her father, the way was now clear for an announcement of the engagement—at least when the Royal Tour was over.

Two final points ought to be made on this question of naturalization. The first is that there was, technically speaking, no need for Prince Philip to have made an application for British citizenship. Under the Act of Settlement of 1701, which excluded from the British throne the Catholic Stuarts, British nationality and royal status were bestowed on the Electress Sophia of Hanover and all her descendants. Since Prince Philip was among these, he had been a British Royal Highness from the moment of his birth. This was confirmed by the decision reached in the case "Attorney-General -v- Prince Ernest Augustus of Hanover". Prince Ernest was a brother to Prince George of Hanover, the second husband of Prince Philip's sister, Sophie. In 1961 Prince Ernest was anxious to claim the rights of a British national. Few ordinary people, and indeed few lawyers gave his claim much chance. But a long legal wrangle led to the decision that the Act of Settlement applied in spite of two World Wars. This seemed so bizarre that the Master of the Rolls felt obliged to comment:

> It seems an extraordinary thing that a man who fought against this country could come along and say that he was a British subject; if he is right he would appear to have committed high treason during the war.[13]

The second point is that the *Express* newspapers, outwitted by Lord Louis in February 1947, did not give up their anti-Mountbatten campaign. Indeed, they enlarged it to include the nephew whom they referred to as "Phil the Greek", ignoring both the legal position resulting from the Act of 1701 and, more pertinently, Prince Philip's individual naturalization. It is not surprising that he should have described the *Daily Express* as a "bloody awful newspaper"[14] and that relations between the Prince and the Press have been, even at their best, brittle.

In common with Lady Airlie (p. 153) and Channon (p. 154) I have continued to use the title 'Prince'.

17

The Question of a Name

IN ONE OF HIS MANY authoritative articles, the constitutional lawyer, Edward Iwi, noted that "Everyone . . . is agreed that a Prince or Princess with the prefix HRH never uses a surname or family name."[1] He went on to point out that even though they had a family name, Windsor, the Royal witnesses who were Edward VIII's brothers, "each signed only his Christian name" to the Instrument of Abdication annexed to the Abdication Act 1936.

Prince Philip was, in at least one sense, worse off than the Royal Windsor Princes, for the Greek royal family simply had no family name at all. We have already seen that when he went to school in Paris and again when he went to Cheam, he simply wrote "Philip" at the top of his essays, and when asked "Philip who?" replied, "Philip of Greece." His midshipman's journal was headed "Philip, Prince of Greece",[2] and when he left Dartmouth the Admiralty issued a special order that he should be addressed by "all ranks" as Prince Philip. This did little to endear him to his fellow-midshipmen and still less to win him the favour of officers. He had enough sense to let it be known that he wished to be known simply as "Philip",[3] rejecting "of Greece" because it was manifestly un-English, and "Prince" because it roused too much antipathy. However, there were still misunderstandings when he was asked to give his name—as to the garage hand in Sydney.[4]

During the final days before the announcement of his naturalization Prince Philip was made acutely aware, yet again, of the disadvantages of not having a surname, for he would need one if the announcement were to be made. After all, the *London Gazette* would not have made much sense if it had carried an announcement that "Philip of Greece now wishes to be known as Philip." And in the event that he became a father, there would have been a problem as to the name by which his children were to be known. So, he, the politicians, the College of Heralds and other members of the Royal Family were driven to find a surname by which the Britisher-to-be might be known.

He was, as we have seen, of Danish stock and that Royal Family was known to the genealogists as the House of Schleswig-Holstein-Sondenburg-Glucksberg. He could hardly be expected to adopt this name which was both too long and far too foreign sounding. Either he[5] or the College of Heralds[6] suggested that the Danish Royal Family had an even older name, Oldenburgh, which was easily translated into Oldcastle. The Home Secretary, James Chuter Ede, who had a better sense both of language and history than either Prince Philip or the College of Heralds, was not happy with this suggestion; Earl Mountbatten was also opposed to the use of this anglicized form of a long forgotten family name.[7]

It was Chuter Ede, acting perhaps as spokesman for Earl Mountbatten, who suggested to King George VI that the Prince be invited to use his mother's family name as his own. As Chuter Ede noted: "It is certainly grander and more glittering than Oldcastle."[8] So it was that when the naturalization was announced, it was, as we have seen, in the name of Lieutenant Philip Mountbatten. Certainly the Mountbatten name was as grand as that of Windsor which was Princess Elizabeth's family name. As Iwi pointed out, ". . . the name of Mountbatten came into being at the same time as the name Windsor and for the same reason."[9] And, in 1947, there was little doubt that it was a "glittering" name, linked as it was with the successes of Earl Mountbatten who was said to have been "delighted" at Prince Philip's choice of name.[10]

It has been suggested that he himself was not "greatly in favour of being given the Mountbatten surname".[11] Certainly by the time he helped Boothroyd write his biography in 1971 he had become less than enamoured with the way in which people linked his name with that of Earl Mountbatten.[12]

He was very pleased that before his marriage to Princess Elizabeth the King gave him the title of Duke of Edinburgh which helped mark him off from the Mountbatten link. Neither did he share Lord Louis's ambition to have the name of the Royal Family changed from that of Windsor to that of Mountbatten; for himself he would have liked the new monarchy to be known as "The Family of Windsor in the House of Edinburgh".[13]

The King felt that it was necessary to give him a title before his marriage so that any children born to him and Princess Elizabeth would not be born commoners. This helps to remind us that while naturalization made it necessary for Prince Philip to acquire a surname it also made it impossible for him to hold on to Greek titles. King George VI, acting on the advice of Prime Minister Attlee and Lord Louis, suggested that he should grant the young man the title "His Royal Highness Prince Philip". It was the young Prince himself who told the King, "with some determination" that "while he appreciated His Majesty's kind offer, he preferred not to take advantage of it but to be known after his naturalization as a British subject simply as 'Lieutenant Philip . . . RN'." This decision both pleased and impressed the King who at once assented to it.[14]

No one knows how Lord Mountbatten felt when he heard that his nephew had turned down the offer of a title with the prefix HRH. It was hardly something which he himself would have done, nor would he have advised anyone else to do so. Philip was using Lord Louis's Chester Street home as his own during this period, making friends with the cook and the valet, John Dean, who has written his own account of life with Prince Philip.[15] Perhaps Lord Louis's disappointment with this refusal of a title was assuaged by the thought that when Philip married Princess Elizabeth she would take the name Mountbatten, for as Iwi pointed out: "Princess Elizabeth, in accordance with the custom followed by all the subjects of King George VI, acquired her husband's name on marriage."[16] This would bring fresh glory to the Mountbatten name.

18

The Question of Marriage, 1941–1947

WE HAVE SEEN HOW Prime Minister Attlee compared the great abilities of "those Mountbattens . . . Prince Louis . . . Dickie . . . and Philip . . .";[1] the same three also made great marriages. Prince Louis married Queen Victoria's granddaughter; 'Dickie' married the beautiful Edwina Ashley, heiress to much of her grandfather's wealth; and Philip made the greatest marriage of the three. But that marriage, and the engagement which preceded it, took place only after a long period of uncertainty. The parental anxieties of King George VI and Queen Elizabeth combined with the political problems arising from the Prince's Greek origins to make it seem that the engagement might never be announced. That it was, on the 10th July 1947, was due in no small part to the stubborn tenacity of Princess Elizabeth who forced her father to allow her to marry the man of her choice.

The eighteen-year-old cadet had not been swept off his feet by the thirteen-year-old cousin whom he met at Dartmouth. We know that before going to Dartmouth he "gallantly, and I think, quite impartially squired . . . all" the "blondes, brunettes and redhead charmers" he met during the summer of 1938 which he spent in Venice.[2] Indeed, some people believe that his relatively poor showing in the entry examinations to Dartmouth was due in part to the good time he had enjoyed in Venice. So he was far too much a man of the world to be 'thrown' by meeting a young teenager. During the war he continued to enjoy female company in many parts of the world. Apart from shore leave in Athens and a short stay in South Africa, there was the time he spent in Australia in late 1944. "Philip, with a golden beard, hit feminine hearts, first in Melbourne and then in Sydney with terrific impact," although always with "one objective: non-involvement. Philip was no longer regardless of gossip." So although "girls had always flung themselves at Prince Philip",[3] he enjoyed their company, found safety in numbers and, "if awkward rumours arose he insisted firmly, sometimes rudely, that they should be scotched immediately."

But the young Princess had "fallen in love" at Dartmouth.[4] At Christmas 1940 she persuaded her father to allow her to use the diplomatic 'bags' to send her Christmas cards to Philip on leave in Athens. Her parents realized that she admired her third cousin, but they did not believe that her interest in the "young Viking" was anything more than cousinly concern. It is symbolic of the difference between the two cousins that while Philip was engaged in active service in the Mediterranean, Princess Elizabeth, at Christmas 1940, acted the nativity story with the children of royal tenants at Windsor. And it is revealing of the father's attitude towards the fourteen-year-old daughter that he wrote in his diary, "I wept through most of it."[5]

In 1941, Lord Louis gave Prince Philip a row for not writing to him more frequently,[6] but Prince Philip found time to write fairly regularly to Princess Elizabeth after he left Britain in January 1940. His cousin Alexandra came across him writing one such letter during his short stay in South Africa in 1941:

> One evening in Cape Town, when I wanted to chat, Philip insisted on finishing a letter he was writing and I, cousin-like, enquired, "Who's it to?" "Lilibet," he answered. "Who?" I asked, still rather mystified. "Princess Elizabeth in England." "But she's only a baby," I said, still rather puzzled, as he sealed the letter. Aha, I thought with family candour, he knows he's going to England and he's angling for an invitation. But as it turned out, I was doing my cousin far, far less than justice. Had they already begun then, the gentle assurances and recognitions of the heart?"[7]

No one knows the answer to that rhetorical question. We do know that he continued to write throughout the war and that the Princess enjoyed receiving his letters, postcards and mementoes of visits to exciting places of which she had heard and read but never seen. In return she wrote, sent parcels and knitted goods—as did many another girl to many another young man during the war.

Some people seemed to have provided their answers to the question which Alexandra posed in the last extract.

In January and February of 1941 Prince Philip had spent some time with his mother when *Valiant* was stationed in the Piraeus.[8] On the 21st January he was at a cocktail party where another guest was the British MP, Sir Henry 'Chips' Channon. In his diary Channon wrote:

> . . . an enjoyable Greek cocktail party. Philip of Greece was there. He is extremely handsome, and I recalled my afternoon's conversation with Princess Nicholas. He is to be our Prince Consort, and that is why he is serving in our Navy.[9]

Princess Nicholas of Greece was the mother of Princess Marina, Duchess of Kent, a reliable source of what was going on in the British Royal Family, so Channon was entitled to take the report as having a substantial element of truth. Indeed, with the hindsight of the fact that the marriage did take place and that he did become Prince Consort, Channon may be seen as the first prophet of that marriage. But Prince Philip will have none of it and he ought to have known better than Princess Marina, Princess Nicholas and Channon.[10] Certainly, as we shall see, King George VI and Queen Elizabeth were not parties to the 'plot' which Channon believes was being worked out. Nor, in 1941, was the twenty-year-old Prince Philip, as he makes clear. Nor, indeed, was the fourteen-year-old Princess Elizabeth who was still the over-protected and immature daughter of very loving parents. Even the Greek Royal Family had other ideas for Philip—one being that he might marry Princess Alexandra, who, after all, was more of an age with him and whose company he had enjoyed for a number of years.

While Philip was in England during the winter of 1941–1942 he met Princess Elizabeth on a number of occasions. King George VI invited him to Buckingham Palace—the sort of thing that one would expect a kindly uncle to do for a young relative returned from action in the Mediterranean. No one should read into these invitations anything connected with a marriage. Indeed, as we shall see, the King was to go out of his way to try to put an end to talk of a marriage in 1944. He would hardly have taken that line in 1944 if he had been 'plotting' a marriage in 1941 or 1942.

Philip also met the Princess at Princess Marina's home, Coppins in Buckinghamshire. Princess Marina, Duchess of Kent, was a popular favourite with the younger members of the Royal Family—as indeed she was with the British people at large. And Coppins was sufficiently remote from London to enable the young people to meet in a degree of privacy, but still there were no indications that the two were other than friendly cousins, albeit of very different ages and experience.

If there was a date when Prince Philip first thought of marriage to his younger cousin it was Christmas 1943. He had returned home in November of that year when *Wallace* was paid off for a major refit and he did not go to sea again for four months. Part of this time he spent on instructional courses, but part he spent on leave. He was invited to spend Christmas with the Royal Family at Windsor. He arrived on Christmas

Eve, "looking more than ever like a Viking, though a drawn and weather-beaten one."[11]

Each year since 1941 the two Princesses had written and performed a Christmas pantomime in which they appeared in traditional costume of gilt shoes, periwigs, brocade and tights. The proceeds from the performances were given to the Queen's Wool Fund and since the prices went as high as *7s. 6d.* (37½p) they were able to raise about nine hundred pounds each year. The pantomimes took place in the Waterloo Room in the Castle where Queen Victoria had built a magnificent stage so that plays could be put on for her entertainment.

For Christmas 1943 the Princesses chose to perform *Aladdin*. The seventeen-year-old Elizabeth played the principal boy in front of an audience which, this year, included Prince Philip. 'Crawfie' noted: "There was a sparkle about her none of us had ever seen before."[12]

There were nine people present at dinner on Christmas Eve—the King and Queen, the two Princesses, Prince Philip and four other guests. Prince Philip told the King about his experiences in *Wallace*. In the drawing-room after dinner the lights were put out and they all sat around the fire to listen to ghost stories. Princess Margaret wrote: "We settled ourselves to be frightened and we were *not*. Most disappointing."[13]

On other evenings there was dancing while on the last evening the party was enlarged by the inclusion of the staff and officers in charge of the guns protecting Windsor Castle. David Milford Haven also arrived and, said Princess Margaret: "David Milford Haven . . . and Philip went mad."[14]

During the three days there was also plenty of chance for Philip and Elizabeth to talk and to get to know each other better. He found, for example, that she had blossomed out into a very beautiful eighteen-year-old and that she had a mind of her own—as her father was to learn to his cost. She found that he was more than someone who could jump higher and dance more madly than anyone else. It was from this time that we can date the fact that Philip's photograph was placed on the dressing-table in her bedroom while he carried her photograph with him when he left to return to duty. It is not surprising then that in Australia he was anxious to avoid any possibilities of rumours of his carrying on with other girls.

It may have been that from this time on, King George VI was made to think of Philip as a potential son-in-law. Certainly his Greek relatives were the first to realize that their kinsman had a very deep interest in Princess Elizabeth. And she, on her part, kept reminding the King of "Philip this . . ." and "Philip that . . ." as Crawfie noted. But still, it seems, the King was unwilling to believe that his daughter could be serious in her feelings for Prince Philip.

During the winter and spring of 1944 Philip had at least one "long heart to heart talk with Marina".[15] By now he seemed to be thinking definitely about marriage—and Channon picked up the gossip. On the 16th February 1944 he noted: "My parents-in-law called to see me, after having had tea with the King and Queen at Buckingham Palace . . . I do believe that a marriage may well be arranged between Princess Elizabeth and Prince Philip of Greece."[16] That "may well be" is very much less definite than the "will be" used by Channon in January 1941.

Princess Marina may have unwittingly been the cause of an unfortunate conversation which took place at the celebration of the marriage of Princess Alexandra to Prince Peter of Yugoslavia early in March 1944. King George of Greece and other members of the exiled families from Greece and Yugoslavia were entertained by King George VI and Queen Elizabeth at Buckingham Palace. The King of Greece took the opportunity to remind King George that many people had supposed that Philip might marry Alexandra—which was now out of the question. However, he went on, this need not be a major tragedy because "we could reunite our families and countries through Lilibet and Philip."[17] The King of Greece continued: "It seems that Lilibet is in love with Philip, and I know that he adores her."

If there had been any substance in the reports which Channon picked up in Greece in 1941, this conversation would never have taken place in 1944. To give added weight to the argument that there was no "plot" to make Prince Philip "our Prince Consort", King George VI reacted angrily—as he did whenever something annoyed him—and let the King of Greece know that he wanted to hear no more on this subject. Later, he wrote to his mother Queen Mary:

> We both think she is too young for that now, as she has never met any young men of her own age . . . I like Philip. He is intelligent, has a good sense of humour and thinks about things in the right way . . . We are going to tell G. [King George of Greece] that P. had better not think any more about it for the present.[18]

It was probably the Queen, remembering her many suitors, who found it hard to believe that her daughter had fallen in love with the first eligible young man she had met. As for the King, he had a special regard for his elder daughter as Lady Airlie noted:

> The King was a devoted father to both his daughters. He spoiled Princess Margaret . . . but Princess Elizabeth was his constant companion in shooting, walking, riding—in fact in everything. His affection for her was touching. I wondered sometimes whether he was secretly dreading the prospect of an early marriage for her . . .[19]

In the hope that there might be "safety in numbers" and to provide the Princess with other eligible young men against whom she might be able to see Philip in a different light, the King and Queen began to organize parties at which young guardsmen, stationed at Windsor, squired the Princesses. Queen Mary, with the wisdom of age and the ability to be objective towards the problem of the Princess's dawning love, laughingly referred to these as the 'Body-Guard'.[20] These young men also accompanied the Princesses to the theatre, to dances outside the Palace and to race meetings. It was hardly surprising that this should have misled the

Press—ever eager to foretell the next development in the lives of each member of the Royal Family. In December 1943 the New York *Journal-American* had confidently predicted the forthcoming marriage of Princess Elizabeth to Hugh Fitzroy, Earl of Euston, *or* (an unusual admission of ignorance by a newspaper) Charles Manners, Duke of Rutland, both of them twenty-four years old and both in the Grenadier Guards.[21] Other magazines and newspapers joined in the guessing game. Only *Time* had Prince Philip's name in a list and even that august magazine put him second after the forty-one-year-old Charles, the Prince Regent of Belgium, ignoring the fact that a marriage to the latter would have created all sorts of religious and constitutional problems.

On the 18th April 1944 Queen Mary gave a party at Marlborough House to celebrate Princess Elizabeth's eighteenth birthday, one which marked her 'coming of age' as a royal person. Prince Philip was one of the guests invited by the ageing Dowager Queen who, as we have seen, liked the young man and was to be among the first to know of the young couple's engagement.

Then Philip was off to sea again in *Whelp* while Princess Elizabeth continued with her training as a subaltern in the ATS. She had forced her father to allow her to do as every other youngster had to do—register for National Service. He did so with mixed feelings; on the one hand he wanted her to see a little more of life; on the other hand he was not sure that serving in the Women's Army was the best way to achieve this desirable end. But she insisted—being as stubborn as he was—and finally he relented. So, "No. 230873, Second Subaltern Elizabeth Alexandra Mary Windsor. Age: 18. Eyes: Blue. Hair: Brown. Height: 5ft 3ins" joined up at Aldershot. While she continued to live at Windsor, she went to Camberley or to London each day for her training. She did a course on vehicle maintenance which involved her working in, on and under motor cars and lorries. She learnt to strip an engine and to service it, to read a map and drive in convoy. Her aunt, Princess Royal, came for one inspection and her father for another—enjoying the joke when she was unable to get her vehicle to start.[22]

She had barely finished her training before the War-in-Europe ended with the German surrender. She was with her parents in Buckingham Palace on the 8th May 1945 when the people of London gathered outside to cheer their victory and to call for the King, Queen and the Princesses. The King told some of the 'Body-Guard' to take the two Princesses out of the Palace so that they could mix with the people revelling in the lit-up streets. In his diary for that evening he noted: "Poor darlings, they have never had any fun yet."[23]

In January 1946 Prince Philip came back to England and the courtship was resumed at a new level of intensity on both sides, but with the King and Queen still showing their opposition to any question of an engagement and marriage. On the first night on which he had leave from *Whelp* Prince Philip went to Buckingham Palace where he had dinner in

Princess Elizabeth's private sitting-room—her sister acting as chaperone. The three of them were in high spirits and, as 'Crawfie' recalled, they chased each other up and down the long corridors of the Palace in a very unseemly way. Prince Philip used Lord Louis's house in Chester Street as his base when in London. When the Royal Family moved to Windsor for the weekends he was often invited to stay with them, impressing King George VI once again.[24]

Still on the side of young love was Queen Mary, as Lady Airlie wrote:

> It was when I joined Queen Mary in Sandringham in January 1946 that she spoke to me for the first time about Princess Elizabeth and Prince Philip. "They have been in love for the last eighteen months," she said. "In fact longer, I think. I believe she fell in love with him the first time he went down to Windsor, but the King and Queen feel that she is too young to be engaged yet. They want her to see more of the world before committing herself, and to meet more men. After all, she's only nineteen, and one is very impressionable at that age."
>
> "I fell in love at nineteen and it lasted for ever," I said. Queen Mary agreed. "Yes, it does happen sometimes, and Elizabeth seems to me that kind of girl. She would always know her own mind. There's something very steadfast and determined about her—like her father. She won't give her heart lightly, but when she does it will be for always. All the same, I think the King and Queen are right to make her wait a while. Apart from anything else there's the problem of Prince Philip's nationality . . . That may take some time, so I suppose my son is wise," concluded the Queen. Then she laughed, "After all, he had to wait long enough for *his* wife, and you can see what a success their marriage is."[25]

We have seen that the politicians advised King George VI against allowing Prince Philip to take up British nationality in 1946, using the confused state of Greek politics as their excuse for suggesting that no action be taken for the moment. And if Prince Philip wanted to become not merely a British citizen but the fiancé of the heir to the throne? The King would have had to take the advice of his Ministers in this as well. As the *Manchester Guardian* noted: "The King would not assert his personal judgement on such a matter against that of the Government."[26] There can be little doubt that this advice, at least in 1946 and perhaps early in 1947, was that such a match would not be in the best interests of the country. There was a civil war in Greece; its King was a sick man and his heir was married to Frederica, Princess of Hanover. The British people were already unsure about whether they ought to continue to allow their soldiers to be killed on the streets of Athens. They would have had even less sympathy with maintaining the Greek throne for a Queen whose family had thrown in their lot with Hitler. And it would be unwise, the Government suggested, to allow the heir to the British throne, to ally herself to a Prince who himself was so closely linked with that uncertain and possibly pro-German throne in Greece.

King George of Greece had tried, in 1944, to get King George VI to agree to the marriage. Now, back on the throne of Greece, he allowed newspapers there to speculate and to 'officially announce' a forthcoming marriage. The *Hellicon Aema* was an 'official' newspaper and when it carried reports about the marriage, newspapers elsewhere in the world took it as a sign that the British too would be issuing a statement soon. So there was a welter of gossip, rumour and speculation. Palace denials merely confirmed popular opinion that "an understanding existed but was being kept secret".[27] The young couple continued to meet—Prince Philip driving to London or Windsor from whichever naval station he happened to be attached to. They also wrote frequently. He gave up his former practice of sending his letters addressed to a lady-in-waiting and sent them openly to "HRH Princess Elizabeth, Buckingham Palace, London," to the delight of the post-mistresses in small country offices.

During one of his short stays at Windsor, Peter of Yugoslavia and Princess Alexandra were at their home in Sunninghill which backs on to Windsor Great Park. While out walking:

> . . . two of the royal corgis dashed through the bracken and when we looked around expecting to see Uncle Bertie and Aunt Elizabeth it was Philip and Lilibet, walking alone. They were so intent in conversation that we decided not to bother them so we just waved and walked on. They seemed relieved to be left in peace. This was only the first of several such encounters.
>
> We used to see them holding hands, disengaging themselves sometimes until we came closer and then could see it was only us.
>
> "I only hope Philip isn't flirting with her," I once told Marina . . . Marina said soberly, "His flirting days are over. He would be the one to be hurt if it was all just a flirtation or if—if it is not to be. One thing I'm sure about, those two would never do anything to hurt each other."[28]

It was foreign to Prince Philip's normal way of doing things—wholeheartedly and exuberantly. He had to have almost clandestine meetings with the Princess in the Great Park away from the publicity that would have attended their meetings in London or at race meetings. That he was prepared to behave in this way is, in some people's opinion, in itself a proof of the genuine love he had for the Princess. It was also a preparation for the sort of life he would have to lead when he married; there would be incessant prying, constant gossiping and overmuch unfair criticism. He had seen enough of this as it affected his other relations and he was too worldly-wise and intelligent not to have foreseen that this would be his fate if he married the future Queen of England. He understood why Queen Victoria had written to thank her fiancé, Prince Albert, for "his self-sacrifice".[29]

In May 1946 Prince Philip accompanied King George VI, Queen Elizabeth and the two Princesses to the wedding of the Hon. Mrs Vicary Gibbs (Princess Elizabeth's lady-in-waiting) to Captain the Hon. Andrew Elphinstone. Almost all the Royal Family was present at the wedding and at the reception afterwards at the Savoy Hotel.

> . . . one of the wedding cameramen caught a beautiful picture of Lilibet and Philip, standing together for all the world like a bride and bridegroom. Wearing her bridesmaid's wreath of orange blossom and lily of the valley, Lilibet was still in fact even holding her bridesmaid's bouquet and practically

> every newspaper in the world used the picture. Yet Uncle Georgie also appeared in the photograph and I think that every newspaper without exception cut him out.[30]

In this way did the Press 'doctor' a picture as a means of informing their readers as to what was going on. This led to a growth of interest in the possibilities of a royal romance. This was increased when it was announced that in the summer Prince Philip was to spend a month with the Royal Family at Balmoral. The King hoped that this would give his daughter a chance to see Prince Philip over a fairly long period, and help her find out whether this was, in fact, the man she wanted to marry.

And, as she herself was to say later at a luncheon in Edinburgh, "beside some well-loved loch, the white clouds sailing overhead and a curlew crying out of sight . . ." Prince Philip proposed to her and she accepted his offer of marriage. The King and Queen accepted Prince Philip as their son-in-law. That, one might think, was the end of this matter. However, Prince Philip's path had never been very smooth nor was his future to be any better, so it is not surprising that even this matter of proposal-acceptance did not lead to an announcement of a formal engagement. Would Parliament agree? Would he get his British nationality? What about that Greek throne? And, still nagging at George VI, did Elizabeth really know her mind?

The young couple were told that they could regard themselves as unofficially engaged, but that the official announcement would have to wait at least until Princess Elizabeth had returned from the Royal Tour of South Africa in the early months of 1947. When Press speculation reached the point of claiming that the young couple were engaged, the Palace issued a denial, in September, although seeming to give the lie to its own denial by announcing that the Prince would spend Christmas with the family at Sandringham.

19

An Engagement—At Last

PRINCESS ELIZABETH SEEMED TO HAVE forced her father's hand, but he still insisted that there should be no public announcement of the engagement, at least until after the Royal Tour of South Africa. Perhaps he hoped that this enforced separation, which would last three months, would give his daughter a chance to forget the young man. After all, she was still only twenty and it could be that the romance which had flourished in the fairly hot-house atmosphere of royal circles might wither once the couple were apart for a longish period.

The King, however, had other than purely personal considerations in mind. He would have to get the approval of his Government—and of Parliament—for a marriage between Prince Philip and the Princess. How would a Socialist government react to the prospects of such a match? We have to remember, once again, the international situation of the winter of 1946–1947 when the British were struggling to keep the Greek King on his uncertain throne, and fighting a civil war against Russian-backed troops of ELAS. Not everyone in the Labour Party agreed with its own government's Greek policy. Would this spill over into criticism of the proposal to allow the heir to the English throne to marry a Greek-born Prince?

How would public opinion react to the announcement of the engagement? The King did not have Lord Mountbatten's charm, nor did he have that personal contact with editors of Fleet Street newspapers which Mountbatten was to use to such good effect in February 1947. But the King was all too well aware of the Beaverbrook line and its anti-Mountbatten campaign which had become increasingly strong once it was known that Mountbatten was to be sent to India to lead that sub-continent to independence. Would the Press, led by Beaverbrook, conduct an anti-Philip campaign and so turn people against the proposed marriage?

As well as being guided by his Ministers, the King also relied on the advice given him by the people who surrounded him at Court. These tended, on the whole, to be against the idea of a marriage between the heir and Prince Philip. Some of them resented the way in which Mountbatten's career had developed during the war and the way in which it was to take off in a new direction in India. Some questioned whether there was any limit to the man's ambitions. Would he, in the event of a Philip-Elizabeth marriage become, in time, a power behind the throne, someone with whom they would be unable to deal?

And in any event, they said, the Princess was too young. Some of the King's advisers pointed out that she was still only twenty, that if the King died in the near future a young, inexperienced Sovereign might naturally turn to her consort for advice and help. This, they claimed, would increase the influence of Mountbatten and might lead to all sorts of constitutional problems. In passing, we might note that Prince Philip was well aware of this argument against him—and since 1952 he has carefully avoided being involved in any part of the Queen's constitutional life. He does not see the Red Boxes, nor does he remain with her while she meets the Prime Minister at the weekly visit to the Palace, or in any other way play an active role as her political adviser.

Other of the King's advisers reminded him that the young Prince was of German descent—and made that tell against him, ignoring the fact that the King himself was of German descent. But again we have to try to remember that in 1946 and 1947 the British people were still living in that age of austerity, rationing and shortages which resulted from the long and costly war. It might, indeed, have been difficult to 'sell' a German prince as the prospective bridegroom for the heir. And if that argument didn't go down all that well with King George, his advisers could point to the Prince's Greek connections which would certainly be held against him by Socialists, at least. These matters were discussed not only between the King and his advisers, they were also part of the general conversation among the family. Princess Margaret, younger and less knowledgeable, and so maybe that much more naïve, was driven to ask, "Not being English—does it make any difference?"[1] For some time at least, it did.

Finally, the King felt that he wanted the tour of South Africa to take place with as much ceremony as possible and with the minimum of distraction.

At the time there was a growing anti-monarchist movement in South Africa. One of the major reasons for the tour was to try to rekindle that loyalty for the monarchy and for Britain which had been a feature of South Africa but which was in danger of being lost under the resurgence of Boer nationalism. The King did not, therefore, want the tour to take place against the welter of publicity which would have followed the announcement of an engagement. This would have to wait until the tour was over—at least.

In October 1946 Princess Elizabeth was bridesmaid at the wedding of Lord Mountbatten's eldest daughter, Patricia, to her father's ADC, Sir

John Knatchbull, 7th Baron Brabourne, whose father had been a temporary Viceroy of India in 1938. The King and Queen were at the wedding and the King allowed Princess Elizabeth to be photographed with Prince Philip—and every newspaper carried this photograph with its overtones of royal romance. For some people, however, this photograph taken against the backcloth of a Mountbatten wedding, was confirmation of their fears that the noble Lord was indeed the influence urging on this romance.

Although there was no official announcement—indeed there was an official denial of any engagement—the Press decided that it knew better. It was not only a matter of photographs and hints. Some newspapers conducted their own opinion polls to find out how their readers would react if, in the future, there were an announcement. As anyone knows who has studied the pseudo-science of sampling public opinion, the nature of the response depends on the way in which the questions are framed. This helps to explain why the Beaverbrook Press reported that only forty per cent of their readers were in favour of a marriage between the Princess and "Phil the Greek", as the *Express* chain continued to describe him even after he had become naturalized. Other newspapers reported that fifty-five per cent of their readers favoured the match with forty per cent being against it, while yet another poll saw eighty-seven per cent coming out in favour of the match. There was, obviously, little credence to be given to such polls with their widely differing results. But the King was disturbed by what he read. He had, after all, come to the throne in 1936, when the country had been bitterly divided over the question of his brother's abdication. He had seen how politicians—such as Churchill—and Press lords—such as Beaverbrook and Rothermere—had dragged the 'King's Matter' into the gutter. He knew, in 1946 and 1947, that the British people were already divided over the question of their part in the Greek Civil War. He had no wish to see the question of his daughter's marriage become the plaything of headline-seeking politicians or headline-making Press lords and editors. So the polls of autumn 1946 tended to strengthen his resolve that his daughter would have to wait.

On the 29th January 1947, two days before the Royal Party sailed for South Africa, the King and Queen with Princess Elizabeth went to dine at the Chester Street home of Lord and Lady Mountbatten where the other guests were the newly-married Brabournes, David Milford Haven—and Prince Philip. John Dean wrote:

> It was by far the most important party I had ever provided on my own, and there was a lot of excitement . . . The Royal engagement was clearly in the air that night . . . I was told afterwards that Princess Elizabeth and Prince Philip wanted the engagement to be announced before the royal tour, but the date was fixed by the King . . .[2]

For the Mountbatten watchers (and fearers) here was more evidence of the great influence of the man they disliked so much. These people did not realize, as did people close to the young couple, that "It was no 'arranged' marriage. This young couple were in love."[3]

Queen Mary was one who appreciated the true position as Lady Airlie reported:

> In the following spring Princess Elizabeth celebrated her twenty-first birthday and as the oldest member of Queen Mary's Household I was asked to head a deputation to present our gift of a silver inkstand to her.
>
> As she would be away with the King and Queen . . . and would be away for her birthday, the presentations had to be made on the 30th January 1947, the day before the Royal Family sailed . . .
>
> In the best clothes I could muster out of my shabby wartime wardrobe I drove to Buckingham Palace where the rest of the deputation had already assembled . . . After the Princess had received us . . . I made a short speech . . . When I had finished she said, rather wistfully, that it would be sad to be away from England on her birthday, and then visibly brightening, added, "but when I come back we will have a celebration—perhaps two celebrations."
>
> This seemed to me to confirm the rumours that soon after she returned from South Africa her engagement to Prince Philip would be announced, but only Queen Mary, who was the confidante of the entire Royal Family, knew the truth. And she never referred to the subject. The one thing certain was that the marriage would have her approval.[4]

But whatever the young couple may have thought and however much Queen Mary knew, when the Royal Family sailed in *Vanguard* on the 1st February 1947 the King insisted "that it wouldn't do at all for Philip to come on board to bid Lilibet good-bye."[5] He was back on duty at the Petty Officers' Training School where he had to endure the rigours of the worst winter that Britain had known since records were kept. The announcement of his naturalization in March may have helped to lighten the gloom for him, as did the regular flow of mail from South Africa in which Princess Elizabeth kept him informed of the rigours of the arduous tour. He may have heard the broadcast which she made on her twenty-first birthday:

> I declare before you all that my whole life, whether it be long or short, shall be devoted to your service and the service of our great Imperial Commonwealth to which we all belong. But I shall not have the strength to carry out this resolution unless you join in it with me, as I now invite you to do; I know that your support will be unfailingly given. God bless all of you who are willing to share it.[6]

She may also have thought of the support she was going to get from Prince Philip. Certainly when the *Vanguard* steamed into British waters in May "Lilibet had danced a little jig of sheer joy on the deck." When she stepped ashore "Lilibet noticeably had an inner radiance . . ." although "Philip was not in the family welcoming party . . ." at the dockside or at the Palace.[7]

But things were no farther forward as regards her father, who "had always liked Prince Philip and had grown to esteem him highly . . . but still found it difficult to believe that his elder daughter had really fallen in love . . . and perhaps he dreaded losing her from that compact and happy family circle, which had been his delight . . . since his early married days in Royal Lodge."[8] Fortunately for the young people, the Queen was more of a realist. "Aunt Elizabeth had reminded Uncle Bertie a trifle sternly that Lilibet was now over twenty-one. Uncle Bertie took this well."[9] Indeed, as I have tried to show in *The Queen Mother* she had great influence over the King, and as he showed in his letter to Princess Elizabeth (p. 156) he fully appreciated the contribution she had made to his development. So perhaps he became more amenable to the idea of losing his elder daughter because of his wife's persuasive powers.

During the late spring Philip came to visit Princess Elizabeth at the Palace and took her to meet his mother who was now living in Kensington Palace. The young couple enjoyed outings into the countryside—even managing to walk hand in hand unnoticed through Richmond Park, "Elizabeth in a head scarf and Philip in dark glasses".[10] There were public outings—to dances at places such as the Savoy—and private evenings with the Brabournes, Princess Marina and other friends. But there was no announcement—nor did Prince Philip receive an official invitation to Windsor Castle for the house party during Royal Ascot week as he had in 1946. Princess Elizabeth had to carry out a number of royal engagements; some she did with her father, as at the Trooping the Colour in June; some she did on her own and at least at one of these the waiting crowds shouted, well-meaningly but hurtfully, "Where's Philip?" It is little wonder that she found this period one of great strain.

So did Prince Philip, whose temper was a short one even at the best of times. He had managed to offend even the servants at the Palace, one of whom had gone to open a door for him only to be "met with the grouse, 'I've got a bloody pair of hands, man.' "[11] Queen Alexandra also tells of his "wrath" which "flashed out one day on a friend who had genially tried to joke, 'You've chosen the wrong girl. Margaret is much better looking.' Rage flared out before Philip answered, 'You wouldn't say that if you knew them. Elizabeth is sweet and kind, just like her mother.' "[12]

No one knows how long King George would have allowed things to drift on in this uncertain, tension-making way. In the end a decision was reached almost accidentally. Philip had been thinking of buying an engagement ring. He asked his mother's advice. It was Princess Alice's idea that he should use the engagement ring which she had received from the dead Prince Andrew and a diamond ring which had belonged to her grandmother. This appealed to Prince Philip's filial piety. She and Prince Philip sketched some designs of how the diamond might be incorporated into the older ring. Then Princess Alice went to a Bond Street jeweller to show the people there what she wanted done. They persuaded her that they knew more about design than she did and she was delighted when they later handed back a solitaire diamond with diamond shoulders set in platinum.[13]

When the ring was ready, Prince Philip telephoned the Palace to ask that he be allowed to bring it to give to the Princess. The King agreed. So on the 8th July "he went to the Palace for dinner but walked up to Lilibet's sitting-room first. When they entered the dining-room together, her right hand covered the fingers on her left hand. But her mother at once went and kissed her. 'It's too big,' Lilibet laughed, as she showed them. 'We don't have to wait until it's right, do we?' she asked anxiously. Uncle Bertie beamed and shook his head."[14] The public announcement was not made for another thirty-six hours:

> Buckingham Palace, July 10th, 1947.
>
> It is with the greatest pleasure that the King and Queen announce the betrothal of their dearly beloved daughter The Princess Elizabeth to Lieutenant Philip Mountbatten, RN, son of the late Prince Andrew of Greece and Princess Andrew (Princess Alice of Battenberg), to which union the King has gladly given his consent.[15]

Queen Mary heard the news "with great pleasure . . . They both came to see me after luncheon looking radiant,"[16] and she gave her grand-daughter the jewellery which she had received as wedding presents in July 1893.

Perhaps the public response surprised the anxious father. The Press, including the Beaverbrook chain, reported that there was "a new upsurging of loyalty and devotion to the Monarchy . . . because it was apparent that the engagement could have had no motive but the impulse of their own hearts to bring this young couple together."[17] Some evidence of this was provided on the 10th July itself when the young couple accompanied the King and Queen on their walk-about among the guests at a Palace garden party. "Rather like throwing him to the lions," reported King Peter of Yugoslavia.[18] One of those at the party was Harold Nicolson who noted in his diary:

> Then I go to Buckingham Palace for the garden party. It is raining slightly, but I wear my top hat. I go to have some chocolate cake in the marquee . . . and then I walk out again. Everyone is straining to see the bridal pair—irreverently and shamelessly straining.[19]

King Peter and Queen Alexandra watched the young Prince walking with "hands clasped behind his back, bending forward protectively over his fiancée . . . he acquitted himself very well, so much so that when the Royal Party reached their tea pavilion, the onlookers gave a little cheer. Uncle Bertie was so pleased that he did a comical little Charlie Chaplin dance, and responsive bursts of laughter came back from the guests."[20]

But if Prince Philip imagined that this was the end of his troubles he was sadly mistaken. Those who had lost the battle over the engagement were determined to win one over the wedding. They were also prepared to carry on their anti-Mountbatten campaign into the longer term and Prince Philip was to find that his role as Princess Elizabeth's husband and, later, as the Queen's consort, was to be the subject of much argument and a good deal of public humiliation.

20

The Wedding—and its Problems

ON THE 10th JULY 1947 *The Times* carried an editorial which was heavily portentous as fitted "the top people's paper", commenting on the announcement of the engagement:

> An event of the most auspicious interest to every subject is announced today in the betrothal of Her Royal Highness Elizabeth . . . to Lieutenant Philip Mountbatten . . . until his recent naturalization a prince of the kingdom of Greece . . .

After giving a brief résumé of the Prince's childhood and career, *The Times* referred to his grandfather, Prince Louis of Battenberg, a reminder, if any were needed, that this was another of those troublesome foreigners who would have to be watched carefully, and a reminder to him that he was now entering "the cage" as Queen Wilhelmina of Holland described the Court.[1]

The question of a home for the young couple seemed to have been settled by the announcement that the King had granted them a grace-and-favour house adjacent to Windsor called Sunninghill Park. It had been used by the Army during the war so that only one wing was fit for occupation and even this would require a good deal of renovation. The local authority had been going to requisition the property to convert it into flats for working people when the King made his decision.[2] There was a certain amount of complaint that they should have such a fine home while thousands of people were living in bomb-damaged homes or in squalid rooms. It seems to have been an act of providence that in August the mansion was burned to the ground.

In its place the King gave them Clarence House on the Mall in London. This dilapidated Regency mansion had been used by the Red Cross during the war and when it was returned to the Crown in 1948 it was badly in need of reconversion, modernization and decoration. Labour and material were very scarce in the post-war years and work on Clarence House took longer than had been expected. The young couple did not move into their new home until July 1949, almost two years after their wedding.[3]

And the Established Church of England presented its own problem. Dr Fisher, the Archbishop of Canterbury, wrote to the King pointing out that:

> Lieutenant Mountbatten was baptized into the Greek Orthodox Church [although] he appears "always to have regarded himself as an Anglican". [This] misrepresents the relations between the Church of England and the Orthodox Church . . . we are always ready to minister to members of the Orthodox Church . . . which is not able to enter into full communion with us. I suggest for Your Majesty's consideration that there would be an advantage if he were officially received into the Church of England . . .[4]

The King agreed that it would be advisable for his future son-in-law to placate the Established Church and, Dr Fisher wrote, ". . . one day he and Princess Elizabeth came to Lambeth (Palace) and I took them into the temporary chapel and in a very simple little service of only a few minutes I received him into the Church of England."[5] Philip had expected "oaths of renouncement but there was nothing of the kind".[6] Indeed, some people argued that he "need not have changed since our Church is in communion with the Church of England."[7]

This was a small matter blown up out of proportion by an archbishop and his advisers eagerly seeking to put the bridegroom-to-be in his place and to surround him with a welter of protocol in which, they hoped, to imprison him. He was, after all, one of those dashing, able and ambitious Battenbergs.

Nor was he allowed to buy his wife-to-be a wedding ring. This, by custom, had to be made from a nugget of Welsh gold—"a present from the people of Wales . . ."—which struck Philip as a little impersonal, but he overcame this objection by composing an inscription to be engraved on the inside, for his wife's eyes alone.[8]

These were but minor problems compared to the one which arose from discussions about the sort of wedding that should be allowed to take place. Left-wing members of the Labour Party and Government pointed out that in 1947 the British economic position was, if anything, worse than it had been during the war. Only now, for example, had it been necessary to introduce bread rationing, a sign of the grave crisis through which the country was passing. Was it right to spend a great deal of public money on a magnificent wedding? The people were enduring a housing shortage, rationing of food and clothes and other controls which made this the Age of Austerity. Would they welcome a 'proper wedding'? And these left-wing critics found unholy allies in the Establishment which was anxious to put the young Mountbatten in his proper place—as they sought to define it. It would be fitting that he should have a simple ceremony as a reminder that he was not to expect too much because he was marrying the heiress.

The King seemed to agree with these initial suggestions. Plans were drawn up for the wedding to be held at St George's Chapel, Windsor, or at the Chapel Royal at St James's Palace. The announcement that these plans were being considered brought a great protest from more moderate members of the Labour Party and from Conservative politicians in the House of Lords and the House of Commons. There were angry letters to *The Times* as well as less influential newspapers and demands that the people be allowed the glamour of a State Wedding which would provide some light in the midst of the economic drabness, and be, as the *New York Times* said, "a welcome occasion for gaiety in grim England, beset in peace with troubles almost as burdensome as those of war."[9] And so the plans were changed and the wedding was "solemnized at Westminster Abbey with the pomp and dignity imperatively demanded by a King's daughter who would be Queen hereafter . . .".[10]

But the Establishment was not beaten as easily as that. Although the wedding was to take place at the Abbey, "someone in the Government advised simplicity, misjudging the English people's love of pageantry and a show. Now it is too late and a great opportunity has been missed—when else in history has the heiress to the throne been married? Never."[11] The list of guests was cut to the minimum, so that, for example, many of the leading politicians did not receive an invitation. As Channon noted on the 20th November:

> Royal Wedding Day. I was not commanded . . . Rab [Butler] wandering about in the crowd outside was affronted at not being asked—a foolish oversight of the Court as Rab may well be Prime Minister one day and is, in any case, a leader of the Opposition Party.[12]

The full impact of MPs' annoyance at their being ignored was to be felt in December during the discussions on Prince Philip's allowance.

Before this the King had decided that he would mark his daughter's wedding by bestowing honours on her and her husband-to-be. He wrote to Queen Mary:

> I am giving the Garter to Lilibet next Tuesday, November 11th, so that she will be senior to Philip, to whom I am giving it on November 19th. I have arranged that he shall be created a Royal Highness and the titles of his peerage will be: Baron Greenwich, Earl of Merioneth and Duke of Edinburgh. These will be announced in the morning papers of November 20th, including the Garter. It is a great deal to give a man all at once, but I know Philip understands his new responsibilities on his marriage to Lilibet.[13]

Although the King had created him "a Royal Highness" he did not go so far as he might. He did not, for example, make him a Prince, although he became popularly known as Prince Philip—probably because of his earlier title. The Queen put this right—but only in 1957. Some people believe that this princely honorific was withheld on the advice of the Prime Minister, Attlee, "who feared the popular effect of too much too soon".[14] Others prefer to think that this was the Establishment's way of showing the newly created Duke that he was not as important as his marriage might have tempted him to believe.

As if to remind the Establishment of their fears, the Garter was given by the King at a family ceremony in Buckingham Palace on the eve of the wedding. Among the family was Viceroy Mountbatten, returned from "liquidating the British Empire in India" to see his nephew wed his Queen-to-be. It was only natural that he should have been there—but to the jaundiced eyes of the Mountbatten-haters his presence was proof that he had plotted this wedding and that he would use his nephew's new position as a means of gaining more influence for himself and the family.

On the eve of his marriage the newly-ennobled Duke of Edinburgh left Buckingham Palace to go to a bachelor party given by Commander Norfolk, who had been his captain on *Whelp*. Most of the guests were young naval officers, including David Milford Haven who was to be his best man, and Lieutenant Michael Parker with whom he had once had a friendly rivalry and who was to become his equerry. The oldest man in the party was Lord Louis. The Press was invited to that party which ended at twelve thirty a.m.—and great publicity was given to everyone's high spirits as noble naval officers chased unfortunate cameramen around the rooms. There was a second party, much smaller, of close friends—and Lord Louis. David Milford Haven drove the Duke of Edinburgh home to Kensington Palace in the early morning, past groups of people already camping out in the streets. But when his valet woke him at seven o'clock in the morning "he was plainly in great form, extremely cheerful and in no way nervous."[15] Nor did he have the support of his usual cigarettes. After arriving home from the stag party he and David Milford Haven had had one final cigarette. As he stubbed it out the Duke had said, "That's the last one." It is one sign of the strength of his character that he has never smoked since.

The week preceding the wedding had been, in Lady Airlie's words:

> . . . an escape from reality; a cut back to the past. It was a week of gaiety such as the Court had not seen for years. There were parties at St James's Palace to view the wedding presents, a royal dinner party for all the foreign Royalties, and an evening party at Buckingham Palace which seemed after the years of austerity like a scene of a fairy tale. It was a wonderful occasion, if only because of the intense pleasure of meeting so many people again. Old friends scattered far and wide by the war were reunited; old feuds and jealousies swept away.
>
> Queen Mary looked supremely happy that night of the party at Buckingham Palace. It was obvious that the marriage of the Princess, who was to her both a dearly loved granddaughter and the future Sovereign, delighted her. In the short time since she had grown to know him really well Prince Philip had won both her liking and her approbation. She told me that when a member of the Royal Family had said to her that the only thing which could be brought against him was that he had been to a crank school with theories of social equality and that it would remain to be seen whether the effects of this training would be useful or baleful to the King's son-in-law, she had replied decisively—"Useful." "And it will be, Mabell," the Queen

added. "The world has changed since you and I were born into it, and it will change still more." Queen Mary was far more broad-minded and progressive than most people imagined.[16]

And, it ought to be noted, "far more" than most of the people who surrounded the King and acted as his advisers. They continued for many years to see the Duke in an unfavourable light as we shall see in subsequent chapters.

All the overseas guests had received, along with their invitations, "our travel tickets and detailed instructions of the best train from Paris, how and where we should be met, and a list of other invitations to the State Dinner and Ball at Buckingham Palace . . . the Golden Arrow boat-train that November night seemed almost a Royal Family special for nearly everyone I met was a relative of mine."[17] Almost all London's hotels had been taken over to accommodate the foreign Royalties: the King and Queen of Denmark, the Kings of Norway, Rumania and Iraq, the King and Queen of Yugoslavia, the Queen of the Hellenes, the Princess Regent and Prince Bernhard of the Netherlands, the Prince Regent of Belgium . . . and royals from Spain, Luxembourg, Rumania, all coming to pay their tribute to the future Queen of England and to the success with which the House of Windsor had managed to hold on to its throne whereas so many of them had lost theirs.

Princess Alice, the new Duke's mother, put away her nun-like costume and wore a laced gown. She was one of the many who signed the register at the wedding. But her daughters were not there. They, after all, had married Germans and the King's advisers thought that the British people were not yet ready to welcome Germans so soon after the war.

Wedding presents came from all over the world and they were put on public display to raise money for charity. 'Chips' Channon went along on the 18th November and noted: "At the reception at St James's Palace to see the Royal presents I was struck by how ghastly some of the presents were, though the crowd made it difficult to see. Queen Mary's was magnificent, as was the wreath of diamond roses given by the Nizam of Hyderabad. My silver box was in a conspicuous position. The King and Queen—and the young couple, were too surrounded to be approachable."[18]

Lady Airlie was with Queen Mary when:

> . . . she went to see the wedding presents and found among them the loin-cloth knitted by Gandhi. Queen Mary was deeply shocked at the sight of "such an indelicate gift" as she described it to me, publicly displayed. "What a horrible thing," she exclaimed.
>
> Prince Philip who was standing by her, being of another generation, did not understand the cause of her displeasure. "I don't think it's horrible," he said. "Gandhi is a wonderful man; a very great man." Queen Mary moved on in silence.
>
> When the Royal Party went around again the next day the loin-cloth was still in a place of honour. But as Queen Mary approached the spot Princess Margaret scenting danger, darted ahead, pounced on the offending garment and hid it quickly behind some other presents.[19]

Finally the great day dawned for what Archbishop Fisher of Canterbury called, "one of the greatest events after the war".[20] Channon . . .

> . . . drove through the crowded streets—many people had waited all night to see the show. I thought Princess Elizabeth looked well, shy and attractive and Prince Philip as if he was thoroughly enjoying himself. There were cheers of love and loyalty for Queen Mary and shouts for Princess Juliana of the Netherlands who is popular and whom the crowds take for a comic, which she is. But the warmest reception was reserved for Winston [Churchill] and I hear that in the Abbey when he arrived, a little late, everyone stood up, all the Kings and Queens.[21]

Prince Philip, as Channon decided to call him, was wearing his regular naval uniform with his few decorations and the Star of the Garter. He wore Prince Louis of Battenberg's beautifully wrought sword, which Lord Louis had worn at his marriage. The Princess wore an "exquisite wedding gown" as she walked up the nave of the Abbey on her father's arm. The service was broadcast—against the wishes of many of the King's advisers who feared that the religious service might be heard by people drinking in public houses! This argument had been sufficiently strong to prevent the broadcasting of previous royal ceremonies such as the Coronation in 1937. This argument was lost in 1947, but the Establishment managed to keep television cameras out of the Abbey. The BBC was, however, allowed to put cameras outside the Abbey so that millions of people living around London had their first glimpse of a royal occasion.

Inside the Abbey the service was, as Dr Fisher reminded everyone, the simple service which was carried out in any village church. The Princess promised to "love, honour and obey" her husband. Then there was the procession back through the crowded streets when, said *The Times*:

> Colour came back, for a little while, into the life of a people starved of visual inspiration. There can be no doubt that the decision to restore the escort of Household Cavalry to the full splendour of their full-dress uniform was right. The brilliant picture had a tonic effect upon the eyes and hearts of all who saw it—and it was seen by many who were not physically present beside the processional way. The lifting of spirits that came with it will be a refreshing memory when they return to their daily task.[22]

Back at Buckingham Palace there was the noisy confusion to be expected as dozens of royal cousins rushed around finding their places at table, greeting one another—and looking for toilets. Whenever Princess Margaret seemed to have organized everyone in line for a photograph one or other of the principals was called to the balcony to acknowledge the cheering crowds. As one of the guests said, "A country which can throw such a party will never go under."[23] For Lord Louis it was a glittering day. He and Lady Edwina had been the most eye-catching couple in the Abbey,[24] and he, the head of the family, was very proud as he heard his future Queen take his family's name on her marriage to Lieutenant Philip Mountbatten. He himself has said:

> This was a great moment in the history of our family—yet such was the state of affairs in India in November 1947 that I had grave doubts whether I ought to go back to London for the wedding or not. Of course, I wanted to very badly—and the Indian Government settled the matter for me by saying that if I didn't that would make the atmosphere of crisis in India appear even worse. So home we went.
>
> Prince Philip, of course, was more like a son than a nephew to Edwina and me. I was pleased to see how well he was doing in the Navy. Princess Elizabeth herself was very close to our family. In age she comes just in between our two daughters, and it was less than a year since she had been a bridesmaid at Patricia's wedding.
>
> For most people in Britain the royal wedding provided a marvellous cheering splash of colour in the midst of austerity. For me it was a splendid interlude in the midst of the hardest work I have ever done in my life. And then it was back to India, where the crisis atmosphere was still intense.[25]

Most of the old aristocracy thought of Mountbatten as the man who was collaborating with their enemies in India which he was busily trying to give away. They thought of him as a traitor to his class and country, ignoring the reality of the situation which was that Britain simply could not have held down India in 1947. Indeed, we were to discover in the 1950s that we could not hold down even an island as small as Cyprus. It was a sign of Mountbatten's intelligence that he saw, as did Attlee and the Labour Party, that Indian independence was inevitable. The Establishment preferred to think otherwise, however, and their hostility towards Mountbatten was intense. Unfortunately for him, some of this hostility spilled over on to the nephew. This helps to explain the subsequent behaviour of the old guard towards the new groom.

The young couple left London for the first part of their honeymoon which they spent at Broadlands, the country home of Lord Louis. This was a mistake—for two reasons. In the first place it reminded the Establishment again of the link between the "great betrayer of India" and the heir to the throne. In the second place it was much too close to London so that hordes of people, including Press photographers, descended on Romsey to try to catch a glimpse of the newly married couple. During the week-long siege, Prince Philip became increasingly annoyed as he spotted photographers up trees, or people standing on sideboards which they had carried to the Abbey Church to glimpse the couple entering or leaving the service on Sunday. This was one of his first confrontations with the Press; it was not a happy one and unfortunately may have helped set the tone for that unhappy relationship which has developed over the years.

On their return to London after this first week of married life they issued a statement which is beautifully euphemistic in its irony:

> The reception given us on our wedding day and the loving interest shown by our fellow-countrymen and well-wishers have left an impression that will never grow faint. We can find no words to express what we feel, but we can at least offer our grateful thanks to the millions who have given us this unforgettable send-off in our married life.[26]

They spent the second part of their honeymoon at Birkhall, a royal castle on the Balmoral estate with its own 6,500-acre estate. Although the weather was very bad and snow covered the hills, at least they were far away from Fleet Street and the London crowds, while the local people, accustomed for so long to the presence of royalty at Balmoral, left them alone to enjoy their stay.

During their honeymoon Princess Elizabeth received a letter from her father which tells us much about his relationship with both his wife and his daughter and which served also to remind the newcomer that he was entering "the royal firm" as George VI called the family:

> I was so proud of you and thrilled at having you so close to me on our long walk in Westminster Abbey, but when I handed you to the Archbishop I felt that I had lost something very precious. You were so calm and composed during the Service and said your words with such conviction that I knew everything was all right.
>
> I am so glad you wrote and told Mummy that you think the long wait before your engagement and the long time before the wedding was for the best. I was rather afraid that you had thought I was being hard-hearted about it. I was so anxious for you to come to South Africa as you knew. Our family, us four, the "Royal Family" must remain together, with additions of course at suitable moments. I have watched you grow up all these years with pride under the skilful direction of Mummy, who as you know, is the most marvellous person in the world in my eyes, and I can, I know, always count on you, and now Philip, to help us in our work.
>
> Your leaving has left a great blank in our lives, but do remember that your old home is still yours and come back to it as much and as often as possible. I can see that you are sublimely happy with Philip—which is right, but don't forget us is the wish of,
>
> Your ever loving and devoted, Papa.[27]

Prince Philip and Princess Elizabeth were back with the "Royal Family" for a family Christmas at Sandringham. During the honeymoon, the King had given some consideration to the question of the young couple's finances. He had sent a message to Parliament, ". . . relying on the liberality and affection of his faithful Commons" to make adequate provision for the Heir and her husband. Parliament had set up a Select Committee which discussed the topic for several weeks. The Committee recommended by thirteen votes to five that the Duke should receive an annual allowance of £10,000 a year while the Princess's allowance should be raised to £40,000 a year. The couple had to pay income tax on these allowances and the King did not think that Parliament had shown much "liberality and affection". Queen Victoria's Consort had been given an allowance of £30,000 a year—and that at a time when the cost of living was a small fraction of what it was in 1947. Prince Philip was thus given a sharp reminder, through his pocket, that the Commons at least did not hold him in high regard. In his diary 'Chips' Channon noted:

> *17th December:* In the afternoon there was a rumpus in the House of Commons and the Royal Family had, I think, a deserved jolt . . . The

> annuity to be paid to the Edinburghs was discussed, and the Socialists were in favour of reducing the proposed sum of £40,000. We then had the unpleasant spectacle of the Royal Family's finances being discussed in the House of Commons for 4 hours. Had they all been invited to the wedding this would never have happened, and the larger sum voted instantly.[28]

This was Prince Philip's introduction to the problem of royal finances, a problem which was to plague him often in the future.

Part V

THE DUAL ROLE OF NAVAL OFFICER AND ROYAL WORKER, 1946—1952

21

The Naval Officer, 1946–1951

AFTER THE *Whelp* HAD BEEN paid off in January 1946 Prince Philip—still a Greek Prince—was posted to HMS *Glendower*. This was a shore establishment—in spite of its nautical name. The Royal Navy had taken over the Butlin's Holiday Camp at Pwllheli in North Wales and transformed it into a training establishment for newly-promoted petty officers. One correspondent remembers:

> . . . when in charge of the Guard Room I was instructed to send out transport to the local station to meet Lt HRH Prince Philip of Greece who had been appointed to our ship's company. The name meant nothing to any of the lads on duty, but along with a Wren driver and an Able Seaman I went along the few miles to the station to meet him. He was no different to any other officer, and in fact we found him quite amusing during the journey back to *Glendower*, the only difference to his arrival to that of any other officer was that the Captain and No. 1 met him on arrival. For a short time there was a little fuss about this new officer who had something to do with Royalty and quite often I had the duty of taking private Buckingham Palace mail to him collected especially from our Mail Office. For a while he was in fact my Divisional Officer and he was always a pleasure to serve, fully observant of his duties and yet always available to take part in any social event . . . always put his hand down to buy a round of drinks for his staff, although I believe that he spent a good deal of his free time at a pub in Criccieth.
>
> Early in 1946 it was decided to pay off *Glendower* and return the camp to Butlin's and the ship's colours were to be placed in Bangor Cathedral. A large parade with due pomp and ceremony was arranged and most of the reduced ship's company and remaining trainees were detailed to go to Bangor along with the ship's colours for the big parade, and coach transport was laid on. I was in charge of the Guard at the gates and the officer of the day was HRH, and I don't think it was by choice, for after the formalities as the last coach left *Glendower* full of officers he pulled a funny face in the direction of the officers at the rear of the coach and his saluting hand changed position to a repeated 'Harvey Smith' type of V-sign and a smile on his face matched the smiles on the faces of the guard and myself. "That's it, Smith," he said, "dismiss the guard and if I am wanted you know where to find me." I saw him later that day for the last time, for he was soon drafted himself, as indeed I was . . .[1]

In fact, *Glendower* was closed down during the summer of 1946 while Prince Philip was on holiday at Balmoral, proposing to Princess Elizabeth. When he returned from that fateful leave he was posted to HMS *Royal Arthur*, another shore establishment at Corsham in Wiltshire, about ninety miles from London. This was a collection of dreary tin-roofed Nissen huts where about two hundred petty officers were engaged on training courses. Prince Philip was one of the two officers giving the course, an attempt to update the education of petty officers as the Royal Navy moved into the new atomic era.

Older readers will remember that the winter of 1946–1947 was the coldest on record to that date. While the Royal Family basked in the sunshine of South Africa, Prince Philip and the petty officers shivered in the uncomfortable huts through which the wind whistled. Electricity supplies were often cut off because of the fuel shortage when the snow prevented the movement of coal from collieries to generating stations. Life at Corsham became even more uncomfortable in the unlit, unheated, windswept hutments.

Philip enjoyed setting up a new course and in helping the trainee petty officers to get to grips with their role in the new Navy: "Strands of discipline in each individual spring from confidence in authority, from loyalty and sense of duty, from anticipation of consequences—pleasant and unpleasant . . ."[2]

One correspondent had a number of reasons for remembering his time at Corsham:

> I attended a Petty Officers' Leadership Course at Corsham in Wiltshire. It was one of the best months I had experienced during my nineteen years' Royal Navy service and Lt Mountbatten, as he then was, was the class instructor. I had joined the Navy as an apprentice Air Artificer in August 1939, three days before hostilities started—and had signed on for fourteen years. As the years went by, I did my best, but knew deep down that I wasn't really cut out for Navy life or aircraft engineering. I welcomed the opportunity to go to Corsham. Lt Mountbatten took drill and public speaking and "The Art of Communication" and the class took turns in addressing their contemporaries on any topical subject. I revelled in it.
>
> Lt Mountbatten must have been intrigued by my service history sheet, as none of the previous Divisional Officers had been particularly complimentary about my ability and had invariably mentioned "a lack of drive".
>
> Lt Mountbatten wrote "that I definitely had talent, was a very good public speaker", and though I might be somewhat unsuited to my Naval career, he was sure that my ability would eventually flourish somewhere.
>
> I read this report on the final morning, and was really keen to question him on these remarks in the afternoon. The chance never came. That day the newspapers were full of his engagement to Princess Elizabeth; he was whisked away and 'Course 21' was the last course he ever took there.
>
> . . . It was another eleven years before I left the Navy as a Chief Petty Officer, still knowing that I hadn't ever realized my full potential and often wondering whether his conjecture would ever come true . . . I left the Fleet

> Air Arm in 1958 determined to make a new career outside of engineering and Service life. I joined this Company in September 1958 . . . In my twenty years with [the Company] I've been credited with more 'drive' than any of my colleagues . . . have had a continuous stream of complimentary letters from Head Office . . . thanking me for the example I have set my colleagues. A complete contrast to all the reports made on me during my Navy career; and I had justified the Duke of Edinburgh's remarks that I had ability and knew it. I was only a twenty-four-year-old Petty Officer then, now I am a fifty-five-year-old Senior Life Consultant, as well paid as an Admiral.
>
> The Duke of Edinburgh was the only Divisional Officer who had even hinted that I would shine one day. A group photograph of "Course 21, Kingsmoore, Corsham, 1947" still sits proudly in my study to remind me of my most enjoyable month in the Navy . . .[3]

But even Prince Philip fell victim to the tedium of the School, partly because he was, naturally, thinking about the forthcoming engagement and wedding, and partly because each batch of petty officers only spent a few weeks at Corsham to be replaced by a new group to whom the Prince had to lecture yet again—and again, as a third group moved in. There are limits to the degree of enthusiasm which even the most inspiring of teachers can bring to talks on: "The force which causes a man to play the part required of him in the organization to which he belongs. It is: A Guiding Force; An Inspiring Force; A Driving Force; A Controlling Force; A Comforting Force."[4]

There were few relaxations available in the small Wiltshire village. Along with his fellow-officers Prince Philip went to the village local, the Methuen Arms, drank beer and played skittles—but was not the "well-remembered", "very popular", "life and soul of the party" which some reporters presented to their readers when they wrote about his time at Corsham.

He spent some of his free time tinkering with his small MG in which he would drive to London whenever he had free time, particularly after the Royal Family had returned from South Africa in May 1947. He stayed at Lord Louis's house in Chester Street where John Dean, Mountbatten's valet looked after him. After the announcement of the engagement this house was besieged by the Press. He then moved into Kensington Palace to live with his mother. John Dean looked after him there too and wrote: "Their rooms were astonishingly poor and humble—not at all what one would expect in a Palace. The floors were scrubbed boards, with rather worn rugs, and the stairs creaked badly . . ."[5]

The Press seemed unaware of this side of the Prince's life, being more concerned to comment on the way in which he drove his MG. As one newspaper said:

> A keen mechanic and motorist, he has a zest for speed which has upset even the Royal chauffeurs, men with accident-free records who are now chary of driving with him. Philip's naval friends credit him with their camp record for the ninety-eight-mile journey from Corsham to London—one hour and forty minutes. While he is likely to conform to Buckingham Palace wishes about his motoring activities, Court circles feel that Lieutenant Mountbatten

is unlikely to curb his independence of mind in most other directions. The future Prince Consort has shown many signs that he has a will of his own and that he intends to act as he thinks.[6]

The small MG, however, was a luxury for the young officer who, when he moved into Kensington Palace, "brought all his worldly possessions in two suitcases . . . his wardrobe was scantier than that of many a bank clerk . . . only one lounge suit—grey—to his name [he] much preferred to knock around in blazer and flannels . . . socks full of darns, and shoes, though good, were well worn."[7]

Although he had a princely title, he had only a naval lieutenant's pay of about eleven pounds per week. This would not have been enough for the fiancé of the Heiress—whom he squired at dances, parties, meals at the Savoy and trips into the countryside in his car. There can be little doubt that Lord Louis—whether present or absent—provided the additional money that was needed for this "extravagance", for servants' wages and the tips expected from a royal person.

After his marriage, his income went up as we have seen, when Parliament voted to give him £10,000 a year. This was money well-earned by the Duke who became an active member of the 'royal firm'. But while he spent time at royal work he remained, after marriage, a young naval officer, eager, as his cousin said, "to earn his promotions" and to emulate the successes of his grandfather and Lord Louis.[8] Soon after his marriage he was appointed to the Operations Division of the Admiralty—its youngest member.[9] He walked across the park each morning to arrive at the Admiralty at nine o'clock and spent his day seeking "eagerly his full quota of duties"[10] in his cousin's opinion, but "shuffling ships around" as "just a dog's body" in his own words.[11] After his work had been completed he then spent most evenings on one or other of the tasks imposed on him as an active member of the 'royal firm'.

In April 1948 he was chosen by his superiors to take a naval staff course at the Royal Naval College at Greenwich. This was proof that he was being considered as suitable for high rank at some later stage. Most of the other people on the course were commanders and captains, very much his senior in rank and experience. They studied history and the strategy of war, naval strategy in an atomic age and also followed a general course which included civics and economics. This was the navy's equivalent of a post-graduate university course and it is not surprising that Philip enjoyed the challenge of the study as well as the level of discussion.

During this three-month course Philip lived at the Naval College during the week, returning to Buckingham Palace only for the weekends. It might be argued that he 'lived in' with the other people of the course to avoid being 'different' and to show his new wife that being married to a naval officer involved periods of separation. It might also be argued that he wanted to get the full benefit from the course, and those of us who have been on such courses appreciate that the greatest benefit is derived not from the lectures and the formal discussions but from the informal arguments and discussions that go on late in the evenings over meals and drinks.

But it has to be said that he welcomed the chance to escape from "the cage". Even at this early stage in their married life he found life in the Palace very constricting and one from which he was glad to escape into the freer atmosphere of the Naval College and the company of fellow-officers.

One of the problems he had to contend with was his father-in-law's obsession with etiquette—so that "his first act on returning to Buckingham Palace after the wedding of Princess Elizabeth was to cause enquiries to be made as to why a certain distinguished Admiral had omitted to wear his sword."[12] Philip's casual approach to dress and to life in general brought him into conflict with this stickler-king. During the Christmas holiday, 1947, at Sandringham, he was told that, as a member of the family, he had to follow the tradition and wear a kilt. He felt that this form of dress hardly suited him, and to overcome his shyness and embarrassment when he wore it for the first time, he made a mock curtsy to his father-in-law. He was not amused and let Philip know this in no uncertain fashion. Courtly dress and family traditions were to be observed and not mocked, however, lightly.

He found it equally difficult to come to terms with the expectations of the Palace staff—that regiment of servants which included fifty house-maids, large numbers of footmen, butlers, pages, chefs and electricians as well as people with duties lowly (flower arrangers) and exalted (private secretaries). They found him prickly, over-concerned, in their opinion, to assert his position as husband and to be master in his household. He claimed that he "naturally filled the principal position".[13] As one of his relatives said: "It was only right that the young naval officer husband should be in charge of his own home. He was the head; that's how it should be."[14]

The atmosphere in Buckingham Palace was, and is, laden with tradition. He found it very heavy, while his valet found it "frigid . . . elderly servants addressed me as 'Sir', which I found embarrassing. I could never get used to the ridiculous distinctions so rigidly observed at the Palace . . ."[15]—and neither could his master.

It is therefore easy to understand why Prince Philip took advantage of the chance to 'escape' to the freedom of Greenwich for three months and why he looked forward to the weekends when he and Princess Elizabeth left London behind to live on their own at Windlesham. But he was even happier when he was appointed to be First Lieutenant of HMS *Chequers*, the leader of the destroyer flotilla in the Mediterranean. He joined the ship on 17th October 1949, almost a year after the birth of Prince Charles. On board he dropped, willingly, his title and became, once again, "Number 1" to his captain and other officers. He was "responsible for discipline, stores, welfare and the general running of the ship".[16]

Lord Louis was Commander of the First Cruiser Squadron based on

Malta—happy to resume his own naval career and now eager to welcome his nephew to the Mediterranean. When the Prince flew into Malta Lord Louis was there to meet him "as an uncle, not an admiral".[17] For both of them, their Maltese experience was "different". During 1948 and part of 1949 the King had been seriously ill so that Prince Philip had been seconded from the navy to take up some of the public duties that would have devolved upon the King. For almost a year he had become used to the idea that he was a "royal worker", receiving the acclaim of the crowds and the homage of officials at national and local level. Now he was back in the navy, having to obey men who in another sphere might have bowed to him at the Palace. And for Lord Louis, the former Viceroy and the first Governor-General of an Independent India, there was a similar change of circumstance. He had once been Commander of SEAC with the rank of "Acting Admiral". Now, back in active service again, he had had to step down to the rank of Rear-Admiral and was under the command of officers who had served under him in South-East Asia. His Commander-in-Chief, Mediterranean, wrote of him: "Ordinary men may climb with distinction; only extraordinary men can climb down without some loss of distinction. He has achieved the latter."[18]

Princess Elizabeth followed her husband to Malta when she could be released from the calls of public duty. For a time she lived with the Mountbattens at the Villa Guardamangia and when Lord Louis returned to London as Fourth Sea Lord, the villa was leased in the Princess's name. This was, by any standard, the freest and happiest period of their married life. He was busily engaged at his job, acquiring more of that knowledge and experience which would qualify him for promotion later on, and while she could not be exactly "like any other naval officer's wife", she did see him off each morning and then have time to herself during the day. Although crowds gathered whenever she went shopping, she managed to escape from formality in the company of other wives with whom she lunched, swam, watched their husbands play polo and dine in the evening.

But neither of them could escape completely from "the cage". She had to open hospitals, schools, fêtes; together they had to go on official visits to various countries bordering on the Mediterranean—Jordan, Iran and Greece among others; and the Governor of Malta gave a ball and a number of dinners in honour of the Princess when both she and Prince Philip had to play their public roles.

Princess Elizabeth's first visit ended two days after Christmas, 1949, when *Chequers* sailed with six other warships to routine patrols in the Red Sea. In April 1950 she was back again, bringing news of the baby Prince Charles and discussing the baby that was to be born in August 1950, and when she had finished nursing the baby Princess Anne, the young wife was back in Malta again in the autumn of 1950.

During these two years Prince Philip's naval career had advanced several stages. He sat his 'command' examination, success in which guarantees an officer a future command of his own. He, along with everyone else concerned, thought that he would pass this examination without any difficulty. It was a shock then when his equerry, Lieutenant Michael Parker, was summoned to the office of the Commander-in-Chief, Admiral Sir Arthur J. Powers, to be told that Prince Philip had been failed "in Torpedo and ASDIC", a subject in which the Prince had shown unusual practical ability. The Admiral explained to Parker that he had read the particular paper himself, thought it was "a damned good pass" in spite of "this bloody examiner", leaving Parker with the impression that the Admiral was going to exert his authority to overrule the examiner and give Prince Philip his pass.

Prince Philip had never tried to use his royal connections to give himself any privileges—at Greenwich or in Malta. He resented the inference that the well-intentioned Admiral might interfere with the natural process—by which he was as entitled to fail as anyone else. He told Parker that "if they try to fix it, I quit the navy for good."[19] The result was allowed to stand and he took the examination again—and passed. In July 1950, while Princess Elizabeth was back at home for the imminent birth of Princess Anne, he was promoted to Lieutenant Commander at the age of twenty-nine—two years older than Lord Louis had been when getting this promotion. But we have to remember that Lord Louis had been in the navy since he was thirteen, while Prince Philip was eighteen when he went to Dartmouth, and his subsequent career had been partially halted by the call of royal duties in 1948 and 1949. He had done as well as his brilliant uncle—and was to do even better.

He was given home leave for the birth of Princess Anne, and the official announcement of his promotion was gazetted on the day of the Princess's birth, 15th August 1950. On that day he also learned that he was to be given his own ship, the frigate *Magpie*, a sister ship of the famous *Amethyst*. He was piped aboard his new command in September 1950 at its Malta base, and told the crew of 186 that he meant to make *Magpie* one of the finest ships in the fleet. "It will be up to you and up to me."[20] This was in the tradition of his grandfather and Uncle Louis.

Aboard *Magpie* he had a cabin under the bridge, and when he entertained guests such as the King of Greece he had to use the officers' wardroom. In this small cabin he wrote the speeches he was to make on his return home, corresponded with people about the National Playing Fields Association and did all the other office work connected with his position in the 'royal firm'.

He quickly showed his men that he intended the *Magpie* to be cock ship in the fleet, in spite of his position of junior in command to all other commanders in the flotilla and fleet. In the annual regatta the crew won six of the ten events, Philip himself stroking one of the boats to victory. That, plus her record in manoeuvres, won her the coveted title of Cock of the Fleet, which allowed him to hoist a huge plywood rooster arrogantly to the top of the single mast. Hahn would have been proud of his former pupil's ability as a leader.

But he might also have commented on his continuing "impatience". Unlike his grandfather and uncle, Philip does not seem to have won the affection of his crews. His cousin wrote: "An officer who was on the *Magpie* glows with warm enthusiasm when he tells me how popular Philip was with his crew."[21] But the truth seems to have been otherwise. Some resented having to serve on what became known as "Edinburgh's private yacht", on which "he worked us like hell", or as another member of the crew said, where he "stamped about like a . . . . ing tiger".[22] I take it as significant that while many people wrote to me with their memories of Prince Philip before and after his time on *Magpie*, no one wrote about his short period of command. This, it seems to me, is a case of "the dog that did not bark".

It was unfair perhaps to describe *Magpie* as his private yacht. Maybe his crew did not appreciate that he was following orders when he dropped anchor in foreign harbours so that he could call, officially, on the Kings of Jordan and Iran and the Presidents of Turkey and Iraq. Maybe they thought that he was satisfying a private whim when they called into Corfu so that he could revisit his birthplace. This was in the early summer of 1950 when Princess Elizabeth was still in Malta. She was assigned to the flagship HMS *Surprise* and sailed to Athens with *Magpie* as one of the escort ships. This trip allowed Prince Philip to "show his homeland off to his wife"[23] so that they were able to combine the pleasure of such reminiscing with the more official part of the voyage which was to enable the heir to the throne to call on the Greek Royal Family in Athens.

In July 1951 Prince Philip's naval career suffered another setback. He was called back to Britain to prepare for a tour of Canada and the USA which the King and Queen had been due to undertake. The King's continuing illness had forced them to give up the idea and the Princess and her husband were to be sent as substitutes. The announcement said that he was going on indefinite leave. In fact he never returned, although the wheels of the Service continued to turn and in July 1952, although not on the active list, he was awarded his promotion to Commander. He was only thirty-one. Lord Louis had been thirty-two when he became a Commander. Who knows, as Attlee said, how far Prince Philip might have gone if he had been allowed to follow his career? But the death of King George and his wife's accession to the throne meant that he did not have that pleasure. Instead, as we shall see, he had to contend with the problem of becoming a royal consort at a Court and amidst an Establishment which made it evident that he was unwelcome.

22

The Royal Worker, 1947–1951

IN THE FIRST FOUR YEARS after his marriage, Prince Philip had to play three major roles. He was, in the first place, a newly-married man, setting up a home, adjusting to the fact that he now had a partner to consider and, after November 1948, that he had children He was also an able, ambitious naval officer, anxious to pursue his career in that service as his grandfather and uncle had done. Finally he was called on—both individually and in partnership with Princess Elizabeth—to undertake a variety of public duties. He was a member of what the King called, "not so much a family as a Royal firm".

When they returned from their honeymoon in December 1947 both Princess Elizabeth and the Duke of Edinburgh were entitled to plan their lives on the assumption that they would have twenty years or so before the Princess would become Queen. King George VI was only fifty-two in 1947. The Windsor men have tended, on average, to live well beyond the biblical three score years and ten. King George V had reached that age, and two of his sons did better; David, later King Edward VIII and, in 1947, the Duke of Windsor, was to live for seventy-eight years while another son, Henry, Duke of Gloucester, was seventy-four years old when he died in 1974. So the young couple were justified in planning their future on the basis that Prince Philip would have about twenty years to fulfil his ambitions as a naval officer while Princess Elizabeth would have the pleasure of the sort of freedom which she was to enjoy in Malta between 1948 and 1950. And both of them looked forward to the pleasure of supervising the upbringing of the children they hoped to have.

Both of them realized, however, that they would also be called upon to play their public roles. Indeed there was early recognition of the Duke's new and public role in the form of the annual allowance voted by Parliament. The Select Committee in making its recommendations to Parliament noted that "the responsibilities falling on the Duke of Edinburgh, as consort of the heiress presumptive, will be at least as great as those falling on the younger sons of a Sovereign."[1] And the fact was, of course, that the Sovereign did not have any younger sons, so that there would be a large number of "responsibilities" of various kinds "falling on" this male newcomer to "the firm". If Lord Louis and Lady Edwina saw the young Prince Philip as "more like a son than a nephew"[2], the King and Queen must have been grateful for the fact that they could, after 1947, call on a young, active male to carry out some of those public duties which people expect of the Royal Family.

The allowance of £10,000 was voted by Parliament so that the Duke would be able to employ the staff he would need to help him fulfil his public role, to pay for the expenses of travelling and to buy the clothes fitting to his new role. It would hardly have done for him to have continued to have only one suit and a blazer and flannels. His valet who has written about his wardrobe, has also told us about the mail that poured into the Palace, and later into Clarence House.[3] There were letters from societies and regiments, charities and institutions, associations and individuals, town and county councils, individual factories and major industries—all asking that the Duke present this, open that, speak here, visit there and so on. To help cope with this flood of mail and to help plan his public work the Duke had to have a number of aides—a Private Secretary, a typist, a filing clerk—and all these had to be paid. There was little left out of the £10,000 when such expenses had been met, maybe enough to pay for the presents which custom dictated had to be given to various people—to servants in homes where the Edinburghs stayed, to those who helped plan a visit or tour, and to some, at least, of the charities which asked for support.

When in December 1947 the Duke examined his new role he arrived, by what he thought of as logic, at certain conclusions. First he took seriously his role as the head of his household. "Within the house, and whatever we did, it was together. I suppose I naturally filled the principal position."[4] He was, after all, much more worldly-wise than his young wife who had been brought up in "the cage" and knew little of the real world outside. He took the view that he would have to give her "the complete low-down on absolutely anything".[5] He also had to help his young wife learn to relax so that she, and he with her, could get some enjoyment out of their life, much of which would have to be lived in the goldfish bowl of publicity. Princess Elizabeth had always been the more serious of the King's two daughters. When Lady Airlie, with Queen Mary, met the King, Queen and daughters in January 1946 she wrote:

> During my visit to Sandringham I saw more of Princess Elizabeth than I had done for several years. In that family setting she seemed to me one of the most unselfish girls I had ever met, always the first to give way in any of the small issues that arise in every home. I thought that no two sisters could have been less alike than the Princesses, the elder with her quiet simplicity, the younger with her puckish expression and irrepressible high spirits . . . Queen Mary described her as "*espiègle*" which was precisely the right word, although it has no complete equivalent in English—adding, "All the same, she is so outrageously amusing that one can't help encouraging her."[6]

> The King was a devoted father to both his daughters. He spoilt Princess Margaret and still continued to treat her as an *enfant terrible*, but Princess Elizabeth was his constant companion . . . in everything.[7]

The constant companion of her father who groomed her for her role of heir, the frequent companion of the ageing Queen Mary with her concept of the dignity befitting "Majesty" and dominated, in some ways, by her more extrovert but younger sister, Princess Elizabeth was considered to be shy, over-conscientious and prim. Prince Philip took it on himself to help this young, constrained wife to learn to enjoy life. As one writer has it: "He piped the tune for their new life together as husband and wife and she was happy to dance to it."[8] In the company of the Prince and his ebullient equerry, Michael Parker, she learned to laugh, to tease and be teased in a way which was "quite foreign to her normally shy and serious nature".[9]

But if Prince Philip saw himself as the head of the household he also saw himself as the one who had to guard his young wife against the pressures of the outside world. He felt that she was too young to cope with the demands that were being made on her—and that increased because of her father's ill-health after 1948. He saw one feature of his role as that of a protector, one who would provide her with the help, the encouragement, the confidence and love which she would need if she were to perform her role properly. In that sense he was to do for her what her mother had done for the shy, stammering, reserved and introverted Duke of York after their marriage in 1923. Some people in the Establishment and Court took this as a sign that he wanted to be "the power behind the throne" after 1952—and this helps to explain their attempts to downgrade him publicly.

He contrived to fulfil this 'relaxing' role even within the confines of Buckingham Palace where the young couple lived while Clarence House was being renovated. But both he and Princess Elizabeth looked forward to the weekends when they escaped from "the cage" to Windlesham Moor, near Sunningdale, a modern country house which the King had leased so that the young couple could have a country retreat. This was the first house which they could call their own and Prince Philip in particular was very happy when down there.[10] He enjoyed driving over to Windsor Great Park where they could ride or walk and also looked forward to the afternoon visits which they made to Royal Lodge, the King and Queen's favourite home.

All this was very different from the restricting life of the Palace where he was often tetchy and showed himself bored with the protocol-ridden atmosphere. When time and weather permitted, Prince Philip escaped from this life and went sailing at Cowes where, in the summer of 1949, he first became friendly with Uffa Fox, the noted sailor and designer.[11] Fox's biographer tells us that "Prince Philip was a first-rate helmsman long before he ever met Uffa, and Uffa greatly admired his ability to handle a boat and his quick and active brain. Uffa was convinced that, had Prince

Philip devoted more time to sailing, instead of being the all-round sportsman that he was, he could have become one of our finest helmsmen."[12] And years later Fox reckoned that Prince Philip was a better sailor than Ted Heath who enjoyed a degree of fame because of his success in international competitions.[13]

Older members of the Royal Family helped Prince Philip to draw out the shy Princess Elizabeth. In May 1948 they were guests at Princess Marina's house, Coppins. 'Chips' Channon was also there and wrote in his diary:

> *30 May 1948*: I stayed with the Herberts, for the dance at Coppins . . . the dance was really for the Edinburghs, who were enchanting. She was in black lace, with a large comb and mantilla, as an Infanta, and danced every dance until nearly five a.m. I am beginning to doubt the supposed pregnancy . . . but Philip of Edinburgh, although as always extremely handsome and pleasing, looked worn out. But he was the success of the ball, and was wildly gay with his policeman's hat and handcuffs. He leapt about and jumped into the air as he greeted everybody. His charm is colossal, like all Mountbattens, and he and Princess Elizabeth seemed supremely happy . . .[14]

But these opportunities to escape from harsh reality were few and far between. During the summer of 1948 it became clear that King George VI was a very sick man, unable to perform many public duties.

The Princess was called upon to take over some of the tasks which her father would, if well, have undertaken. This, in turn, meant that the Duke was asked to devote more of his time to his public role. The Navy gave him a long leave on half pay so that he could be more readily available to help his wife in her public work and so that he could undertake some of the King's work on his own.

Few people appreciate the nature of some of this public work. The newspapers may report "A royal visit to Edinburgh"—as they did in 1948. That visit was in connection with the Scottish Playing Fields Association. "Before the day was out, the Duke of Edinburgh had inspected three guards of honour, walked in procession to the church with the magistrates, lunched with the Lord Provost, visited a local mariners' club, taken an Army salute, watched a fly-past and been vociferously cheered through the city."[15] And even then, no doubt, there was some organization or society, some club or institution that felt aggrieved because he had not managed to squeeze in a visit to their home, centre or whatever.

John Dean gave us an insight into the typical royal tour:

> Often, on industrial tours, we would travel on the royal train, leaving London about ten or eleven at night and pulling into a siding conveniently close to where the next day's engagements were to begin . . . The Royal visit usually began at ten in the morning, with civic dignitaries and great crowds at the station . . .
>
> When we were on these tours the Princess, leaving the train with the Duke, would be wearing a pair of fresh white gloves. I noticed that when she

> rejoined the train in the afternoon or evening that her gloves were by that time absolutely black, through shaking hands with so many people. She never complained, but sometimes said that her wrist felt very tired . . . The Duke seemed tireless.[16]

In May 1948 he and Princess Elizabeth went to Paris to open an exhibition of eight centuries of British life. This was supposed to be a semi-private visit but it "rapidly assumed the proportions of a full State visit . . . and offered Philip a trying test of the royal discipline to which kings and queens, princesses and consorts are subject in the twentieth century."[17] On arrival in Paris they went to the British Embassy where they were to stay. Then they began their crowded engagements ". . . calling on the President, and laying a wreath on the Unknown Warrior's Tomb at the Arc de Triomphe . . . On Sunday after church there was a formal lunch . . . races at Longchamps in the afternoon . . . a ball in the Embassy."[18] As if this were not enough, on his return to England it was to read the attack made on him by a Scottish clergyman who was appalled at the visit to the races on a Sunday, "a dark day in our history,".[19] He was learning that whatever he did—in or out of the Palace, in private or in public—would be noted and probably criticized.

In the summer of 1948 Princess Elizabeth withdrew from public life because of the imminent birth of Prince Charles. This threw an even greater burden of work on the Duke of Edinburgh. There were regiments to be reviewed and colours to be presented, memorials unveiled and factories to be visited. There were days in small towns and large cities with municipal receptions and endless speeches and tours of factories, housing estates, dockyards and industrial estates.

When Princess Elizabeth was fit to take up her duties after Prince Charles's birth, the young couple were assigned, each month, to a two-day tour of the provinces. They travelled in the royal train, were ceremoniously greeted, signed vellum civic parchments with golden pens and laid foundation stones. The Duke thought that much of this ceremony was "rather futile",[20] but he enjoyed his visits to industrial centres. As Dean noted:

> . . . It was swiftly apparent that the Duke was a man of firm and forthright views, progressive in his outlook to science and with a genuine interest in the mines, the factories and the engineering works he was invited to visit. He goes down well, everywhere, because he is completely without 'side'. He gets on well with the working people because, from the highest to the lowest, they are all the same in his eyes. And he genuinely adores children.[21]

Philip also had to learn to make the required public speeches. At first the Establishment tried to make him read one of 'their' speeches. As his cousin noted: "On one occasion, the comptroller of the 'Clarence' household, Sir Frederick Browning, actually wrote a speech for Philip. At the banquet Prince Philip pulled out his notes, put them aside and then began an entirely different speech—and a very successful one—of his own . . . Philip was soon being hailed as the best after-dinner speaker in

London."[22] While making allowances for the cousinly exaggeration of that last line there is little doubt that Prince Philip became a very welcome and popular speaker at a number of functions. People began to see him not as "merely a glorified courtier, not a husbandly cipher, and his nominal position as second fiddle was strictly relative."[23]

On his twenty-seventh birthday he was appointed a personal ADC to King George, a recognition by that perceptive monarch of the work that his son-in-law was doing. It was a happy coincidence that his first official function in his new post was to meet Lord Louis at London Airport on his return as the last Viceroy of India.

On the 14th November 1948 Prince Charles was born at Buckingham Palace. In my *Our Future King* I have described how the Duke received the news while he was at the Palace swimming-pool with Michael Parker with whom he had been playing squash. He rushed to tell the King and Queen about the birth of their first grandchild. Queen Elizabeth was heard to say, "Isn't it wonderful," as many another grandmother has been known to say. The delighted father then went to see his wife and son, taking with him a bouquet of roses and carnations. Queen Mary, in nearby Marlborough House, had seen and heard the huge crowds that made their way up the Mall to gather at the Palace gates after the radio announcements of the imminent birth. Although it was midnight when she was told the news she insisted on going across to the Palace to see the new Prince. When she left the Palace the crowds outside cheered and shouted their congratulations to the royal great-grandmother. She noted in her diary: "I gave the baby a silver gilt cup and cover which George III had given to a godson in 1780, so that I gave a present from my great-grandfather to my great-grandson 168 years later."[24]

By the time Queen Mary left the Palace the floodlights in Trafalgar Square had been changed to blue in honour of the baby Prince, and the crowds outside the Palace and down the Mall were singing, demanding: "We want Philip" and dozens of taxis and cars were tooting their horns in good-humoured mood. After Queen Mary had left, a police car moved slowly among the crowd, the loudspeaker repeating the message: "Ladies and gentlemen, it is requested from the Palace that we have a little quietness, if you please." But little notice was taken for a couple of hours or more until finally a senior royal official came out to say, "Please, Princess Elizabeth wants some rest, Prince Philip is with her and there will be nothing more tonight." Slowly, unwillingly, but cheerfully the crowds began to make their way home—most of them on foot because the last buses and tubes had gone.

Lord Louis and no doubt Prince Philip were proud of the fact that the second in line of succession to the throne bore the family name, Mountbatten. But Prince Philip was more than merely a proud father. He and Princess Elizabeth were loving and caring parents, and when she left Charles behind to join her husband in Malta, Princess Elizabeth knew that he would be happy with his grandparents—as they were with him.

In particular she knew that he had "a doting grandmother". After the birth of Princess Anne in August 1950 Princess Elizabeth rejoined the Duke in Malta, but both of them kept in touch with the children—by telephone and by letter. And as the King wrote to his daughter, "Charles is too sweet, stumping around the room. We shall love having him at Sandringham. He is the fifth generation to live there and I hope he will get to like the place . . ."[25]

In July 1949—after the birth of Prince Charles and before the birth of Princess Anne—the Duke and the Princess moved from Buckingham Palace to their own home at Clarence House. The house had once been the home of King William IV, the Duke of Clarence, before his accession in 1830. Later it had belonged to the Duke of Connaught who had, however, retired just before the First World War to live in Bagshot. During the Second World War King George VI had lent the almost derelict house to the British Red Cross who had converted it into offices. When it was returned to the Royal Family in 1948 it was badly in need of reconversion, modernization and decoration.

The success of that work may be seen by anyone who has had the privilege of visiting the house—as I did when working on *The Queen Mother*. My first visit to Clarence House took place on the day after the arrival of the President of Rumania. As I walked down the Mall I watched a procession in which he drove from the Palace, where he had stayed for the night, to a reception in the City. Then, as if further to confirm the fact that Clarence House is part of a political-cum-diplomatic complex, I had to make my way past a line of official cars waiting to take ambassadors away from a reception which had just been held at St James's Palace. Then on through the aptly named Ambassador's Court to the back entrance to Clarence House. A black door was opened by a uniformed footman. One of my first impressions of this back portion of the house was of going up and down small flights of stairs. It was explained to me that the house in fact is a series of back-to-back houses and the stairs are needed to link these together. The morning-room, a corner room on the ground floor facing the garden and Stable Yard, is a long sunlit room. It is linked by double doors to the library, a square high room which was once the hall of the House. There is a large dining-room off the library. This is a long room dominated by a beautiful chimney-piece of white and grey marble. The walls of this room are hung with portraits of the original occupant, King William IV, and of King George III and Queen Charlotte, his father and mother. The west side of the first floor of the house is occupied by a double drawing-room and a private sitting-room.

In 1949 the staff at Clarence House was headed by a comptroller, Sir Frederick Browning, husband of the novelist Daphne du Maurier. Apart from the private secretaries to the Prince and Princess, there were housemaids, a steward, a housekeeper, a butler, footmen, pages, a cook, John Dean, valet to the Prince, and 'Bobo' Macdonald, the Princess's private servant. While they were drawing up plans for the renovation of their future home, the Prince and Princess consulted their staff about "the design of the places where they were going to work, with the result that the staff quarters were as near ideal as could possibly be imagined." After they had moved in both of them continued to take a great personal interest in their staff so that "everyone who left did so with very real regret . . ."[26].

Clarence House then, as now, is part home, part office and part official base where visiting statesmen and other guests have to be entertained. The Prince was reminded in this home that he had his three roles to play—as husband, naval officer and public figure. In 1949 King George VI seemed to have recovered sufficiently to allow the ambitious Prince to return to the Navy. But as we have seen, even in the Mediterranean he was continually being reminded of his triple role. As a naval officer he earned his promotions and made *Magpie* the cock ship. As a husband he welcomed his wife to Malta and helped her to enjoy a period of freedom which she was to remember with pleasure in the hard years ahead. He was also called on to pay official or semi-official visits to the various countries around the Mediterranean, both with his wife and on his own.

As we saw at the beginning of this chapter he had every right to hope, in 1947, that he had about twenty years during which to act out each of these three roles. But unfortunately King George's health deteriorated rapidly in 1951 and Philip was compelled to take an indefinite leave from the Navy. We know that he never returned to the service. He had lost one role and would, in future, have to learn to adjust to a life in which his wife was not merely heiress but Queen.

23

The King's Illness and an American Tour

ON THE 26TH APRIL 1948 KING GEORGE VI and Queen Elizabeth celebrated their Silver Wedding Day. It was made a day of great public rejoicing. In the morning the royal couple drove in a State landau to a ceremony at St Paul's. The streets of London were crowded with cheering people. In the afternoon they drove in an open car through twenty miles of London streets and again were given a continual ovation. In the evening they were called several times to appear on the balcony of the Palace to acknowledge the great crowds that had gathered in the Mall.[1]

This was the British people's way of thanking their two monarchs for a job that had been well done. In 1936 they had come unwillingly to the throne; between 1939–1945 they had stayed with their people throughout the bombing of London and had not sent their children to the safety of Canada or the USA as some had urged. They had shown in their private as well as in their public lives a splendid example of devotion and service. Both of them were surprised at the warmth of their reception. As the King wrote to his mother:

> We were both dumbfounded over our reception. We have received so many nice letters from all and sundry thanking us for what we have tried to do during these years. It does spur us on to further efforts.[2]

Among the "further efforts" was a tour of Australia and New Zealand. The decision to make this trip had been announced on March 6th prior to the Silver Wedding celebration. They had visited Canada in 1939 and South Africa in 1947 and the King was anxious to visit his Australasian Dominions as soon as possible. He and the then Duchess of York had enjoyed a great triumph when they visited these Dominions in 1927—their first great public work together.[3] They hoped to repeat that triumph in 1949.

However, the King was not enjoying good health. The strains of monarchy had been relatively greater for this shy, introverted and uncertain man than they would have been for someone better prepared, and the additional strain of being monarch of wartime Britain had taken its toll. Even during the tour of South Africa he had lost seventeen pounds in weight. He first began to suffer from cramp in both legs in January 1948, and by October his left foot was numb all day and the pain kept him awake at night. During October he saw a number of doctors, including heart specialists; he had a number of X-rays and blood tests and finally was examined by Professor James Learmouth of Edinburgh, one of the greatest authorities on vascular complaints.

He examined the King at Buckingham Palace on the 12th November—while in another part of the Palace, rooms were being prepared for the imminent birth of Princess Elizabeth's first baby. Learmouth confirmed that the King was suffering from a form of early arteriosclerosis, and that there was a danger that gangrene might develop, in which case the right leg might have to be amputated. This news was made public on the 23rd November when it was also announced that the tour of Australia and New Zealand would not go ahead.[4]

This was the reason why the Duke of Edinburgh was not allowed to take up a posting until late in 1948—by which time the King's health had imporoved under a regimen of medication and rest. He was able to enjoy the traditional fare of a Sandringham Christmas—walking and shooting—although he had to rest each afternoon.

There was, however, a set-back in March 1949. His doctors realized that he would be unwilling to lead the life of an inactive invalid which alone would ensure that his condition improved, because that would have meant putting a stop to most of his public duties—those "further efforts" he had written about. He was advised that, if he wanted to live fairly normally, he ought to have a right lumbar sympathectomy operation. This was carried out at the Palace on 12th March 1949. By the 29th March he had recovered sufficiently to hold a Privy Council and in the following two months he carried out a number of public duties, although on the 9th June he drove in an open carriage to the Trooping the Colour, Princess Elizabeth riding at the head of the parade for the first time. By the end of November he had recovered sufficiently for plans to be made for the tour of Australia and New Zealand to take place in 1952. Princess Elizabeth was able, as we have seen, to enjoy Christmas 1949 with her husband in Malta. All seemed well again.

The King and Queen were to have left for Australia in December 1951, but in May the King went down with an attack of influenza, which developed into pneumonia which was checked only by heavy doses of penicillin.[5] During June and July he rested—but was unable to regain his strength. In July, as we have seen, Prince Philip returned to Britain on "indefinite leave". He and the Princess were told that they were to go on a short tour of Canada and the USA.

The King spent August and the beginning of September at Balmoral and although he wrote "I am getting stronger every day",[6] the truth was otherwise. Late in August he developed a chill and a sore throat; he was sent back to London for more X-rays and examination by the specialists who had seen him during his earlier illness. This time they called in Mr Clement Price Thomas, a leading surgical authority on malignant diseases. On the 11th September the King was told that he would have to have an operation to remove a portion of tissue from the lung for examination.

This operation took place on the 15th September and the examination confirmed that the King was suffering from cancer; this would necessitate yet another operation. This news was given to the Queen who decided that Prince Philip ought to know. Both of them kept the news from their partners, so that neither the King nor Princess Elizabeth knew how gravely ill the King really was. The doctors feared that one result of another operation might be a coronary thrombosis—which was, in fact, to be the cause of the King's death in 1952. There was, however, a further problem. During the operation on Sunday, 23rd September, Price Thomas found that the cancer had spread to the larynx. It was decided that certain portions of this organ had to be removed, even though this might mean that the King would only be able to speak in a whisper.

The operation was a success, but recovery was slow. The Canadian

Government asked that the Princess and Duke should postpone their projected visit to Canada until recovery was assured. On the 9th October it was announced that the King would be unable to undertake the tour of Australasia in 1952.

Princess Elizabeth and Prince Philip were supposed to have left for their tour of Canada and the USA on the 25th September, but the King's operation had taken place only on the 23rd September and no one thought that it was advisable for the heir to the throne to leave the country until the King's recovery seemed certain. So their departure was delayed. As the King's condition improved he insisted that they go. They should have sailed in the liner *Empress of Britain* and taken a leisurely few days crossing to Canada. By the time the King's recovery was assured, it was the 3rd October and if the Princess travelled by sea she would throw out of gear all the arrangements for the bulging schedule of the tour. Originally this was to have been a modest tour, a gentle introduction for both of them to the arduous nature of overseas visits. Both governments had agreed that they would visit three cities in a tour lasting ten days. But during the detailed planning and after further talks between governments, this developed into a gruelling 15,000-mile journey which was to last fifteen days and involve the crossing of the North American Continent twice.

To travel by liner after October 3rd would make it impossible to adhere to these arrangements. The sensible thing to do—said the Duke and Princess—was to fly and so save a few days of travel time. This would allow them to 'catch up' on the arrangements which had hinged on their sailing on the 25th September. But the politicians and the Court Establishment would not allow the heir to the throne to travel such a long distance by air. It is difficult now to think of flying across the Atlantic as dangerous. But the politicians—Prime Minister Attlee and Churchill, the leader of the Opposition—and the Establishment were old men. Their ideas were 'fixed' for them as far back as 1914, and although they knew that during the Second World War heavy bombers had flown across the Atlantic, they also knew that until 1939 there had been no passenger service across that Ocean and that even by 1951 it was still something of an adventure to fly to Canada and the USA.

They were unwilling to expose the heir to the throne to the dangers, real or imagined, of flying. It was Prince Philip who 'managed' it all. He saw the King and explained the problem to that monarch, namely that either they had to be allowed to fly or the tour would have to become a rushed and overtaxing affair. The King agreed and played his part. He let it be known that the tour might have to be cancelled because of the problem of timing. The Governor-General of Canada, Field Marshal Earl Alexander of Tunis, protested that the Canadian people would be bitterly disappointed. The British Government then faced the dilemma of either facing up to Canadian ill-will or of allowing the Princess to fly. So on the 8th October 1951 the Duke and Princess Elizabeth left London Airport for

Montreal. The Duke had won a battle with the politicians and the Establishment—but there would be others which he would not win.

When they left he had another reminder of the position in which he and his wife might find themselves. In their luggage they carried a sealed envelope which contained a message to both Houses of Parliament as well as a draft Declaration of Accession. These were to be opened in the event of the King's death while they were in Canada.[7] This was a burden which the twenty-five-year-old Princess had to bear. It was one which her older, more experienced and very able husband shared with her. His own knowledge of the gravity of the King's illness and the drafts in the Princess's luggage, made him all the more protective of her during the long days of the Canadian and American Tour.

The tour on which the Edinburghs now embarked was due to last thirty-five days and was to take them over fifteen thousand miles. They crossed the vast Continent twice, in the Governor-General's special train which was preceded by a train carrying the corps of Pressmen covering the tour. Sometimes the day lasted as long as fourteen hours; other days were spent largely in travelling—on one day, for example, they covered a thousand miles.

Both of them appreciated that the tour was part of their royal training. This aspect of their lives was also reflected in the Princess's reading. She "was always anxious to see the airmail edition of *The Times* as soon as it arrived . . . to keep abreast of events . . . She also received the Hansard Parliamentary Reports each day, and went through them conscientiously . . . the *Observer* and the *Sunday Times* . . ."[8] It may help to remind us of how politically aware she is if we remember that, at that time, most of the members of the present government were not even MPs and many present-day MPs were still in school. The Queen's awareness of political affairs was part of the training she received from her father and helps to explain why all her former Prime Ministers have paid great tributes to her 'nous'.

The Duke learned more than ever that one of his tasks was to help the Princess to fulfil her expected public role. He was so assiduous at this that "hardened professionals were impressed".[9] When they were in one of the many receiving lines, shaking hands with a long queue of eager people, the Prince would give her a slight rest by holding on to the next in line, keeping them chatting. During public receptions they tended to talk separately to groups of people, but the Prince always had an eye on what was happening around his wife and, when necessary, would move over to take some of the crowd away from her and so relieve the pressure.[10]

It was, of course, their future Queen that the crowds turned out to see in their thousands—students, children, women, workers, old and young. Some waited for hours at some wayside station where the royal train made only a ten-minute stop, so eager were the people to see her. But it was the Prince who charmed the crowds. It was easier for him to make a wisecrack, insist that cameramen move out of the way so that a child could get a photograph of the Princess and in general act more naturally than the more restrained, shyer, less worldly-wise and protocol-conscious Princess. Another of his tasks was to help the Princess to relax, to ease the tensions that tended to make her more nervous than she had a right to be. Sometimes he did this by playing practical jokes on her so that at times "we heard screams of laughter coming from the Royal car as the Duke chased his wife wearing a particularly horrible-looking set of false teeth."[11] There was an imitation tin of nuts out of which a snake popped out, and a gadget which gave a mild electric shock when pressed. In cold print these may appear to be senseless exercises of princely humour. In fact they were deliberately intended to help the Princess to forget the letters she had in her luggage and the drudgery that lay ahead at the next town or city.

It was the Governor-General who suggested that they should go to a square dance at Government House in Ottawa. Both of them dressed in the highly-coloured outfits fitting to the occasion and the world's Press carried pictures of the two of them swinging their way through the dances. For the Canadians there was an even greater pleasure when it transpired that there was no time for the two of them to change out of this garb before catching the royal train. The onlookers were delighted to see them dressed in this informal way—and the Canadian Press made a great deal out of this incident which helped to make them even more popular than they had been.

A Canadian reckoned that "Philip worked like a beaver to make the tour a success."[12] It was his brain-wave which led to the fixing of a plexiglass top to the royal car so that the Princess could be seen by more people and during all weathers.[13] The Press reported this story and earned him and the Princess even more credit. But his relations with the Press were not always friendly. He could not understand why photographers always wanted "One more, Princie," after they had posed for minutes while cameras clicked. When he and the Princess were saying farewell to the members of the Press who were not coming with them to the USA, he found that some people who were, in fact, staying with the Royal party had gatecrashed so that they could get an additional shake of the royal hands. "This is a waste of time," he growled and left.[14] One can sympathize with him; they had, after all, shaken tens of thousands of hands. This particular party had been laid on for a section of the Press and the royal goodwill had been abused by another section of the corps, but this did little to endear him to certain reporters who were to report unfavourably on him whenever they saw a chance.

Fortunately, this moment of ill-will bore no fruit immediately. The royal couple were popular before they arrived in Canada—where the King and Queen had enjoyed a great triumph in 1939[15] and from where thousands of Canadians had sailed or flown to take part in the war against Germany. And they became more popular as their trip progressed. The Canadians approved of the way in which, whatever the weather 'the royals' turned up to do their job. When she broadcast at the end of the tour, Princess Elizabeth was obviously emotional. It was not, she said, a goodbye but an *au revoir*. "I am leaving a country which has become a second home in every sense."[16] And in his one major speech the Duke showed his appreciation of Canada: "Canada is wrong in insisting it is a young country. Youth means inexperience and lack of judgement. How can this fit a nation that rushed a railway through the Rockies, developed the prairies and is steadily pushing the last frontier northward?"[17]

A Canadian wrote: "Here at least is something that the Americans have not got. Almost universally Canadians feel that Americans are always one gadget ahead of them. Here the Canadians had royalty, and it was their own, and the Americans had not got it."[18] But the Americans showed that they would have liked to have "got it" when the Royal Tour went south to Washington. Police estimated that half a million people lined the streets as they drove from Washington Station to Blair House to be met by President Truman who was "moved by the youth and charm of his guests and spoke repeatedly of the highest admiration of the responsible and attentive manner in which they carried out their engagements."[19] He later wrote to King George VI:

> We've just had a visit from a lovely young lady and her personable husband. They went to the hearts of all the citizens of the United States. We tried to make their visit a happy one.
>
> As one father to another, we can be very proud of our daughters. You have the better of me—because you have two.[20]

The King and Queen had themselves had a triumphal tour of the USA in 1939, a tour which the Queen declared at the time had "made us".[21] It seemed that her daughter had repeated that success.

The bed-ridden King was delighted to read such glowing reports about his daughter and son-in-law. He was given a similarly glowing account by Sir Oliver Franks, the British Ambassador in the USA.[22] To mark his approval he wrote to the Princess on the 28th November:

> To mark the return of this country from your and Philip's most successful visit to Canada I propose to have you both introduced into the Privy Council. In other words to make you Privy Councillors. I am holding a Council next Tuesday, December 4th at 12.15 p.m. which I wish you to attend. Will you please come at 12.00 so that I can show you what you will have to do.
>
> From
>
> Your very loving and devoted,
>
> Papa.[23]

This was to be more significant for Prince Philip than the King could have known, as we shall see in Chapter 25, but neither he nor the King appreciated that in November 1951. Both of them were more concerned, for example, with Prince Charles. He had stayed with the King and Queen while his parents were away, and has vivid memories of that holiday. In particular he remembers sitting with his grandfather on his third birthday while a photographer took a picture that has become well-known. To help keep him quiet, Richard Colville, Press Secretary to the King, swung his watch which Charles remembers now only as "something shiny".

Charles was taken to Euston Station to meet his parents and "stole the show with his wide-eyed admiration for the parading Mounties from Canada".[24] The three-year-old was seen to have many of his father's mannerisms—the hands tucked behind the back as he walked, but he was not with his mother and father when they drove, in State, to the Guildhall for a 'welcome home' from the City of London and so took up again the threads of their public life at home. The family was together again at Sandringham for Christmas 1951 to celebrate the King's fifty-sixth birthday on the 14th December and to listen to his Christmas broadcast in which he referred to his illness and "with confidence" to his recovery. This hope and confidence was to be proved to be misplaced.

24

The Death of King George VI

WHEN PRINCE PHILIP RETURNED FROM Canada he thought that he was on the verge of returning to playing the three roles which he had occupied immediately after his marriage, that of husband and father, public worker on behalf of the Royal Family and, most significantly for him, a naval officer.

Back home again in Clarence House he enjoyed being a father. If Princess Elizabeth was "in and out of the nursery all the time"[1] Prince Philip was with her whenever he was at home. In particular the staff remember him enjoying the young Charles's bathtime which was turned into a playtime with plastic ducks, toy boats—and wet clothes when his son learned the pleasure of splashing. He was to continue to play an active paternal role in his son's life for many years to come.

But he was not always at home, because he was the *active* young royal. Almost as soon as he had adjusted to life in England again, he was back on the treadmill. There was a new university building to be opened in Durham, laboratories to be opened in the Potteries in Stoke-on-Trent, honorary degrees to be accepted at London University and a Hebrew Service to be attended at the oldest synagogue in Britain. These were the headline-catching events in his busy life. There were, too, the seemingly endless inspections, dinners and sporting events which filled the day—and often the night—of a busy worker-Prince.

On top of this busy schedule there was the planning of yet another tour. Only two days after they had left for Canada it had been announced that the King and Queen would be unable to undertake the already postponed tour of Australia and New Zealand proposed for 1952. Instead, Princess Elizabeth and Prince Philip would go on their behalf. Prince Philip applied himself to ensuring that this tour would be as successful as the Canadian one. He went through the list of towns to be visited, "adding new towns",[2] and explained to the planners why certain things could not be done—as he had discovered by experience in Canada. He read widely about Australian affairs and even went to the London Wool Exchange to get a better idea about sheep-farming and the vocabulary of those connected with the wool trade. Hahn would have approved of the way in which his former pupil applied himself to excel at the work he had to do.

But over and above all this—his children, his home life at Clarence House, and the activities of a royal worker—there was the seeming promise of a return to the Navy. Although he was on indefinite leave, his length of service and his success at examinations meant that during 1952 he would qualify as a commander. He confidently expected that, on his return from Australia, he would be given command of his own destroyer and return to sea in 1953.[3]

Prince Philip was with the rest of the family at Sandringham for the traditional Christmas holiday. The King was in great form. His friend and wartime Prime Minister, Churchill, had been returned to office on the defeat of the Attlee-led Labour Party in the October general election. As 'Chips' Channon noted: "I do not think that he [the King] concealed very skilfully his dislike of the Socialists . . .".[4] He made a well-received Christmas broadcast and spent time discussing the forthcoming tour.

The original plan was for the royal couple to sail on the liner *Gothic*, but Princess Elizabeth wanted to visit Kenya so that she could see the Royal Lodge at Sagana which the Kenyan people had given her as a wedding present. It was therefore agreed that she would fly to Australia. So, an advance party sailed on the *Gothic* on the 12th January, while the more important members remained behind at Sandringham. On the 30th January the King took the Queen, Prince Philip and Princess Elizabeth as well as other members of the Royal Family to Drury Lane to see *South Pacific*. On the following day he went to see the party off at London Airport. Lady Pamela Mountbatten was there as the Princess's lady-in-waiting, Lieutenant-Colonel Michael Charteris as her equerry. Michael

Parker, Prince Philip's equerry, John Dean, his valet, and 'Bobo' Macdonald, the Princess's confidante and dresser completed the party. John Dean wrote:

> I heard the King say to Bobo Macdonald: "Look after the Princess for me, Bobo. I hope the tour is not going to be too tiring for you." Bobo said afterwards that she had never known the King look so upset on parting from his daughter.[5]

A number of people have left their vivid recollections of the King's appearance at the farewell to his daughter and son-in-law. Miles Thomas was the Controller of London Airport and one of the official party. He wrote of "the bitterly cold wind . . . [the King] bracing himself against some inner tension as a man does when he is determined not to let an aching tooth or a sprained muscle interfere with his normal deportment . . . left quickly with the Queen."[6]

Oliver Lyttleton, later Lord Chandos, Colonial Minister in the Churchill government, was another of the official party. Later he wrote:

> I was shocked by the King's appearance . . . he seemed much altered and strained. I had the feeling of doom, which grew as the minutes before the time of departure ebbed away. The King went on to the roof of the building to wave goodbye. The high wind blew his hair into disorder . . .[7]

Both of these were recollections of men who had the benefit of a sad hindsight. 'Chips' Channon wrote his impressions at the time:

> *2nd February*: I watched the television, and saw the King, bare-headed, cross, almost mad-looking, waving farewell to the Edinburghs, who have flown to Kenya en route for Australia. He is reported to be going out duck shooting next week, suicidal.[8]

The visit to Kenya was meant to be the private part of the tour, but on February 1st there was a reception at the Governor's residence with the inevitable line of people waiting to shake royal hands. Then on Sunday, 3rd February, the royal couple drove the ninety miles up country to Sagana Lodge—a six-roomed bungalow, built of cedar wood on stone foundations. They stayed there during the night—getting a taste of 'wild Africa' as an elephant trumpeted through the servants' quarters. On the 4th February they went out riding and enjoyed the views of forests and mountains. After lunch the Duke played a game of polo at Nyeri. On February 5th they went on to Treetops, the famous observation lodge built in a fig-tree in the jungle. This 'hotel' overlooked a water-hole used by buffaloes, rhinoceroses and elephants. It had been specially decorated for the royal visit and some baboons which broke in and ate some of the new lampshades were unpopular. "For this visit the Princess wore a bush scarf and brown slacks, walking with her escorts along a narrow, quarter-mile track through the forest. Every few yards along the track there were escape ladders—just in case!"[9] From their perch in Treetops they watched the animals come to the water-hole to drink. The Princess made a film to show the children when she got back home. This was "a wonderful holiday which gave great pleasure to us all."[10]

On the same day, back in England, the King had enjoyed himself out shooting on the Sandringham estate. He seemed so well that the Queen and Princess Margaret felt able to leave him while they went across Norfolk to visit Edward Seago, the artist. In the early evening the King had his tea and a short rest. Then he went, for the first time ever, to the nursery, where Prince Charles and Princess Anne were having their supper. He stayed with them, helped to tuck them into bed and knelt to say a prayer with them before saying good-night. Then he went downstairs to dine with his wife and daughter on their return. While his elder daughter was enjoying the night life at the water-hole at Treetops, he went to bed—and about midnight was heard fixing the shutters on the window in his bedroom.

The King's valet went to bring him his tea early on the morning of Wednesday, 6th February. He thought that the King was still sleeping and left it. Only when he went to call him for his bath did he realize that the King was dead—of a coronary thrombosis which the doctors had feared ever since his cancer operation. Although the Queen was told of the King's death at seven thirty a.m. no public announcement was made until ten a.m. in the hope that the news might be sent to Kenya and the new Queen told of her father's death before it was announced over the radio.

At Treetops the 6th February was another fine day. The Governor had left Nairobi so that he might be at Mombasa, Princess Elizabeth's next stop. The Whitehall machine was unable to get in touch with him to tell him of the King's death. Nor was Treetops in easy communication with the outside world. During the morning the royal party had gone fishing. John Dean and Bobo Macdonald . . .

> After lunch . . . were sitting on a doorstep cleaning shoes. Clarke, the detective, took a snap of us . . . Clarke was called by Lieut-Commander Parker . . . Clarke came out to tell us: "There is awful news from London—the King has died."[11]

The news had been released in London about ten a.m. and telephoned through to the Nairobi offices of the *East African Standard*. It was a reporter on that paper who had telephoned the Princess's Private Secretary. He had rung from the hotel across the valley to the Treetops Lodge where Parker had answered the telephone. He tried to get the news confirmed officially, but was unable to contact the Governor. He managed to pick up a BBC programme. Although this did not immediately give an announcement of the King's death, Parker realized from the solemn music being played continually that the reports of the death must be true. It was about two forty-five p.m. Kenya time. John Dean again:

> When the first news agency flash came from London the Duke was asleep. The Princess was resting in her room. Bobo and I carried on cleaning shoes . . . nothing else to do. Then the Princess, still unaware of her father's death

> [still unconfirmed] came out to talk to us. She said that she and the Duke would be riding earlier than usual the next morning. I wanted to express my deep sympathy to her, but dare not show . . . that I knew what she did not.[12]

Michael Parker woke the Duke and gave him the news. "I never felt so sorry for anyone in all my life. He looked as if you'd dropped half the world on him."[13] As there had been no official confirmation of the news reports, the Duke insisted that the Princess should not be told, and said that when such a confirmation came through he would be the one to inform her.

He then got his wife out of the house on the pretext that they ought to look at the horses they were going to ride the next day. It was two hours before the official confirmation came through. Parker caught the Duke's attention and drew him away from Princess Elizabeth to give him the news that the death was now officially confirmed. John Dean wrote:

> Then he sent for me and the Princess called Bobo. The Duke said to me; "I am afraid we shall have to return home as soon as we can. The King is dead." He had just told me this when the Princess came into the room. She was composed but looked pale and worried. She did not speak.[14]

Prince Philip's first thoughts were that the Princess needed even more help and protection than ever. While arrangements were made for their departure and for the flight back to London, he walked with her for an hour along the bank of the Sagana River. When they came back for tea she was dry-eyed and composed although still pale. All her life had been a preparation for her accession although she was unable to accept the way in which it had happened so suddenly. But the Queen now reigned and the letters which she carried in her luggage had to be sent to the governments of the Dominions and to the governors of Colonial Territories. Her Private Secretary came to her to ask by what name she would wish to be known as Queen, and as if she had known all her life that one day she would have to answer such a question she replied, "Elizabeth. Elizabeth II."[15]

By five o'clock they were ready to leave. Along the forty-mile journey to the airport, natives stood with bowed heads, "not grinning or clapping as they had done on the outward journey, but offering a silent tribute to their Queen's grief which I found most moving."[16] A small East African Airways plane took the party to Entebbe in Uganda where they boarded the BOAC plane, *Atlanta*. It was late afternoon when they dropped down through the clouds to London Airport. By this time the Queen had changed into a plain black dress, coat and hat. As Dean wrote:

> . . . the Queen always had something black in her luggage, and I always carried a black tie for the Duke, in case . . . something would happen . . .[17]

The *Atlanta* landed at London Airport at about five o'clock on the 7th February, just twenty-four hours after the party had left Kenya. The Duke of Gloucester and Lord and Lady Mountbatten boarded the plane and "went into the rear compartment where the Queen and her husband received them."[18] Lord Louis "gave Philip's shoulder a hard squeeze of comfort"[19] as they left the plane.

The Queen came down the steps, a small figure dressed in black. Waiting at the bottom of the steps representing the Privy Council were Prime Minister Winston Churchill, the former Prime Minister Attlee and Foreign Secretary Anthony Eden. Even Churchill was "unable to speak"[20] and all three bowed their heads in homage to their new Monarch.

She went by Royal Daimler not to her home at Clarence House but to Buckingham Palace where Queen Mary was waiting for her. She did not get to Clarence House until later that evening where her son Charles was waiting expectantly. He may not have noticed that as she arrived back 'home' the royal banner was run up on the flagstaff, an outward sign of the changes that were to take place in their family life. For even as she was greeting her children her father's Private Secretary, Sir Alan Lascelles, came to say, "Ma'am, the Boxes are in your office." The Boxes with their State papers and Foreign Office telegrams had to be attended to and the private grief of a bereaved daughter had to wait.

The Queen did not see her mother at Sandringham until the afternoon of the following day, because she had to spend the morning at her Accession Council. She walked in procession with her mother, sister and husband to the small church at Sandringham where the King's body lay overnight before being taken the next day to lie in state at Westminster Hall. 'Chips' Channon left a moving description of the scene in the Hall on the afternoon of the 19th February:

> At the House of Commons everyone was in black . . . at 3.40 we filed to Westminster Hall . . . recently refurbished and re-lit, spacious and empty . . . Slowly, solemnly, silently, sedately, the gorgeously apparelled Heralds followed by the various Heraldic Kings, all of them in red and blue and gold tabards, advanced and went out . . . preceded by Bernard Norfolk as Earl Marshal who walked with Roc Cholmondeley, the new Lord Great Chamberlain of England . . . superb in a splendid uniform . . .
>
> At length . . . the Heralds, followed by the Heraldic Kings, returned. Behind them, bearing the King's coffin, were eight Grenadiers . . . very slowly they made their way to the catafalque . . . The Great Hall was cold, splendid and impressive . . . a few paces behind, the Royal Family followed . . . the young Queen, all in black . . . behind her the Queen Mother . . . On her left was Queen Mary . . . Then the others . . . The service was short. At the end there was a brief pause and I watched the new Queen nod to Norfolk and then the Bellini-like procession left slowly.[21]

Some photographers caught a very moving picture of the three Queens paying homage to their dead son, husband or father, their faces tearless but grief-stricken behind their long black veils of mourning. Channon did not mention Prince Philip in his long account of the proceedings in the Hall, but throughout the long nine days which now elapsed before her father's funeral, the Queen relied very much on his continued help. He was with her almost all the time "attentive to her every need, giving her strength by a touch on her arm, a whisper of encouragement''.[22] By this time, however, Prince Philip was already well aware of the hostility with which he was regarded by the Establishment which had shone so resplendently at Westminster Hall and which moved in to surround the new, young and inexperienced Queen with their tradition-laden protocol. There was no room for the Prince, the husband, in their plans.

Part VI

THE ESTABLISHMENT -v- THE PRINCE 1952–1953

ith the Queen on their
turn from Kenya on 7
ebruary 1952 when, as
ince Philip said, "the whole
ing changed, very, very
nsiderably".

lking in King George VI's
eral with the Dukes of
ndsor, Gloucester and
nt.

Giving the kiss of fealty to the Queen during her Coronation. At this point his cloak seemed to fold around the Queen as if to symbolize his protective part in her future.

Above: Prince Philip arriving to open the King George V playing fields in Stepney, 20 October 1952. The President of the NPFA was an assiduous and successful worker. *Below:* Prince Charles and Princess Anne, with their grandmother Princess Andrew (Alice), arrive at Portsmouth on 5 August 1955 to join their parents on the eight-day cruise to Wales, the Isle of Man and Scotland.

A study by Baron taken on Prince Philip's 35th birthday in the Pine Room at Buckingham Palace. For this portrait he chose to wear the tie of the Edinburgh University Union.

One of a collection of photographs taken in Octobe 1957 by Antony Armstrong-Jones. This one shows the Royal Family in the grounds of Buckingham Palace.

Another from the October 1957 series taken by Armstrong-Jones. This one was taken in the Music Room at Buckingham Palace, with Prince Philip wearing the uniform of an Admiral of the Fleet.

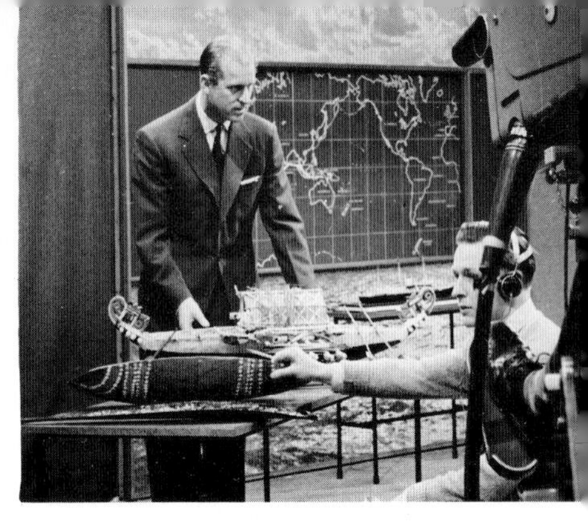

Above left: The Prince with his friend and former shipmate Commander Michael Parker relaxing during a visit to Gambia in 1957. Just after this photograph was taken Commander Parker resigned from his post of Private Secretary to Prince Philip because of his impending divorce. This persuaded some members of the Press that Prince Philip's relationship with the Queen was also under strain which made their meeting at the start of the State Visit to Portugal all the more newsworthy. *Above right:* Later in 1957 the Prince addressed a crammed audience at the Festival Hall when he gave an account of his world tour in *Britannia*. The talk was adapted for transmission on BBC Children's Television on 17 May 1957 when it was illustrated by films and slides which he had taken during his long tour. *Below*: A photograph taken during the Royal Tour of India in 1960 showing the 9ft. 8in. tiger shot by the Duke of Edinburgh. The Maharajah of Jaipur is on the Queen's right and the Maharanee on her left. Some people find it difficult to reconcile the Prince's hunting with his concern for wildlife – but he distinguishes between the process of culling or of organized killing and wholesale slaughter of wildlife.

Above left: The Duke at a luncheon of the Grand Order of Water Rats on 11 March 1960, organized to raise funds for the London Federation of Boys' Clubs. *Above right:* The Duke climbing into a Centurion tank during his visit in May 1960 to the Queen's Royal Irish Hussars of which he is Colonel-in-Chief and which was then stationed at Bergen Hohne in Germany. *Below:* 1963 and another uniform – that of Colonel-in-Chief of the Queen's Own Highlanders. The Prince was inspecting his men on their return from service in the Far East as part of the ceremony of presenting new colours to the 1st Battalion at the Palace of Holyroodhouse.

Prince Philip has always found it easy to relax with children during royal tours. On 16 March 1963 he and the Queen touched down at the small township of Katherine in the Northern Territory of Australia. The small population (600) was swollen by about 1,000 'invaders', some of whom had travelled up to 150 miles to see the royal couple in whose honour the township even closed its pub for the first time in its history.

Prince Philip talks to some o the men involved in the rescu attempts after the Aberfan disaster in October 1966.

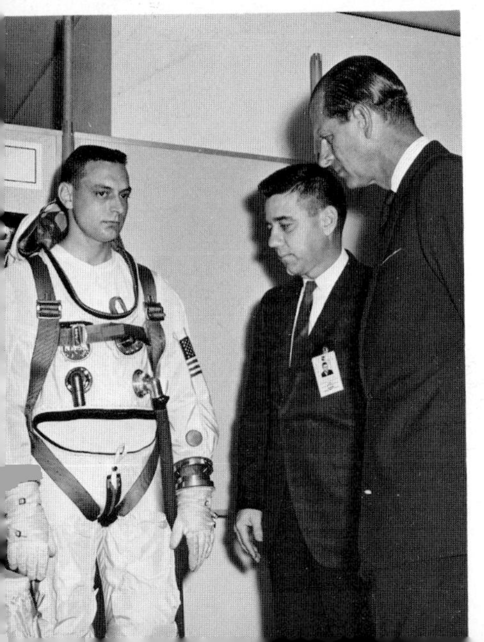

Prince Philip on a visit to the Manned Spacecra Centre, Houston, Texas in March 1966 listening to a explanation of the new soft space suit worn during t 14-day Gemini 7 space flight in December 1965.

25

The Humiliation of the Accession Council

ALL THE YEARS OF TRAINING—from her father, mother and Queen Mary—came to fruition in that discipline and self-control which the young Queen showed in the first few days of her reign. How else does one explain the wave of 'good-bye' that she remembered to give when going aboard the BOAC *Atlanta* in Entebbe? Or the 'royal' way in which she went to thank the crew of the aircraft after she had met the waiting party at London Airport? Or the immediate answer when asked what name she intended to use? Or the prompt dealing with the Red Boxes on her arrival in Clarence House on that first sad evening at home?

In spite of all the training, she knew, as did Philip, that there was a world of difference between sitting with a father-King as he worked through his boxes, listening to him as he discussed some meeting he had had with an ambassador or visiting statesmen—and being called on to do these things for herself. And to add to her burden was her grief over the death of a well-loved father who was, to her, an ideal, both as father and as King. On the 21st October 1955 she unveiled a memorial to the late King in the Mall. She spoke of the way in which he had been called, unexpectedly, to the throne in 1936, the "fortitude, determination and confidence" he had shown throughout the war, his "friendliness and simplicity . . . human sympathy which was one of my father's most lovable qualities." And she concluded:

> Much was asked of my father in personal sacrifice and endeavour, often in the face of illness; his courage in overcoming it endeared him to everybody. He shirked no task . . . and never faltered in his duty . . . Throughout all the strains of public life he remained a man of warm and friendly sympathies . . . who won for himself such a place in the affection of all of us that when he died millions mourned for him as a true and trusted friend . . .[1]

And none mourned more than did his daughter-successor. Her mourning made it all the more traumatic that she had to undertake all those duties which devolved on the Monarch as well as the peculiar duties involved in such ceremonies as her Accession Council which took place on February 8th. Throughout the long nine days before her father's funeral there were documents to be signed, official appointments to be made, and meetings with foreign statesmen from the USA and Europe. There were audiences with her ministers and precious minutes to be spent with the ageing and grief-stricken Queen Mary.

The Queen Mother and Princess Margaret were her almost constant companions at Clarence House where she also had the benefit of the company, support and encouragement of Prince Philip and the distractions of the children with whom she tried to lead, as far as was at all possible, a mother's life. As if to remind her that her life was no longer to be her own, the Government insisted that she had to move from Clarence House to Buckingham Palace. She had suggested that while she might use the Palace as her office, she should live at Clarence House which provided a family atmosphere which she knew could never be reproduced in the museum-like and much larger Palace. Prime Minister Churchill, however, had a romantic idea of "the Queen in her Palace", and as a constitutional monarch she had to accept that decision and prepare to move her family from their home.

This period was almost equally traumatic for Prince Philip. As a husband he was anxious on behalf of his young wife. He feared that she might be asked to do more than she could bear—particularly in the short term when she was coming to grips not only with her new role but also trying to help her mother and grandmother through their mourning. He had always felt the need to protect her; he felt this even more emphatically in February 1952.

One effect of her Accession was to end his hope of a return to the Navy. This was the major sacrifice that he would be called on to make as part of his role of royal Consort, but what exactly that new role involved was far from clear. No one in a position of authority tried to help him understand his new role. On the contrary, every effort seemed to have been made to make his position as untenable as possible; this was made clear to him at the Accession Council of the 8th February.

Originally the Monarch's Privy Council was, as its name suggests, a small group of people who acted as the Monarch's advisers. It was established by Thomas Cromwell in the sixteenth century. He chose a few important members of the much larger King's Council to sit and deliberate with Henry VIII. It was, in Tudor times, the nerve centre of government, took all the important decisions and concerned itself with every aspect of English life. In 1641 Parliament executed the King and, not surprisingly, abolished the Privy Council—the King's Council could hardly exist if there were no monarch.

Nevertheless, tradition-laden England soon found a way to restore this Tudor institution, and it continues to exist today although a pale shadow of its former self. In these days of prime ministerial government, the monarch continues to issue 'orders-in-council' and the Privy Council continues to act as a Court of Appeal for decisions of courts in the

Colonies and some Commonwealth countries. All members of incoming Cabinets have to be sworn in as members of the Privy Council, giving them the right to be known as 'The Right Honourable . . .'. Their appointment is for life, so that today there are about three hundred members entitled to attend meetings, but the convention is that only people who are in the Cabinet—or are non-Cabinet Ministers in the government—attend regular meetings. It is for the Lord President of the Council, a government minister, to issue invitations and agendas for meetings. In its working form the Council meets at least once a month with only four or five members being called to attend.

But for the accession of a new monarch the whole Council is invited to attend. Lord Woolton was Lord President of the Council in the Churchill Cabinet of 1952. He wrote:

> . . . the death of the Monarch [made it] my duty to summon the Privy Council and the Lord Mayor of London and—as the phrase goes—"certain gentlemen of quality" to attend at St James's Palace that same day [6th February] and to be officially informed of the demise of the Crown. Concurrently, they were invited to sign the Roll of Allegiance to the new Monarch. This being done, it was customary for all except the members of the Privy Council to retire and the new Monarch to meet the Council.[2]

This could not be done on the 6th February. On behalf of the Council, Churchill, Attlee and Eden went with Lord Woolton to meet the Queen when she arrived at London Airport on the 7th February, and the whole Council reassembled on the morning of the 8th February for the second part of the ceremony of Accession. In the interval Churchill had broadcast a message to the British people, of which Macmillan, a member of his Cabinet, wrote:

> It was the best piece of prose I have heard or read from him. Some phrases will live long such as "during these last months, the King walked with Death as if Death were a companion, an acquaintance whom he recognized and did not fear. In the end Death came as a friend." His references to the Queen Mother and Queen Mary were very fine. The last sentence was memorable, "I, whose youth was passed in the august, unchallenged and tranquil glare of the Victorian era, may well feel a thrill in invoking once more the prayer and anthem *God Save the Queen*."[3]

It is possible that the historian in him would have compelled Churchill to look up Greville's account of the last Accession Council of a young Queen—that same Victoria to whom he referred in his broadcast. If he did, then he read of:

> . . . the first impression she produced . . . and the chorus of praise and admiration which is raised about her manner and behaviour . . . Her extreme youth and inexperience . . . The first thing to be done was to teach her her lesson, which for this purpose [Lord] Melbourne [Prime Minister] had himself to learn . . . She went through the whole ceremony, *occasionally looking at Melbourne as if for instruction when she had any doubt what to do* . . .[4] (My italics.)

Churchill already knew from his study of history that the young Victoria had come to rely on her first Prime Minister, Lord Melbourne. He may have thought that he might play a similar father-figure part to the young Queen Elizabeth II, but he had some initial doubts about this. "I don't know her," he told his Private Secretary, Jock Colville. "She's a mere child. I knew the King so well."[5] Queen Victoria, after all, was not married when she ascended the throne in 1837. When she did marry, she quickly came to rely on Prince Albert, the Prince Consort. Maybe it occurred to Churchill that the young but married Elizabeth II would rely on her husband, Prince Philip.

On the morning of the 8th February the majority of the Privy Councillors had assembled in the Levee Room at St James's Palace. As the clock struck ten Lord Woolton named a small number, including Churchill and Attlee, to "wait upon Her Majesty" in the Throne Room and to escort her into the Levee Room.

Meanwhile she had been preparing for the ordeal in Clarence House. As many readers will know, this is the next house down the Mall from St James's Palace—which itself was, originally, the Monarch's residence. Indeed, overseas ambassadors are still accredited officially to 'The Court of St James', and a good deal of official state business is carried on at that palace. As a reminder of this there are the crown-topped lamp-posts in the area, and the huge ironwork gates, the aptly named Ambassador's Court, as well as guards and watchful policemen who patrol the area of the Palace and Clarence House. The more one sees of these two houses the more the Queen's suggestion that she should live at Clarence House makes sense.

A minute or two before ten she left Clarence House and walked across the road and cobbled yard to St James's—on the arm of her husband. They had walked together along the banks of the Sagana River when she first received the news of her father's death; they had walked together to and from the various aircraft that had brought them home; he had been her constant companion throughout the long journey and later during that long first night home at Clarence House. So it is hardly surprising that as she walked to face the ordeal of her Accession Council she wanted him to be at her side, to encourage with a touch, a look and a smile—much as her mother had often helped her father through a public ordeal.[6] When they reached the Palace, however, this natural—and, on her part, desirable—arrangement came abruptly to an end. So, at least, I have been forced to conclude, although as I try to show, others deny most of what follows.

In the preparation of this book I met a number of people who were kind enough to give me their help while insisting that they had to remain anonymous. From one such source I learned of the humiliation which the Duke of Edinburgh suffered at St James's Palace. I was told that he was forbidden to enter the Throne Room where Woolton, Churchill and a few others were waiting. The officials handling the Accession ceremony insisted that, constitutionally, he did not exist and had no right to accompany the Queen. Officialdom determined that the Queen should go into the Palace on the arm of her uncle, Henry, Duke of Gloucester—who as a member of the Royal Family had a place in the lists of precedence so loved by the Establishment.[7]

Prince Philip in the meantime, unable to get into the Palace via the front entrance, entered by the back entrance, accompanied by his secretary, Michael Parker. He then made his way to the larger room where the rest of the Privy Councillors were waiting for the Queen to appear. But even here his entrance was marred by another official's initial refusal to allow him in, since, it was argued, only Privy Councillors had been invited. Fortunately for Philip, one of the late King's last acts had been to make him a member of the Privy Council. Maybe the official was unaware of this, but Prince Philip knew and forced his way into the room to take his place with the bulk of the Council.

That, as I say, is the story as given to me by what I have to regard as an unimpeachable, albeit anonymous, source. The person concerned suggested that I write to Michael Parker in the following words:

> In my enquiries about the early days after the death of King George VI I have come across the story that the Duke of Edinburgh, accompanied by you, entered by the back entrance to the Accession Privy Council meeting at St James's Palace, whereas the Queen was accompanied by her uncle, the Duke of Gloucester, through the front entrance. This obviously caused a good deal of talk at the time and I would be grateful if you would just confirm that this is exactly what happened . . .

From Australia Michael Parker wrote to say that I "should talk to—", naming an official who had helped in the organizing of the Accession Council. Parker went on to say that "It may well be that the innuendos that you have been getting are somewhat exaggerated . . ." But, as can be seen, he did not either confirm or deny the story that I had been given.

I then wrote to the now-retired official, using the same form of words as I had used when writing to Michael Parker. The reply, again, was unsatisfactory.

> Together with all the other Privy Councillors present, both His Royal Highness the Prince Philip and the Duke of Gloucester assembled in the Council Chamber in the usual way. Her Majesty the Queen then entered the Council Chamber from the Throne Room alone. Her Majesty was *not* accompanied or escorted by the Duke of Gloucester.

This was *not*, however, an answer to the question as to what had happened *before* she entered the Throne Room—which was the essence of my original enquiry. I pointed this out in a second letter and asked that I be allowed to come to discuss this matter with the retired official. Unfortunately, he replied that "I do not think any useful purpose would be served by a discussion." Nor were the Prince's present staff of any more help. When I asked for a comment on the story, the reply was invariably: "I am not really in a position to provide any useful evidence whatsoever . . ." which leaves all sort of questions hanging in the air. In particular it left me with the question: why does no one deny the story I was given? For no one did—which left me to conclude that, given that the source was unimpeachable, the story was correct. As to why no one denied or confirmed the story I am reminded of something that Robert Lacey wrote in *Majesty*:

> For many good reasons—and a few bad—great secrecy surrounds the Queen; coupled with the extraordinary reverence attached to the most trivial pieces of information that are released about her, it makes chronicling her life an obstacle course beset with booby traps. To anybody else venturing into the field I would suggest inverting a widespread journalistic rule of thumb; if you get information that only one source can confirm, it may possibly be true; if two sources confirm it, tread warily, and the more people who repeat it thereafter, the higher you have risen into the clouds of what the world would like to believe true—and probably isn't.

Emboldened by this advice I have decided to stick to the story which came from that one source.

As to the Accession Council itself, Harold Macmillan wrote:

> The Queen's entrance; the low bows of her Councillors; the firm yet charming voice in which she pronounced her allocution and went through the various ceremonious forms of the ritual (including the oath to maintain the Scottish Church) produced a profound impression on us all. Of course, the effect would have been much more brilliant had we all been in full dress like the Earl Marshal, the High Steward of Westminster (Lord Halifax), and one or two others . . . In contrast our dark coats and striped trousers presented rather a scruffy appearance.[8]

During her speech the young Queen showed "magnificent self-control"[9] while saying:

> On the sudden death of my dear father, I am called to fulfil the duties and responsibilities of Sovereignty . . . My heart is too full for me to say more to you today than that I shall always work, as my father did throughout his reign, to uphold the constitutional government and to advance the happiness and prosperity of my peoples, spread as they are the world over . . . I pray that God will help me to discharge the heavy task that has been laid upon me so early in my life.[10]

Woolton wrote:

> It was deeply moving and emotion might well have taken charge . . .[11]

Churchill, the latter-day Melbourne, and maybe a mainspring in the hostility shown towards the husband of the wife facing "the heavy task . . . laid upon me so early in my life", was very moved. He spoke of "too much care on that young brow".[12] Another Councillor was Oliver Lyttleton who wrote that he "could hardly control my emotions. All the pageantry of the Coronation did not convey so clearly the great burden which the Queen was called upon to carry so early in life", and of the members of her Council suddenly looking "immeasurably old and gnarled and grey".[13] Yet no one thought that she might have been allowed the support of a young, unwrinkled and fair-haired husband. Oliver Lyttleton went on to write:

> The Prime Minister was captivated by his Queen. I often recalled the relations between Disraeli and Queen Victoria and here an equally felicitous relationship was growing, though in a different way and with a very much wider gap in age.[14]

But Lyttleton overlooked the fact that when Disraeli developed his "felicitous relationship" with Queen Victoria she was "the widow of Windsor" while the young Elizabeth II had an active, able and anxious husband. Maybe it would have been more proper to have allowed that relationship to develop rather than promote one between a fading Churchill and a blooming Queen.

After the Council, the Accession was officially proclaimed by the various Heralds Kings of Arms at St James's Palace, Charing Cross, on the steps of the Royal Exchange in the City, and at the Mercat Cross in Edinburgh. As the young Queen made her way back to Clarence House—and her children—she may have heard the sonorous tones ring out:

> We do now hereby, with one voice and consent to Tongue and Heart, publish and proclaim that the High and Mighty Princess Elizabeth Alexandra Mary is now, by the death of the late Sovereign of Happy Memory, become Queen Elizabeth the Second, by the Grace of God Queen of this Realm and of all Her other Realms and Territories, Head of the Commonwealth, Defender of the Faith, to whom her lieges do acknowledge all Faith and Affection, beseeching God, by whom Kings and Queens do reign, to bless the Royal Princess Elizabeth the Second with long and happy years to reign over us.

The young Queen had come through her first ordeal, but hardly unscathed because of the way in which her husband and, indirectly at least, she, had been treated by officialdom. Although she lost the battle over Clarence House—moving to Buckingham Palace during the spring of 1952—she did win one battle. Leastwise she appeared to have done so. On the 30th September 1952 the *London Gazette* carried a notice:

> The Queen has been graciously pleased by Warrant bearing date the 18th instant to declare and ordain that His Royal Highness Philip, Duke of Edinburgh . . . shall henceforth upon all occasions . . . except where otherwise provided by Act of Parliament have, hold and enjoy Place, Pre-eminence and Precedence next to Her Majesty.[15]

She, at least, was determined that he would not be humiliated as he had been at the Accession Council and as he had continued to be in the official prayers of the Anglican Church and at ceremonies where loyal toasts were drunk. In these prayers and toasts the Queen was followed in order of precedence by her mother, Queen Mary, the Duke of Gloucester and so on—with the Duke of Edinburgh coming well down the list. The Queen's announcement was meant to put an end to this public attempt by the Establishment to "keep him in his place".[16] His place, from the 30th September onwards, was to be next to her.

But if "man proposes, God disposes." And in this instance, while the Queen proposed, the Establishment, resplendent in title and uniform, close-knit and protocol-bound, unthinking of the best interests of the Monarch and thoughtful only for its own prerogatives, disposed otherwise.[17] As we shall see, the next nine months after September 1952 were to continue to be months of frustration for the Queen and above all for her husband.

As a footnote, there came, long after I had written this chapter, the episode of the opening of the Battle of Britain Museum at Hendon Airport on the 22nd November 1978. There were, in 1978, only about five hundred surviving members of that "few" of whom Churchill had spoken so feelingly in 1941. They had got together to raise the money needed to fund a museum which would serve to commemorate the exploits of the men who had saved Britain during its "finest hour". On the 22nd November 1978 the Queen Mother went to Hendon to open this museum. The Establishment had assumed responsibility for organizing the opening—having done nothing about providing the money. It had invited only two of the five hundred to attend the ceremony. The invitations went out to politicians—many unborn when the Battle of Britain was fought—and to a variety of dignitaries. But in spite of protests from the RAF and the former airmen's own organization, there was no room at the ceremony for the men whom the museum was meant to honour. The official mind is indeed a peculiar thing. In 1952, 1978—and no doubt in 1981—it is more occupied with the rules of protocol rather than the human.

26

The Family Name

IN THE COURSE OF Chapters 25–28 I am trying to show that there was an organized campaign to exclude Prince Philip from any active role in the new Monarchy. I appreciate that it is possible to become paranoiac about 'conspiracies' and, depending on taste, to blame the Jesuits, the

Calvinists, the Marxists, the Imperialists or Lord Mountbatten for whatever ills one is describing. I hope that I have been able to avoid this danger while examining the events of 1952–1953.

I think it significant that Lord Woolton made no mention of Prince Philip in his *Memoirs.* He was, after all, the Lord President of the Council in Churchill's government and he does have a number of pages devoted to the Queen and the Queen Mother. It might be that he never met Prince Philip, or that his omission of any mention of his name is accidental. It might, however, be a case of a man doing his best to ignore issues and events which if presented might show him in a bad light. For surely no sensible person could now approve of what was done at the Accession Council.

I also think it significant that in the years of Accession and Coronation, the Prime Minister was the dominating and very popular Churchill, remembered even now as the great wartime leader. We have seen that he took a protective attitude towards the new Monarch—modelling himself on the ageing Melbourne, or, some say, the equally ageing Disraeli. Whatever doubts there may be as to who was his model, there can be no doubt about Churchill's attitude. After an audience in 1952 he reported to his colleagues in Downing Street: "What a *very* attractive and intelligent young woman."[1] He was almost as euphoric about his Queen as were those reporters who imagined that they were witnessing the start of a 'New Elizabethan Era' in which, they hoped, Britain would once again emerge as the world's leading nation. On the 11th March 1952 'Chips' Channon went "to the House for the Budget" in which the Chancellor R. A. Butler cut taxes in the first Conservative budget since their victory in the general election in October 1951. Channon went on: "Rab [Butler] had a great triumph . . . a wave of enthusiastic relief has surged over the House and later in the City. There is a new festival spirit aboutl A young Queen: an old Prime Minister and a brave buoyant Butler budget. Has he put us in for a generation?"[2]

The answer to his question was "No", but he was right to draw attention to the "young Queen" and her "old Prime Minister". Each Tuesday evening the Prime Minister went to the Palace to have an audience with his Queen—he agreed to come an hour later than was customary so that she could help bath the children. Churchill enjoyed these audiences which often lasted so long that he was asked to stay for dinner.[3] This gave him an even stronger impression of the important part which he thought he should play in the life of the Monarch.

And if he had any doubts about this there was always his long-time friend, Lord Beaverbrook, to offer advice and guidance. They had been together at Cap d'Àil in 1948 when Churchill had his first stroke; and Beaverbrook was aware that in 1952 the Prime Minister had had a second "arterial spasm" which led to a loss of control of speech for a time. Churchill's doctor, Lord Moran, has told in his diaries that after this second attack Churchill became sluggish and apathetic. Beaverbrook urged him to become a "lazy Prime Minister", to allow his Ministers a free hand and not to try to read all the papers and telegrams that came across his desk.[4] As well as being Churchill's friend and adviser, Beaverbrook was also the bitterest enemy of the Mountbattens—and hence of Prince Philip.

And if there was the brave talk of the 'New Elizabethan Era' there was an 'Old Guard' at the Palace anxious to ensure that little if anything changed. Basil Boothroyd wrote of "crusted old operators at Court, tending the constitutional Juggernaut," who "closed their ranks round it, hoping to rumble on without a lot of tinkering from a newcomer for whom there was literally no place."[5] It was their job, as they saw it, to advise and guide the new Queen and they wanted no interference from a young, energetic consort who might have some ideas of his own, and who, "above all is a Battenberg."[6]

As a sign of the strength of the Palace 'Old Guard' was their treatment of the staff that had served Princess Elizabeth at Clarence House. Her former Private Secretary and the rest were given junior posts at the Palace. Sir Alan Lascelles, her father's Private Secretary, remained at his post, acting as her mentor and adviser; Sir Michael Adeane, the late King's assistant Private Secretary, continued in that post and was groomed to take over from Lascelles when he retired. Then there were the host of men with ancient titles—Keeper of the Privy Purse, Master of the Household, Lord Chamberlain, Master of the Horse and so on—many of whom are entitled to wear what Lacey called "pack-of-card uniforms".[7] One sees these gaily-garbed but "gnarled" men[8] gathering around the young Queen on her throne and presenting a set of hostile faces to the young consort.

He was well aware of what was happening. In 1947 and 1948 he had faced a period of adjustment to marriage. In 1952 and 1953 he went through a much longer period of even greater adjustment. Before the King's death he had had a certain position in his own home, in which he was master to whom people went to ask what had to be done. But after the Accession everything changed. The Household now reported to the Queen and refused to agree with Prince Philip's suggestion that, for some things at least, they might come to him and save the Queen some of the burden of her job. As he argued, when there was a king on the throne, people went to the Queen about some things and she acted as the King's assistant. He went on to argue that, logically, now that there was a queen on the throne he ought to play the role of assistant. But the Establishment would have none of it.[9]

His anxiety to help was not a sign that he was "moving in on the monarchy". It was the natural attitude of an anxious husband who had given up his own career in 1948 and again in 1951 so that he could help his wife in her public work when she was only the Princess. He was surely right in thinking that she needed that help even more now that she was Monarch. As a naval officer he had first been taught and then learned by experience that the commander of the ship does not try to do everything nor does he allow everyone to come to see him about incidentals. He had a chain of command, executive officers of varying grades. Philip saw his role as that of an executive officer who would take some of the day-to-day decisions on Palace life and so allow the Queen the freedom to concentrate on the important constitutional roles which she alone could play.

She certainly had a great deal to do—and to learn, in spite of the training she had received from her father and grandmother. She was an assiduous worker, reading all the documents that she had to sign, all the letters that came from the Foreign Office, and all the Cabinet Papers—so that she was able to catch out Churchill[10] and, later, Wilson[11] when they came for their audiences.

The politicians, however, did their best to help the Palace Guard exclude Philip from affairs. He may have brought something of their hostility on himself, for he has never been able to hide his contempt for the double-talking and devious politicians. "To understand what ministers are saying sometimes, you must buy a gobbledegook dictionary and add an arbitrary ten years to every promise they make."[12] Those of us who have lived through the generation of promises of Utopia only to see it end in economic decline may have some sympathy for his outspoken comment, but it was hardly calculated to endear him to the self-important occupiers of ministerial chairs. In any event he was a Mountbatten, and "no Prime Minister would be caught dead acting 'in accordance with what *he* said'."[13]

He may have thought that the humiliation he suffered at the Accession was a nadir and that he could not fall further. He was wrong, for almost immediately there was the beginning of the campaign to compel the Queen to give up the name she had taken on her marriage—Mountbatten—and to revert again to the name of Windsor. This campaign bears some close examination because of what and who was involved and how it was concluded.

In the Westminster Abbey marriage register the record shows that "Elizabeth Alexandra Mary Windsor" married "Lieutenant Philip Mountbatten". This has to be pointed out, because in 1952 the Home Office declared:

> As a Princess of the Royal Blood there was no occasion for the Queen to use a surname either before or after her marriage and the question [of her surname] is academic . . .[14]

This is manifestly untrue for she did have a surname and she did use it at her marriage. Presumably the constitutional lawyer, Edward Iwi, was right when he wrote:

> At the time of her marriage, Princess Elizabeth, in accordance with the custom followed by all the subjects of King George VI, took her husband's name of Mountbatten.[15]

Now, if "Elizabeth . . . Windsor" had become "Elizabeth . . . Mountbatten" on her marriage, then on her Accession she was the last of the Windsor line and the first of the Mountbatten line. A change of lineage would be nothing new in British history. Queen Elizabeth I was the last of the Tudors, James I the first of the Stuarts. Queen Anne was the last of the Stuarts while Queen Victoria was the last of the Hanoverians. She married after her Accession and her son, Edward VII, took his father's name and was the first of the Saxe-Coburg-Gotha line. We have already seen that during the First World War King George V acknowledged the German name and took steps to change it—to Windsor.[16]

Earl Mountbatten was in no doubt about the position. In *The Mountbatten Lineage* he wrote:

> Princess Elizabeth legally took her husband's name, Mountbatten, on marriage, for there was no legal provision for any female, not even an heir presumptive to the throne, to retain her maiden name on marriage . . .

and he went on:

> . . . she succeeded to the throne as a Mountbatten . . .[17]

But the Establishment, the politicians and their friends, as well as sections of the Press were unwilling to allow this to become the name of the Royal Family. They forced the Queen to change her name. On the 9th April 1952 the *London Gazette* announced:

> The Queen today declared in Council Her Will and Pleasure that She and Her Children shall be styled and known as the House and Family of Windsor, and that Her descendants, other than female descendants who marry, and their descendants shall bear the name of Windsor.[18]

It is worth noting that the Queen referred to *herself* as well as her children. If, as the Establishment argued, she had never had a surname why was it necessary for her, now, to announce that from 9th April she, as well as her children would be named Windsor? She, at least, seemed to have accepted the Mountbatten-Iwi argument that, on marriage, she had changed her name to Mountbatten.

Why did the young Queen accept the arguments of those who urged her to adopt the older family name of Windsor? It may have been an act of filial piety in memory of her father; it may have been a justifiable attempt to show that, although she was a Queen, she intended to carry on the traditions of the Windsor Kings, George V and George VI.

There is evidence that not everyone in the Establishment agreed with the way in which Prince Philip's name was expunged from the royal pedigree—and the way in which the father was deprived of the normal paternal privilege of having his children carry his name. Dermot Morrah was Arundel Herald of Arms Extraordinary, an expert on constitutional usage. He claimed that the ruling "did less than justice to Prince Philip as the progenitor of the dynasty to come."

The pressure for the change seems to have come from the ageing Prime Minister, Winston Churchill. He advised her that "the feeling of his

Government reinforced by public sentiment was that she should drop the Mountbatten name and reign under her father's name of Windsor."[19] He, at least, accepted that she had taken her husband's name in 1947. This was the opinion of Professor Iwi who devoted a good deal of time to a study of the whole affair. Writing in the *Law Journal* in March 1960, he argued:

> This [the Family of Mountbatten] continued for only two months because, it is said, as a result of great pressure by Sir Winston Churchill, a change was made.[20]

There is no obvious explanation of Churchill's attitude. It may have been the result of the influence of Beaverbrook; it may have been an old man's wish to see a tradition maintained—although he had boasted of having lived under the last of the Hanoverians, the first of the Saxe-Coburg-Gothas and the first of the Windsors, so he ought to have been able to accept this latest change. It is difficult to avoid the conclusion that he, along with many others, feared that the use of the Mountbatten name would indicate that the Mountbattens were "moving in on the monarchy".[21] Churchill had 'betrayed' Prince Louis in 1914; it is suggested that his generous treatment of Lord Louis in the Second World War was his attempt to make amends for that earlier failure. But after 1945 he had seen Lord Louis push through the Independence of India. When, in 1951, he came Prime Minister again, one of his first declarations had been "I have not become the King's First Minister to preside over the liquidation of the British Empire." During the earlier debates on Indian Independence Attlee described him as "strongly opposed . . . thought we were being precipitate. The argument always is 'Go slow, and things will get better.' "[22] It is easy to see why Churchill would have become disenchanted with his former protégé and a willing listener to Beaverbrook.

We have seen that when she had gained in confidence the Queen promoted Prince Philip in the order of precedence. On the 8th February 1960, a mere eleven days before the birth of her third child, she tried to put right—at least in part—the damage that had been done in the 1952 decision over the family name. The *London Gazette* announced her decision in Council that:

> . . . while I and my children shall continue to be styled and known as the House and Family of Windsor, my descendants, other than descendants enjoying the style, title or attributes of Royal Highness and the titular dignity of Prince or Princess, and female descendants who marry and their descendants, shall bear the name Mountbatten-Windsor.[23]

By this time Churchill was dead and most of the 'Old Guard' who had surrounded her in 1952 had either retired or died. A Palace spokesman commented: "The Queen has always wanted to associate her husband with their descendants. She has had this in mind for a long time and it is close to her heart."

This was only a small step in the right direction; the Mountbatten name would not stand on its own as it had done for two months in 1952, nor, according to most observers, would the Mountbatten name be used until Prince Charles had two grandsons—only the second of whom would be known by the new name. But even this tentative step on the road to justice was severely criticized. Only the *Daily Telegraph* wrote in favour of the Queen's decision, commenting:

> . . . It was the normal practice of the Queen's subjects that a child uses the name of his father's family, and this personal wish, natural in an expectant mother, had become stronger than ever.[24]

The lower quality Press was highly critical. The *Daily Mirror* asked:

> Is the decision prudent? If it is prudent, is it necessary? If it is necessary, is it well-timed? . . . it is only fifteen years after the Second World War against Germany that the British nation are abruptly informed that the name Mountbatten, formerly Battenberg, is to be joined willy-nilly with the name of Windsor . . . were the Prime Minister and the Cabinet merely informed, or did they agree? . . . Earl Mountbatten was fully aware of what was going on.[25]

The *Daily Mail* sank a little lower in its attack on the declaration

> . . . which will hyphenate the newly-forged Mountbatten name indissolubly with the British Crown, can have brought profounder gratification on to no one more than Earl Mountbatten, son of Prince Louis of Battenberg, whose name did not ring sweetly in British ears, and uncle of Prince Philip . . . certainly the most controversial figure in this forcefully successful family . . .[26]

The Mountbatten name was no more "newly-forged" than was the Windsor name—as the *Daily Mail* may have known. And this attack in 1960 on the memory of Prince Louis—reminiscent of the hysterical attack by the *Globe*, Lord Beresford and others in 1914—was worthy of the *Mail*.

But the longest and most virulent attack on the proposal came from Lord Beaverbrook who had his own 'conspiracy theory'. In the *Daily Express* he wrote:

> While he sat in his office in Whitehall and pondered the problems of defence, or the Navy, or whatever high position he happened to be holding, one spectre has always confronted Earl Mountbatten of Burma; that his family name should finally die out. For he himself has two daughters now both married . . . and he has a nephew who is the Marquess of Milford Haven. And another who holds perhaps the greatest honour and responsibility than any other member of his ancient family. Prince Philip. Small wonder then that Lord Mountbatten, whose devotion to his heritage is little short of fanatical, has for many years nursed a secret ambition that one day the name of the ruling house of Britain might be Mountbatten . . . Within the conclave of the family, Lord Mountbatten has raised the matter more than once; suggested that even if the name of Windsor be retained, the name of Mountbatten might also be included.
>
> Prince Philip was less concerned than his uncle in the future of the name, though he took pains to see that the Prince of Wales should know of his

> heritage. He sent over to German genealogists to secure a complete family tree for Prince Charles to see. Through all this, the Queen remained steadfast in one respect. She could never see the name of Windsor, chosen by her grandfather, abandoned by the royal house. On the other hand, she sympathises with her husband's feelings—and more particularly with the overtures of his uncle. So, the compromise. Her descendants, though not those who stand in direct line to the Throne, shall carry the name Mountbatten-Windsor.[27]

This vicious attack is shot through with error, innuendo and unsubstantiated claims. Lord Mountbatten's name will not "die out". By a Special Remainder it will descend through the female line. Only if we think that Lord Louis organized the chicken-pox/mumps attacks at Dartmouth in July 1939 can we credit him with arranging a marriage—and even then we have to see him, often *in absentia,* influencing the emotions and determination of Princess Elizabeth between 1939 and 1947. It was not only Lord Louis who raised the question of the family name—there was also Dermot Morrah, the constitutional lawyer, Iwi, and others who thought that like all other wives, Princess Elizabeth had taken her husband's name on her marriage. And the prophecy in the last line was as false as the claims in the rest of the passage, for thirteen years later, on the 14th November 1973, Princess Anne married Mark Phillips and signed the register "Anne Mountbatten-Windsor". But perhaps this was the act of a rebel?

27

The First State Opening of Parliament

AS CONSORT OF THE REIGNING QUEEN, Prince Philip has been called upon to play a variety of roles. In one sense the remainder of this book is an examination of different ways in which he has interpreted those roles. In Chapter 32 we will look at the peculiar position of a consort and see how Prince Philip looked to his predecessor, Prince Albert, and his contemporary, Prince Bernhard of Holland as models.

But in this chapter I would like to examine in some detail just one part of the consort's duties, a part which he plays on only one day a year, when the Queen rides to the State Opening of Parliament. This ceremony serves to remind us that today we are ruled by the 'Crown-in-Parliament'. That, at least, is the constitutional theory even if, as we all know, power really lies elsewhere. Where exactly that power may be found is still a matter of constitutional conjecture. Aneurin Bevan, once a member of the radical Left, but by his death a respected member of the hierarchy of the Labour Party, once told the House of Commons of his search for power. His father had told him that he would find it in the local council, but once elected to that body he found that power had fled down the valley to the county council. Having become a county councillor he discovered that this had little real power because, he was told, power now rested in the Commons. So, he told his audience, he became an MP only to find that the constitutional theory was no longer true. For, he declared, power had fled from the Commons. It now rested with the Cabinet.

In the 1960s and 1970s a number of writers, notably Richard Crossman, wrote about "Prime Ministerial Government", arguing that a modern Prime Minister is now so powerful that he has in his hands all the reins of real power. About one third of the ruling party's MPs are office holders, dependent on the Prime Minister for their positions and salaries. Another one third will be eager for a position and so will be amenable to Prime Ministerial persuasion, while the remainder will be bought off by the promise of 'something to be done' for the constituency or interest which they serve. It is the Prime Minister who heads the Inner Cabinet; he alone who has access to all the papers produced by the Cabinet Committees which are today the lynchpin of the constitution. It is he who appoints the Heads of the Civil Service who can assure that the Departmental Heads—of the Treasury, Foreign Office and so on, are men who will not rock the Prime Minister's boat.

But in the late 1970s we saw that the Commons does have some power—to deny Callaghan the sanctions he wanted to give his 5% pay policy some backbone; to cut income tax rates against the wishes of the government and to annul the government's proposal to raise the level of tax on petrol. So the Prime Minister may not, *pace* Crossman, be as powerful as he was thought to be. Indeed, given the way that trade unions have undone a Conservative government (1974) and a Labour government (1979) we may wonder whether a modern Bevan would look now for power in the TUC.

But the theory is that the country is governed by the 'Crown-in-Parliament'. Parliament is the legislature whose main function is law-making. The Crown, in theory, is the head of the Executive which is responsible for putting those laws into effect. The reality is that the Cabinet is now the heart of government. But the ancient convention is honoured and the Cabinet has to be officially described as "Her Majesty's government".

Each Parliamentary session lasts from October to the following

October, when shortly after the summer recess, Parliament is dismissed (or prorogued) by the Queen. At the beginning of each session after a prorogation, or at the first meeting after a general election, Parliament is re-opened by the Queen.

The Sovereign drives in state from Buckingham Palace to the Palace of Westminster, surrounded by a guard of honour drawn from the Household Cavalry. She drives to the House of Lords—which is still called the Upper House, a constitutional position it has not occupied since at least 1911. Having put on her crown in the Robing Room, the Queen then enters the Chamber of the House of Lords surrounded by members of her family and by various members of her official household, many arrayed in their 'pack-of-cards uniforms'. She goes to the Throne set on a dais and waits while the members of "my loyal Commons" are summoned by Black Rod to attend on Her Majesty. The Prime Minister, who leads the troop of MPs from the Commons through the long corridor which links the two Houses of Parliament, most Ministers and some members of the Opposition Front Bench will manage to secure a place at the Bar of the House of Lords from which they can see and hear the Queen. The rest of the six hundred or so MPs will collect in an awkward gaggle along the corridor striving to get as near the front as they can so that they, too, might have a glimpse of the ceremony.

The Queen then reads a speech handed to her by the Lord President of the Council—a leading member of the government. The speech has, in fact, been written by civil servants acting on the advice of the government—their political masters. Each year the speech reads like one produced by a committee which, it is said, if asked to produce a horse would instead give birth to a camel. In stilted phrases the Queen is heard to say that "My ministers will . . ." and that "My government will . . ." thus giving credence to the convention that the Crown plays a significant role in government.

The ceremony was once enjoyed only by the members of the Lords and a few members of the Commons. Today we are all invited to enjoy the colourful occasion since television cameras are allowed into Parliament; they are also present along the road from the Palace to Westminster so that we enjoy, with the crowds along the pavements, the spectacle of the jingling harnesses, the colourful uniforms and the tossing plumes of the guards accompanying Her Majesty in her state coach as she drives through the streets.

What part does the Queen's husband play in such a ceremony? Anyone who has seen a televised State Opening will know that Prince Philip, normally in a naval uniform, enters alongside the Queen following behind the Sword of State carried by a distinguished former soldier. The Prince helps Her Majesty to ascend the four steps leading to the dais where he then sits on a throne alongside Her Majesty seated on a similar throne. To Her Majesty's right, but at floor level, the Prince of Wales sits on an armchair much less splendid than the thrones occupied by his parents.

There seems no reason in logic why the consort should not help his wife up the steps, and sit alongside her as she faces the rows of wigged judges, gowned bishops, ermined lords and the rest. But reason has played little part in official thinking. In 1952 if Prince Philip had had time to make a detailed study of the life of Prince Albert he would have been forewarned of the sorts of arguments that would be used against him. Today Prince Philip sits on a throne while the heir, the Prince of Wales, is relegated to a mere chair and at floor level at that. In 1841 Edward Walpole had written of Victoria and Albert:

> Then again as to Precedence—it is very laudable that she should be attached to her husband and show him all *due* respect. But the Prince of Wales is Heir Apparent to the Crown of these Realms—Prince Albert is utterly without any position in *the State*—therefore that he should take Precedence of the Prince of Wales is flagrantly wrong and unjustifiable . . . If the Queen does not know right from wrong, those about her should set her right, for a Sovereign may not indulge in whims and caprices which would be immaterial in a subject of private station.[1]

In 1952 court officials and "those about her" insisted that the Queen should sit alone on a throne while the consort should occupy the seat which one day would be occupied by the Prince of Wales. That this might offend Queen Elizabeth's feelings or be hurtful to Prince Philip seemed not to have occurred to the Establishment. Nor had anyone given thought to what would happen when, one day, Prince Charles became old enough to occupy the seat set aside for him. What would happen then to Prince Philip? Maybe, like Walpole, the Establishment was trying to show him that, like Albert, he was "utterly without any position . . ."

Prince Albert was, as we know, of German stock. So was Prince Philip with the Battenberg name which "did not ring sweetly in British ears".[2] Albert never managed to get on with the British aristocracy whom "he went out of his way to antagonize and upset".[3] Albert was too well educated to fit easily into the ranks of men who thought more of sport than of mathematics. He had too high an opinion of the value of reason and logic to please the stuffier class which relied on tradition and convention to maintain the social divisions which kept them in a place apart. In 1902 Sidney Lee produced the first authorized biography of Queen Victoria. Of Albert he wrote:

> Outside the domestic circle the Prince was not liked. He was cold and distant in manner, and his bearing, both mental and physical, was held to be too characteristically German to render it acceptable to Englishmen. His temperament was out of harmony with the habitual ease and levity of the English aristocracy.[4]

No one could accuse Prince Philip of being cold or distant in manner. Indeed, some officials thought him too friendly and too unconventional with his practical jokes on his wife[5] and the antics at the children's bathtime.[6] But, like Albert, he had and has a preference for efficient people and a dislike for time-wasting[7]—and there was not a surfeit of efficiency in official circles, while there was a good deal of time-wasting. Maybe, in the eyes of Queen Elizabeth's officials, this was reminiscent of that "characteristically German" manner which had made Albert unpopular.

Like Prince Philip, Albert was made to feel an outsider. He was constantly snubbed by the nobility, most of whom "came from families that were interrelated and knew one another well".[8] In Prince Philip's case the resentment came not so much from interrelated members of upper-class families but from long-serving officials who had served King George VI, knew each other well, had their own conventions and traditions, and who feared that the Battenberg new broom might sweep these aside—much as his uncle was to do with the Defence system in the next few years.

Queen Victoria married Prince Albert in February 1840. In August she drove to the prorogation of Parliament. This was the occasion for two notable storms in official circles. Queen Victoria had discovered that Queen Anne had taken her husband with her in her carriage as she drove through London. Victoria insisted that Prince Albert be accorded the same privilege. Those who thought, with Edward Walpole, that he was "utterly without any position" were outraged. The Master of the Horse was "particularly obstructive".[9] Nor were the opponents made any less obstructive when the Queen won this victory, for she went on to win another, having discovered that Queen Anne's husband had sat by her side while she read the Speech from the Throne. Victoria insisted that there should be a second throne on the dais, "specially built for me" wrote Albert jubilantly.[10] The second throne was built; Albert did sit at Victoria's side—and she considered that she read her speech the better because he was there.[11]

That, one might have thought, would have been sufficient of a tradition to have shown the protocol-minded Establishment what ought to be done when Queen Elizabeth came to open the first Parliament of her new reign. The previous consorts—of Queen Anne and Queen Victoria—had sat alongside their wives as they read their speeches. There were, in any event, already two thrones on the dais where, since 1937, King George VI had sat with Queen Elizabeth to read his speeches.

But the downgrading of the new consort was relentlessly pursued; the second throne was removed and Prince Philip had to sit on the Chair of State. When arguing for her husband's presence at her side Queen Victoria had had the support of her Prime Minister, Lord Melbourne. It was he who had led the research into the way in which Queen Anne's consort had been treated. It was he who had written to the young Queen Victoria to tell her that, in spite of opposition, she could have her husband with her in the carriage and on the dais.[12] But Prince Philip had no such staunch political ally. In 1953 the Queen's Prime Minister was the ageing Churchill. We have seen that he had a romantic view of the young Queen and of his position *vis-à-vis* the new, young monarch. We have also seen that many of his friends—such as Beaverbrook—and many of the members of his party were opposed to Prince Philip.[13] So there was no latter-day Melbourne to come to Philip's aid when he was faced with the opposition of a Court Establishment which advised the Queen in her first uncertain years on the Throne.

John Dean gives us an insight into the way in which the Prince reacted to life at the Palace—and so gives us some understanding of the reasons for the opposition of the Court officials to the newcomer.

> The Duke's forthright views about work in the Palace caused a certain amount of headshaking among some of the older members of the staff. He though that the best way to keep staff to a minimum number was for everyone to do a fair share of work. He also cut across a lot of Palace formalities by walking through the basement passages of the Palace—they are like a rabbit warren—carrying in his own luggage from his car, and calling for any help he required instead of ringing a bell.
>
> The Palace is run a lot more sensibly than it was in the time of Queen Victoria, who, when she wanted a fire in her dining-room, was told by the Master of the Household that it was not his responsibility, as it was the business of the Lord Steward to get the fire laid and the Lord Chamberlain to see that it was lit. But there are still a lot of departments, each responsible for its own job, which no one else must do.
>
> For instance, for even the smallest dinner, when the Queen and the Duke are alone, a man will come up from the glass pantry to put the glasses on the table, another from the silver pantry will attend to the silver, and a third from the china pantry. In fact, it seemed to me, the whole job could have been done very well by one footman. In addition to all this there is one footman responsible for bringing the food from the kitchen, and another on duty to run any errands required by the page who is waiting at table. In all, about six men for one small dinner.[14]

This is a servant's view of the wasteful way in which the Palace was run at his level. There were similarly entrenched positions at higher levels with officials insisting on doing things in the way in which they had always been done. It is little wonder that the efficient-minded Philip, anxious that all should "pull out their fingers", should have clashed with the people in the Household, and they did their best to see to it that he was kept firmly in his lowly place.

Only a handful of officials and Establishment-figures were aware of the struggle taking place over Prince Philip's place in the constitutional life of the country, for in 1952, once the people had got over the death and funeral of the late King George VI, they were bombarded with the preliminaries to the Coronation, fixed for June 1953. 'Chips' Channon caught the spirit of the time in his diary. He wrote:

> *24 November* [*1952*]: People are prattling of the Coronation already, of whom will or will not be summoned, of their robes and places and arrangements. The Dowager Peeresses are nervous lest they are not invited. Members of Parliament too, are in a ticklish position. In fact, conversation has taken on a Gilbert and Sullivan quality. Coaches and robes, tiaras and decorations. Winnie Portalington announced at luncheon that she has harness but no coach; Circe Londonderry has a coach but no horses; Mollie Buccleuch has

no postillions—but five tiaras. People are obsessed by their Coronation prerogatives. There is something unreal about it.

26 January [*1953*]: The fashionable complaint is now known as Coronation Thrombosis. People talk of nothing else, except who is and who is not "Abbey Happy" and people prattle all day about places, tiaras, coaches, postillions, robes and coronets. One peer, who had been divorced, suggested to the Earl Marshal that he feared he would be ineligible for a place in the Abbey; the reply is said to have been "Of course you will; this is the Coronation, not Ascot."[15]

28

From Accession to Coronation

'CHIPS' CHANNON JOKINGLY NOTED THE onset of "Coronation Thrombosis". On the official level, the preparations for the Coronation began within days of the funeral of King George VI. The Ministry of Public Works set up a Coronation Committee and the first of its weekly meetings took place late in February 1952. At a more frivolous level, the Press began to speculate on the date of the Coronation. The *Empire News* had a headline: "Coronation on August 7". The *News of the World* predicted: "Early Coronation Prospect". In fact it was June 1952 before the young Queen fixed on 2nd June 1953 as the date on which she would be crowned. There would not be an "Early Coronation". Maybe the *News of the World* had been misled by the short period which elapsed between her father's Accession and his Coronation. This had been an accidental result of the abdication of Edward VIII. George VI was crowned on the day originally set by his brother when he had ascended the Throne. The sixteen-month gap between the Queen's Accession and her Coronation was not unusually long. It provided sufficient time for the official mourning for the death of George VI, for various committees and organizations to supervise the works they had to undertake—such as the building of the miles of stands in and near the Abbey—and for foreign guests to fit the date into their own timetables.

In the autumn of 1952 the Government recognized Prince Philip's changed position by granting him an annual allowance of £40,000 subject to income tax. This was only £10,000 more than had been granted, tax-free, to Prince Albert, Victoria's consort, and was one more example of official meanness. King Peter of Yugoslavia met him after the funeral of King George VI and noted: "It was as if a volcano had been stoppered up. I don't know how long he can last . . . bottled up like that."[1] It is one of the objects of the remainder of this book to demonstrate that the "volcano" did remain "bottled up"—or, at least, that the energy in the "volcano" was diverted to worthwhile fields so that there was no untoward explosion.

But even this miserly allowance became the subject of criticism—in Labour Party circles and in some sections of the Press. Even more undeserved was the criticism levelled at the Prince about the new royal yacht *Britannia*. One politician named this a "costly toy", while another labelled it "Philip's Folly". In fact the proposal to build a new yacht as a replacement for the old and unseaworthy *Victoria and Albert* had been made early in 1951 long before Prince Philip had any say in such matters.

The inflation from which Britain had suffered since 1945 was the main cause of the increase in costs from the estimated £1,750,000 to the £2,139,000 the yacht cost before it was launched. But the critics preferred to blame the new consort.

John Dean, Philip's valet for many years, found that he could not stand the pressures of life at the Palace. He decided to leave to rejoin Lord Mountbatten's staff. Later he wrote:

> Of course I took the first opportunity of mentioning my intention to the Duke. When I told him, he asked whether I had thought about what I was doing. I said "Yes," and explained that I did not think I could adapt myself to the ways of the Palace permanently, for all the years that remained of my working life. He said, "It affects us all, this new life, and we should at least give it a fair trial. But if you feel you are going to be happier elsewhere, John, I quite understand."[2]

This was the view of an employer who had his own difficulties in adapting to "the ways of the Palace" but for whom there was no chance of "going to be happier elsewhere". He was now the spider in the official web—of protocol and tradition. As evidence of this was his sudden promotion to the position of Admiral of the Fleet. This came early in 1953—too late to prevent the distribution and sale of thousands of pictures, mugs and other Coronation souvenirs showing him in the uniform of a commander. Later he was granted the dignities of Field Marshal and Marshal of the Royal Air Force; the man who might have made it on his own[3] had been advanced to these high positions because protocol demanded that this should be so.

In March 1953 a symbol, indeed almost a part, of that tradition died. Queen Mary, the Dowager Queen, had sat in her sitting-room with Lady Airlie to watch the funeral procession of George VI going up the Mall. Lady Airlie wrote:

> We sat alone at the window, looking out into the murk and gloom. As the cortège wound slowly along the Queen whispered in a broken voice, "Here *he* is," and I knew that her dry eyes were seeing beyond the coffin a little boy in a sailor suit. She was past weeping. My tears choked me. We held each other's hands in silence.[4]

But within a few weeks, the aged Queen's grief for her son-King was "sublimated in loyalty to the new Sovereign . . . by the end of May 1952 she was already occupied with plans for the Coronation of Queen Elizabeth II . . ."[5] However, on 24th March 1953 the old Queen died. The Duke of Windsor attended the funeral—but was not invited to the family dinner at Windsor on March 31st,[6] a little more than a year after the funeral of King George VI. Prince Philip's cousin, Alexandra, thought that "It was as if a new reign, the new Elizabethan era, were being tidied up and freed from all the furbishments of the old."[7]

Not all the old world was swept away. Indeed, within a month Prince Philip participated in a ceremony which reminded him, if he needed reminding, of the tradition surrounding the Throne and of one of the strongest upholders of that tradition, Winston Churchill. On the 24th April 1953 Churchill was given the Order of the Garter by the Queen at Windsor. As 'Chips' Channon noted in his diary: "What a romantic picture—the aged Prime Minister kneeling at the feet of the young Queen; like Melbourne and Queen Victoria."[8] But Victoria was not married when Melbourne first knelt at her feet and, indeed, when she did marry Prince Albert, it was Melbourne who went out of his way to help her and the consort to win their victories over the Establishment. Churchill was no Melbourne to Philip's Albert.

The young Queen found herself surrounded by her father's advisers and officials. She also found herself deluged with a welter of public work—documents to read and sign, audiences to be granted, ministers to be received and so on.

For the Queen the first year or so of her new reign were the busiest she had ever known. We have already noted that although she had been trained by her father, there was a deal of difference between doing things under his supervision and tackling the same tasks on her own, and, because of the constitutional position and the prickliness of her advisers, she could not turn to her husband for help and advice. She was guided by Sir Alan Lascelles, the late King's Private Secretary, Sir Piers Legh, his Master of the Household and Sir Ulick Alexander, the Keeper of the Privy Purse. Under their guidance and that of her Prime Minister, Sir Winston Churchill, she spent long hours studying documents, signing royal warrants and Parliamentary Bills. She had to sign hundreds of official portraits, carry out numerous public engagements, and receive the steady stream of official visitors who came to pay their respects to the new Sovereign.

Increasingly she found herself separated from her husband, no longer free to drive out to watch him play polo as she had been when they lived in Malta. But she had the sense to realize that there was a danger that he might not have enough to do while she was being guided in her new role. It was she who appointed Prince Philip to a number of offices which gave him some chance to spend his energies. One, which "caused some little amusement among his relatives",[9] was that of Ranger of Windsor Great Park. The Queen gave him the powers to introduce schemes to reorganize and modernize the royal estates. He examined the way in which the estates at Windsor and Sandringham were being run. He showed a quick grasp for essential detail of things such as estate management of which he had no experience, and many changes were made at his suggestion. One result was that Sandringham, for example, ceased to be the drain on the Queen's purse that it had been on her father's.

He also set about the modernization of Buckingham Palace. He produced a scheme for a small, modern kitchen on the same floor as the royal apartment—which John Dean would have welcomed if he had still been at the Palace—but the Duke failed to persuade officials that it would be economic for the Palace to have its own laundry and bakery; the capital cost, it seems, would have been too great. He supervised the installation of a modern system of central heating, brought electric typewriters and tape recorders into the royal offices and radio telephones in royal cars.

The Queen appointed Prince Philip chairman of the Coronation Committee—the first time that a Queen Regnant had appointed her husband to be "general manager of her Coronation".[10] The Commission set up the smaller working Coronation Committee which was controlled by the Duke of Norfolk, the hereditary Earl Marshal, and who was the grand strategist of the ceremony. Prince Philip's commission also helped to link the Commonwealth with the ceremonies and celebrations surrounding the Coronation.

Prince Philip got on very well with the Duke of Norfolk, already a close friend of the Queen because of their joint interest in horse racing. He enjoyed the task of tackling the specialized sort of organization surrounding the traditional ceremonial of the Coronation. He studied the descriptions of previous coronations, followed the traditions when this seemed best—but suggested changes when it seemed valid. He had a certain advantage at meetings of the Commission for he acted as the Queen's spokesman. Few of the members of the Commission dared stand out against a suggestion preceded by the words, "I know the Queen would want us to do . . ."

The Queen also appointed him a member of the Court of Claims which had to examine petitions by all those who claimed an historic right to perform special services for the Queen at her crowning. This Court consisted of the Lord Chancellor (President), the Lord Chief Justice of England and the Lord Justice General of Scotland, the Lord Chief Justice of Northern Ireland, the Master of the Rolls, a former Lord Chancellor and a Lord of Appeal, the Duke of Norfolk—and the young Duke of Edinburgh. It was this Court which had to agree that the Dean and

Chapter of Westminster Abbey had the right to "instruct the Queen in the rites and ceremonies, to assist the Archbishop of Canterbury, and to retain the robes and ornaments of the Coronation in the vestry of the Collegiate Church of St Peter in Westminster . . ." The Court also agreed that the ceremony should be performed by the Archbishop of Canterbury, "supported" by the Bishop of Durham and the Bishop of Bath and Wells, while the Barons of the Cinque Ports had the right to bear the canopy over the Queen. Lord Hastings and Lord Churston won the right to bear the Golden Spurs but the Duke of Newcastle lost his claim as Lord of the Manor of Worksop that he should present the embroidered Glove which the Queen wore on her right hand while holding the Sceptre and Orb. At the Coronation this Glove was presented by Lord Woolton, the Chancellor of the Duchy of Lancaster.

The Court had to decide who should carry the Orb, the Sceptre and Cross—and even a towel to be used by the Queen. The legal wrangling over these and other claims ensured that the Duke became fully aware of the weight of tradition and the importance which the Establishment attached to it.

This Court met at intervals after October 1952 in the oak panelled room of the Judicial Committee of the Privy Council in Downing Street. Prince Philip was thus walking in "the corridors of power" as a member of this prestigious body. The Queen also appointed him President of the Committee to advise the Royal Mint on the design of the new seals, coins and medals of the realm. This introduced him to the work of a number of artists—and proved to be a stepping stone to his work at the Industrial Design Centre.

As the date of the Coronation approached he was pleased to discover that relations between Germany and Britain had eased to the point where his three sisters with their husbands and children could be officially invited to the Coronation of their sister-in-law. They stayed at Buckingham Palace and the Queen arranged a family dinner party to celebrate the reunion.

But, as if to remind him of his peculiar constitutional position, there was a debate over whether he should have a separate coach, ride alongside the Queen's coach, or ride inside that coach. There was no precedent to which anyone could turn. Queen Victoria had been crowned before her marriage to Albert and Queen Anne had been carried to the Abbey in a chair. Her consort had walked—some say tottered—just ahead of the nobles carrying the Regalia.[11] This debate was happily resolved and, as the photographs show, the Duke travelled with the Queen, taking great care at the Abbey door to ensure that her train bearers had everything right before the procession set off into the Abbey.

Prince Philip realized that the preparations for the Coronation would not be sufficient to occupy his energies and time. In any event, these calls on his time would come to an end after June 1953. So after the Accession he started to carve out a niche for himself. He undertook a series of visits to Lancashire coalfields, industrial workshops, research laboratories and the like. In Lancashire, miners banged their mugs in approval when they found him sharing their everyday lunch about two thousand feet below the ground. This was typical of the novel way in which he tackled his job. Before undertaking a visit he found out enough about the place—mine, workshop, factory, laboratory, town or school—so that he could ask intelligent questions as he went on the royal round.

The Queen approved of his proposal to take up flying, so that he could get his pilot's licence before taking up the appointment of Air Marshal. The Prime Minister was opposed to this suggestion—in spite of the argument that it would save time on one-day engagements. But when it was pointed out that both King Edward VIII and King George VI had acquired their pilot's licences, and that Prince Bernhard of the Netherlands also held a licence, Churchill gave in. So in November 1952 Prince Philip began his training in a Chipmunk at White Waltham. He made his first solo flight on the 20th December and two months later he transferred to heavier and faster planes. His final handling test was in April 1953 and on the 4th May 1953 the royal pilot received his wings in a ceremony at Buckingham Palace. A week before the Coronation he flew, by helicopter, from the lawns of Buckingham Palace to a review of Commonwealth troops at Pirbright.

During May 1953 there were regular rehearsals for the Coronation ceremony. Everyone arrived at the rehearsals with their individual plans prepared for them by the Garter King of Arms. As in the making of a film, the rehearsals took place in separate parts, not always in the order in which they would happen on the great day itself. This gave some people the impression that chaos would ensue in June.[12] What was happening inside the Abbey had also to be co-ordinated with what would happen outside. Seven separate processions had to reach the Abbey and pass up the Nave to their places before the arrival of the Queen and the Duke of Edinburgh. These various members of the royal family, foreign royals and representatives of foreign governments had to be marshalled and escorted by the Heralds and Pursuivants through the five long lines of people already waiting in their places. There would have been a great tangle of confusion if there had been any delay. While these processions were coming to the Abbey from one direction there had to be a procession of the clergy from the other direction. The bishops were slow to learn their parts. After several rehearsals the Duke of Norfolk shouted, "If those bishops don't learn to walk in step we'll be here all night!"[13]

The Queen and Prince Philip attended some of the rehearsals. The Queen had to practise the difficult descent from the Throne Chair. At one rehearsal Prince Philip had to kneel before his wife to swear that he would become "Your liege man of life and limb and of earthly worship, and faith and truth. I will bear unto you to live and die against all manner of folks. So help me God." In the cold atmosphere of a rehearsal the Prince mumbled his words as quickly as possible and jumped up, to give the crown a flip of the hand and to kiss the air about a foot from the Queen's cheek. It was the young Queen who called out, "Come back, Philip, and do it again—properly."[14]

This is not meant to be an account of the Coronation. This has been more than adequately covered in *When the Queen was Crowned* by Brian Barker, OBE, one of the civil servants responsible for its organization. Millions of people watched the ceremony on television—but only after great public protest had forced the Earl's Committee to reverse its original decision that "still photography will be allowed within Westminster Abbey during the ceremony. Live television will be restricted to the procession west of the choir screen."[15]

Few viewers failed to be impressed by the religious nature of the ceremony in which the young Queen was consecrated by the Archbishop of Canterbury and in which, it seemed, she consecrated herself to her new role. This was not surprising to those who recalled the broadcast made by the twenty-one-year-old Princess Elizabeth. Speaking from South Africa on the 21st April 1947 she had declared:

> I declare before you all that my whole life, whether it be long or short, shall be devoted to your service and the service of the great Imperial Commonwealth to which we all belong.[16]

She had renewed this promise to serve at her Accession Council when she said:

> My heart is too full for me to say more to you today than that I shall always work, as my father did throughout his reign, to uphold constitutional government and to advance the happiness and prosperity of my peoples . . . I pray that God will help me to discharge worthily the heavy task that has been laid upon me so early in life.[17]

In her first Christmas broadcast she had spoken of the forthcoming Coronation:

> Pray for me on that day. Pray that God may give me wisdom and strength to carry out the solemn promises I shall be making.[18]

So it is not surprising to read that the "sense of spiritual exaltation that radiated from her was almost tangible."[19]

No one seemed to feel this sense of the Queen's "spiritual exaltation" more than Prince Philip. After he made his oath of fealty, he rose to kiss his wife. As he did so his cloak seemed to fall, naturally, around her as if he were indicating that he would act as protector and guardian of this young Queen-wife. But, as we shall see, he would be faced with many problems while trying to play that role.

Part VII

AS BROTHER-IN-LAW AND FATHER

29

Prince Philip, Princess Margaret and Peter Townsend

FOLLOWING THE CORONATION SERVICE THE QUEEN, Prince Philip and other members of the Royal Family went to an annex in the Abbey for a picnic-type lunch of smoked salmon, foie gras, cheese and biscuits.[1] Among those in the royal party was Group Captain Peter Townsend, Comptroller of the Household of the Queen Mother. Few of the general public knew him and even none of these were aware of the important part he was to play in the lives of the Queen and Prince Philip during the next two or three years.

But as the Royal Family waited in the entrance to Westminster Abbey for their carriages to come to take them back to the Palace, cameramen and reporters were quick to spot the way in which Princess Margaret brushed her hand along his row of medals. Donald Edgar, a noted reporter, said, "At first I thought this slight man in RAF uniform was a member of the Royal Family", because of the way he held out his hands to the Princess and she almost fell into his arms in a half-embrace.[2]

Photographs and reports of this incident appeared in the foreign Press. As in 1936 the British Press remained silent—but only for two weeks. Then the *People*, outlining the stories in the foreign Press, argued:

> The story is of course utterly untrue. It is quite unthinkable that a royal princess, third in line of succession to the throne, should even contemplate a marriage with a man who has been through the Divorce Courts.[3]

Little did they know.

The Townsend affair began when King George VI appointed Equerries of Honour to his Household Staff to show his admiration for the bravery of young servicemen. One of those appointed was Wing Commander Peter Townsend, DSO, DFC and Bar, one of "those few" who had won the Battle of Britain.

He quickly won a special place at the Palace, largely because he proved able to calm the easily-angered King who came to rely on the discreet support which Townsend gave him. The King admired his ability to organize the day's timetable during the last hectic weeks of the war. As an indication of the King's approval, Townsend and his wife were given a grace-and-favour home next to Windsor Castle. The King gave a second mark of his approval when he stood as godfather to Townsend's second child. It was hardly surprising that the fourteen-year-old Princess Margaret tended to hero-worship the man whom her father admired and who became, in one sense, a member of the family.

Townsend was a well-established figure in the Royal Household by 1946 when Prince Philip began to pay regular visits to the Palace. The two men did not get on. One writer says that when they "brushed against each other it was like ice floes passing on the Arctic".[4] Both of them were attractive; one had the ear of the King, the other had the heart of his daughter; one was a naval officer, the other an officer in a younger but proud service.

There were, however, more solid reasons for the clashes between the two men. Townsend was a confidential aide to the King and advised him to delay an announcement of an engagement. Philip is reported to have exploded: "What a cheek, for a man who was already heading for a break-up with his wife to set himself up as a marriage counsellor . . ."[5] And even when it became clear that Princess Elizabeth would not be daunted, it was Townsend who suggested that the young couple be separated early in 1947 by the royal tour of South Africa.

Townsend helped to organize that tour when, once again, his efficiency won the praise of both the King and Queen who told him, "I don't know what we'd do without you, Peter."[6] The arduous tour lasted for nine weeks when the royal party covered six thousand miles. Townsend proved to be an admirable companion for the two Princesses and especially for Princess Margaret. The elder sister, after all, saw the tour largely as an enforced separation from her fiancé.

During the King's periods of illness, after 1948, the Queen tended to turn to Townsend for the male support which she needed, confirming his position as an important member of the staff. In 1952 the Queen Mother drew on her own inner resources to overcome the traumatic effects of the King's death. Princess Margaret was equally affected by the death of the King who had spoiled her as a child and with whom she shared a boisterous sense of humour. It is not surprising that she turned to Townsend for that mature male companionship which her father had once provided. When the Queen Mother and Princess Margaret moved into Clarence House, Townsend, now a Group Captain, moved with them to take charge of the running of what had to be at one and the same time, a home, an office, and a State establishment. As one of the Queen Mother's present staff explained: "He had seen how the Palace was run and not many people had that experience."[7] One side effect of this appointment was that Townsend's marriage broke up. In December 1952 he obtained a divorce on the grounds of his wife's misconduct.

Up until this time no one seems to have noticed anything special or untoward in the relationship between Townsend and Princess Margaret. Indeed, on reflection, no one seems to have paid much attention to the development of Princess Margaret at all. Her father had spoilt her when she was young; Queen Mary had found her "so outrageously amusing that one can't help encouraging her"[8] and everyone had laughed at the ability of the mimic and piano-playing leader of family get-togethers. But no one had thought of the part which she might play in the life of the 'royal firm'. There was a defined role for Princess Elizabeth which tended to separate the sisters from one another. Her marriage in 1947 left Princess Margaret even lonelier than she had been. It is perhaps not surprising that given her character and other people's failure to plan a role for her, she should have found her friends among actors, music hall entertainers and others connected with the theatre. 'Chips' Channon met her at Ascot in 1949 and in a moment of perception noted: "Already she is a public character and I wonder what will happen to her."[9] What happened was that she fell in love with Peter Townsend, who, after his divorce, was free to re-marry. Some people in royal circles, then and now, blame the much older Townsend for having allowed the matter to develop to that point. John Dean shared the view of most members of the staff who watched what seemed to be a ripening friendship. ". . . Our view was that it would be regrettable if a man in Mr Townsend's position allowed Princess Margaret's interest to grow into anything stronger than the friendly feeling which would naturally exist between them, meeting as often as they were bound to do."[10] Others, more highly placed, told Townsend that he was "either mad, or bad, or both".

In April 1953, a few weeks before the Coronation was due to take place, Princess Margaret told her mother that she intended to marry Peter Townsend. However, she was bound by the Royal Marriages Act of 1772 to ask her sister's permission to marry. This Act laid down that no descendant of King George II could marry under the age of twenty-five without the Sovereign's consent. But it ran on:

> . . . in case any descendant of George II, being above twenty-five years old, shall persist to contract a marriage disapproved of by His Majesty, such descendant, after giving twelve months' notice to the Privy Council, may contract such marriage and the same may be duly solemnized without the Consent of his Majesty . . .[11]

The new Queen, deeply involved with the plans for her Coronation, was presented with a major problem which had overtones of 1936 about it. We do not know her private attitude towards her sister's plans to marry a divorced and older man. Happy in her own marriage she may have wanted to allow her sister to marry the man of her choice. She and the Queen Mother knew and liked Townsend, and may have thought him a suitable partner for the younger Princess. But since the Royal Marriages Act is a statute, the Queen had to ask her Prime Minister to tell her what answer she should make to her sister's request. In 1936 Winston Churchill had wanted the government to allow Edward VIII to marry the "woman he loves". In 1953, as Prime Minister, he told the Queen that a marriage between her sister and a divorced commoner was impossible. The required permission should not be given; the Princess should be told to wait for two years when, under the terms of the 1772 Act, she would be free to marry without the Queen's consent. The Queen was constitutionally bound to follow this advice. She was not, however, obliged to accept her Prime Minister's suggestion that Townsend should be dismissed from Clarence House and sent abroad on some government mission or other. This explains why Townsend was with the Princess at her sister's Coronation in June 1953.

The Press speculation about Princess Margaret's possible marriage tended, in Prince Philip's opinion, to diminish and threaten the dignity of the Crown.[12] He was fully aware of 1936 and the effect that the Abdication had had on the Monarchy. He did not want the first years of his wife's reign to be clouded by a new controversy which would open up old wounds. He was in favour of a radical solution and was "against pussy-footing".[13] It was he who had suggested that the couple should be separated—not temporarily as he and his wife had been in 1947, but more permanently. This, he believed, would soon bring the two lovers to their senses.

Townsend had been due to travel with the Queen Mother and Princess Margaret to Southern Rhodesia after the Coronation. The Prime Minister advised the Queen that he should be sent abroad as an air attaché to a British Embassy of his choice and that he and Princess Margaret, while free to write to each other, had to promise that they would not meet for a year and that they would meet after that only "in circumstances of absolute discretion". So it was that Princess Margaret travelled to Southern Rhodesia with her mother while Townsend went to the British Embassy in Brussels.

Prince Philip's constitutional position was affected by the controversy over Princess Margaret. Under the Regency Act 1937 she was "the person, twenty-one years or older, who was next in succession to the Throne . . ." who should have become Regent in the event of the Queen's death while Prince Charles was still under the age of eighteen. Although Prince Charles had been born in 1948, no one had done anything about changing the terms of the 1937 Act. But in 1953 Churchill advised the Queen that Princess Margaret had forfeited her right to this position. He proposed a new Regency Act (1953). In support of this the Queen sent a message which was read in the Commons by the Home Secretary, Sir David Maxwell-Fyfe (later Lord Kilmuir). She wrote:

> The uncertainty of human life leads me to put you in mind of the possibility that a child of myself and my dear husband may succeed to the Throne whilst under the age of eighteen years. And I would recommend to your consideration whether it be no expedient to provide that, in that event and also in the event of a Regency becoming necessary during my lifetime, whilst there is no child or grandchild of ours who can become Regent, my husband should be the Regent and be charged with the guardianship of the person of the Sovereign.

In retrospect it seems very sensible to have the father of the future monarch as Regent. But it is doubtful if Prince Philip would have attained that position if it had not been for Princess Margaret's unfortunate behaviour in 1953.

In my book, *The Queen Mother*, I have outlined the way in which the Townsend affair developed and shown how it soured relationships inside the Royal Family. The Queen Mother believed that her late husband would not have wanted a marriage between his younger daughter and the divorced Townsend—so she opposed it. The Queen herself was torn between wanting the happiness of a sister who had supported her during the testing days before her own engagement was allowed—and fearing that a Margaret–Townsend marriage would have overtones of 1936 about it and would be a poor way in which to begin a new reign. Prince Philip, not surprisingly, supported the Queen in her opposition which, personal feelings apart, was forced on her by the advice she received from Prime Minister Eden.

Eden gave the Queen his advice during a visit to Balmoral on 1st October 1955—a few weeks after Princess Margaret's twenty-fifth birthday. The Prime Minister pointed out that the Princess might wait for a year when she would only have to give notice to the Privy Council of an intention to marry and would not be bound by the terms of the Royal Marriages Act. But, the Prime Minister explained, Parliament would have to debate the application to the Privy Council and while it was likely that it would accept the Princess's right to marry the man of her choice, it would in all probability object to the Princess retaining her royal status and her allowance under the Civil List. Indeed, Parliament might advise the Monarch that the Princess and her husband should live abroad.

No one knows for sure what part the various arguments played in driving the young Princess to the decision she reached and announced on 31st October 1955. The cynics will argue that she was unwilling to sacrifice her position and income for marriage; the more charitable will point to the fact that on 25th October she had had an interview with the Archbishop of Canterbury and, they will claim, was made to realize that as the sister of the Head of the Established Church she could not go through with her plan. Others will suggest that she found it impossible to resist the arguments of the Queen Mother and the Queen, both of whom called on the memory of her late father. But whatever the reasons, the decision was final; there would be no marriage to Townsend who published his own account of the affair in 1978.[14]

30

Prince Philip, Princess Margaret and Lord Snowdon

IN 1955 THE POPULAR PRESS tried to show that the Archbishop of Canterbury, Dr Fisher, had played a major role in the matter of Princess Margaret's decision not to marry Peter Townsend. Headlines such as "The Archbishop Must Go" and "The Archbishop Has Gone Too Far" with their apparent contradictions enabled him to find "some humour in the situation".[1] In fact the Archbishop had played no immediate part in the Princess's decision-making as he made clear in an interview with Richard Dimbleby on television.[2] Randolph Churchill came to the Archbishop's support in a long article in the *Spectator* on the 23rd May 1957, long after the matter should have been allowed to fade away. Churchill showed that the Princess had arrived at her decision on her own and that she went to see the Archbishop at Lambeth Palace on the 27th October 1955 merely to inform him of her decision. Churchill, gilding the lily in the hope that this would help his case, had Princess Margaret say, "Archbishop, you may put your books away; I have made up my mind already." In fact, as the Archbishop said, "I had no books of any sort spread around. The Princess came and I received her, as I would anybody else, in the quietness of my own study. She never said, 'Put away those books' because there were not any books to put away."[3]

There were, of course, a number of forces working against Princess Margaret in 1955. The Eden government, and in particular Lord Salisbury, represented a powerful political force which was opposed to the proposed marriage. It is likely that the Princess had been informed that in the event of such a marriage she would lose not only the £15,000 to which she was entitled on marriage, but even the £6,000 a year she was paid as a single person. The arguments of the politicians were reinforced by the attitudes of leading members of the Royal Family—the Queen, Prince Philip and the Queen Mother. They did not want the first years of the new reign to be tarnished with the public controversy which would inevitably follow such a marriage, particularly if the government took a strong line against it. The family name would be dragged into the public arena, the wounds of the Abdication would be re-opened and the Queen as Supreme Governor of the Church of England would find herself in an embarrassing position if her sister flouted the laws of that Church and married a divorced person.

The Queen had let her sister know that she was opposed to the proposed marriage and she, in riposte, turned to attack Prince Philip. She told the Queen about the rumours of his involvement in a car accident while driving an unnamed lady—a rumour which had no substance in fact.[4] She repeated other rumours about Prince Philip's close friendship with the photographer, Baron, and the supposed goings-on at the photographer's studio in Park Lane. Other rumours to which the angry Princess gave credence in her rage concerned the Thursday Club of which the Prince and Baron were members. This met at Wheeler's Oyster Bar in Soho every Thursday for a private lunch. The Princess suggested that the "harmless frolics" in which the Club's members indulged were distasteful to say the least.

This was merely malicious gossip and there was no evidence to buttress the rumours. The Queen was angry at her sister's retailing of such gutter gossip and for more than a year there was a breach in their relationship. This was only healed when the Queen went out of her way to show that the Princess was back in favour in the summer of 1956. But Prince Philip, the subject of these rumours, felt a deeper resentment against the Princess whom he condemned for not having the sense to see where her public duty lay—*vis-à-vis* her sister as an individual and as Queen.

The popular Press had been robbed of its prey when the Princess decided not to marry Peter Townsend in which Prince Philip played only a background role. There was little Press speculation on his part in the controversy and no mention of his conflicts with the two major players in that drama. But the Press, robbed of its opportunity in 1955, was soon on its Royal-baiting trail in 1957—and this time the Prince was at the eye of the storm.

He had been invited to open the Olympic Games in Australia in October 1956. He took advantage of the chance to visit a number of other Commonwealth countries during the journey to and from Australia. During his trip of almost forty thousand miles he travelled partly by air and partly in *Britannia* with his secretary, Michael Parker, as his constant companion. During the tour he visited not only Australia and New Zealand but St Helena and Ascension Island whose people had never before seen a royal visitor. He sailed in the research ship *John Biscoe* down through the Antarctic to visit twelve of the research bases in that cold continent.

As he sailed home in January 1957 he had a right to feel that he had done a good job. Then shortly after *Britannia* had left Gambia came British newspaper reports that Mrs Michael Parker was going to divorce the Prince's secretary and close friend; because of the Queen's well-publicized attitude towards divorce, Parker felt that he had to resign immediately. He left *Britannia*—and a bitter Philip who felt deeply the loss of the man with whom he had had a close relationship for many years.

Back in London the rumour-mongers and the Mountbatten-haters gave support to the tittle-tattle that Parker and the Prince had indulged in wild parties—without being able to present any evidence of such goings-on. There were stories about Wheeler's Bar and Baron's studio, to which Princess Margaret had referred in 1955. And there were people who transposed the difference between Parker and his wife into a difference between the Prince and his wife. Of such things are rumours born. None of the British papers printed any of these wild stories, but American newspapers have less regard for people and face fewer and looser libel laws than do their British counterparts. So the London correspondent of the *Baltimore Sun* won himself a moment of glory by sending back a story that London was "seething with rumours" of a serious row between the Queen and the Duke of Edinburgh.[5] His story began "The whisper started last summer . . ."[6] without stating who started the whisper or on what evidence. Other American papers sent their reporters to dredge up what stories they could. It was hardly surprising that one inventive journalist hit on the notion that the Prince's long trip to and from Melbourne had been in the nature of a punishment, claiming that he had been "got out of the country to cool off".[7] Each succeeding report piled another falsehood on the existing tissue of rumour. In *Scoop* Evelyn Waugh has shown how competing newspapers fabricated an African war to satisfy their owners and to drive up their circulations. Much the same happened with American newspapers during January 1957.

None of this was known to British readers until a reporter from the Associated Press in London telephoned Buckingham Palace to ask a Press Officer for his view on the American stories. It was unfortunate that the Press Officer was hardly up to his job. Instead of referring the matter to someone who might have had the gumption to deal with the Americans as they deserved, he issued a statement: "It is quite untrue that there is any rift between the Queen and the Duke of Edinburgh."[8]

This gave the British Press its opportunity. Using the Palace statement as the base of their stories they described what was being said, by whom, and why. In all, the Press had themselves a good time at the expense of the Queen and the Prince. It is hardly surprising that he is bitter towards the Press.

When the story broke in the British Press the Queen was planning her journey to Gibraltar where she was due to meet Prince Philip on board *Britannia* before going on with him to a state visit to Portugal. It is hardly surprising that she was very bitter about the "terrible things".[9] She knew how carefully the two of them had planned his long tour so that it would yield the maximum advantage to the Commonwealth and the Crown. She knew how Prince Philip had maintained close contact with her and the children during his long absence—during which their ninth wedding anniversary came around, which Philip had prepared for so that the

Queen received his customary present of a huge box of white blooms when she came down to breakfast. On Christmas Day 1956 he had opened his Christmas present from the Queen—a tape recording of her and the children—which he responded to with a radio-telephone call from *Britannia* to the Queen almost as soon as she had finished her Christmas broadcast. He had introduced that broadcast from his cabin in *Britannia*, concluding his contribution with the words: "The Lord watch between me and thee when we are absent one from the other." In her broadcast the Queen told the millions of listeners: "You will understand me when I tell you that of all the voices we have heard this afternoon, none has given my children and myself greater joy than that of my husband."

So it came as a great shock to the Queen when the British Press seemed to give credence to the American-based rumours, and when she met Prince Philip at Gibraltar she found that he was even more bitter. After all, he had worked hard on his tour—as he and the Queen do on all their tours. Their well-publicized reunion showed that he was not bitter with the Queen nor she with him—but both of them resented the unjust Press speculation.

In trying to 'make up' to the Royal Family the British Press merely gave them even greater offence. For after their meeting at Gibraltar the Press headlined stories about the "Radiant Queen" and "Smiling Prince" ensuring their readers that all was well in the royal household. But the more they made these needless assurances the more they drew attention to the false reports which they had printed.

Within twenty-four hours of their return to London the Queen made the announcement that her husband was now to be a Prince of the United Kingdom (p. 151). Maybe this was a wife's way of 'cocking a snook' at the Press—but it did little to soothe the relationship between that Press and the Prince.

Before Prince Philip had gone to open the Melbourne Olympics he had introduced the Queen to a young photographer, Antony Armstrong-Jones. He had been an assistant to Baron, Philip's photographer-friend who had recently died. Armstrong-Jones had already done some work for the Duke of Kent and the Queen approved of the portfolio of photographs which Prince Philip showed her. She agreed that the young man should take pictures of Prince Charles and Princess Anne, and his pictures were adopted as the official portraits released on Prince Charles's eighth birthday in November 1956.

At that time Princess Margaret was on a tour of the West Indies and so she missed the newspaper reports about the début of "a cameraman with the magic touch, London's most talked-about photographer, twenty-five-year-old Tony Armstrong-Jones."[10] The well-publicized young man was different from most photographers. Educated at Eton and Cambridge he had coxed the Cambridge crew in its victory in the boat race of 1950. His father was a lawyer, Ronald Armstrong-Jones. His mother and her second husband, the Earl of Rosse, lived in Birr Castle in County Offaly in Southern Ireland. One of his uncles was the outstanding theatrical designer and interior decorator, Oliver Messel, who helped introduce him into society and to important clients. By 1956 Armstrong-Jones had a reputation for having unorthodox girlfriends, a studio in a former ironmongery in Pimlico where he lived 'beneath the shop' in a flat decorated with Regency grotesques, lapis lazuli and other pieces of extravagance—and a looking-glass in which the majority of the Mayfair and Belgravia sets had etched their signatures with the aid of a diamond kept conveniently to hand.

Princess Margaret had for a long time been a leading member of this set with its 'jet-set' image and its constant seeking for the strange or *louche.* Noël Coward, Eddie Fisher, Danny Kaye and other notabilities from the world of theatre and Hollywood were brought into the set where they helped the Princess get the impression that she was a talented music-hall star *manquée.*

It was not surprising then that in 1957 she got to know the latest trendy figure, the photographer of whom everybody was talking. She enjoyed his company and he, on his part, was far from over-awed in her presence. She found him an attractive, stimulating companion whose tastes fitted her own.

The Queen and Prince Philip were fully aware of the developing friendship. At first they had only one thought—that there might be more unwelcome publicity if Princess Margaret's name became too closely linked with that of Armstrong-Jones. For him to have his name appear in gossip columns was one thing—and a considerable help to his work, but the Queen and Prince Philip had no wish to see the Princess's name appear in those columns. They had already suffered more than their fill from newspaper speculation in January and February and were frightened that there might be more of the same because of the Margaret-Tony friendship.

Princess Margaret, however, found an ally in her mother. They lived together at Clarence House and the Queen Mother approved of the friendship between two who were, she argued, "two of a kind". The anxious mother was pleased to notice that the Townsend affair seemed to have left no permanent scars.

The Princess became a frequent visitor to the new flat which Armstrong-Jones had found in Rotherhithe where there were no servants and where she and her newly-found friend opened the bottles, laid and cleared the table and shared the washing up. As the gossip about their friendship grew throughout 1957, so did royal anxiety. Was it possible that Margaret would allow herself to become involved in a romance with a young man whose unorthodox way of life might create another scandal? There was a heated argument between the two sisters in the autumn of 1957 which led to Princess Margaret's absence from the Palace dinner arranged for 20th November 1957 to celebrate the tenth wedding anniversary of the Queen and Prince Philip. It was a family affair—the Queen Mother, Earl and Countess Mountbatten and their daughters and son-in-law came to join the royal couple. But Princess Margret defiantly was not there. Instead, in a blaze of publicity, she went to the Coliseum to see *Bells are Ringing* and then went on to an ostentatious dinner at the Grill Room in the Savoy. It seemed as if she were indicating that she resented the celebration of ten years of her sister's marriage while she, owing to the Townsend affair, was still unmarried.

And she resented the way in which the family seemed to be opposed to her developing friendship with Armstrong-Jones, especially after the unhappy outcome of the Townsend affair. All would have been well, she claimed, if she had wanted to marry one of Philip's clan—a German princeling or duke.

In March 1958 she went out of her way to give the Press something to talk about—and to cause the family more worry. She let Peter Townsend know that he would be welcome to come to Clarence House when he came to England. He arrived about four o'clock on the 26th March 1958 surrounded by journalists and photographers. The Press trumpeted "Together Again". It is small wonder that one of the Queen's household described her conduct as "perverse" and that a newspaper reported that the Queen was "irked".

But the Queen Mother proved a little wiser than the Press and the Palace spokesmen. She knew that the Townsend affair was over. She watched the developing relationship between her younger daughter and Tony Armstrong-Jones. And she approved. In 1959 his name appeared frequently on the list of guests at official dinners and luncheons given at Clarence House. He often stayed with the Queen Mother and Princess Margaret at Royal Lodge, Windsor, and spent part of the summer holiday with them at Birkhall on the Balmoral estate. On the 26th February 1960, a week after the birth of Prince Andrew, the Princess and Armstrong-Jones announced their engagement.

Prince Philip had little in common with his prospective brother-in-law, who was too artistic and almost uninterested in things which interested the Prince, but he realized that the newcomer to the royal circle deserved some help from its leading male. It was Prince Philip who coached Armstrong-Jones in such things as coping with the crowds that would surround him when he went on official engagements. It was noticeable that, for example, Armstrong-Jones adopted the hands-behind-the-back which Prince Philip had almost copyrighted.

The Queen on the other hand liked the newcomer—and has continued to show him a great kindness even now that he is divorced from the Princess. Invitations to the wedding were issued by the Queen Mother. Actors, Tony's friends from Pimlico and Rotherhithe and film stars of the jet set received the invitations—and accepted. So did Tony's father, twice divorced and three times married, and his mother who was married for the second time. But the royal families of Holland, Sweden, Belgium, Norway and Greece turned down their invitations.

Two days before the wedding the Queen gave a reception at Buckingham Palace for the young couple and those who would be attending the wedding. Armstrong-Jones saw his close friends mingling with royal establishment figures who came from widely different backgrounds. He himself was uneasy at this reception, unsure whether to choose the informality of his long-standing friends or the dignity and solemnity of the royal circle. Bandleader Joe Loss caught the mood when he ordered the band to play 'Fings Ain't Wot They Used T'Be'.

The wedding took place at Westminster Abbey on the 6th May 1960. Prince Philip escorted Princess Margaret through the crowded and decorated streets to the Abbey. Throughout the ceremony the Queen remained unsmiling, as millions of television viewers noticed. It was a strange wedding for her to attend and one which indicated the swift changes that were taking place in morals and beliefs; here was the girl who had renounced a marriage to Townsend because of her supposed belief in the Church's teaching on marriage, becoming the daughter-in-law of parents who were twice and thrice married.

On the 3rd October 1961 Antony Armstrong-Jones was created the Earl of Snowdon and a month later on the 2nd November he drove his wife from their home at Kensington Palace to Clarence House where, on the 3rd November, was born a son, David Albert Charles, Viscount Linley. Almost four years to the day after their wedding was born a daughter, Sarah Frances Elizabeth. On the surface at least this marriage seemed to be working.

In fact there were a number of factors which put this marriage under a stress which, as we know, finally proved too much. In part the blame for this lay within the Royal Family itself. Although the Queen and the Queen Mother approved of the marriage, and since its break up have continued to maintain a close friendship with Lord Snowdon, Prince Philip was less than welcoming to the first commoner to marry into the Royal Family for over five hundred years. In 1963 J. A. Frere, formerly Chester Herald of Arms and a close observer of the royal scene, wrote: "[Prince] Philip has not actually made things difficult for Tony in any way, but he has done nothing to try to make things any easier."[11]

The Queen was disturbed by Princess Margaret's constant changing moods and the frequent rows which broke out in the Margaret-Tony household. Prince Philip shared with her the suspicion that the newcomer did not quite belong—with his wish to continue his work as a photographer and his involvement in the design of the Aviary at the London Zoo. Prince Philip gave vent to his feelings at a Saints' and Sinners' Lunch. Here, in front of television cameras, he said, "Unlike my brother-in-law . . ." adding with a smirk, "well, he isn't really, but you know the chap I mean . . ."[12]

The Queen was annoyed at this public display of family feeling. Prince

Philip tried to repair the damage by over-praising the Aviary when he spoke at the Zoological Society's annual meeting. But, as in his own case in 1957, this merely drew attention to the divisions in the family.

In part the cause of the stress lay within Antony Armstrong-Jones himself. On the one hand he seemed to want to become an accepted part of the Royal Family; he took a title and sometimes travelled in style with Princess Margaret as a sort of mini-version of the Queen and Prince Philip. On the other hand he wanted to continue to follow his career as a photographer; to maintain his friendship with designers, actors and other people in the 'pop' world. It was difficult, if not impossible, to reconcile the two worlds in which he wished to move and it might have been better if he had chosen either the royal world—as Prince Philip had done at the cost of his career—or the business world—as Angus Ogilvy did when he married Princess Alexandra of Kent but refused a title and insisted on carrying on a life of an involved businessman. Lord Snowdon, in accepting the title but continuing with his career, tried to have the best of both worlds.

But a good deal of the blame for the break up of the marriage in 1976 and for the divorce which was announced in 1978 must lie with Princess Margaret. On the one hand she wished to be treated as the Queen's privileged sister and as such she carried out, faithfully, a number of public engagements. On the other hand she wanted to identify herself with the trendiest fashions of the 'swinging sixties'. While at one time she wanted her husband to behave towards her as Prince Philip did to the Queen—walking deferentially one stride behind her—at other times she wanted him to join her at the latest club or some jet-set disco. It is not surprising that she had to receive psychiatric help in an effort to find a cure for her neurotic concern for her real identity. Nor is it surprising that in the late 1960s she and her husband had blazing rows in public. Increasingly they tended to lead a separate social life. She tended to find most happiness in her holiday home in the West Indies, a wedding gift from Colin Tennant. It was here in the 1970s that Princess Margaret lived in a well-publicized 'relationship' with Roddy Llewellyn, the son of the Olympic horse rider, Colonel Harry Llewellyn of Foxhunter fame.

The young Llewellyn had 'dropped out' of society. In the 1950s Princess Margaret had sought happiness in the shape of a man sixteen years older than herself. In the 1970s she looked for happiness in the shape of a man seventeen years younger than herself. It came as no surprise when Lord Snowdon announced that he had decided, after consulting the Queen, to seek a divorce.

31

The Father of the Royal Children

IT MAY BE A MATTER OF JUDGMENT as to whether Prince Philip is more able, more intelligent and harder working than Prince Albert, Queen Victoria's consort, but there can be little doubt that he has been a more successful parent. There is, in one sense, nothing unusual about that—for there are millions of equally successful fathers in millions of other British homes. In that sense, Prince Philip is merely 'one of us'. But we have to see him, as a father, against the peculiar royal background to which Randolph Churchill referred in his biography of the Earl of Derby. Churchill attributed to King George V the statement:

> My father was frightened of his mother. I was frightened of my father and I am damned well going to see to it that my children are frightened of me.[1]

There is some doubt as to whether the King ever made this statement, but his son, later Edward VIII and the Duke of Windsor, recalled the fear and eventual dislike he felt for the autocratic father. George V had recorded Edward's birth in his diary: "A sweet little boy was born." These, according to Edward, were the last kind words his father ever used about him. It is possible that the unfortunate Duke of Windsor was hardly the best judge of his father's capacity as a parent. Maybe a fairer view could be expected from Harold Nicolson. He wrote the official biography of King George V, each line of which was read and approved by Queen Mary and by the present Queen Mother. Nicolson was compelled by all the evidence that he gathered to conclude that:

> There is no doubt that King George V and Queen Mary failed in their relationships with their children and were for different reasons temperamentally unsuited to parenthood. King George was a strict disciplinarian who was often harsh in word and deed to his children. The Queen found it difficult to stand between the children and the sudden gusts of their father's wrath.[2]

The first break in this royal pattern of parent-children enmity was made during the childhood of the Queen, and it was her mother, the present

Queen Mother, who was mainly responsible for that change. Herself the youngest daughter of Lady Strathmore with her "genius for family life",[3] she brought a new life and gaiety to the Royal Family after her marriage to the then Duke of York in 1923.[4] It was she who ensured that the shy, introverted Duke found a warmth and security in his home which allowed his hidden talents to develop. It was she, rather than the Duke, who created for her daughters a happy framework in which to grow up.

It is not, therefore, surprising that in her turn the present Queen—both when Princess Elizabeth and, after 1952, as Queen, sought to give her children the same background of a secure and happy home.

Both she and Prince Philip did their best to ensure that their children received much less publicity than she and Princess Margaret had suffered when they were young. In trying to achieve this they sought the co-operation of the Press, as we shall see when looking at the question of their children's education, but it has to be noted here that the Press did not always allow the royal children the privacy which their parents wanted them to enjoy.

When the children were young both the mother and father did their best to help them enjoy as normal a life as was possible. Both of them were often away from home and even at home there were frequent calls on their time so that they have not been able to live what most of us would regard as a normal family life. Nevertheless, given those constraints, the Queen and Prince Philip have provided their children with some, at least, of that 'normalcy'. There was always an hour after breakfast when the mother and/or father played with the under-fives. In the evenings there was a family tea, a nursery playtime and the ritual of the bath when Princess Elizabeth would put on a waterproof apron and both mother and father would enjoy the splashing of the excited children playing with their bathtime toys.

We have seen that the marriage between Princess Elizabeth and Prince Philip was certainly not one of those 'arranged' mariages, and we have seen that the once-persistent Princess was happy to be the wife of the young naval officer in Malta. During those early years he was, as he said, the master in his household. Even today he continues to be the old-fashioned *paterfamilias*.[5] The Queen who first encouraged him to run the estates at Balmoral and Sandringham, who allowed him to reform some features of Palace life, has shown herself willing to allow a fairly free reign to her able, energetic and much-loved husband.

It was he, more than their mother, who insisted that the children should be disciplined and taught to do things for themselves. Princess Anne remembers being sent from the table because she had not bothered to wash her hands;[6] both she and her brother were punished—sometimes being deprived of television, sometimes being smacked—by their father. They were taught to say 'please' and 'thank you' and when a young Prince Charles addressed a detective by his surname the Queen spoke sharply to him and sent him to apologize and to 'mister' the embarrassed policeman.

Life for royal children could never be normal in the full sense of the word. Even today Princess Anne curtsies when she meets the Queen Mother and throughout her childhood she will have seen others in the Palace bow or curtsy to her parents. But the parents did their best to make things as 'real' as possible. When Charles left a door open and a servant went to close it, the irate father snapped, "Leave it alone, man. He's got hands. Let him do it himself." In complete contrast to such sharp disciplining, there were the games and chases along the long corridors which turned the Palace from the morgue it had once been into something resembling a normal home.

We have seen that Prince Philip went out of his way to show that he had a deep respect for his father and his dead father's memory. But his cousin wrote, "I feel sure that he was aware that he did not see enough of his father. He always wanted to 'make this up' to Charles . . ."[7] And, it must be added, to the three other children as well. If it was the mother who taught the children to read, it was the father who taught them to swim, to ride, to play tennis, cricket and other games. As soon as they were old enough he took them shooting on the Norfolk Broads and on the Balmoral estates, and also took them sailing—often in "roughish weather at an age when many boys would still be in the charge of their nannies".[8]

During the long summer holiday at Balmoral the relaxed father was at his best. The children dressed casually in jeans and sweaters, the older ones in tweeds or tartan skirts or kilts. After the parents had gone through their mail and the Queen dealt with her boxes, the family were free to enjoy a day on the moors. There was riding, fishing, shooting, stalking or photography. Often there was an out-of-doors lunch or an evening barbecue—the Prince enjoying the chance to show off his prowess as cook. There were nights spent out of doors, the boys and father rolled up in sleeping-bags on the floor of a remote cottage, waking to a breakfast of bacon and beans.

In *Our Future Monarch* I have written at some length about Prince Charles's education. Since then I have been amazed at how many have been unaware that Charles was the first child to be sent from the Palace to an outside school. Not even the progressive Queen Mother went that far with her daughters. They, like all their predecessors, were taught by a series of governesses and private tutors within the walls of the Palace. The author of this particular revolution was, undoubtedly, Prince Philip. In the matter of their children's education, the Queen bowed to his wider knowledge and greater experience. So, in November 1956 Prince Charles left the Palace to become a day pupil at Hill House School in Hans Place, Knightsbridge. Then, when he was only nine, he was sent to board at Prince Philip's old school, Cheam—now established at Headley on the Berkshire Downs.

Before sending him to Hill House the parents had tried to gain the support of the Press for their enterprise. On the 11th April 1955 Richard Colville, the Queen's Press Secretary, issued a statement:

> I am commanded by the Queen to say that Her Majesty and the Duke of Edinburgh have decided that their son has reached the stage when he should take part in the more grown-up educational pursuits with other children.
>
> In consequence, a certain amount of his instruction will take place outside his home; for example, he will visit museums and other places of interest. The Queen trusts, therefore, that His Royal Highness will be able to enjoy this in the same way as other children without the embarrassment of constant publicity. In this respect, Her Majesty feels that it is equally important that those in charge of, or sharing in, the instruction should be spared undue publicity, which can so seriously interrupt their normal lives.
>
> I would be grateful if you will communicate the above to your members and seek their co-operation in this matter . . .

Unfortunately, the Press showed that it had a small share of respect for the royal wishes. Hill House was besieged; so, when he went to Cheam, were the stations at Paddington and Reading as well as the school itself. This helps to explain the decision to send him to Gordonstoun—another of Philip's former schools. This, it was hoped, would be too remote for even the hardiest reporter, but even in Scotland there were eagle-eyed royal-watchers. The incident of the cherry brandy was blown up into a matter of major significance—at least for a publicity-gaining day or two.

If Prince Charles broke new ground by leaving the Palace to go to school, it was even more adventurous to allow him to go to university. Other members of the family had gone to university—but under peculiar arrangements. The future Edward VII had gone to Cambridge but had not been allowed to live with other students or to take examinations. The future Kings Edward VIII and George VI had followed a similar course. In 1967 Prince Charles entered Trinity College, Cambridge; he lived 'on a staircase' like other students and studied alongside his peers from various walks of life. He took part in amateur dramatics, played games, and took examinations, gaining a Second Class Honours BA in 1970—all this despite a term spent at Aberystwyth, the interference involved in his Investiture in 1969, and the calls on his time resulting from his work as an active member of the 'royal firm'.

It was Prince Charles who was the 'guinea pig' in the matter of education. His sister and younger brothers have, in a sense, followed the trail that he blazed, or at least have followed it for part of the way. Princess Anne, for example, went to Benenden in Kent in the autumn term of 1963. In 1968 she took her A-levels—but did not go on to university as Charles had done. Her parents encouraged her in her horse riding and were at Burghley in 1971 when she became the European Champion at three-day eventing. In 1968 she had been a reserve for the British equestrian team in the Mexico Olympics. Here she met Mark Phillips. They became engaged at Easter 1973 and married on the 14th November of that year. In 1977 they presented the Queen and Prince Philip with their first grandchild.

Princess Anne has shown herself to be very different, in character, to Prince Charles. She is more like her father, while Charles has many of the quieter traits of his grandfather, George VI, and his grandmother, the Queen Mother. It is Anne who has the dash, rashness, impatience and temper of her father; she has shown his intolerance and like him is often outspoken.

The two younger Princes, Andrew and Edward, have had a less public childhood than the two older children. In part this is due to the fact that the Press now finds nothing unusual about a royal child going to school, playing a game, climbing a tree or whatever, so there has been less public attention paid to their development. And the Queen and Prince Philip no doubt felt they were better fitted to be parents in the 1960s and 1970s than in the 1950s. Then they were new to both sides of their lives—as parents and as Monarch and Consort. Andrew (born 1960) and Edward (born 1964) have benefited from the fact that the parents have been able to look back on the childhood of the two older children. Like many of us, they think they have learned from the experience and are better parents. At the same time, they no longer find their royal work as tiring and demanding as they did when they first tackled the job in 1952. So it is not surprising that Palace officials see Andrew and Edward as "very ordinary youngsters".

On the 4th December 1966 Prince Philip gave an interview to Gomer Jones, the Court Correspondent of the Press Association. The subject of the interview was the decision to allow Prince Charles to go to university. The interview[9] showed that the Queen and Prince Philip had given a great deal of thought to the education of the future monarch. Only the future will show the extent to which their work as parents has been a success. Certainly, at the time of writing, the signs are that they will be seen to have been more successful than Victoria and Albert and George V and Queen Mary. The future Edward VIII was scathing about his father. Prince Charles, on the other hand, has spoken of his mother as "a marvellous person and a wonderful mother. Terribly sensible and wise." His father he has described as "a great help and a strong influence".[10] Only during the next reign will people be able to see the extent of that influence.

Part VIII

PUBLIC DUTY AND PRINCELY INTERESTS

32

The Queen's Consort

ONE OF THE MORE PLEASANT tasks involved in writing this book has been to visit Buckingham Palace. It would be idle to pretend that I did not enjoy the walk across the gravelled yard, the entry through the Privy Purse door and the reception by the polite footman. It did strike me as odd that, in the winter of 1978–1979 I was not searched nor my case opened either by the policemen at the Palace gates or by anyone inside the Palace itself. There was a casual air of acceptance in the well-carpeted house (the scuffs masked as best as was possible) which is part museum (with its art gallery now opened to the public), part private home for the Royal Family, part state office where major receptions are held and part private office for the individual members of the family.

Prince Philip was no stranger to palaces in general or to Buckingham Palace in particular, when Queen Elizabeth ascended the Throne in 1952. But ever since 1947 he had found it hard to 'get on' with Palace staff—and this unease increased after 1952. Palace staff use words such as "prickly", "arrogant" and "defensive" to describe his attitude in those early years.[1] His valet recalled: ". . . in those early years the Duke was uneasy in the atmosphere of the Palace, with all its formalities, footmen and pages . . .".[2]

During the first four years of his marriage he had enjoyed a period of semi-freedom before he was finally confined to 'the cage'. During this time he was "master in his own household". He enjoyed the task of bringing some light relief to the life of Princess Elizabeth and undertook willingly the various public duties he was asked to perform. But at the same time he had his eyes fixed firmly on a naval career. Then in February 1952 it all changed. The young Monarch was inexperienced and unsure. Her continual question when faced with a problem was, "What did my father do?" And when told she would answer, "Then I will too."[3] Her husband was not able to offer her any help in this situation—for he had even less experience and constitutional training than she had. So the Establishment web closed around her—protectively—and he was excluded for many hours of his wife's life.

Indeed, there were many of the old Court and Establishment who were anxious to downgrade him as we have seen. One "waxed indignant because he dined with a group of publicans" as part of his work to raise money for the National Playing Fields Association. Others thought he was "going too far" when he allowed himself to be photographed at a nightclub with newly-divorced Frank Sinatra and Ava Gardner as part of an evening devoted to raising money for the same charity.[4] Nor were the members of his own family of much help. His cousin, Queen Alexandra of Yugoslavia, wrote:

> . . . My Aunt Helen, Marina's mother, pointed out that, when his wife was not present, Philip came below the Dukes of Gloucester and Windsor . . . as a junior royal duke, yet, strictly speaking, the ruling house now bore his name; it was the House of Mountbatten . . .[5]

We have seen how the Establishment quickly dealt with the name of the House. It may come as a surprise to learn that not even his aunt was prepared to back him in the matter of precedence.

During his study of the life of one of his consort-predecessors, the young Duke might have read of the way in which Prince Albert was treated by the politicians and by the Royal Dukes. Queen Victoria's uncles, the Dukes of Cambridge and Sussex, reluctantly agreed to give precedence to Albert. But Uncle Ernest, Duke of Cumberland, refused to give precedence to what he called a "paper Royal Highness". It was only a use of the royal prerogative which gave Albert his place after his wife.[6] And, as we have seen, it was a similar declaration by Queen Elizabeth II in September 1952 that finally settled Prince Philip's place, but in February 1952 he was made to realize that he had no position.[7]

In reading about other consorts of queens regnant, Prince Philip found little to encourage him. The first consort was Lord Dudley, husband of Lady Jane Grey. She only reigned for nine days so that Dudley's life offered no guidance to the Duke of Edinburgh. The next consort was Philip of Spain who married the ill-starred Mary Tudor. She made sure that all the power of the Crown remained within her control. Philip on his part was more concerned to be King of Spain, the Netherlands and Naples and was little more than a temporary visitor to England. So there was not much guidance here either.

The next consort was William of Orange, the husband of Queen Mary II, daughter of the deposed James II. William refused to come to England unless he was allowed to share the Throne with his wife, and while they started off as co-Sovereigns, William soon elbowed Mary from affairs and so in practice ruled as a sole Monarch. His successor, Queen Anne, was married to Prince George of Denmark—"very fat; loving news, the bottle and the Queen" in that order. He was a nonentity whose experience offered no lessons to the young Duke of Edinburgh.

It was Prince Albert, Consort to Queen Victoria, whose life offered the best guidance. Prince Philip made an intense study of the various lives of the Prince Consort as well as searching through the royal archives to find out as much as he could about his famous predecessor. But the more he studied the more it became clear that there was little of any practical value to be gleaned here either. Albert and Philip were two diametrically opposed characters; Albert was a deeply religious, humourless, self-righteous, conscientious, highly intelligent and deadly solemn German. Only some of those adjectives might, with much straining, be applied to the lively, impatient, fun-loving husband of Queen Elizabeth II. And while they were both of foreign birth, and as such were suspect by many in the Establishments of their different periods, the fact was that they lived in very different periods. Soon after her marriage, Queen Victoria received a message from her Prime Minister, Lord Melbourne, urging her to show all foreign dispatches to her new husband; in return, Albert had the satisfaction of "seeing him act entirely in accordance with what I have said."[8] Philip was too intelligent to think that he was going to be allowed any such position of influence. The politicians had shown what they thought of him in the matter of his allowance and the name of the House. He also knew that there was a widespread mistrust of the Mountbatten name. To have given him a position of influence would have given strength to the argument that "Mountbatten was moving in on the monarchy". In any event, the Monarchy in 1952 had little if any chance to exercise the sort of power and influence wielded by Victoria and, through her, by Albert.

Since 1947 Prince Philip had seen that he had one major role to play in helping his younger, more inexperienced wife to come to terms with life in the modern world. He may have wished to have had the sort of role which was allowed to Prince Albert who was praised by both the Whig Prime Minister, Melbourne, and by the Tory Prime Minister, Peel, for the ways in which he helped the young Queen Victoria with her papers. Albert was always with her when she read her papers and opened those famous red boxes. It was he who advised the appointment of Gladstone to the Cabinet in 1843 and who considered himself to be the Queen's "permanent Minister".[9] But Philip never had, was never allowed or ever sought such a constitutional position. He does not have keys to the boxes; he does not sit with his wife when she meets her Ministers; he does not seek to play any part in the constitutional side of her life.

In his thorough-going way, Prince Albert had written an account of how he saw his role as the husband of England's Queen. "The position of the Prince Consort requires that the husband should entirely sink his own individual existence in that of his wife; that he should shun all attention, assume no separate responsibility before the public, but make his position entirely a part of hers."[10] There is little evidence that, in practice, Albert lived down to this submerging of his personality. In a letter to the Duke of Wellington, Albert wrote of his position:

> As natural head of her family, superintendent of her household, manager of her private affairs, sole confidential adviser in politics and only assistant in

> her communications with the officers of her government, he is besides the husband of the Queen, the tutor of the royal children, the private secretary of the Sovereign and her permanent Minister.[11]

This presents a much more real picture of the role which Albert carved out for himself. Indeed, Albert's power was so obvious that when King Louis Philippe of France stayed at Windsor in 1844 he told Queen Victoria, "Le Prince Albert, c'est pour moi le Roi." The Queen was not at all outraged by this observation. She noted, "How lively, how sagacious."[12]

There was never any danger of Philip becoming a king *manqué*. An American interviewer pointed out that his grandfather was a King, his great-great-grandmother was a Queen and his wife was a Queen. "Have you ever thought, maybe it would be nice to be King? Or have you thought, I'm glad I'm not King?" Philip said that he was glad not to be King. "Why wouldn't you like to be King?" "Well, I'm not. It's a hypothetical question."[13] And life is too short for time to be wasted on the might-have-beens of the hypothetical.

As well as studying the lives of his predecessor-consorts, Philip also discussed his role with Prince Bernhard of the Netherlands, the Consort to Queen Juliana. Bernhard is reported to have told him:

> You are new to this thing and you probably don't realize what you are up against. Practically everything you do will be a subject of criticism. You can't ignore it because some of it may be justified, and even if it isn't, it may be politic to heed it. But don't let it get you down. In this job you need a skin like an elephant.[14]

Alden Hatch believed that Philip tried to "emulate Bernhard" but that "the British tradition which makes the British apprehensive of anyone connected with the Royal Family having any ideas about anything",[15] made him less successful than the Dutch Consort, who, said Hatch, made a "truly valuable contribution to their military, industrial and cultural life and to bettering international relations." Hatch was unlucky in that he wrote his book in 1964–1965. He did not know that at that very time, Prince Bernhard was a subject of concern to the Dutch Government. His "marriage to the Queen had had some difficulties and his extra-marital activities had been extensive . . . in the early sixties he had a mistress in Paris who had a young daughter."[16] Even worse was to be revealed in the 1970s when the US Government found various armaments manufacturers guilty of spending millions of dollars on bribes to potential customers. The scandals surrounding the Lockheed, Northrop and other firms shocked the world in 1975–1976, and right at the centre of the European web of bribery and corruption was Prince Bernhard who was forced to resign all his public posts.

It is perhaps fortunate that Philip decided that he would emulate neither Bernhard, the living consort, nor Albert, the dead one. Instead he decided to shape his own role to suit his own abilities and preferences and the particular period in which we live. It was a coincidence that one of his first actions as consort was to visit the House of Commons, just as Albert had done. Only a week or so after his wife's Accession he "slipped away from Clarence House one evening—the place was in a turmoil of packing and dismantling—and spent four hours in the House of Commons listening to a debate. He went to the House again to hear the Chancellor of the Exchequer's Budget speech, and there were none of the hostile references from Members that had marked Prince Albert's first and last attendance."[17] Albert had gone to the Commons in January 1846 to hear Prime Minister Robert Peel announce his programme for the repeal of the Corn Laws. Albert's presence was taken as a sign that he supported Peel. The Conservative gentlemen opposed to Peel's policies raised such an outcry that Albert was forced to make this his last attendance at a Commons' debate.[18] Maybe Philip's presence in the Commons raised no storm because MPs in 1952 knew that neither he nor any member of the Royal Family had the influence that Victoria and Albert had exercised in the 1840s.

Philip also gave his attention, as Albert had done, to reforming the Palace. He installed the intercom system which did away with the centuries of message-carrying pages; royal footmen were no longer required to whiten their heads with a mixture of flour, starch and soap; and state liveries were lightened by the removal of the heavy and expensive gold trimmings which had adorned them. This was all of a piece with the informality with which the Queen treated visiting ambassadors and ministers.

He encouraged the Queen to abolish the annual débutante presentation parties and to have larger garden parties to which a more representative selection of guests could be invited from the Commonwealth as well as from Britain itself. In keeping with this wish to meet as many people as possible there are evening cocktail parties for guests from the worlds of business, entertainment, arts and letters, politics and sport. There were and are the informal luncheon parties at which the Queen sits not at the head of the table but in the middle on one side facing Philip sitting opposite so that they can chat to a number of their guests drawn from a wide spectrum of British life—trade unionists, bankers, businessmen and entertainers from the worlds of football, stage, television and horse racing.

He saw his major role as a link between people and Monarch. It is easier for him to talk to people. In their turn people are more likely to speak more openly to him than they might to the Queen. He is then able to come back—from some place in Britain or some part of the Commonwealth—and report to the Queen who is thus the better informed for his work as a liaison officer. He has, at times, been an outspoken commentator on things—and this, in turn has led to a good deal of criticism. Sometimes, particularly when abroad, he has been too outspoken. Andrew Duncan told of one detective who spent hours trying to calm the Dutch chauffeur who had listened to Philip's comments on the drive from Amsterdam Airport. "What a po-faced lot these Dutch are. Look at them."[19] As

Duncan noted, the Queen has had to exercise much of her charm to soothe those who have been irritated by her husband's moods.

In general Philip has shown a public face that has won him a reputation for being genial, natural and relaxed. In this he resembles the Queen Mother. He has also felt free to indulge in wit and spontaneous expressions of pleasure—and anger. The Queen, on the other hand, has felt bound to adopt that serious face fitting to 'Majesty'. In acting more freely Philip has given the Monarchy a more human appearance.

During the twenty-nine years which have elapsed since her Accession the Queen has, not surprisingly, become much more confident in her role. In 1952 she allowed herself to be guided by her father's former advisers. As the years have passed most of these have retired and/or died and her current advisers came to their jobs with less experience than she had. It has been the same in regard to her Prime Ministers. In 1952 she had a very old and experienced Winston Churchill, but as the years have gone on she has had to deal with a succession of younger men, none of whom have had her experience and all of whom pay tribute to her ability, intelligence and grasp of affairs.[20]

It is not surprising, therefore, that the relationship between the Queen and Prince Philip has changed, or that he has allowed his role to widen and change. Now he feels less need to act as her protector and guide—although he continues to take care that, for example, during walkabouts she is not overwhelmed by the informality.

During their first years of marriage he took it on himself to transform the shy, fussy, over-conscientious, prim young Princess with his extrovert and happy-go-lucky character. In this he succeeded, so that until 1952, at least, life was less serious and more carefree. But there has been a two-way influence. If he is less rude, less arrogant, less impatient and more compassionate today than he was in 1947, a deal of the credit for these changes-for-the-better are due to the Queen's influence.[21]

Like Prince Albert, Philip involved himself in the country's industrial life. Unlike Albert, he has proved to be a splendid father with progressive views on the sort of education that his children should have. And he has shown himself to be an excellent consort for a popular queen. In November 1972 they celebrated their silver wedding. The City of London entertained the royal couple at the Guildhall. When she rose to speak the Queen started, "I think everyone will concede that today, of all occasions, I should begin my speech with 'My husband and I'." She then told of the bishop who had been asked what he thought of sin. He simply said he was against it. Her answer to anyone who asked her the same question about marriage and the family was equally simple. "I am for it."

33

In the Public Eye—At Home

ONE OF THE TASKS OF THE Duke of Edinburgh's Press Secretary is to liaise with the Press secretaries of other members of the Royal Family and to produce a daily Court Circular. Sometimes this is a very brief document. On the 9th November 1979 the Circular gave details of the various ambassadors, politicians and foreign statesmen who "had an audience of Her Majesty the Queen" on the morning of Thursday, 8th November. The Circular then gave a four-paragraph outline of the way in which Prince Philip spent the afternoon and evening. There was a train journey to Exeter, a lecture at Bath for the Royal Bath and West and Southern Counties Society and a quick return to London for a reception at the Sail Training Association in Fleet Street followed by a dinner of the Royal Yachting Association for the Permanent Committee of the International Yacht Racing Union in Pall Mall.

At fairly regular intervals throughout the year the Circular is much longer, as was the one for the 2nd November 1979.

COURT CIRCULAR
Buckingham Palace

November 2: The Queen and The Duke of Edinburgh having arrived at Chester Station in the Royal Train this morning were received by Her Majesty's Lord-Lieutenant for Cheshire (the Viscount Leverhulme) and drove to the Town Hall where Her Majesty and His Royal Highness were received by the Mayor of Chester (Councillor J. H. Jones).

The Queen and The Duke of Edinburgh attended a Service of Thanksgiving in Chester Cathedral on the occasion of the 1,900th Anniversary of the City of Chester and were received at the West Door by the Bishop of Chester (the Right Reverend H. V. Whitsey) and the Dean (the Very Reverend T. W. Ingram Cleasby).

Afterwards Her Majesty and His Royal Highness walked to the Town Hall and later visited Grange Farm. Mollington (Chairman and Managing Director, Mr W. Oulton Wade).

The Queen and The Duke of Edinburgh drove to the Civic Hall, Ellesmere Port, were received by the Mayor of Ellesmere Port and Neston (Councillor J. F. Price), toured Ellesmere Port Boat Museum where Her Majesty unveiled a commemorative plaque.

The Queen and The Duke of Edinburgh having arrived at Runcorn Station in the Royal Train this afternoon, drove to West Bank, Widnes, where Her Majesty and His Royal Highness were received by the Mayor of Halton (Councillor E. N. Gleave), and viewed a photographic exhibition.

The Queen and The Duke of Edinburgh drove to the Town Hall, Warrington, were received by the Mayor (Councillor H. G. Edwards), and walked through Golden Square Shopping Centre where Her Majesty unveiled a commemorative plaque.

The Queen and The Duke of Edinburgh later arrived at Ringway Airport and were received by Her Majesty's Lord-Lieutenant for Greater Manchester (Sir William Downward) and the Lord Mayor of Manchester (Councillor Gerard Fitzsimmons), and subsequently left in an aircraft of The Queen's Flight for London.

And so ended a one-day trip to the North-West. On other occasions there are two-day visits to Lancashire, four-day visits to Yorkshire and other northern counties, dozens of conferences and receptions, hundreds of inspections and dinners interspersed with the protocol surrounding the state visits from Premier Hua of China, President Kaunda of Zambia and other heads of state. There are regimental anniversaries to be commemorated, breweries to be inspected, aircraft establishments to be visited, industrial associations to be honoured and tours around universities, technical institutions and schools. There is too, as we shall see, the work for the Award Scheme, Wildlife Fund and other highly-favoured interests.

A journalist-critic who "had an opportunity to follow a typical royal procession through towns on the south-east coast" in 1968 commented on the "unremitting series of handshakes, addresses, visits and presentations . . . a bewildering succession of Sussex folk bowed and curtsied . . . mayors and mayoresses, aldermen, sheriffs, chief constables, schoolmasters, schoolmistresses, clerks to the local councils, magistrates, deans, vicars, vicars' wardens, managers of building works, hotel-keepers, college students and school prefects, the odd Lord and Lady . . ."[1]

One might have thought that such an observer would have shown some sympathy for the Queen and the Prince as they went about "their usual intense royal round".[2] For if it was Sussex today, it was somewhere else tomorrow and so on throughout the year—and for years before and after 1968. Prince Philip has never found it easy to see the point of a great deal of the routine which accompanies such visits and tours. One correspondent has officiated at 520 royal functions. Having written about Prince Philip's preference for "efficient people" and his dislike for "time wasters", he went on:

One day at London's Mansion House he was the guest of honour, and he made the usual interesting speech, to the point and not too long. But one other speaker was boring and all the guests were fed up and some started looking at their watches. H.R.H. of course listened intently although I felt he was just as bored. On the way out he smiled and said in a quiet voice so that no one else should overhear: "At least you get paid to listen." I replied, "Sir, I should have asked for danger money as I was in danger of going to sleep."[3]

There are the critics who believe that on these royal tours and visits there is "no real communication between the crowds and the visiting members of the Royal Family". Certainly there is not—nor can there be—any "real communication" between the Queen or Prince Philip and each individual in the crowds. For most people the royal visit is "a fleeting moment" in which they catch a glimpse of the Prince, maybe overhear some formal greeting as they poke their heads around the bodies of the detectives and others accompanying him. Increasingly as the years have gone both the Queen and Prince Philip have relaxed during these tours and the 'walkabout' has allowed some people in the vast crowds a chance to have an individual greeting, and it is evident from the many letters I received that people treasure the memory of "their day". One lady wrote of the day on which her husband, then a policeman, spoke to Prince Philip when he was visiting Glasgow. She writes, "You may think me an old fool keeping this old *Port of Glasgow Express* but my husband is now dead twenty years. Well, we old folks like to hold on to memories."[4] Another lady noted that "Prince Philip . . . is not above speaking to ordinary folks like myself. My husband and I were on holiday in Torquay in Jubilee Year and my husband was waiting for the Queen and the Duke to come so's we could use the remainder of our film trying to get a nice photo of them. We were lucky getting the Queen but it was not so easy getting Prince Philip with the jostling of the crowd and the Prince on the move. Then the Prince noticed what my husband was trying to do and he came over with a cheery word and stood for my husband to get a close-up of him. It certainly made our day . . ."[5]

And the journalist-critic had his comeuppance when he asked a Sussex schoolboy whether it had all been worth it, standing in a crowd waiting for hours only to see the royal couple pass along their route. At first he must have though he'd got some good copy. The schoolboy complained, "I blinked and missed her going past." But then he confounded the eager critic, with, "Was it worth it? Well, she means more to me than Harold Wilson does anyway."[6]

During these public tours and visits Prince Philip has, over the years, helped the Queen to relax. It has been easier for him to be the genial figure, the one with the ready word and quip. In this he has followed the example of the Queen Mother and has become the example to his eldest son. But behind the public visit there has always been a less publicized part of the royal work. There has been, for example, the Prince's work as Patron of the School of Tropical Medicine in Liverpool with its close association with the ex-Far East Prisoner of War Association. The Secretary of the School wrote of the value of the continuing interest which Prince Philip has shown in the work of the School[7]. There are also the many receptions, luncheons and dinners for various societies and institutions. The Secretary of the Institution of Public Health Engineers wrote about the regard which their Institution has for Prince Philip, since 1967 an Honorary Fellow of the Institution. When he accepted this award in June 1967 Prince Philip made one of the three hundred or so speeches which he made in that year. It is worth remembering that he writes each of these himself and does not employ a ghost-writer, and he has the happy knack of always saying the right thing to the right group of people as can be seen from the following speech.

Mr President, Ladies and Gentlemen:

First of all may I say how very grateful I am for your kind welcome and also for this very excellent lunch.

It is, of course, a very great pleasure and an honour for me personally to receive this Honorary Fellowship at such a gathering of distinguished members of the Institution, and in retaliation it also gives me a convenient opportunity to pay a very well deserved tribute to the work and achievements of Public Health Engineers, and I think that on the whole this sort of tribute comes best from an outsider, and apart from some experience with one of those rubber-ended suction things and the inevitable tinkering with the ball-cock flushing devices, I think I can claim to be a complete outsider to Public Health Engineering.

I am, as it were, a customer and on the whole a satisfied customer. I am impressed with regularity with which water comes out of the taps and I appreciate the fact that it is clean and germ-free even if its taste suffers on occasions, and looking around I notice that no one has been over-keen to sample any of it here. I am also equally impressed by the efficiency with which sewage is removed and disposed.

Now this may sound very simple, but everyone here knows that a good water supply and efficient sewage are the essence of good public health and the two most important factors in the prevention of disease. The trouble is that I think we as laymen have become spoilt and we take these things for granted. Well here I am, at any rate one person, one layman, today who would like you to know how much he appreciates the work of Public Health Engineers.

Now water supply and sewage disposal affect all citizens, but the collection of water and the ultimate disposal of sewage are also of considerable interest to more specialized groups of citizens. May I say that I have been very pleasantly impressed by the increasingly liberal attitude towards the use of reservoirs and catchment areas for various sporting purposes. I remember only a few years ago having a discussion with some Public Health Officers—that was when I at one time was President of the British Medical Association—about sailing on reservoirs and being told that it was quite out of the question because the paint and tar from the boats would pollute the water. I found it extremely difficult to point out politely that the art of boat-building has changed somewhat since Noah built the Ark.

I am also very impressed by the growing recognition that pumping untreated sewage into rivers and estuaries and also into the sea is the cause of very serious pollution. In many cases it is human sewage which has cleared rivers of fish rather than industrial effluent. As Public Health Engineering improves its methods, I think we can look forward to many rivers and estuaries regaining a thriving fish population to the delight of the growing army of anglers.

I have certainly personal cause to know that Public Health Engineers are alert to this. I think it was about ten or twelve years ago that we had to install a new sewage plant at Balmoral. I may say that it has made not the slightest difference to the salmon who continue to show a marked reluctance to come up the Dee and get themselves caught in any greater numbers, but it is pleasant to think that the standard of public health in Aberdeen has gone up as a result.

Anyway, having said such nice things about Public Health Engineers, I think you will forgive me if I say that there is one subject which seems to need somewhat closer attention. My impression is that the whole process of collection and disposal of waste and rubbish, and particularly of derelict motorcars although I am not sure what sort of health hazard they represent, is not quite as good as it might be. I think the methods now in use are certainly hallowed by tradition and I dare say those could be improved somewhat. However, we are constantly being told that we are living in a technological age—and we've even got a Ministry of Technology—and I can't help thinking that an entirely new approach to this problem, making use of all the modern technological knowledge and ability, might pay handsome dividends in the long run.

Mr President, I am most grateful to you for this Honorary Fellowship which you have given me today, and for the very kind welcome you have given me, and again for this very excellent lunch.[8]

In his early days as an active member of King George VI's 'royal firm' Prince Philip annoyed many members of the "old school who believed that royal speeches should be written in formal terms and read with equal formality."[9] But he quickly showed that he intended to be his own man, making his own brand of very unroyal 'pep' talks such as the one he gave to the Chamber of Commerce and Manufacturers in 1952:

America has invented the phrase 'yes-men' for those who flatter great executives. In England we are more troubled by 'no-men' who make it their business to employ clever ignorance in opposing . . . every scheme suggested by those who have energy, imagination and enterprise. I am afraid our 'no-men' are a thousand times more harmful than the American 'yes-men'. If we are to recover prosperity we shall have to find ways of emancipating energy and enterprise from the frustrating control of constitutionally timid ignoramuses. There is a school of thought which says "What was good enough for my father is good enough for me." I have no quarrel with this sentiment at all, so long as it is not made an excuse for stagnation, frustration and inefficiency and I am quite sure our fathers would be the first to agree with this. The great name of British commerce was founded on honesty, fair dealing and hard work. But do not forget that the great position of British industry was won when we led the world in inventive imagination and the spirit of adventure.

Some of the Prince's critics argue that since 1952 Britain has failed to live up to the expectations of those who spoke then of a 'New Elizabethan Age'—and somehow contrive to blame him for the national failure. Others who have worked more closely with him are aware of the various ways in which he has tried to help Britain become more attuned to the modern world. In 1964 he became the first President of the Council for National Academic Awards, an autonomous body which was established by Royal Charter in September 1964 with powers to award degrees, diplomas, certificates and other academic awards to persons who have successfully pursued courses of study approved by the Council at educational establishments other than universities or who have successfully carried out research work under the supervision of an educational or research establishment other than a university. The Council awards degrees and other academic distinctions, comparable in standard with awards granted and conferred by universities, to students who pursue their higher education in establishments for further education which do not have the power to award their own degrees. The Council deals with Scottish colleges as well as colleges in England and Wales, promoting the bulk of the new technologically-based courses at the new polytechnics and at universities. As the chief officer of the CNAA wrote: "The President has always taken a keen interest in the development of the activities of the Council and has attended and addressed Congregation Ceremonies at which award holders are presented to the President."[10]

In 1964 Prince Philip accepted the post of President of the CNAA, and in 1970, after six years (although no specified term of office had been agreed upon), the Council asked him to serve for a further period. "His Royal Highness intimated that he would be willing to consider a further term as President, but only if a time limit for service for President was first incorporated in the Charter." The Charter was amended so that the President may no longer serve for more than ten years in all.[11]

As an active President he visited many of the colleges and polytechnics where CNAA courses were being taught, and every year presided at degree-giving ceremonies at some of these institutions. In December 1972 he spoke at the second honorary degree ceremony of the CNAA and said:

> As far as students are concerned, degree courses must be good education in themselves and under-graduate courses should provide a foundation for the personal development of the student. Vocational courses should enable the student to be versatile and capable of progress and development within the broad limits of his career.
>
> All these requirements are best met by the sandwich type of course which is always strongly advocated by the Council in suitable cases.
>
> The ultimate purpose of the whole effort of the Council is to enable young men and women to provide themselves with the necessary qualifications to exploit their talents to the full in their future careers. A degree is not an end in itself but merely a means to an end. The Council therefore has the further responsibility to consider the attitudes and interests of the employers whether in industry, commerce or the Government service.
>
> It is worse than useless for the Council to ignore the point of view of the employers or to be unrealistic about life beyond the moment of graduation. If employers are not falling over themselves to employ graduates, it may, of course, be due to the lack of intelligence and appreciation in the employers, but the fault is more likely to lie with the course and with the student.

In July 1973 he made his first 'capping ceremony' in Scotland when he presided at the degree-giving ceremony at the Paisley College of Technology. The *Paisley Gazette* reported:

It was dull but warm when the helicopter carrying the Duke from the grounds of Holyroodhouse flew into the Abbotsinch Airport. Crowds thronged the balcony on top of the airport building for a good view of the Royal visitor as he stepped out of the helicopter to be met by County dignitaries.

Parents held up children for a better view of the welcoming party who included the Lord Lieutenant of Renfrewshire, Viscount Muirshiel, and Mr Robert Robertson the County Convener.

While the party made their way from the airport the crowds who had gathered outside the Town Hall witnessed a colourful procession as college governors and academic staff made their way from the cloisters of Paisley Abbey to the Town Hall.

Cars filled the Bridge Street car park as students and their parents along with 100 guests arrived for the ceremony.

When the royal convoy pulled into the Town Hall the Duke was met by Paisley Provost John S. Smart, and the Paisley Town Clerk Mr J. Aitken.

Two others to meet the Royal visitors were Mr Robin Elles, the chairman of the college's board of governors, and the college principal Mr Tom Howie.

Other guests present were Sir Norman Graham of the Scottish Office and the Paisley Member of Parliament Mr John Robertson.

The Town Hall was a blaze of colour with students and visitors wearing university and college robes.

A quiet calm which seemed to add an extra dignity settled over the building as the first of the students prepared to receive their degree. Apart from newspaper photographers seeking an advantage spot and television crews focussing on the official party the 1,100 people in the building were keenly awaiting the capping ceremony to begin.

The first to receive their degrees were the post-graduate students who took up their positions, they had the honour of being capped in the long-standing traditional manner but with the extra distinction of being honoured by a member of the Royal Family.

The Duke capped the students who then received their scroll from the college secretary. The three schools of study at college, Science, Engineering and Social Planning and Management, were represented at the ceremony and at one part of the proceedings the three college deans presented to the Duke, students from their respective studies.

Prince Philip in his remarks described the awards system of the Council of National Academic Awards as the best thing that has happened to higher education for a long time.

The council set out to make provision for the exceptions to the accepted system. It was a useful compromise between the bureaucratic ideal, what had been inherited from previous generations, current needs, and the need to make provisions for the exceptions.

In Scotland the council had accepted twenty-six courses in three central institutions in Paisley, Dundee and Aberdeen and other colleges in Edinburgh and Glasgow.

Considerable expansion was expected in the next few years.

Parents and young wives watched with pride as students, many from various parts of Renfrewshire, stood before the Duke of Edinburgh to receive their diploma.

In 1976 he gave up this particular position but has continued to show an active interest in the work of the CNAA which he encourages with visits, speeches and willingness to attend receptions and other functions organized by the Council. During his time as President, and since, he showed a happy knack of being able to convince people that somehow he knew a great deal about what was going on—in varied fields of study. This has been true of his links with many other associations and societies. The secretaries and/or presidents of societies or institutions with interests in civil engineering, concrete, tropical medicine, education, animal welfare, industrial welfare and many others all tell the same story. Sir Miles Thomas was Chairman of Monsanto when that company opened its new offices in Victoria Street, which . . .

> . . . gave us a splendid opportunity of seeing state processions as visiting royalty came to London. On one occasion when discussing his Oxford Study Conference, of which I had been given charge of the public relations facet, Prince Philip told me how well our building looked from a ceremonial coach.
>
> I asked if he would honour us by taking lunch, and he said that he would. It was a private affair, very informal, but we were all very much impressed by His Royal Highness's intimate knowledge of business affairs of the day and particularly with his deep understanding of labour relations. His grasp of scientific discoveries in the field that was our own concern—chemicals and plastic—was equally impressive.
>
> Over the subsequent years I have had the privilege of working in connection with his 'Oxford' Conferences often. Prince Philip naturally took the leading part. He was efficiency itself, even spending a couple of hours in the large ancient buildings in Oxford where the inaugural ceremony in 1956 was held so that the ciné and television cameramen could get the lighting right and the microphones could be properly adjusted.
>
> I belong to a dining club composed mainly of Fleet Street people. It is a rigid rule that anything that our speakers of this '30 Club' say is absolutely off the record. During my year of Presidency, Prince Philip was our guest of honour and speaker at a regular dinner. He left us in no doubt about his reactions to the way some sections of the Press handle royal affairs, particularly those connected with the ladies of the Royal Family. His blunt, well-delivered opinions did much good.[12]

Here, then, a picture of the man behind the genial smile with time for "ordinary folks" trying to take a picture of him. Sir Miles Thomas saw him with the eyes of a successful industrialist; others who have written have seen him with the eyes of compassionate doctors, involved educationalists and social workers. Everyone writes or speaks of his intelligence, wide-ranging interests, efficiency, ability and drive. In Victoria's reign people spoke and wrote like this about Prince Albert, the Prince Consort, and one wonders, with A. P. Herbert, about Prince Philip . . . "why on earth is he not Prince Consort?"[13]

The Duke talking to 9-year-old Allan Stamford, a young artist in the Art Craft section of the Christchurch United Clubs, Kennington Oval, during his tour of boys' clubs in Kennington, Bermondsey and Wapping on 15 December 1959.

Prince Philip at the Howard House, Brunswick, Boys' Club Belsize Avenue, Hampstead on 25 October 1967 during a whirlwind visit to boys' clubs in London.

The Royal Family at home.

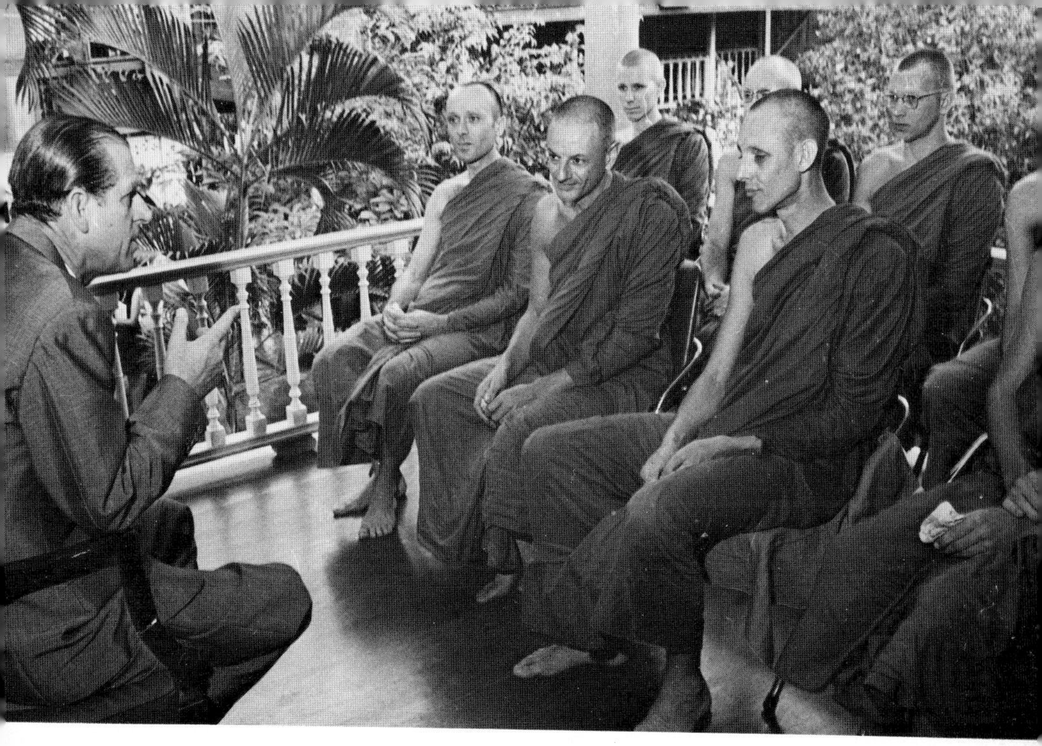

Above: Prince Philip talking with a group of Britons who have chosen to follow the life of the Buddhist monks in Thailand. He met them at their monastery on 11 February 1972 at the start of a seven-week tour of South-East Asia on which the Queen, the Prince and Princess Anne were embarking. *Below:* On a Balmoral picnic, outings enjoyed by members of the family, Prince Philip and Princess Anne barbecue sausages and steaks during the summer of 1972.

Above: Prince Philip (nearest the camera) actively involved in a polo game at Windsor Great Park 1956. Injury forced him to give up polo in 1971. *Below left:* With his close friend, Uffa Fox, on *Cowslip*, 1968. *Below right:* After he had been forced to give up polo Prince Philip became an enthusiast of four-in-hand driving. This photograph shows him in charge of his team during the 1980 Windsor Horse Show.

Above: On 9 April 1975 he and Prince Edward braved the snow at the Windsor Horse Trials as Prince Philip drove his son in a horse and cart through the Great Park to watch Princess Anne take part in the dressage section of the Trials. *Below left:* A beer, an apple and a time for reflection during a visit to Hilbre Island on the northwest coast where he had gone with the naturalist Eric Hosking to study bird life on the Island. *Below right:* An historic pint – the first pub pint to be sold in Britain on Sunday 20 July 1975 – forty-five minutes before official opening time. The Prince made a stop at the Tunnel House Inn, near Cirencester, during the National Carriage Championships. The Prince's host, Lord Bathurst, had arranged for the occasional licence, granted to the Championships, to be transferred to the pub – but the beer didn't work wonders since the Prince only finished fifth in the Championships.

Above: Three royal experts on the polo field – Prince Charles relaxing after a game getting the benefit of the advice of an old hand, the seventy-seven-year-old Lord Mountbatten with Prince Philip as an amused bystander. *Below left:* Prince Philip greeting Sheik Rashid of Dubai during the historic visit to the Gulf States in 1979 when the Queen was welcomed into the male strongholds of these Arab states. *Below right:* The Duke wearing the Balmoral tartan as he and the Queen dance the Gay Gordons at the annual Ghillies' Ball at Balmoral Castle on 31 October 1972 when they were also celebrating their Silver Wedding.

n reflective mood at the 1980 3adminton Horse Trials.

study made in 1975.

A study taken by Karsh of Ottawa in the Drawing Room at Buckingham Palace in 1967, showing the Prince in the full dress uniform of an Admiral of the Fleet with the Sash and Star of the Order of the Garter and the Star of the Order of the Thistle. From the collar hangs the badge of the Grand Master of the Order of the British Empire.

34

At Work—Abroad

SINCE THE ACCESSION OF THE Queen in 1952 Prince Philip has made about 60 tours and visited about 120 foreign countries. On some of these tours he has accompanied the Queen and has played a subordinate role; on others he has gone 'solo'. Some of these tours have been short ones, others have been longer and more official state visits. We cannot examine the role of the Prince-consort without looking at the part he has played in these overseas tours.

We have seen that he had gone on such overseas visits before the Accession and that, indeed, the Queen's reign began during just such a royal visit. It was not surprising that, following the Coronation, the Queen and Prince Philip embarked on a long world tour—partly to make up for the cancellation of the 1952 tour and partly to allow the peoples of the world-wide Commonwealth to have a glimpse of their new Monarch.

The Prince played some part in the preparations for pre-Coronation visits. But, inevitably, he was, as Princess Elizabeth's husband, very much an onlooker in this matter. After the Coronation he played a far greater part in the elaborate preparations for tours. In 1959 *The People* carried extracts from a letter sent out by the Queen's Private Secretary, Sir Michael Adeane, addressing the various hosts who hoped to entertain the Queen and the Duke of Edinburgh during their forthcoming tour.[1] 'Letter' is perhaps hardly the word to describe a six-thousand-word document carrying detailed instructions as to what was and was not permissible or expected. "The Queen does not normally lay foundation stones. The Duke of Edinburgh does so only rarely. Her Majesty and His Royal Highness much prefer visiting institutions which are already in full use to opening new ones." The document gave details as to what gifts were acceptable—stressing that the royal couple would not accept commercially-produced articles for fear that this might lead to their being used in advertising. But, the document explains, "very small presents of purely sentimental value offered by children, veterans, etc. are accepted when a refusal would lead to hurt feelings." Gifts of perishable fruit or food as well as of flowers were acceptable as long as it was understood that some, at least, of these gifts would be handed on by the Queen to some local hospital.

The document deals with the question of church services during which the offertory plate should be passed to the Queen "in the normal way" while "the Duke of Edinburgh is sometimes prepared to read the New Testament lesson". While the royal couple wanted to have Sunday kept as free as possible they did want Saturdays to be a full working day so that as many people as possible should have the chance to see the royal visitors. The document asked that the Queen should be provided in advance with brief notes on each of the communities, institutions and places she was going to visit.

Sir Michael Adeane explained in his document that the Queen did not want to spend long at meals. On a working day she considered that an hour was quite long enough for lunch while in the evening mealtimes might be lengthened to about an hour and three quarters—"including speeches". There were details of the wines that might be offered at table and the food that might be served—with oysters, lobsters and other shellfish forbidden because of the Queen's fears that they might lead to tummy upsets.

At the same time as the overseas hosts are busy with their manifold preparations for the royal visit preparations have to be made in Britain. The royal couple have to be inoculated against tetanus, polio, yellow fever and sundry other diseases; anti-malaria pills have to be packed, along with crates of wine, packets of shortbread, jars of jam, bottles of sour cream, tins of chipolatas, packets of parsley, "three tins of Dundee cake . . . bottles of mint sauce, and three tiaras".[2] For a royal tour is not so much a journey as a way of life for the royal couple and the politicians, policemen, pages, doctors, secretaries, valets and maids who accompany them. The luggage must therefore include such mundane things as tea-making equipment as well as barley sugar to be sucked before speech-making. The royal couple also have to be ready to make the presentations expected of them—which explains the "ton of silver-framed photographs and assorted presents . . ."[3]

An important part of the luggage will be the various dresses and suits which the Queen will wear. Until his death Norman Hartnell had the privilege of designing the Queen's clothing and helped to ensure that whether travelling in the heat of the African day or appearing in the glitter of a royal banquet the Queen was fittingly dressed. Prince Philip admired the work of Hartnell and worked with him to ensure, for example, that when touring Nigeria the Queen was protected from the equatorial sun by "a crown-topped canopy, a square of gilded aluminium draped with lightweight velvet which could be carried about or used on a saluting base. This proved highly successful."[4]

It would be tedious to give a blow-by-blow account of even one overseas tour let alone all of them. But it is worth looking closely at one or two tours from the point of view of the Prince and the Queen and to see how such tours appear to the people on the ground. The Coronation Tour of 1953 took the royal couple on a journey of about 40,000 miles during which, in 173 days, they visited 12 Commonwealth countries. Part of their journey was made by air although as their plane crossed the Atlantic its route was covered by a relay of eight ships—so hazardous was flying considered in 1953.

Their plane arrived in Gander, Newfoundland at 3.23 a.m. and "in the middle of the night Philip woke up, puzzled, to hear distant shouts of 'We want the Queen!' and 'Come out, Phil!' For a moment he thought he was dreaming. The plane had touched down at 3.23 a.m. and even there, at that unearthly hour, people were waiting." And so "the travellers dressed in the middle of the night over their nightclothes to respond to the greetings [of] this unofficial reception and then wisely went back to snatch what sleep they could."[5] Meanwhile the plane went on to the West Indies where the temperature and scenery were very different from that of Gander while the crowds were more frenzied. The royal couple now embarked on that endless round of tours, banquets, receptions and speeches. There was some relief from the razzle-dazzle—in Jamaica, for example, they "were lulled to sleep by the songs of the people".[6] But there were various crises to be met; in Bermuda, for example, there was an outcry because, in a population which was two-thirds coloured, there was not a single coloured man among the thirty who sat down to a welcoming dinner at Government House. Later, in Panama, "Philip experienced the most fantastic and probably one of the most frightening welcomes of his life."[7] There were no police on duty along the route taken by the royal procession. It was hardly surprising that the dancing, yelling crowds swept off the pavements where they had been waiting and surged around the cars carrying the royal couple. The Duke and the Queen had been placed in separate cars. The Duke was frightened when he realized that the Queen's car and his own had been slowed to less than a walking pace by the press of the crowd. Some of the excited people rang hand-bells, others tried to jump on the bonnets and roofs of the royal cars. To make matters worse, ordinary cars began to cut in from side streets and the procession had to come to a halt. Fortunately, royal equerries and detectives managed to fight their way through the crush of the crowd to help Prince Philip to make his way from his own car and join the Queen. Then they changed to a closed car as a precautionary measure—in time to escape from the torrential downpour which helped break up the crowd and allow the royal couple to drive slowly on.

The royal couple had flown on the first part of their tour. In Jamaica they boarded the liner *Gothic* on which they had been scheduled to sail in 1952. Now late in 1953 they travelled on this same liner from Jamaica through the Panama Canal to the Commonwealth islands in the Pacific. Here they visited Fiji where they were entertained by Fijians dancing a frenzied war-dance and invited to take "a ceremonial draught of *kava* which had first been brewed before the visitors' eyes by black arms up to their elbows in the mixture. 'You will find it tastes like soap,' Philip warned the Queen as she was handed the potion in half a coconut shell. The Queen drained it bravely."[8] Then it was on to Tonga where they were greeted by the very tall Queen Salote who had won the hearts of the crowds along the Coronation route. Now she drove with her royal visitors in a London taxi-cab which she had ordered when in London. She and the Queen and Prince Philip shared in an exotic feast spread on the ground. When the official guests retired from the meal, the tables were thrown open to the public and in a short time there was nothing left. Then "Philip gleefully reported home that the local musicians played the flute by blowing down their noses . . ."[9]

After the Pacific it was on to New Zealand where their arrival was marred by the worst railway disaster in New Zealand's history. On Christmas Eve a railway bridge collapsed into a flooded river carrying with it a crowded train in which 166 people were killed. In a small country like New Zealand there was "scarcely a family which did not know someone affected by the crash."[10] The Prime Minister asked the Queen not to change the programme which had been arranged for her tour. She and Prince Philip agreed—although they insisted on visiting one of the families which had survived the crash to hear the story from their lips and "Philip was up at 5 a.m. to fly 300 miles to attend the mass funeral service in Wellington. The previous night he had been engaged till nearly midnight at a civic dinner. The funeral journey, however, was the Prime Minister's idea; Philip readily agreed. Personal considerations of fatigue were set aside, as they always must be, though one can sympathetically record that he snatched a cat-nap as he flew back after the service to rejoin the Queen. They had engagements that evening and he had in fact carried out thirty-six hours of engagements with only five hours for sleep."[11]

Having toured the two islands of New Zealand the royal couple then went on to Australia where "the one-time naval lieutenant and his wife were met by ten miles of cheers in Sydney"[12] and by dense crowds in township after township. But amid the crowded programme of a royal tour the Prince insisted that time be found for him to share with the Queen his memories of his previous visit to Australia as a mere midshipman. They motored off to visit a sheep station in Tasmania and arranged to stay at a private home so that the Queen might get some idea of the hospitality the Prince had received there when on wartime leave.

But the royal procession had to go on—to Canberra where the Queen opened the Australian Parliament wearing her Coronation gown which had been flown out from London. Then it was on to Melbourne, Ballarat, Brisbane, Perth and Fremantle, the round of banquets and receptions broken by such things as a visit to the semi-desert area of Woomera with its rocket range and a visit to the Great Barrier Reef where the royal couple enjoyed a day off on one of the tiny coral-edged islands. A day's sunbathing and swimming was a welcome relaxation after "the most lavish carnival that had ever interrupted Australian work and play." Some people camped out for days on the streets merely to be able to glimpse the royal couple as they swept by. "Philip said afterwards that it was just as well he and his wife had been prepared for the excitement of the tour by the welcome in Canada and drilled for parades and the ceremonies by the Coronation season. He felt that the good to be accomplished by such a tour far outweighed the toll to be paid in physical exhaustion."[13] After Australia it was back to the *Gothic* for a journey to the Cocos Islands, Ceylon, Aden and finally Uganda—to make up for the visit which had been cancelled because of her father's death in 1952. Then it was back to meet up with the royal yacht at Tobruk where the children were waiting to accompany them to Malta where they stayed with 'Uncle Dickie' before returning to England.

And what of Prince Philip in this, the longest of the many tours they were to make? Andrew Duncan spent a year following the Queen in 1968–1969 and his *Reality of Monarchy* gives an entertaining account of a year in the royal life. He describes Philip as one who "liked to be the centre of attraction [with] the penetrating way of looking below the listeners' eyes, [an] easy assumption of authority, the background to be convincing, the height to inspire trust."[14] But this is only to describe the man's appearance. There is and was much more to him than that. There was the very humanly concerned man who, having heard about differences between the New Zealand Government and its Maoris took it on himself to try to heal the rift. During their progress through New Zealand the royal couple were scheduled to visit Waikato where the Maoris were to chant an address of welcome. Unfortunately, the crowded schedule did not permit time for the Queen and the Duke to go into the Maoris' meeting-house—and this had annoyed the Maoris. "Philip solved the problem in his own way. The royal cars stopped. The address of welcome was chanted. But just before they turned back to the car Philip nodded at the meeting-house and murmured, 'Couldn't we just take a peep?' Immense Maori cheers greeted this genial move. It was nothing and it was everything. The tour would have been an immense solo triumph for Elizabeth, but with Philip the success was underlined most decisively."[15]

He won the approval of the crowds with his many friendly gestures and humorous asides. When asked to join in the demonstration of sheep-shearing he refused: "No thanks. I might nick it and we've had enough mutton." A homely joke which was repeated in many headlines. The Press also noted how it was Philip who constantly drew the Queen's attention to small illustrations of people's loyalty and affection—a tiny railway station decked out with a message in flowers, a parade of children's pet lambs, the groups of children waiting at outback stations. Yet there was also the serious level—at which he showed that characteristic of appearing to know enough to be "convincing". There was the two-hour visit to a research institute where he discussed pest control with the experts—and won the plaudits of New Zealand's farmers. At Woomera there was a chance to question the experts on inter-continental ballistic missiles, and "all New Zealand felt that no more homely or moving touch could have been contrived" than his reading of the lesson in the old wooden church of St Paul's in Wellington.

During this world tour and throughout his subsequent overseas visits the Prince has shown himself to be much more relaxed than the Queen. In part this is a matter of personality—she the shyer and more introverted of the royal couple and quite unlike her mother with her eye to the camera and the crowds. When they were in Jamaica a wildly excited schoolmaster had tried to play the part of Walter Raleigh by throwing down his raincoat in a puddle. The Queen looked at it carefully, then stepped around it. Not for her the off-the-cuff remarks such as were made by Philip when, in Melbourne, the university students offered him a pair of crutches. He handed them right back with the comment, "Your need is greater than mine." The Queen seems to be hampered, too, by her sense of what is fitting to 'Majesty'. It may be in order for her mother, husband, son and other relatives like Princess Alexandra to radiate charm. The Queen seems to share the opinion of one of her staff who is quoted as saying, "Our capital is stuffiness. We don't exist to convert or divert people. We Are."[16]

Andrew Duncan thinks it unfair to describe the Queen as "grim"; rather he thinks she is "a timid woman doing a job that provides more than the usual amount of idiocies." And Prince Philip has seen it as one of his tasks to help her relax. In Brazil in 1969, for example, she was standing in line with the President of Brazil and other notables while the Press photographers took the 'official' pictures. "The Queen [had] a blank miserable expression. He smiled, touched her arm and she relaxed, smiled nervously back, a tender look of tragic implications . . . and the photographers took more pictures . . ."[17]

Maybe it is inevitable that the Queen has had to stick to the rigid conventions—although as time has gone on she has learned to relax and to play her active part in the now famous walkabouts. But Prince Philip has always had this ability to break through the official barriers. In the Muslim region of Nigeria the womenfolk were forced to stay at home while their menfolk lined the roads and saw the royal procession as it made its way through their country in 1954. "Philip noticed the all-male element and discovered the difficulties. A few minutes later a woman in a hutment heard a quiet voice at the door. Philip was asking, 'May I come in?' "[18]

But there are hazards in being so free in behaviour and speech. In 1968, for example, the Prince was annoyed when the Prime Minister of Chile, Dr Allende, turned up at a state banquet wearing a lounge suit. "Why are you dressed like that?" "Because my Party is poor, and they advised me not to hire evening dress." "If they told you to wear a bathing costume, I suppose you'd come dressed in one?" "Oh no, Sir, our Party is a serious one."[19] Hardly the diplomatic way to win friends and influence people, but then he has little regard for politicians as a breed. Addressing American correspondents in London he said, "I sometimes think that it is a pity the peace of the world if left to politicians who are a quarrelsome lot." But if he has little respect for politicians he seems to have less for those who elect them. As he told the dictator-President of Paraguay, "It is a pleasant change to be in a country which is not ruled by the people."

During the period of the Suez Crisis Prince Philip was out of the country opening the Olympic Games and, later, on his long tour of the southern hemisphere. The Queen is quoted as having confided to one of the family that it was a good job he was not at home during those troubled months. "He would have been hell to live with." In 1965 he came down firmly on the side of the white government of Ian Smith with its illegal Unilateral Declaration of Independence. Like the Queen Mother, Prince Philip has a great deal of sympathy for what they see as the beleaguered whites of Southern Africa. This led to him being attacked by the *Daily Mirror* in July 1965, but the real reason for that attack only became clear with the publication of Cecil King's *Diary* in which we read:

> Tuesday, July 13th, 1965.
> Letter from Cecil King to Harold Wilson.
> CONFIDENTIAL.
> Dear Harold,
> Our attack on Prince Philip was not really caused by his pretty innocuous remarks about Rhodesia. But a few days earlier he had been the guest at lunch of Denis Hamilton (of the *Sunday Times*) at which various newspapermen were present . . . At this lunch Prince Philip's main theme—following the Queen's visit to Germany—was the urgent importance of the re-unification of Germany . . . we cannot have Prince Philip saying in public anything like what he said in private at this lunch. Hence the decision to seize on his remarks about Rhodesia to fire a shot across his bow. We are informed from the Palace that the point has been taken . . .
> Yours sincerely,
> Cecil King.[20]

Throughout his career the Prince has shown little wish to compromise—as a politician might have done—or to observe the silences which are forced on the Queen by convention. He has not seemed to mind if he offends politicians or diplomats. He has been more concerned, on his many foreign tours, to respond to the fervour of the welcomes that have always been waiting and to carry out the many tasks which have to be performed by the royal visitor. At a Mansion House luncheon he tried to explain why he was willing to travel through the heat of Nigeria and the cold of Antarctica. "I believe that there are some things for which it is worthwhile making some personal sacrifices. I believe that the British Commonwealth is one of those things, and I am, for one, prepared to sacrifice a good deal if by so doing I can advance its well-being by even a small degree."[21] And, in spite of his attitudes to Rhodesia and South

Africa, there is little doubt that he has done much to maintain a close link between the multi-national Commonwealth and the Crown.

He is, nevertheless, fully aware that there are other reasons for many of the royal tours. He knows, for example, that one of the reasons for the tour of South America in 1968 was to promote British trade. At that time British firms were trying to get the Chilean Government to sign a contract for the purchase from Britain of a nuclear reactor. By the time the royal party had arrived in Chile it seemed as if the deal might not come off and that the Chileans might buy a French reactor, so Prince Philip was asked to draw Chilean attention to British industrial progress and the advantages of trade between the two countries. He did so in a speech to the Chamber of Commerce in Santiago on the 13th November 1968:

> Co-operation and collaboration between Chileans and British works, and works well. This is the best possible basis for the further development and expansion of trading and commercial activities of all kinds. I am certain this is possible and indeed desirable for both countries.
>
> The pattern [of trade] has changed dramatically in the last twenty years alone. The Chilean economy is totally different and vastly more developed. Equally, British industry has become immensely more sophisticated technologically and scientifically.
>
> And that is not all. Trade is no longer a simple matter of exporting and importing, or of straightforward financing and investing. Many other factors have entered into the business, and today credit terms, co-operative enterprises and all sorts of subtle variations have to be devised to keep the wheels of trade turning smoothly to the mutual benefit of both partners.
>
> As far as British exports to Chile are concerned, there can be no doubt whatsoever that British industry has a very great deal to offer Chile. Every kind of advanced technological equipment is available, but someone has to make it his business to convince potential customers in the teeth of efficient and ruthless competition.

The agreement—worth at least £635,000 initially—was signed on December 19th.

In spite of his dislike of politicians, Prince Philip has been willing to allow royal tours to be used for political purposes. The visit to North America in 1957, for example, was designed in part at least to heal the rifts in Anglo-American relations which had followed from the débâcle over Suez in the autumn of 1956. This visit, like their earlier visit to North America in 1951, took the Queen and Prince Philip first to Canada where they were followed by over three thousand accredited journalists before they left to land on American soil at Jamestown, Virginia. This visit was especially to commemorate the three hundred and fiftieth anniversary of the establishment of the first British colony in the New World. After an eight-hour programme of junketing with people dressed in Elizabethan costumes and bewigged with curls they flew off to Washington where President Eisenhower was waiting to welcome them at the airport. There was the usual round of children's hospitals, receptions, visits to art galleries, wreath laying and the rest—a total of 114 ceremonies in a mere 81 hours.

The political side of the visit was stressed on the final night in Washington. An Australian was the senior Commonwealth representative in Washington and the traditional dinner by the Queen for the host-President was staged in the Australian Embassy. This was a reminder that the Queen was visiting Washington as the representative of many peoples and that whatever isolationist Americans might think Britain and the British Commonwealth could be neither isolated nor isolationist. The good effect of that visit and dinner may be gauged by President Eisenhower's parting impression of the Queen as confided to a friend: "She's a good girl. She's all right." And as for Philip, the saying went round, "He's regular!"[22]

But if Britain wished to show the USA that it was still the centre of a world-wide Commonwealth, British politicians, industrialists and economists were well aware, in 1965, that Britain was no longer holding its own in the industrial world. Some people believed that if Britain became a member of the EEC the cold *douche* of competition would compel industry to modernize and invest and force trade unions to accept the realities of economic life. It is hardly the fault of the royal family if these hopes have not been realized. But the royal couple were used by politicians to try to make it easier for Britain to join the EEC. President de Gaulle had vetoed Britain's first application for membership in 1961. In 1965 Harold Wilson hoped that the other members of the Community might bring pressure to bear on the ageing President and force him to agree to Britain's application. In order to arouse enthusiasm for Britain the politicians arranged for the Queen and Prince Philip to make a state visit to West Germany in the spring of 1965. Not everyone in Britain welcomed the news of this proposed tour. The *Daily Express* complained: "They are precisely the same people who held the dagger to our throats." The royal visit—the first by a British sovereign since 1913—was meant as a gesture of reconciliation after the world wars, all the more welcome to the Queen and Prince Philip because of their many German relatives, and the crowds in West Germany and those who gathered at the infamous Berlin Wall gave the Queen and her husband a rapturous welcome.

Overseas tours are, in general, arranged at the dictates of politicians, but in the autumn of 1961 the Queen showed that she was not always willing to be treated as a puppet. In September 1961 she was preparing for her tour of Ghana, but the news from that unhappy country was of strikes and demonstrations against the rule of Dr Nkrumah who responded by putting fifty of his leading opponents into jail. There were bomb explosions and threats against the life of the unpopular President. Elder statesmen in Britain—such as Churchill and Eden—argued that the Queen ought not to be allowed to go to Ghana where she might be killed by a bullet meant for the President. They knew that if she went she would insist, as always, that there would be no motorcycle outriders between her and the crowds, and that she be allowed to make that contact with ordinary people which she regarded as the most important part of her work in the Commonwealth. The Queen listened to the politicians' arguments against her proposed tour. Then she declared that unless the Cabinet imposed a veto (with all its constitutional implications) she would insist on making the visit. As she said, "If I were to cancel now, Nkrumah might invite Khrushchev instead and they wouldn't like that, would they?"[23] She did go after all, and the tour was a great success, much to the delight of her Prime Minister, Harold Macmillan.[24]

Not everyone agrees that these foreign tours are worthwhile. Some criticize them on the grounds of cost, others complain that they are merely a part of a royal soap opera which serves to disguise realities. In a speech to the Mansion House in 1957 Prince Philip recounted some of these attacks on the tour which he had made to Australia and Antarctica. He then went on to say: "You cannot please all people all the time. You do not please the half-hearted, the defeatists, the players for safety. But you delight and thrill the eager, the energetic and the brave, the men and women who look to the future."[25] And, as the crowds that gather everywhere reveal, the appeal is to ordinary people in general.

This was denied by journalist and author Colin MacInnes. Writing in 1969 he refuted the belief that the monarchy helps to preserve the Commonwealth.

> This is believed to some extent in England, a little in Australia, a very little in Canada, but nowhere else, so far as I can discover from enquiry among citizens of other Commonwealth countries. That a visit from the Queen to some part of the Commonwealth may be welcomed is still probably true—but so would one from Mrs Jacqueline Kennedy, or for that matter, Mrs Elizabeth Burton . . .[26]

Notice the *may be welcomed* with the subliminal implication that really the truth is otherwise. This flies in the face of all the evidence of the welcome received by the Queen and Prince Philip during the years since 1969. Notice, too, the journalist's belief that Mrs Kennedy (later Onassis) or Mrs Burton (once Taylor) would be as welcome as the Queen. One only has to read this in 1981 to realize how trite are the criticisms of the critics who are concerned with the trivia and ephemeral.

MacInnes's criticism appeared as part of a symposium. It was unfortunate for him that another contributor, writing from the viewpoint of a Frenchman, should have written:

> On the continent the Queen enjoys wild and dazzling success. In France, Germany and Italy the mere fact that her photograph appears on the front of a newspaper or magazine virtually ensures its success . . . In Berlin, Rome or Brussels the Queen attracts more attention than any other Head of State, at home or visiting there. In Paris itself, she would draw more crowds than General de Gaulle who has such a mystic fascination for the French . . . and the husband of the Queen [is seen] as the devoted husband, doing his utmost to support his wife in the prodigious, complex and well-nigh hopeless task for which she seemed so ill-prepared. Where the Queen went, he went too, discreet and attentive, always ready to fly to her rescue with word or gesture . . . radiating confidence and manly charm.

For several years now this heartening political and matrimonial image has been superseded by a third; the emancipated husband. He is still there to bear the brunt, but he is no longer the Sovereign's faithful shadow. He has on occasion taken the leading role, and does not hesitate, if the opportunity arises, to take a bold initiative even if it runs contrary to the strict tradition of royal protocol. He sometimes looks a trifle bored, as if he found the whole thing rather silly. He ducks Pressmen, harangues industrialists, sets off on a voyage around the world and grows his beard to show that he is a free man.

This is no Prince Charming but a mature man, thinking for himself and living his own life. Some people would go so far as to say that it is he who is the King . . .[27]

35

The National Playing Fields Association

EVEN HIS CRITICS AGREE THAT Prince Philip has carried his kindness and concern for children outside the walls of the Palace. In walkabouts he goes out of his way to talk to them, and although there are reports of his rudeness to some adults—from the Press, in yachting clubs in the Bahamas and so on—there is no report of his having been unkind to a child. As his valet recalled:

> All youth movements interested him, and soon after his marriage he spent a lot of time at boys' clubs in the poorest parts of London, drinking coffee and soft drinks with them in their canteens. Inspector Usher, who went with the Duke—in plain clothes of course—was amused one night when a shrewd little Cockney at a boys' club correctly guessed his occupation and called out to his pals: "Look mates, Philip's got his copper wiv 'im."[1]

As Consort he has maintained that interest in the boys' clubs movement. Indeed, one reporter believes that he ". . . is, of course, at his best in the . . . atmosphere of boys' clubs . . . Each year he spends a night visiting London boys' clubs—he has visited sixty altogether—informally and with great enthusiasm . . ."[2]

During his early visits to industrial areas "the Duke was appalled to see children playing in the street and anxiously determined that green spaces should be found for them."[3] This determination to make things better for urban children led him to accept the post of President of the National Playing Fields Association, a post which he held for twenty-five years. Normally he will accept a patronage only for a short period. The fact that he held on to his post at the NPFA until 1972 is evidence of his interest and concern.

According to his cousin it was King George VI "who saw that the post would help forge civic links for Philip throughout Britain's intricate national life, and the late King more or less dragooned Uncle Dickie out of office."[4] The King's involvement with the Association dated back to the First World War. In August 1918 the then Duke of York was a serving officer in the still-new Royal Air Force. At the RAF headquarters at St Leonard's the Duke of York was in command of a squadron of the No. 5 RAF Cadet Wing. He took a "keen interest in the physical and technical training of young men . . . and an enthusiastic pride in the cadets under his charge."[5] According to his official biographer it was this work with RAF cadets which "fired his imagination and in fact it was at . . . St Leonard's . . . that he first became imbued with those early ideals of sport and fitness which in later life he made a slogan in his public speeches and which found expression in his work with the Industrial Welfare Society, the National Playing Fields Fund and, above all, in his own Duke of York's Camp."[6]

That King George VI should have 'pushed' Prince Philip into a position of authority in his Association may be seen as a mark of signal regard; he must have known that his son-in-law would prove a fitting occupant of the place which not only he himself once held, but which "the magnificent Mountbatten" had also held.

'Uncle Dickie' or Lord Mountbatten had become the President of the Association in 1947, but he had all too little time to devote to the progress of the Association. He had, after all, only recently returned from India and was trying to catch up on his own naval career. The Association was badly in need of someone with energy and drive to put its affairs in order. By 1949 it was saddled with heavy mortgages, overdrafts and other debts; the long years of the war had seen the work of the Association almost come to a halt. That the King should have thought Prince Philip suited to undertake the work of rejuvenating the ailing Association is a tribute to the energy, initiative and enthusiasm that the Prince had shown for his other work.

Prince Philip became Chairman while he was still attending the Staff Course at the Naval College at Greenwich. At his first meeting he told the committee, "Gentlemen, I want to assure you that I have no intention of being a sitting tenant in this post."[7] And his work since then has shown how well he has lived up to his assurance.

He invited the council and the Association's officials to come to a luncheon at the Palace. This was done with "Uncle Bertie's full approval . . ."[8] It was the first of many such unorthodox luncheons at the Palace.

Philip then got down to drafting an appeal to be sent out with his name on it. He used his contacts to squeeze the greatest amount possible from the largest number of people. He rallied support from industrialists, from people in the worlds of sport and show business and from the public at large.

When he had completed the Staff Course at Greenwich he used to spend each morning at the offices of the NPFA, walking from Clarence House to reach the Buckingham Gate office at about nine o'clock. This allowed him to supervise the progress of his appeal, to make fresh suggestions and to enthuse others with his own drive, energy and imagination. Hahn would have approved of the wholehearted way in which his former pupil tackled this project.

The Prince showed himself willing to undertake almost any task to help raise the desired £500,000. It was he who hit on the idea of labelling it the Silver Jubilee Fund. This linked his appeal with the very popular King George VI and Queen Elizabeth. It also set a date by which he wanted to raise the money—for Their Majesties' Jubilee was to be celebrated in 1952.

It soon became apparent that he was aware of the importance of every aspect of publicity to help the appeal. There were posters, speeches, broadcasts—but there was much more. There was attendance at Variety Club matinées, to one of which Frank Sinatra came and performed for nothing. That raised £16,000. There was the film which he made in Malta with Bob Hope as its star. The film showed poor children whose only playgrounds were the neighbourhood streets. That film raised £84,000. There were charity cricket games in which he played alongside Test stars such as Bill Edrich and Denis Compton, and a reunion of Butlin holiday campers at the Albert Hall to accept a cheque for £7,000. There was a visit to another holiday camp, at Skegness, to accept a cheque for his fund—and to endure "the gaze of 5,000 bright-eyed girl campers singing 'All the nice girls love a sailor' ".[9] Jack Solomon, the boxing promoter, ran a tournament for the benefit of the fund—and was invited to the Palace to present the cheque, "wearing his NPFA green-striped tie".[10]

This sort of activity raised fears among the 'old school' and the 'old dears' that Philip was going too far, but he was willing to risk this sort of condemnation provided that what he was doing helped raise the necessary money. He always tried to fit in a meeting to do with the NPFA whenever this was possible. As his cousin wrote:

> A day in Edinburgh happened to be scheduled in the Duke's appointment book as a Scottish Playing Fields committee. Before the day was out, the Duke of Edinburgh had inspected three guards of honour, walked in procession to church with the magistrates, lunched with the Lord Provost, visited a local mariners' club, taken an army salute, watched a fly-past and been vociferously cheered through the city.[11]

In 1979 I met officials from the Association in the course of preparing this work. I discovered that they were all too aware of the heavy burden of public work which still falls to their President. He is still an active

President; he attends meetings regularly, and arranges small functions and meetings at the Palace where benefactors and organizers of the Association can be thanked. But when asked in 1978 to attend a luncheon to discuss informally some future development he had been obliged to reply that the earliest date he had available was in May 1979.

His initial appeal was a great success. By 1952 he had raised the planned £500,000 and then set about ensuring a steady flow of money into the Association's coffers; today it has a steady income of about £270,000 a year. His initial success was reflected in the rapid increase in the number of playing fields opened each year. In 1949 when he took over as President about thirty fields were opened or being planned. In 1952 over two hundred fields were opened. By 1960 the Association had raised the staggering sum of a million pounds and Prince Philip was using television to open five fields at a time. In all over 2,500 were opened in the 1950s and, as he said, "I will go almost anywhere to see a new playing field opened."[12]

One of the main and regular sources of the funds for his Association is the Variety Club of Great Britain. This was founded in 1949 and, like all other national variety clubs, was modelled on the first such club formed in Pittsburgh USA in 1928. Because of its name "the general public believes that the Variety Club of Great Britain derives its name from the variety or vaudeville stage. *This is not so*. The Variety Club movement was founded by eleven men associated with films and other forms of entertainment and today's membership is drawn from motion pictures, the theatre, television, theatrical costuming, sport, fairgrounds, radio, records, the circus, holiday camps, Press, juke-boxes and other subsidiaries of the entertainment world in general. In brief, Variety, as used in the club title means—*a variety of the show business professions*."[13]

Both Lord Mountbatten and Prince Philip were enrolled as 'gold card life members' of the Club in 1951. The Club raises and spends huge sums of money on a wide variety of projects. In 1977 it raised and spent £1,200,000; in 1978 over £1,500,000. Some of this money goes to the National Playing Fields Association; some of it goes to support youth centres and boys' clubs; some to help develop sports and recreational centres such as the one in Islington which was sponsored by Variety through an initial contribution of £1,100,000 donated by a member of the Club, Sir Michael Sobell.

Prince Philip has been glad to receive the help of the Club for his own Association. In return he supports the wider work of the Variety Club. He visits boys' clubs and youth centres sponsored by the Club; he and other members of the Royal Family attend various functions planned to raise money for the Club. There are, for example, Royal Charity Première evenings at theatres and cinemas. On the 23rd October 1978 "HM The Queen, HRH The Duke of Edinburgh and Earl Mountbatten of Burma were guests of honour at the Royal Charity Première of Agatha Christie's *Death on the Nile* at the ABC 1 & 2 Theatres, Shaftesbury Avenue, London

. . . to aid the Variety's Heart Fund and the Royal British Legion. The event, one of the year's biggest film first-nights, raised a sum of £26,000 . . ."[14]

In 1966 Prince Philip was touring America to raise funds for the Variety Club's many charities. In Miami Beach an American businessman offered to donate $100,000 if only the Prince would take a swim in his private swimming-pool. The Prince stripped, dived in, swam—and collected the cheque. This unprincely behaviour was matched when he gave his patronage to the English-Scottish Tiddly-winks Championships. He designed the Silver Wink which is presented to the winner. The annual championships resemble the more rowdy features of students' rag-weeks, but each year the participants raise over £1,000 for the NPFA.

Prince Philip is patron of a number of charities. I have dealt with the NPFA at some length largely because it is the one with which he was associated for the longest time and consideration of his work for the Association enables one to see something of the work which he puts into his patronages. But it would be wrong to see him as being only or mainly concerned with the extroverted side of money-raising or with meeting children. He has shown a concern for drug addicts, visiting centres where young people are being treated, and he has visited Borstals and tried to understand what leads young people into crime. It is, of course, easier for Prince Philip than for the Queen to be relaxed and at ease—with film stars, boxing promoters, handicapped children and people at large. He presents the Royal Family's human face—as the Queen Mother has done over many more years. The Queen has, until very recently, seemed to be concerned to show the dignity of Majesty. She seems to think that her formality is balanced by the geniality of her husband, her mother and her son. In this sense, her husband-consort is her complement for which we ought to be grateful.

36

The Duke of Edinburgh's Award Scheme

PRINCE PHILIP'S INTEREST IN YOUNG PEOPLE in general is dismissed by some of his critics as merely a liking for "the jockstrap-scented atmosphere of boys' clubs".[1] This illustrates the fact that he and other members of the Royal Family are on a hiding-to-nothing in regard to their activities and interests. If he went regularly to the Saddle Club, it was claimed to be a sign of his wish to escape from 'the cage' and to "live it up"; if he played a game, he was criticized as "the polo-playing playboy"; if the family play only a traditional role they are attacked as being "stuffy"; yet if they allow the BBC to make a television film of life at the Palace they are accused of "cheapening" royalty.

Prince Philip's interest in young people is best illustrated by his Duke of Edinburgh's Award Scheme. He claims that "It has probably done more for people than anything else I have been interested in." This is a sweeping claim when we consider his interest in the National Playing Fields Association, London boys' clubs, youth clubs in general and the Medical Commission for Accident Prevention. His carping critics do not think much of his Scheme. It is, they say, "an attempt" to encourage leisure activities among young people that seems "slightly square" in spite of attempts to enliven it.[2]

The Scheme has, in fact, been much more than "an attempt"—a term that suggests failure. It has, on the contrary, been a great success, both in Great Britain and overseas. It has also done much more than encourage "leisure activities", a term which suggests merely recreational pursuits and/or merely physical endurance tests. Its basic concept has been one of service to the community. I find it almost impossible to comment on the accusation that the Scheme is "slightly square" because the criticism itself is almost meaningless, but I find the squareness of the Scheme and its participants preferable to the trendiness of much that was beloved of the critics in the 1960s when the Scheme flowered.

The Duke of Edinburgh had first suggested some form of Award Scheme in 1954. He chaired an Originating Committee which met throughout 1954 and 1955 to work out details for the Award and in 1956 a pilot experiment was launched—for boys only. The intention was to offer boys between the ages of fifteen and nineteen the opportunity of participating in a challenging programme of leisure time activities which were both enjoyable and purposeful. At the request of local education authorities the starting age was lowered to fourteen. They argued that if young people were allowed to start the Scheme in what was then the last year of compulsory attendance at school they might be encouraged to carry on after they left. In this way the Award would provide a bridge between school and further education or work.

The organizers made it clear that the objects of the Scheme were "to encourage in the individual the spirit of voluntary service, self-reliance and perseverance, a sense of responsibility and the pursuit of hobbies and other leisure activities through a programme of activities, divided into five sections: Service, Expeditions, Interests, Design for Living and Physical Activities." In these various ways the Scheme was intended to play an important role in fostering a sense of community and nationalism as well as helping young people towards finding employment. The Duke of Edinburgh issued his own statement on the Scheme:

> BUCKINGHAM PALACE
>
> Young people growing up in an industrial society have many difficulties to face and not many opportunities for personal achievements. At the same time parents, schools, voluntary organizations and industrial firms who recognize their responsibilities also have to overcome many problems. This scheme is intended to help both the young and those people who take an interest in their welfare. It is designed as an introduction to leisure time activities, a challenge to the individual to personal achievement, and as a guide to those people and organizations who are concerned about the development of our future citizens.
>
> I hope that all those who take part in this scheme will find an added purpose and pleasure in their lives. I am quite sure that all who enter for this scheme and all those who help run it will gain that special sense of satisfaction which comes from the discovery of hidden abilities and from helping others to overcome a challenge.
>
> PHILIP

It is worth noting that this scheme was started in 1956 and that "community involvement" and "participation" have only become trendy words in the 1970s. The Scheme was, in that sense, ahead of its time in wishing to prepare young people for carrying responsibility—at play and at work—and for wishing to develop their self-reliance, initiative and breadth of vision.

In 1979 the Award authorities issued *Outline* which summarized the way in which the Scheme works:

> **The Scheme in Outline**
>
> The Award Scheme offers young people in the United Kingdom and in other Commonwealth countries a challenge to endeavour and achievement through a balanced programme with a wide choice of leisure activities. Those involved are encouraged to develop existing interests or undertake

something new. Thousands of young people find not only fresh ideas but also wider opportunities for enjoyment, excitement and satisfaction in their leisure time.

Young people take part in the Scheme; they do not belong to it as members of an organization. They may gain Awards through their schools, as employees through their firms, within a youth organization or on their own.

An Award may be gained by anyone, between their 14th and 25th birthdays, who qualifies in four of the sections of the Scheme, each section relating to activities of a different kind. The qualifying standards are variously defined in terms of proficiency, perseverance or sustained effort. Participants are assessed on the use which they make of their individual aptitudes and abilities and not in competition with others. Success depends more on effort and persistence than on either brains or brawn, and physical handicap need not deter anyone from taking part.

There are three Awards which may be gained by participants of differing age and maturity. There is no necessity to progress from one to another, but certain exemptions are allowed for those who do.

The Bronze Award is for boys and girls over 14 years of age. Their participation involves adult help and encouragement to discover their own capabilities and new possibilities.

The Silver Award is for young people over 15 years of age. Its attainment involves both discovery and development of the use of their leisure time, with the help of adults.

The Gold Award is for young men and women over 16 years of age. They are expected to play a large part in planning their own programmes to meet the requirements. The Award is recognition of individuality, effort and achievement.

The latest date for entry into the Scheme is the 23rd birthday and the upper age limit for all Awards is the 25th birthday.

An important feature of the Scheme is the contribution made by adults, who are not necessarily connected with schools, youth organizations or vocational training, but who, as members of the community with hobbies of their own are prepared to give some of their leisure time to pass on their knowledge and interest to a younger person. Mutual understanding between the generations is more easily achieved when a shared enthusiasm provides common ground.

The Sections

For each Award, those taking part have to meet the requirements in activities of their own choice, in four out of five sections. Each of the five sections includes a different category of activities. The range of activities within a section and the choice of sections is different for Bronze, Silver and Gold Awards.

Service. This involves either practical community service after necessary briefing or training; or specialized training in, for example, first aid, life-saving, care of animals, fire service or home nursing. For the Gold Award both briefing or training and practical voluntary service are required, together covering a period of twelve months.

Expeditions. After training and practical preparation, journeys are planned and undertaken in small groups on foot, or using cycles or other means of travelling. For young men some physical challenge is involved but for young women the emphasis is more on a journey of discovery.

Interests. Participants are required to choose and sustain an interest in an activity such as music, shooting, driving, painting, judo, canoeing or craft work. There is no emphasis on fixed standards of attainment.

EITHER *Design for Living*. Assessment is made at the end of short courses on subjects which relate to the individual, the family and the community. The very wide range includes floral decoration, entertaining, courtship and marriage, acquiring a home, and topics such as money matters and local and national government.

OR *Physical Activity*. Assessment is based partly on training for physical activities and partly on attainment of standards in events chosen from physical efficiency, athletics, swimming, individual sports and games.

At the Gold stage participants are required to have some *residential experience* away from home, lasting at least five days. This can be gained on a course, work camp or other events of a similar nature.

Any organization which is concerned with young people within the Award age range may apply to the National Awards Office to be licensed as an Operating Authority. These include education authorities, voluntary youth organizations, armed and police forces and many firms, independent schools and government establishments. The Operating Authorities are authorized to grant Awards on behalf of HRH the Duke of Edinburgh. They are responsible for ensuring that the conditions of the Scheme are complied with and that its standards are maintained. They make all arrangements for young people to enter, train and be assessed and they distribute all necessary literature within their own organizations.

In some overseas countries the Scheme has been renamed; in Ghana it is known as the Head of State Award, in Lesotho as the Prince Mohato Award, in Kenya it is The President's Award, as also in Sierra Leone and Trinidad and Tobago, while in Nigeria it is known as The Nigerian National Youth Award.

Each National Award Authority is entirely independent but can call on the services of the Overseas Department of the International Headquarters in London which supplies each Authority with Award publications, advice and assistance when requested.

When the Scheme was first launched seven thousand boys were enrolled as the first participators. No one could have foreseen the way in which the Scheme would flourish. In 1977 there were 200,000 people participating in the Scheme which had made well over one million Awards. The Scheme had initially been intended for boys only, but even as the first boys enrolled in the Scheme there was a demand that girls should be allowed to take part. This demand grew and in 1957 a working party was set up to produce a programme for girls. This working party was made up of women well experienced with teenage girls. The aim was to produce a challenging programme of leisure activities attractive to girls within the age group 14–21 years. The working party was careful to produce a programme specifically aimed at girls and not merely a 'watered down' version of the boys' Scheme. The pilot Scheme for girls was launched in September 1958 after a series of Planning Conferences involving the local education authorities and voluntary youth organizations who pioneered the girls' Scheme.

If the originators were caught by surprise by the numbers participating in Great Britain, they must have been even more surprised by the way in which Commonwealth and other countries sought to be allowed to take part in the Scheme. In 1977 the Scheme was operating in Anguilla, Antigua, Ascension, Australia, Bahamas, Barbados, Belize, Bermuda, Botswana, British Virgin Islands, Brunei, Canada, Cayman Islands, Dominica, Falkland Islands, Fiji, Ghana, Gibraltar, Gilbert Islands, Grenada, Hong Kong, India, Jamaica, Kenya, Lesotho, Malta, Mauritius, New Zealand, Nigeria, Papua New Guinea, Seychelles, Sierra Leone, Solomon Islands, Sri Lanka, St Helena, St Kitts-Nevis, St Lucia, St Vincent, Swaziland, Tonga, Trinidad and Tobago, Tristan da Cunha, Turks and Caicos Islands, United Kingdom, Western Samoa. There were also schools licensed as Individual Operators in Cyprus, France, Spain and West Germany. And, through the International Office, Awards have also been made to nationals in Burma, Denmark, Ethiopia, Finland, Greece, Iran, Italy, Malawi, Malaysia, Pakistan, Poland, South Africa, Thailand, Uganda, United States of America and Tanzania.

In 1978 the United States of America gave the accolade to the Scheme, by introducing the Congressional Award based on the Duke of Edinburgh's Award. The introduction of that Award was marked by a visit by Prince Philip to Washington in October. He attended a reception hosted by the Senators and Congressmen responsible for initiating the Congressional Award and he also chaired the inaugural meeting of the Award Authority. A Bill to promote the Award had been sponsored in both the Senate and the House of Representatives. The Americans plan to appoint a full-time National Director and to launch the pilot scheme in Minnesota. It is worth noting that among members of the Committee which sponsored the promotion of the Congressional Award Scheme were three holders of the Golden Award issued by the International Office. They wish to bring to the youth of the USA some of the benefits which they feel they have derived from their participation in the Award Scheme.

The first Gold Award was made in 1958. One of the ways in which the Duke of Edinburgh tried to enhance the Scheme was to arrange for Gold Award presentations to be made in Buckingham Palace. When there were a small number of people gaining the Gold Award the presentation was relatively a simple affair. Today, with about five thousand young people gaining this Award, things have to be organized differently. The Awards are now presented at Buckingham Palace, Holyroodhouse in Edinburgh and in various provincial centres. Today, too, the Award is not always given by the Duke himself. He has drawn other members of the Royal Family into his Scheme so that the Duke of Kent, Princess Anne and the Queen Mother have given the Gold Award to some people. The Duke has also used many well-known personalities to reward Gold Award winners; Jimmy Savile, Henry Cooper and others have played their part in the giving of Awards.

But the State Apartments at the Palace are still used for Gold Award presentations. The Apartments consist of ten rooms—the Picture Gallery, Blue Drawing-Room, Music Room, White Drawing-Room, Throne Room, Green Drawing-Room, East Gallery, Supper Room, Ballroom and State Dining-Room.

Three presentations are normally held a year, each of which is attended by some eight hundred recipients from England, Wales and Northern Ireland. As well as Gold Award recipients, one parent for each young person is invited to the Presentation and also a representative or adult helper from the school, youth organization, club or firm through which the participant took part in the Scheme, bringing the total number of people in Buckingham Palace to nearly two thousand.

A presentation is also held at Holyroodhouse in Edinburgh during the summer months for Gold Award winners from Scotland.

The Award Scheme in England is divided into seven geographical regions—North-East, North-West, East Midlands, West Midlands, Eastern, London and South-East, South-West. For the Presentations these regions, together with Wales and Northern Ireland, are each allocated a different room of the State Apartments and the young people are divided into groups of about twenty.

Each group is supervised by a marshal, who is chosen from the adult helpers or representatives nominated to attend the presentation. There is also a room steward in charge of each individual apartment.

The times of entrance and departure for guests into Buckingham Palace are staggered to make sure that those attending do not have too long a wait before the ceremony.

His Royal Highness, the Duke of Edinburgh, enters the Picture Gallery at two thirty p.m. accompanied by his Equerry, the Director of the Award Scheme and the Senior Deputy Director. His Royal Highness proceeds from the Picture Gallery, to the Blue Drawing-Room, on to the Music Room and White Drawing-Room, crosses the Picture Gallery to the Throne Room and Green Drawing-Room then through the Tapestry Room into the East Gallery and so on to the Supper Room and Ballroom, which has the largest number of groups and finally to the State Dining-Room, ending the ceremony at approximately four-thirty p.m.

As His Royal Highness proceeds through each room, the Director of the Scheme presents the marshals to him and before leaving each group his Equerry hands the certificates to His Royal Highness who gives them to the marshal for subsequent presentation.

One correspondent remembers the day her son received the Gold Award at Holyroodhouse in Edinburgh in 1964:

> I still have the invitation card for myself and my husband to attend the Palace of Holyroodhouse.
>
> The Duke, piloting his own private helicopter, alighted on the lawn of the house in front of a spellbound audience of boys and girls and parents on a beautiful day in July (22nd). To our delight, the Duke stopped and spoke to

my son and his two friends, asking about their particular travels in the Lake District which led to their Gold Award.

We were thrilled to speak to the Duke and he had a wonderful send-off when he stepped in departure into his helicopter.

This is a day we will always remember . . .[3]

The Duke also presents Gold Awards in various parts of the country. At first he undertook to visit two centres each year. Today, as a result of the expansion of the Scheme, he undertakes more and longer tours. In 1978, for example, he undertook three tours, visiting Cornwall, Devon, Avon, Somerset and Gloucestershire in May, Surrey and Hampshire in June and West Yorkshire in October. He also toured Award Scheme activities in the Channel Islands during the course of the state visit there in June. On these tours he met not only the winners of Gold Awards but also many thousands of the participants in the Scheme as well as leaders, helpers and other people connected with the Scheme.

Originally there were to be two annual presentations at Buckingham Palace, today there are five. Originally the Scheme was administered by a very small headquarters staff in London with Territorial Offices in Cardiff, Edinburgh and Belfast. But as the Scheme grew so too did the Organization have to expand and in 1967 six Regional Offices were established; and as the number of people participating in the Scheme grew each year so too did the organizers try to keep the Scheme up to date. In the 1960s the trend in education was towards mixed schools and clubs with boys and girls taking part in joint activities. This made it more difficult for the two separate Schemes—for boys and girls—to work properly. A Working Party was set up in 1967 to look at both Schemes. The result of the Working Party's Report was the introduction of the single revised Scheme under the title of 'The Award Scheme for Young People'. This Scheme was welcomed by young people as was shown by the continued rise in the number of new entrants.

The Scheme was also welcomed by local authorities, many firms and teachers as well as leaders of voluntary organizations. Bradford has been one of the first cities to adopt the Scheme in 1959. The local authority had set aside the Deversham Street School as a centre where for five nights a week boys and girls went to work on part of their programme. In 1972–1973 the Lord Mayor of Bradford was Mrs Audrey Firth, JP. She marked her year of office by appealing for support for her proposal to provide a purpose-built Duke of Edinburgh Award Centre and in July 1974 the Duke visited Bradford to open this new Centre. It has two lecture rooms, a social area and coffee bar. The lecture rooms can be adapted to serve as dormitories for residential courses while the kitchens have been equipped to provide three-course meals. The Centre also has offices, tutorial rooms, a garage/workshop where motorists among Award seekers can undertake their work. The Centre is meant to provide a base for the five hundred or so young people in Bradford engaged in the Scheme, but it also serves as a Training Centre for leaders in the Scouts,

Boys' Brigades and other youth movements who want to set up new groups aimed at achieving the Award.

It is not surprising that the former Lord Mayor is proud of "the very first purpose-built Duke of Edinburgh's Award Centre in the country—indeed in the world."[4]

The organizers of the Scheme have continued to be ready to adapt their Scheme to changing conditions. In June 1978 they published details of new conditions—the result of "wide consultations over the past three years" with Operating Authorities and Award users. The main difference between the old and the new conditions is that the four sections of the Scheme—Service, Expeditions, Interests and Physical Recreation—are mandatory for all participants. In the Service section greater emphasis is given to forms of practical service to the community. As an example of such service the *Award Journal* published details of the work of one young team:

CARLSBERG SPECIAL

A made-to-measure wheel-chair powered by twin 12-volt batteries has opened up a new world for little Andrew Buckby aged nine. The chair has been built by three young people taking part in the Duke of Edinburgh's Award Scheme. Andrew, who is paralysed from the waist down and has never walked, is thrilled with the new freedom it gives him.

"I'm just learning to drive it in dad's garage, but one day I will be able to go out in it to see my friends," he said with delight.

His mother, Mrs Rita Buckby, said at their home in St Luke's Close, Spratton, Northampton: "It really does make a world of difference. Whenever he wanted anything he had to shout for me to get it, but now he will have the freedom to do so many things for himself."

The chair is the 'Carlsberg Special'—built in the workshops at Carlsberg Brewery's UK headquarters in Northampton with backing and finance from the Danish lager company.

The design team members are nineteen-year-old apprentices Neville Evelyn, Martin Starmer and Errol Damerun. Secretarial trainee Bernadette MacMahon, also nineteen, and Gerrard Mavian, aged twenty, a personnel trainee, handled the clerical work. "We phoned round the local children's handicapped centres to find a needy case, and that is how we came upon Andrew, a lovely little boy," they explained.

"We then contacted the various wheel-chair manufacturers to get the latest design ideas which we have modified to suit his special needs. We have made it possible for him to operate his own chair with only his left hand, in which he has most strength." Their gift to Andrew is part of their Community Service.

Mr Jim Edwards, Managing Director of Plessey Connectors Ltd, is Chairman of the Industrial Project for Northampton, and ex-policeman, Michael Stevenson, the county's full-time Award Officer for the Industrial Project.

Mr Stevenson explained: "Carlsberg was one of the first companies to support us, but several are now involved and we have over seventy young working people aiming for Awards. We want all the support we can get and achievements like this help one to illustrate the reason why."

Christian, Lady Hesketh of Towcester, who is chairman of the entire Award scheme for the county, commented: "It is wonderful to hear of the special job that has been done for Andrew, and exciting to know that when given encouragement, young people are so willing to help. I hope they all achieve their Gold Awards."[5]

Under the revised Scheme a two-day expedition on land or water will be a requirement for all participants in the Expeditions section at Bronze level. At the Silver and Gold levels participants will have the option of a three- or four-day expedition or of an exploration of similar length. In the Interests section more emphasis will be placed on the social and cultural aspects of the activity being followed. This revised Scheme came into operation on the 1st September 1980.

The Award Scheme has, from the beginning, been open to all young people, although for those with a physical or mental handicap their ability to participate has obviously been limited. The physically handicapped, however severely disabled, enter for the Award with medical consent provided that their physical condition will not be harmed by its activities. A set of conditions enables variations of conditions to be applied without making their scheme 'a soft option'. The mentally handicapped—slow learners and the educationally subnormal—may enter provided that their intelligence enables them to understand the challenges involved and allows them the chance to undertake it.

Since the Award's inception there have been significant increases each year in the number of handicapped young people entering—and gaining the Awards. In 1975 the Sir Halley Stewart Trust offered to carry out an evaluation for the Award Scheme in the field of "disadvantaged youth". Over the period 1975–1978 two major reports were produced. One was on the Physically and Sensorily Handicapped, the other on the Slow Learners. The two reports were based on field work centred on special schools in the United Kingdom admitting pupils of Award Scheme age. It was found that the Award had taken root in all categories of handicap. The largest numbers entering came from the schools dealing with the educationally subnormal (ESN)—a sign of the preponderance of this kind of handicap and of this type of school. It was found that the Award was in use in special schools as follows:

130 ESN (m) out of 604—i.e. 22%
44 Physically Handicapped & Delicate out of 171—i.e. 25%
14 Deaf & Hearing Impaired out of 42—i.e. 33%
12 Blind & Partially Sighted out of 36—i.e. 33%

Some 800 to 1100 ESN young people were found to take part each year and some 700–800 physically and sensorily handicapped. These figures suggest that some 6% of the special school population in the former category and 10% in the latter participate annually in the Scheme—a substantially higher proportion than in normal schools.

The reports found that there was no cut-off point or any minimum IQ requirement for participation in the Scheme. It recommended:

(i) A basic vocabulary.

(ii) Ability to undertake an Exploration/ Expedition, self-reliance and self-orientation.
(iii) Comprehension of the challenge of the Award. A will to try for it—rather than a willingness to be led through it.

Provided they can meet these criteria, it is clear that the ESN are capable of benefiting from the Award, whatever their handicap in terms of IQ, social competence, reading age, etc.—given the right training and understanding by adults. The report mentioned successful Award winners with: spina bifida, anterior poliomyelitis, muscular dystrophy, congenital heart defect, profound deafness, blindness, cerebral palsy, and limb deficiency, amongst others.

The report contained the evidence from research among twenty-two special schools dealing with educationally sub-normal children. Three questionnaires had been completed by staff at these schools, and one by two hundred pupils. The aim of these questionnaires had been to attempt a 'before' and 'after' comparison. The report found that the main effects on the young people were cited as: helps to get a job, self-confidence, enthusiasm, good social value/education, incentive/something to aim for, aid to maturation/reliability.

The main effects on the schools: good pupil/teacher relationships, outsiders involved in the school, wider scope of work, new interest/ challenge in the school.

The young people were found to have particularly enjoyed: companionship/working with others, new interests/activities, being trusted to work on own, and actually achieving something.

Similar research had been undertaken at twenty-nine special schools for the physically/sensorily handicapped. In these schools the report found that the Scheme has had beneficial effects in all categories of handicap in a number of ways: introducing participants to new and purposeful leisure activities; giving opportunities for service to others, an important fact to many handicapped participants; finding a sense of achievement; bringing opportunities for integration and making friends.

These reports were considered at a two-day residential conference of all the senior staff at the Scheme's headquarters in February 1978; further discussions were held by the National Handicap Panel, the Advisory Committee and the Trustees; and there were discussions at various local centres. All this helped to prepare the way for the reception of the Government's Warnock Committee Report on the education of handicapped children and young people which was published in May 1978. This advocated the integration into ordinary schools of children classified as handicapped in various ways. This was in accord with the Award's philosophy—"the handicapped have as good a chance . . . as the able-bodied, but no better."

During 1978 and 1979 the recommendations of the Sir Halley Stewart Trust were carried out; Territorial and Regional Officers were given more responsibility for approving programmes for the handicapped at Gold level; new guidance and instructional literature was produced; the Variety Club gave a generous grant to the Scheme to enable it to expand the use of the Award in the field of handicap and to help it extend the Award to new fields.

During 1978—as if to illustrate the truths of the various reports—came the news of the first blind winner of a Gold Award, Miss Sue Newman of Australia and the success of Tony Murray of Doncaster, a spastic confined to a wheel-chair who now works with the PHAB. The success of these winners should serve to encourage other physically handicapped young people.

One correspondent remembers her contact with this side of the Award Scheme's work:

> In 1970 I worked as a Supervisor of Dormitories at a home for mentally retarded and epileptic children in Brighton, South Australia. As an extra-curricular activity I prepared some of the residents for participation in the handicapped section of the DEA scheme.
>
> My group worked to put on an exhibition arranged for the visit of the Duke (I am not sure whether it was 1972 or 1973). We were to dance the Circassian Circle, and the organizers asked us to forward the music so that it could be taped for broadcast over the public address system.
>
> On the day in question the children were very apprehensive, but when the music started began dancing. Then the music stopped, as the Duke was approaching. I told the children to stand still. After being introduced the Duke asked me what had happened. I explained. He then asked me what I would have done if no music had been available. I replied, "Count and call." He told me to do so. I explained to the children what we were going to do and they again started dancing. The Duke watched while they completed the full figure and said, "Well done."
>
> Later all the participants were gathered together for an address from the Duke. On his way to the dais he stopped by my little group and once again told the children they had done well. His kindness created a good impression which will not be forgotten by those present on that day in South Australia.[6]

The Duke of Edinburgh has shown in various ways that he is interested in the welfare of young people who do not conform to the rules of society—his visits to Borstals, detention centres, centres for the treatment of drugs addiction and the like indicate this. He has welcomed the interest in his Award Scheme which has been shown by Home Office officials responsible for the administering of custodial centres. In 1978 over 380 young people at such centres took part in the Scheme, 35 of them gaining Awards including 5 Silver Awards. Some juvenile offenders were sent to detention centres for short periods of no more than six weeks. This makes it impossible to gain an Award during their time at the centre. However, even the fact of having started on an Award and having worked on it for this short time seems to have a beneficial effect on some young people who continue to work on their project when they leave the centres. The problem has been to try to devise some means of following up, those who have started on the Scheme while at a centre. There is some hope that a Bristol-based scheme may become more widely adopted. A probation officer in Bristol now sends out to fellow-probation officers, social workers and Award organizers full particulars of boys as soon as they begin the Award at the Bristol Detention Centre at Eastwood Park. This means that the information is available to each appropriate officer some four weeks before the detainee is released. It is hoped that the enthusiasm for the Scheme will be maintained by the young person involved—sustained perhaps by similar enthusiasm from his supervising social worker. Reports to date encourage the hope that this may be the case.

One of the more recent developments has been the formation of an association for winners of Gold Awards. There are a number of local associations whose formation has been encouraged by the Gold Award Holders' Co-ordinator at the International Headquarters. By 1978 there were over fifty thousand such Award winners and the organizers of the Scheme are anxious to use their experience and enthusiasm to help as instructors to other young people, to sponsor small groups, help Award Committees, serve on Advisory Committees or Panels of the Award Scheme or speak to groups of young people and adults about their experience of the Scheme. In September 1979 sixty representatives from twenty-five countries met in Australia for the International Gold Award project to carry out a variety of Community Services. Thirty-one UK Gold Award holders attended a weekend selection conference at Losehill Hall, Derbyshire, so that the five UK representatives could be chosen. They undertook a series of projects and discussions throughout the weekend which left the selection panel with the unenviable task of choosing the five. Those chosen were: *Steve Campbell*, a Guyanan now living in London. Aged twenty-four and a student at the South Bank Polytechnic, Steve is a part-time youth leader at Catford, has been active on two Award Scheme Advisory Bodies and has been involved with work in PHAB clubs; *Patricia Hamilton*, a twenty-two-year-old policewoman from Belfast. She trains a group of girls participating in the Award Scheme and is a cadet leader in the RUC in Belfast; *Gerald Black*, a twenty-four-year-old Civil Engineering Assistant from mid-Glamorgan. He works in his spare time with young offenders through the Caerphilly Probation Service and helps them to work towards their Awards; *Amanda Summerhaye* is a twenty-four-year-old Laboratory Assistant at Wills Cigar factory in Bristol. She is an assistant leader at a youth club, Award co-ordinator at Wills where she introduces new employees to the Scheme and guides them through their Awards; *Alasdair Seal* is a twenty-one-year-old director of his own company. Since gaining his Award he has been President of the Edinburgh Gold Award Holders' Association which helps to train Award participants and to organize expedition courses.

It will be clear that the Gold Holders' Association covers a wide ground—geographically, socially and in terms of employment. What is also clear is that the Duke's initial hopes are being realized in the ways in which his Award winners continue to serve their communities.

This concept of serving the community is one which Prince Philip learned from Kurt Hahn. The idea that young people should be taught to extend themselves and to take risks is one which he has applied in the bringing up of his own children. His involvement with his Award Scheme continues some twenty-five years and more since its inception. Presentations at royal palaces, tours to provincial centres, visits to design centres and attendance at conferences take place regularly, and always, as can be seen in the many pictures in the *Award Journal* and elsewhere, with a sense of his own real participation of what is going on. One correspondent wrote for many:

> I have had the great pleasure of being in contact with Prince Philip during my period of time as Liaison Officer for the Duke of Edinburgh Award Scheme for the Corporation of Glasgow Education Department.
>
> As you know, Prince Philip takes a very lively interest in the operation of the Duke of Edinburgh Award Scheme. I have met him on six occasions, three of these were at Edinburgh Castle when he had come to present Gold Awards and to meet the Co-ordinators. The other three occasions were as follows: (a) at the Design Centre in Glasgow where he and the Queen were present to examine the work carried out by some of my participants who were taking the Design for Living Section as part of the Award; (b) at Bradford at a bi-annual meeting of executives which Prince Philip chaired—I was one of the speakers, and (c) at Buckingham Palace where I was presented to Prince Philip when he told me he had a great love for Glasgow people and enjoyed immensely their particular sense of humour.
>
> On all these occasions I found the Prince to be a most charming gentleman, very interested and very knowledgeable in all aspects of the Award Scheme. I also found him so friendly and he had the happy knack of putting people, both young and old, completely at ease.

It seems that there are more "square" people than the critics allow for.

37

The Medical Commission on Accident Prevention

"WHAT DOES HE DO WITH HIS TIME?" "What does he do to justify the money he gets?" These are two of the commonest questions asked by critics of the Duke of Edinburgh. Most of them get their idea of what he does from the gossipier columns of the popular newspapers and from occasional glimpses of the "Prince at play" on television. They know, for example, that he once played polo but with advancing age he gave this up in favour of less demanding activities such as the driving of four-in-hand coaches. They know that he sails whenever he can and that some of his time is spent on official or semi-official tours at home and abroad. Almost inevitably, however, newspapers and television reports provide only the most superficial accounts of these parts of the ceremonial façade which the Duke of Windsor claimed, "actually disguises an occupation of considerable drudgery . . . the relentless daily round."[1] So the popular picture of the Prince is that of a former polo-playing sportsman who accompanies the Queen on her visits and who, occasionally, drops a brick in an address to a group of industrialists.

Some of his critics ought, by virtue of their own jobs, to be better informed. Willy Hamilton, MP, is one such critic. In his *My Queen and I*, as well as in his speeches inside and outside the Commons, he has given credence to the idea that the Duke does little to deserve the privileges he enjoys. He and others who share his attitude either know better (in which case their hostility is grossly unfair) or they do not know of the various activities undertaken by the active Prince (in which case they are not doing their own jobs properly).

In this chapter I propose to examine the Prince's part in the setting up of a little-known commission, whose work is ongoing and important and which involves the participation of a wide variety of important bodies and individuals. This is the Medical Commission on Accident Prevention.

The Commission may be said to have been born out of a discussion between Kurt Hahn and the then President of the Royal College of Surgeons, Sir Arthur Porritt. Hahn, while still Headmaster of

Gordonstoun, had helped found the Outward Bound Sea School at Aberdovey—a sign of his interest in young people and, in particular, of his wish that they should be faced with challenges and helped to learn how to overcome them. In 1953 he gave up the headship of Gordonstoun but in 1957 came back into the education field when he set up the Atlantic Colleges Project. Hahn's idea was that boys (and later, girls) of different nationalities should spend two years together in a residential college in their last two years at school—immediately before entering universities in their own countries. He hoped that such international colleges would promote educational understanding through education and that in this way education might become a force which united people rather than a nationalist-based force which tended to divide. This once-modest project has flowered into the World Colleges scheme of which Prince Charles is now the active President.

In 1961 Hahn suggested to Sir Arthur Porritt that the Royal College of Surgeons and other medical bodies ought to look into the question of accident prevention. It was the doctors and surgeons who had to deal with the results of accidents; why should they not devote part of their energies to discovering ways of preventing the accidents which brought so many people to their professional attention?

In October 1961 Sir Arthur Porritt held an informal meeting of "persons interested in the problems of youth and in particular to consider the needless loss of life and the serious amount of disability resulting from accidents of all kinds."[2] This meeting led the Royal College of Surgeons to set up a "Working Party in conjunction with other professional bodies to study this problem and to make recommendations upon the human problems involved and upon the more directly medical aspects of life-saving and first-aid."[3]

The setting up of the Working Party was approved by the Council of the Royal College of Surgeons in January 1962. Under the chairmanship of a member of the Royal College the Party consisted of twenty eminent men drawn from the Royal College, the BMA, the Ministry of Health, RoSPA, University Departments of Psychology and Medicine and various societies concerned with health and safety. Many meetings were held in 1962 and the early part of 1963. This led to the calling of a public convention at the Royal College of Surgeons on the 14th and 15th May 1963.

This Convention was "honoured by the presence of HRH the Duke of Edinburgh."[4] His interest in this Convention and in the work of the Working Party which preceded it may be seen as yet one more reflection of his interest in young people in general—as shown by his work for the Award Scheme. It may also be seen as a reflection of that Scheme's interest in handicapped young people. But his interest and later involvement with the work of the Royal College of Surgeons' scheme may also be seen as his response to the challenge of a new outlet for his energies. In 1938 Hahn had reported on his pupil: "Prince Philip is a born leader, but will need the exacting demands of a great service to do justice to himself." He had been denied the call of the "demands" of a naval career in 1952. Hahn's report went on: "Prince Philip will make his mark in any profession where he will have to prove himself in a full trial of strength. His gifts would run to waste if he was soon condemned to lead a life where neither superior officers, nor the routine of the day forced him to tap his hidden resources."[5]

There can be little doubt that the "routine of the day" did not "tap his hidden resources". He has shown his impatience with the 'drudgery' of the royal routine—the shaking of hands with a constant round of local dignitaries, the compulsory dinners and need to listen to yet another speech of welcome. So it is not surprising that Hahn's former pupil saw in this latest of Hahn-inspired ideas a chance to do something worthwhile and which would provide him with the necessary challenge.

In 1963 the Working Party presented a long report to the members of the Convention. This report was based on evidence collected from a widely representative number of societies, associations, institutions, firms and individuals. Having shown that accidental injuries cost the country £500m a year, cause incalculable distress to individuals and their families and make heavy demands on the nation's medical services, the report argued that accidents were:

> . . . the modern epidemic plague . . . a disease which is endemic and universal, continuous and increasing . . . nowhere better illustrated than in a report on the health of children published by the Office of Health Economics. With advances in medical and social progress there has been a sharp decline . . . in the mortality of such diseases as tuberculosis, pneumonia . . . measles in children under fourteen years of age, and . . . similar though less dramatic fall in mortality from road accidents . . .[6]

The report found that "the home has special hazards" and that industry was a major source of accidents with "adventure and sport" being a third important cause of accidents to young people.

On the 14th May the Duke of Edinburgh took part in the discussion which followed the presentation of this report. I spoke to one of the people who took part in this Convention, a man who had worked with the Prince in other of his pet projects. It may be that "no man is a hero to his valet" and that "familiarity breeds contempt". On the other hand it may be thought that people who work with the Prince and other members of the Royal Family are anxious to glamorize their own activities by over-praising the work of the 'royals' with whom they work. My own experience is that those who work or have worked with Prince Philip have been well able to see him in the round. Of his work at the Convention my informant had nothing but praise. Having pointed out the varied qualifications of the other participants at the Convention he spoke of the way in which the Prince was able to participate in the discussions which took place. I asked whether Hahn's report was right and whether "Prince Philip is a born leader . . . will make his mark in any profession . . ." The answer was an unhesitating "Yes". I appreciated that this might be the answer of a loyal servant-companion, so I asked him to try to imagine that Prince Philip had not been a Prince and one married to the Queen. Did my informant think that his innate qualities were such as would have allowed him to succeed without the advantage of birth and marriage? Again the answer was an unhesitating "Yes". I took this as all the more sincere because the interview had already brought out my informant's criticism of the Prince and Prince Charles in regard to their seeming inability to appreciate the problems of, for example, children who live in tower blocks in deprived inner cities or the children of reckless one-parent families. His criticism was forthright and almost bitter for he felt that much that might be done was not being done. The Prince and Prince Charles give their support to the Award Scheme and Silver Jubilee projects—and these are publicized and supported. My informant felt that if the two Princes showed an equal interest in the problems of social deprivation and inner city stress there might well be something more done about these problems.[7]

My informant's praise for the Prince's participation in the Convention was supported by his Address. The speech shows an ability to get to the roots of the various problems; to say, simply and succinctly, what has to be said and to make what turned out to be the most important suggestion of all. The Duke said:

> Everybody concerned with the prevention of accidents as well as every individual and organization involved in rescue, first-aid and hospital services welcomes this Convention. I am certain that all of them would like me to express their gratitude and appreciation to the Royal College of Surgeons for their initiative in this matter and for the programme which they have arranged.
>
> The speed and complication of modern life is such that the ordinary person in his home, at work or in recreation is subject to many more and greater risks than at any time in history. The scourge of disease is being lifted but in its place has appeared this new scourge of accidents. The reasons are not particularly obscure: conditions of living and working are changing; specialization is growing so that experience is limited. Mechanical contrivances are beginning to work faster than we can think. More and longer holidays and leisure offer opportunities to take part in new activities. In the kitchen, crossing the street, in a factory, in a boat or on a mountain we are surrounded by dangers and risks.
>
> Adequate casualty departments, hospital beds and cemeteries are certainly essential, but by the time they are needed the accident has already happened. Rescue and first-aid are even more important because so often serious consequences can be prevented by correct action taken promptly on the spot. Most important of all is action beforehand, to prevent accidents happening.
>
> It is far more dangerous for an inexperienced untrained child cyclist to pedal to school than it is for a pilot in the Royal Air Force aerobatic team to go through his paces. The aerobatic team takes to the air fully trained and prepared and with every known risk and hazard planned out.
>
> Exactly the same must apply to every activity where there is the smallest element of risk. An accident is frequently the result of a breakdown in training, preparation and planning.

This Convention has already started to look into the detailed problems of accidents in the home, on the roads, at work and in sport and recreation. I am interested in all these aspects, but I am probably more intimately concerned with the last—sport and recreation—because I take part in what could be a very dangerous sport, and I am closely connected with Outward Bound, the Award Scheme, the Royal Yachting Association and the Central Council of Physical Recreation. It may be one thing to get after manufacturers of dangerous household equipment or to make rules and regulations for factories and roads, but recreation is different. It is meant to be enjoyment and therefore it should be as free from regulations as possible, but there must be some rules and they should be self-imposed.

Recreation is different because there is an inescapable element of risk in adventurous activities and because one of the attractions is in daring to face such risks: this is implicit in adventure. But this does not mean rushing out blindly to court the risks: that is sheer folly. In fact it is worse than folly for it is likely to involve other people. The real satisfaction lies in accepting the risks of which you are fully aware only when you are prepared in every sense to measure up to them.

It is therefore immensely important that people taking part in any kind of adventurous recreation should voluntarily undergo training and preparation. It is quite obviously impossible to avoid risks and dangers if you are blissfully unaware of their existence. Only by knowing the risks and by knowing how to overcome them can you avoid unnecessary accidents.

There are some genuinely misguided people, in my opinion, who are prepared to accept a few deaths or serious accidents in some hazardous recreation as inevitable, and who believe that without them the activity would be somehow less exciting. I cannot emphasize too strongly how much I disagree with this conception; no activity is worth the death or serious injury of any individual that can conceivably be avoided. Furthermore I believe that every serious accident in any recreation other than organized games should be investigated very carefully and thoroughly.

Accidents on expeditions on land or at sea can take a long time to happen even if the immediate cause appears to be quite sudden. More likely than not they are due to an omission in training, to a fault in planning or to a mistaken decision. Think of the number of small boats which get into trouble off our coasts during the summer and compare it with the achievement of Hiscocks, for instance, sailing around the world without an incident of any kind.

Let us get it out of our minds for ever that the risks and dangers of any activity can be measured by the number of accidents which it produces. This is the philosophy of those who worship toughness for its own sake. It is certainly necessary to be tough to withstand the hazards and privations of any expedition; it is necessary to be tough to stick to the rules and maintain the discipline which alone can bring success. It is definitely not tough to take unnecessary risks, it is not tough to be ignorant of the rules, and it is certainly not tough to create dangers where none need exist.

I think it is important to use the word 'tough' in the right context. I believe that a concert pianist who practises eight hours a day is tough; a painter struggling along at starvation level is tough. But a bully is not tough. An athlete in training, a climber on a mountain, crewing an ocean racer, is tough. But a nitwit barging about in a fast car or on a powerful motor-cycle and behaving as if he were an accident looking for somewhere to happen and scaring the daylights out of other people is not my idea of toughness.

Physical toughness and fitness are a necessary part of the safety factors in arduous activities. Toughness for its own sake is quite pointless.

The real satisfaction only comes from the successful exploit, and the more difficult it is the more training, preparation and planning are needed. Pointless death has no part in any adventure.

While unforeseen circumstances must be reduced to a minimum some will always remain, and it is here that the rescue and first-aid services are so important. Mountain rescue teams, surf life-saving clubs, lifeboats and all the first-aid organizations are there to prevent an incident becoming a serious accident, to stop a minor injury or an unforeseen circumstance resulting in a death.

We know that the casualty departments in hospitals are prepared for the worst, but the weakness of the present arrangement lies in the preparation for the leadership in hazardous activities and in the lack of training in first-aid and rescue work.

I have two suggestions to make. I should like to put forward the idea that all organizations concerned should meet together in conference and discuss the possibility of establishing a series of Instructors' or Guides' certificates for the various activities. These certificates would demand reasonably high standards of knowledge and experience, and I feel they would be popular and invaluable to the growing number of organizations making use of new-found adventurous opportunities. Knowing that groups of boys and girls in expeditions on the water, in wild country and on mountains were in the hands of qualified instructors or guides would be a great relief to many organizers and parents.

My second suggestion is that all the rescue and first-aid organizations should make more use of young people in responsible duties, provided of course they are properly qualified.

The Surf Life-Saving Clubs of Australia, and more recently of this country, are an excellent example. Incidentally, they were responsible for ninety-seven rescues around our coasts in 1962. Young people are trusted to do the serious and responsible job of life-saving, and for this reason they are prepared to undergo rigorous training. They give up much of their spare time to provide regular weekend patrols.

There are similar possibilities in mountain rescue, pothole rescue, forest fire services and canoe patrols. The junior members of first-aid organizations do a magnificent job and there are signs that young motor-cyclists are offering their services to the hospitals as messengers. I see no reason why the police and fire services should not make use of their services as well. There is no quicker way to develop a sense of responsibility than to offer young people the chance to undertake a responsible duty and to combine this with some activity which demands careful training and preparation, skill and endurance.

Speaking one moment for the Award Scheme and Outward Bound, I would very much like this Convention to consider the possibility of establishing some kind of permanent medical commission of appeal. It would be immensely valuable for these two organizations and, I am sure, for many others doing similar work, to be able to turn to some recognized authority for advice on such things as exposure, exhaustion, and the limits of endurance of different age groups.

The commission might also keep the techniques of first-aid and rescue under constant review for the benefit of all the organizations concerned with these matters. It would draw together all the immensely valuable work which is being done by so many independent groups at the moment.

I also hope that this Convention will do what it can to encourage all schools, colleges and universities to take first-aid and rescue training very seriously. No one should have to pass by or avoid an accident for lack of the ability to give prompt attention.

Let me repeat the very great importance I attach to this Convention. It has the power and the opportunity to change the whole picture of accident prevention and first-aid treatment in this country; it can bring the callous and the thoughtless into deserved contempt; it can rouse a conscience for safety; and it can give advice which will help to save thousands of lives and which only fools would disregard.

I wish this Convention and everyone taking part in it a very great measure of success.[8]

The Convention lasted for two days, and led to the publication of the Working Party's Report as well as a report on the work of the Convention. In its conclusions this second report noted:

We believe that doctors should take a bigger interest in these matters [of accident prevention]. This was emphasized by HRH the Duke of Edinburgh when he said: "I would very much like this Convention to consider the possibility of establishing some kind of permanent medical commission of appeal." The need for such a commission has repeatedly been brought before the Working Party during the past eighteen months.[9]

In February 1964 the Council of the Royal College of Surgeons approved the proposal to set up a permanent medical commission in conjunction with all the Royal and other Colleges and the British Medical Association. The Medical Commission on Accident Prevention was created in May 1964. Within a short time it had set up seven committees to look into the various aspects of accident prevention. It also acted on another of the Prince's suggestions. Addressing the Convention he had said:

My second suggestion is that all the rescue and first-aid organizations should make more use of young people in responsible duties, provided of course they are properly qualified . . . There is no quicker way to develop a sense of responsibility than to offer young people the chance to undertake a responsible duty and to combine this with some activity which demands careful training and preparation, skill and endurance.[10]

Between the 17th and 19th May 1967 a Conference on Training Young People for Rescue, Relief and Service was held at Ditchley Park. Prince Philip chaired this conference of experts from Britain, Europe and the USA. Once again he showed an ability to exercise "firm and efficient control".[11] Hahn was one of the participants at this Conference and he must have been pleased with the evident success of this former pupil. A more public sign of this success was taken by the Medical Commission which had been set up in 1964. In 1968 the Commission invited Prince Philip to become President for "a period of three years", and was pleased when in 1971 he "extended his Presidency for a further year."[12]

Even when his official links with the Medical Commission ended the Prince continued to give it his support. In 1978, for example, he initiated and opened a two-day Conference on 'Recreation, Risk and Reward'. In his Presidential Address in 1968 the Prince said:

I am firmly convinced that the formation of the Medical Commission on Accident Prevention was one of the most important events in the whole progress of our social and community existence.[13]

It is perhaps inevitable that the media should fail to present this side of the work of the Duke of Edinburgh. There is little headline-making in the sort of serious discussion involved in the Conferences of the Commission or in Training Conferences; there is no chance of a 'juicy picture' or a 'dropped clanger' at such meetings. Other critics of the media have accused it of 'trivializing" other important issues—politics, industrial relations, the state of the national economy and so on. It has sought to maintain its low standards in its treatment of Prince Philip, ignoring the intelligent and hard work he has done in many fields of which the Medical Commission is one. It has preferred to draw attention to the "hands behind the back walk", "the thinning hair", "the bored look", and so on. This helps to explain his own hostile attitude towards the media in general and the Press in particular.

38

The World Wildlife Fund

"I DOUBT WHETHER I'VE ACHIEVED ANYTHING LIKELY TO BE REMEMBERED," says Prince Philip. This may be taken as the remark of a man regretting that he had not had the chance to live up to Prime Minister Attlee's belief that he too, like his Uncle "Dickie' and grandfather, Prince Louis, could have climbed to the top of the naval tree. It may also be seen as the sort of thing that a man might say having taken part in 300 official engagements and made 130 major speeches during the previous year; he might almost be described as being 'engagement-drunk' and may be forgiven for doubting the value of what he has done.

But in making such self-deprecating remarks he gives hostages to fortune and opportunities to some of his critics. In *The Monarchy and the Future* the television-journalist Clive Irving compared, unfavourably, the contribution made by the British Royal Family with that made by the Kennedy family to the 'life-style' of their respective countries. Irving claimed that while John Kennedy was President, the mainstream of American cultural life flowed from or at least through the White House.

But, he claims, "the mainstream of British cultural life does not flow down the Mall . . . The Monarchy . . . are unashamedly . . . philistine . . . The Duke of Edinburgh has striven to make a virtue out of this philistinism. He has become the leading propagandist for mercantile endeavour, for ruthless reforms of British management . . . for pulling our fingers out and putting in technology . . ."[1]

This word-picture of a tough, abrasive Prince "at home in the sweating and thrusting society of polo players, yachtsmen, and all manifestations of the spartan philosophy of Gordonstoun"[2] is one which is created by many of Prince Philip's critics. There is a danger that this might be taken as the definitive description of this complex character. To people who have been willing to accept this picture at its face value it may come as a corrective shock to learn about his deep involvement in the work of the World Wildlife Fund—something which the British public associate with gentler characters such as Sir Peter Scott or with members of societies such as The Friends of the Earth.

There are various explanations for the Prince's interest in the world of nature and the dangers to that world arising from technological development. Some people think that they find the source of that interest on the shores of the Sagana River in the Aberdare Forest game reserve in Kenya where the Prince and the then Princess Elizabeth spent their last carefree day together and where he had to tell her about the death of her father. The memory of the pleasure they had from watching elephants, rhinoceroses and water-buck come to the watering-hole and salt-lick, and of the film which they made to show to the rest of the family back in Britain, was a lasting one. People claim that it was easier for Peter Scott and others to win the Prince's approval for their project because of that pleasurable memory.

Other people claim that his interest in wildlife in general was really aroused by the tour of the Antarctic which he made after opening the Olympic Games in Melbourne in 1956. When he had agreed to perform the opening ceremony he had looked at the maps and suggested that since he was going that far he might also visit parts of the world which the Queen never visited—the Falkland Islands and the Antarctic. This extended journey would give him a chance to escape from 'the cage' for a while and would also allow him to enjoy again the satisfaction of captaining his own ship in an all-male atmosphere. It was during this trip that he took a series of photographs of sea-birds, did some oil painting under the tuition of the artist Edward Seago and enjoyed the companionship of Sir Raymond Priestley who had been with Scott on his expedition to the South Pole. Following this long tour Prince Philip gave an illustrated lecture about his trip to an audience of 1,800 children in the Royal Festival Hall. This was such a success that he produced a forty-minute version of the lecture for a television programme shown during Children's Hour. This, in turn, led to his inaugurating International

Geophysical Year when he acted as a commentator in a seventy-five-minute television programme.

In 1959 during a trip through the Central Pacific the Prince took a large number of photographs of the very different sorts of birds found in that region. He used these photographs and the ones taken in 1956 when he edited his best-selling *Birds from Britannia*, the text of which showed that he had developed a keen interest in the varied types of wildlife that he had seen during his various journeys.

By the time this book appeared he had already become Patron to the Council for Nature which was set up in 1958. This Council had the enthusiastic support of Sir Peter Scott who had already formed the Wildfowl Trust at Slimbridge in Gloucestershire. By July 1961 Scott and others interested in the future of the environment had held many discussions and prepared papers which were to lead to the formation of the World Wildlife Fund. In that July Prince Philip was "confined to the Palace" because of an injury received in a polo match. Scott went to see him, taking some of the papers dealing with the proposed Fund. On the 19th July Prince Philip agreed to be the President of the British National Appeal which Scott proposed to launch as a fund-raising exercise. In addition, Prince Philip suggested that Scott ask Prince Bernhard of the Netherlands—then visiting London—to accept the post of President of the World Wildlife International Trust. With Prince Bernhard's acceptance of this post, Scott could boast that he had gained the support of two most influential men in his new project.

The International Trust fixed its headquarters in the small town of Morges on the shores of Lake Geneva. From here the Trust issued its appeal to the governments and peoples of the world. At first their work was dismissed as that of a few 'eco-nuts', but their work received a boost in 1962 from the publication of Rachel Carson's best-selling *The Silent Spring*. It was brought home to people that the survival of man as a species was linked with that of other types of life and that concern for the environment and a policy of conservation was something which thinking people could not ignore. The conservationists called for a more rational use of the world's diminishing store of resources. They asked that governments, local authorities, firms and individuals should take an interest in the preservation of and a wise management of those resources and of the environment. In particular they drew attention to the ways in which species of animals and of plants were being destroyed so that many species were already extinct while others were in danger of becoming so.

It was the conservationists who first drew attention to the dangers of pollution—by industry, expanding new towns and chemically-based agriculture. As Prince Philip said:

> Pesticides, insecticides, poison and pollution have destroyed more life than man has ever taken, and by affecting the capacity to breed and by destructive interference in the food chain, whole populations of species are being exterminated.

> What man as a hunter has failed to do in millions of years, man as a businessman and scientist is achieving in a couple of generations, and with every general approval. We seem to exist with a rather strange morality in this country. Everything which is pleasant must of necessity be sinful, and everything that is done for money—that is professionally—cannot possibly be enjoyable.[3]

The World Wildlife Fund set itself two major tasks. In the first place and in the short term it wanted to set up what can best be described as a holding operation whereby no more areas of the world's surface would be plundered and no more species of animals or plants put in danger of extinction, while new laws were brought in against pollution. The second task of the Fund was a longer term one; they wanted people to give their attention to solving the problems linked with conservation. How was man to get enough food without plundering the land and sea? How was the world to get the fuel it needed without denuding the existing resources? How was living space to be provided without destroying the countryside? How were underdeveloped nations to be helped to become more self-sufficient and industrialized without further inroads being made into the dwindling stocks of natural resources?

Most of these questions have become the common parlance of a wider public during the last few years. The western world has been shocked by increased oil prices into a realization that there is not a limitless supply of oil. New laws concerning fishing have led to 'cod wars' with Iceland and disputes between so-called partners in the European Economic Community—but have also caused us to realize that the sea, like the land, can be plundered.

When these questions were first posed in 1961 and 1962 they roused too little interest. The World Wildlife Fund then had to undertake a gigantic task of converting governments and their peoples. This helps to explain the Fund's appeal for money and it is to Britain's credit that the first National Appeal was launched under the patronage of Prince Philip in 1961. Other countries have since followed suit and Prince Philip has been called on to help many of these appeals. The Fund also organized a series of studies and surveys in which national and international bodies of scientists were involved. From the reports of such surveys and studies the Fund has been able to show governments why new laws are required—and has been able to claim a limited success as one country after another has, albeit reluctantly, passed laws on pollution, urban development, the use of the countryside and the use of natural resources.

In 1962 Prince Philip criticized young men in the Lebanon prowling about the olive groves with shot guns to shoot small birds. "Why? Merely so that they can swagger back to the cities with tiny sparrow-sized birds dangling from their belts. Supposedly symbols of achievement—in fact they are badges of barbarity."[4] Many of his critics have seen a contradiction between such strong words and his own personal behaviour in killing for pleasure, for one of his means of escaping from 'the cage' has been to take his sons for shooting weekends on the Sandringham estate. Each year he is reckoned to shoot around seven thousand pheasants. He argues that owners of estates such as Sandringham have been the great conservers and not destroyers, as implied by those who criticize his "massacre of birds with enthusiasm and expertise".[5] If they did not pay attention to the breeding, feeding and preserving of game there would soon be none left. He claims:

> The shooting of small birds for no other purpose than to show-off seems to me barbarous. Controlling the size of a wild population of usable or of eatable animals or of pests, I would say was quite a different matter.
>
> I find it difficult to differentiate clearly between rearing chickens under factory conditions for slaughter and rearing pheasants for shooting. The fact that someone killing chickens in a slaughterhouse is paid for his work, whether he likes it or not, and that someone else likes it or not, and that someone else likes to shoot pheasants without being paid does not really alter the case. If killing is immoral, whether you are paid for it or enjoy it, really makes no difference.[6]

In 1962 he spoke at a World Wildlife Fund dinner in New York. Here he attacked the poachers of wildlife in Africa and elsewhere describing them as "the get-rich-at-any-cost mob". He also criticized "people who want ivory chessmen or a new set of billiard balls" as being responsible for the activities of many poachers. He asked that, if there is a demand for ivory and if governments wish to make money out of an ivory trade, they ought also to be concerned to see that game laws were enforced. He wanted a properly organized system of humane "cropping" by authorized hunters. This, he thought, would lead to the decline of the work of poaching methods "which are inevitably cruel" and of the activities of poachers who "are certainly not concerned with such conservations as sustainable yields."

In 1962 he helped plan the Nature Week Exhibition which was followed by the first of three major conferences on 'The Countryside in 1970'. His interest in this theme was stimulated by the way in which the British countryside was being raped by the development of motorways, urban sprawl and scientific farming. He was angered by the way in which government, local authorities and planning bodies seemed to be unaware of the harm that was being done and by the lack of public interest in what was being done to them and in their name. The limited success of this first conference in 1963 led the organizers to hold others in 1965 and 1970 itself. By 1970 he and his fellow-workers in this field could claim some success. In 1968 the Government passed the Countryside Act and set up the Countryside Commission. In that year one of the country's first country parks was opened on the Sandringham estate and over 100,000 people visited the park in its first year, an indication of the need for such natural outlets for an increasingly urban-based people. Earlier, in 1967, he had taken part in the making of a television film, *The Enchanted Isles*, which was shown on Anglia Television in December 1967 and which brought home to people the beauty of the wildlife of the Galapagos Islands. This film was shown on American television in January 1969—the cost of its showing borne by Quaker Oats.

In 1969 he drew attention to the environmental problem caused by the justifiable attempts by Third World countries to develop:

> I sympathize with people who work up a passionate concern about the all too many examples of inhumanity, injustice and unfairness, but behind all this hangs a really deadly cloud. Still largely unnoticed and unrecognized, the process of destroying our natural environment is gathering speed and momentum. If we fail to cope with this challenge, all the other problems will pale into insignificance.[7]

He believes that sensible conservation practices are desirable "whatever the country, the political situation, the poverty, injustice or under-development . . . I do not think the end can be made to justify destructive means." He would have "the industrially advanced countries concentrate on the more sophisticated end of the spectrum, stop subsidising their relatively simple industries, at great public expense, and allow them to be transferred to the developing nations and then importing the products. Something like this is bound to happen anyway sooner or later although it is bound to be resisted on the grounds that it might cause unemployment."

In 1970 he spoke at a conference in Strasbourg to launch European Conservation Year—a sign of the widening interest in the problems of conservation. He argued that Britain, as a former imperial country, had a special part to play in international conservation. Many countries in the Commonwealth still looked to Britain as the model for their legal, political and civic life-styles. He hoped that Britain would give them a lead in the world of conservation. He claimed that human failings had led to the pollution of the countryside, the sea and rivers so that in the case of Lake Erie: "If anyone falls into it they don't drown, they just decay." The Mediterranean Sea has been converted into a cess-pit because of the failure of the countries bordering that inland sea to develop proper sewage disposal systems. Everywhere in developed countries rivers have been ruined by industrial and sewage pollution. Equally, the scientific farmer had destroyed not only the pests but also the rest of the wildlife in the countryside while the exploitation of the sea by mass fishing and fleets centred on factory-ships was leading to the disappearance of fish stocks. Some people dismissed this as "mere doom-watching". He himself has been critical of the doom-watchers but defended his Strasbourg speech on the grounds that he was not speculating about future possibilities (as do gloomy doom-watchers) but about existing problems.

Later in 1970 he went to Australia to take part in the Australian Wildlife Appeal. He made a major speech in Canberra in which he argued that "conservation is life freedom, it can only be maintained by constant vigilance . . . The last phase of revolution is the return to apathy." He went on to explain that while many people have become concerned about the man-made environment they have tended to ignore the natural environment—to their ultimate loss and cost. He expressed his concern about the needless clash between people at two extremes; those who "protest and revolt against indifference" and those who were "demanding a halt to all development". He saw conservation as "a matter of compromise", due in large part to the constant growth of the world's population and the ever increasing number of development projects resulting from the growth. He pointed out that in spite of all man's efforts it was the poor who suffered most from poor environment. They are the ones who suffer first and longest from "a bad water supply, bad sewage and drainage, derelict land and lack of facilities of all kinds . . ." This was his answer to critics who claimed that "conservation was a cosy middle-class movement for its own benefit".

It was at Canberra that he drew attention to the exploitation of forests "as if they were an inexhaustible bounty provided by a benevolent God for a people determined not to know the facts". The destruction of the tropical rain-forests in Australia, Amazonia, Africa and South-East Asia he saw as "the most worrying factor of all", and even in 1979 thought that in this regard "matters were getting worse".

In 1970 the Prince contributed articles to *World Wildlife Crisis*, a publication which helped rouse international opinion and led to the calling of a United Nations Conference on the Human Environment in Stockholm in 1972. This, he claimed, was "the climax of the environmental revolution . . ." This conference drew the attention of many previously unconcerned people to the problems. Unfortunately, from this point of view " . . . a very large proportion of the time was devoted to the problems of the human environment. This is obviously very important but in many instances the human interests are not compatible with the interests of nature."[8]

In 1975 he accepted the post of President of the United Kingdom Association for European Architectural Heritage—a sign of his realization that the environment was more than "plants and animals". But as early as 1971 he was addressing an Edinburgh Medical Group on the problems of world over-population while in 1977 in New Zealand he was arguing that "the conservation of nature needs to be an international project, and it can only succeed by international co-operation." He was disappointed with the poor quality of support which the United Nations Organization was giving to projects such as the International Union for the Conservation of Nature and that "UN agencies such as UNESCO, WHO and FAO are [not] particularly conscious of the problems of conservation."

In 1978 in New Zealand he drew attention to the failure of the International Whaling Commission: "If certain governments simply ignore the rules it is virtually impossible to do anything about it." While he refused to "be quite so indiscreet" as to name the countries which flouted international laws on whaling he complained of the lack of any workable sanctions against such law-breaking countries.

Interest in the environment is greater today than it was when he and Peter Scott started on their work. He argues that it was the World Wildlife Fund which stimulated governments into action—so that in Britain we have gone from having no government department involved in the work of the environment, to having this job deputed to a junior minister, to the point where there is now a Minister for the Environment in the Cabinet. When the Fund was started its supporters were too often dismissed as eccentrics; today the question of energy conservation, the problems of the tropical rain-forests and of depleted fish stocks are fairly commonly understood. In 1962 there were few laws on pollution; today rivers are being cleaned up, industry is forced to organize its waste disposal without polluting the rivers, sea or countryside; in 1962 few local authorities showed much concern for the environment; today the GLC boasts of having salmon back in the Thames, one indication of the way in which local authorities have been stimulated to take an interest in the natural environment.

It seems that we have every justification for contradicting Prince Philip's remark: "I doubt whether I've achieved anything likely to be remembered." In 1978 a selection of the Duke's speeches on the conservation theme was published in *The Environmental Revolution*. This drew public attention to his long standing interest in a subject which has become increasingly important to fuel-conscious nations. But the popular Press cannot resist the temptation to trivialize this interest. On the 1st May 1979 each of the 'popular' dailies had a report of an incident which took place in Western Australia:

THE DAY PHILIP CRAWLED AFTER NOISY SCRUB BIRD

Prince Philip described yesterday how he crawled through bushes on his stomach during an Australian tropical storm to save the Noisy Scrub Bird. And his efforts persuaded local officials to abandon plans to develop a new town in Western Australia and preserve the habitat of the world's rarest birds.

Prince Philip related his crawl in an interview with David Mitchell, public affairs director of the *World Wildlife Fund*, which is based in Morges, Switzerland. The interview is published in the Fund's bulletin.

"What happened was that a place called Two People Bay in the southern part of Western Australia was zoned for town development," said Prince Philip.

"About the same time, various naturalists in Australia discovered that this bird, reported sighted in the early days and then not seen at all, had suddenly been found again in this area and nowhere else. I heard about this through Peter Scott and went to see the then State Premier, who looked at me in astonishment.

"I could almost see his mind working: 'Do I take this man seriously or is he pulling my leg? Is there such a thing as a Noisy Scrub Bird? And does he really think that plans for a new development should be shifted because of it?' Then, to his eternal credit, he suddenly thought, 'Perhaps he's right.' And they moved it a short distance."

In the interview, held in Buckingham Palace, Prince Philip described how he tried to see the bird.

"It was raining and there was a force eight gale, and the bird only lives in thick scrub. We crawled about in these bushes and I got within about two yards of the thing and noisy is absolutely right. It made a hell of a racket—but I failed to see it."

It seems a pity that the Press should devote so much space to this one incident while it ignores the more serious aspects of the work of the World Wildlife Fund and of Prince Philip's work in connection with this Fund. This tendency is on a par with the comment of a reporter who dismisses his work for the Fund in the assertion that "he makes films for the World Wildlife Fund of which he is an international trustee, and some of his trips abroad are at their expense."[9] True, of course, but as with much Press reporting only partly true and only at the trivial level.

39

Working in His Office

HOW CAN AN AUTHOR HELP READERS TO understand that Prince Philip works much harder than most other people? People who work in the same firm think that the 'real' work in the business is done in their own department. The management 'knows' that it works harder than the men on the shopfloor who, in turn, are convinced that management has a 'soft' job. I am writing this during the lorry drivers' strike of the winter of 1979. They and their leaders claim that no one works as hard, as long or on such a dangerous job as do haulage men. But fellow-unionists in the railway, water-supply, electricity supply and a host of other industries are queuing up to prove that *they* are the ones who work the hardest, longest, *et alia*.

If people who work alongside each other can't agree about the nature of the work of fellow-workers, how does one show that a Prince works hard? Even in these emancipated days, the very words 'Prince' and 'Palace' conjure up—maybe in spite of ourselves—ideas of 'happy ever after', or of fairy godmothers who wave wands to put the world to rights—and do all the work.

And who, struggling to work in snow-bound Britain, does not envy the Prince when they see newspaper pictures of him on the deck of *Britannia* making its way through the Southern Seas? And what work is involved, some ask, in standing in an open car being driven through cheering crowds in some sun-drenched town or city? I have tried to show that royal tours are very hard work, as are the visits made to towns and industries in Britain itself.

But even these public appearances are the tip of an iceberg of work which goes on every day at Buckingham Palace where Prince Philip has his own office-study and a staff which occupies a set of offices on the ground floor of the building. During my research I was contacted by a lady (whom I will call Mrs Smith) who had worked on Prince Philip's staff for many years. She has subsequently worked for a number of industrial and commercial firms and has been able to set her Palace experience against a wider background. Much of what I have to write in this chapter is based either on what she told me or on her confirming what I already knew from other sources. But I think it worthwhile noting here that she is still convinced that "I have never worked as hard since . . ." and "no other office in which I have worked has been as efficient and well-run as Prince Philip's."

Prince Philip's own study is part of the royal apartments on the first floor of the Palace, its windows looking out on to Constitution Hill. Like most of the other rooms in the Palace it is large and multi-windowed. At one time it was also high-ceilinged—a reminder of the fact that the Palace was originally designed in the more spacious days of the eighteenth century for the Duke of Buckingham. One of Prince Philip's first innovations was to have a false ceiling installed giving the room a more streamlined appearance. He also installed a number of labour-saving gadgets so that, for example, the window curtains can be opened or closed at the press of a button. He has his radio and television sets which enable him to keep abreast of what's going on in the world outside, and an intercom dictograph to allow him to communicate with any part of the Palace. He also has a tape machine on which he records his speeches in advance so that he can hear how they will sound.

He does most of his Palace work in this study—writing his own speeches in long-hand before sending them downstairs to be typed out, signing the hundreds of letters that go out each day and meeting his close advisers. When he first went to the Palace as Consort he took with him as Private Secretary his former equerry, Michael Parker. Today Lord Rupert Nevill is Private Secretary and Treasurer—as well as a close personal friend of both the Queen and Prince Philip.[1] William Heseltine is the Prince's Press Secretary and as such the second of the men in close touch with His Royal Highness. He also has a number of equerries, men on short-term secondment from one of the armed forces. Unlike Lord Nevill and William Heseltine, they come and go so that they never become intimate members of the family circle. Equerries were traditionally employed to look after the horses, but now their aiglets are merely decorative; originally they were used to tie up the horses. Today the equerries are concerned with the 'nuts and bolts' of the Prince's work. They run messages inside the Palace, see that the right car comes at the right time and that the driver has the right instructions.

Lord Rupert and William Heseltine each have their own individual offices on the ground floor, beneath the royal apartments. Here too are the offices in which work the five secretaries under the supervision of an office manager.

For many years the office manager was Mr Leslie Treby who was responsible, with the Prince, for the introduction of a high level of efficiency into the office. Mrs Smith had nothing but praise for the way in which, in her day, Leslie Treby ran the office. This efficiency is of a piece with the Prince's own constant seeking for perfection in everything he does or is responsible for. In 1962, National Productivity Year, he persuaded Palace officials to let in a group of business efficiency experts to go through the Palace. He also called in a firm specializing in Organization and Methods to examine the work of his own office in the 1970s. On both occasions the report was favourable. Indeed, as a result of the 1962 examination pay was increased and six more people taken on to the general Palace staff. Mrs Smith saw no change as a result of the later study in the 1970s, but she remains convinced that "we were underpaid for the work we did, compared to what people get outside the Palace."

So much for the people who work for the Prince. We will see more of that work as we examine the Prince's own daily work at the Palace. To set this in a context I would like to examine, in turn, a royal year, a royal week and a royal day. Few people will be surprised to learn that 'making up' the royal year resembles, in one sense, the making up of a school timetable with the weeks replacing the hours which figure on the latter.

There are certain things which have to be pencilled in on the year's calendar. Traditionally the Royal Family spend Christmas at Windsor and Sandringham. Then there is the summer holiday which is spent at Balmoral, as well as other fixed points. Some of these are public engagements such as the Trooping the Colour in June, and the State Opening of Parliament in October. Others are less publicized but nonetheless state occasions, such as long-standing visits to overseas countries or by foreign heads of state to this country. There are also engagements connected with a royal charity which have to be attended.

It is, therefore, possible for people to ink in certain months, weeks or days during which the Prince's engagements are defined. Twice a year the Prince gets together with all his staff—Lord Rupert, William Heseltine, the current senior equerry and the secretaries to consider the make-up of his diary for the next six months. These Programme Meetings start at about ten thirty in the morning and go on until everything has been done. Mrs Smith remembered these meetings well. Here, she felt, was the 'family circle' planning ahead. Like all families the various members had their differences which sometimes led to raised voices. But like most families, these people had come to know each other so well that each could interpret the other's half-suggestions so that the meeting seemed to consist of half-completed sentences, groans, mutterings and inexplicable silences.[2]

Only those at such a meeting would be able to understand how a decision had been reached as to a particular visit. Each year the Prince receives about a thousand requests to visit some place or other in Britain. Each one of these is considered at the six-monthly Programme Meeting. Some have to be rejected immediately. He can't do this one because he will be abroad; he can't do that one because it takes place on the same day as the state visit of some foreign head of state; another has to be turned down because it takes place on a Sunday while another is thrown out because he has an engagement to visit the Rhine Army during that week. And so on and so on. Each of the requests has been transferred, by one of the girls, on to an 'Engagements Possible' card—a crisp white card which shows when the proposed engagement is due to take place, what organization or town is involved, why it seems right that a royal visit might take place, when this town, society or institution was last visited, whether the Prince has either accepted or refused a previous invitation from the town or society—and why he refused—and who, if anyone, of influence is anxious for this particular engagement to take place.

At each six-monthly meeting the Prince and his 'family circle' have to deal with about a thousand cards, and dealing with some of the cards will lead to sending for a bundle of files. So, a consideration of a visit to, say, Plymouth may lead to files being brought in which contain all the correspondence arising from previous visits to that city, to naval establishments in the area and to neighbouring institutions.

In the course of researching this book I wrote to the Prince and to members of his staff and I also visited the Palace. On my first visit I was surprised to learn that my initial letter had led to my being given a file, a number and a place in the secretarial pile-up. I shuddered to think of what files were involved by a proposed or realized visit to a major city. There must be files for the local council, the local industrialists, local schools and so on almost *ad infinitum*. It is not surprising then that during the Programme Meetings girls and equerries are constantly coming and going with bundles of files as the discussion revolves around this and that.

A first run through the 'Engagements Possible' cards leads to the immediate rejection of about half of them. This still leaves many hundreds to be considered for the second time. Only about one in four of the invitations—to visit, tour, inspect, open, attend, speak, launch, lunch or dine can be lucky. Requests stand no chance if they suggest a visit 'next week'—for the royal year is filled in at least six calendar months in advance. The invitation has a better chance if it comes from some organization for which the Prince feels a special concern—as he does for projects involved with wildlife, industrial design, business efficiency and so on. Some will stand or fall because of the country's geography. He can't be seen to go to ten visits to the North-East and one to the North-West: nor, having gone down coal-mines this week can he be expected to repeat the adventure the following week. Nor, if he has to be on duty at Epsom on Derby Day can he be expected to fulfil an afternoon engagement in Durham on the same day—although he will accept engagements for the mornings of such days, using his helicopter or aircraft to get him there and back.

And geography plays another trick of fortune. If, for example, he has accepted an engagement to visit a steelworks in Port Talbot he will then look for other invitations which might be accepted in the same area on that day. This explains why a visit to a town becomes in itself an almost endless run around. If he is in London this might involve interviews at the Palace with important visitors, an official lunch, a couple of annual general meetings of societies which he heads, a speech to write, and an official cocktail party followed by an official dinner. And then, as Mrs Smith remembered, he would come back to the Palace to read, write, plan or set about initiating some other project. There are no fixed hours but it can be said that they are long—and most of them spent in the public eye with little chance for relaxation.

A typical visit to a town in Britain may involve a review of a guard of honour at a railway station or airfield, a meeting with officials at the town or city hall, visits to local schools, factories and other industrial centres, a tour of a housing estate or shopping centre and an official luncheon and tea, with one, two or more speeches during the day. Then maybe back to London for an official engagement in the evening. Throughout the day he has to try to remember that what is for him merely another visit—to factory, works, farm, school or institution—will be for those being visited probably the only chance they'll ever have of seeing a member of the Royal Family at close hand. So however he may feel he has to be pleasant, smiling, with a word here and a glance there—and all the time conscious of the cameras of reporters and television crews.

Back to the six-monthly meetings. To help bring some order to the proceedings there are a set of cards for 'Engagements for week ending . . .'. As each invitation is accepted so the detail is pencilled in on one of these cards. There would be little point in accepting for the same day invitations to Inverness and Penzance, and a glance at these partially completed cards helps the consideration of each 'Engagements Possible' card. If the Prince has agreed to go to Plymouth on Tuesday then he may also be able to visit the Royal Marines at Lympstone on the same day. Sometimes this attempt to dovetail things leads to a lengthy correspondence with the various interested parties. If only so and so would agree to bring forward the date of the proposed visit to such and such, then he could accept. Or, if this visit could be cut by an hour he could go by helicopter to fulfil that engagement—and so the girls troop to their machines and the files grow bulkier.

Out of the apparent chaos of these six-monthly meetings order finally emerges and his diary is completed. This then shows him what he has to do each day of each week—at least it shows this in part, each day is different from the next and has its own unexpected developments. He rises early, reads the newspapers, and takes breakfast with the Queen and others in the family who may be at the Palace. This gives him a chance to discuss with the Queen the day's events—where they'll be, who they'll meet, what he'll say to him and she to her and so on. Then he goes to his study to tackle the morning mail. This falls into three categories. There is the large mail which arises from his patronage. He receives annual reports, letters from heads of societies or charities—and each of these he reads, initials and, when required, plans an answer. Mrs Smith remembered that he has a great capacity for reading quickly—not carelessly, because he always showed that he had taken the gist of whatever it was he had read so that he could ask the pertinent questions, make the required reply or suggest the necessary follow-up.

He also has to deal with what may be called 'household mail' which is to do with the work of his office which we have just examined. There will be letters from chief constables who want to know how he will travel in their area, what guard he wishes to have provided and so on; town clerks will write about this, factory managers about that. Most of this 'nuts and bolts' work will be answered by one of the equerries—but only after the Prince has read the letter, sometimes suggested the answer—and always read the final reply.

Every day there are about a hundred letters which 'just arrive'. Mrs Smith remembered the dozens which came, each with a supply of Polo mints, when some reporter commented on his liking for that sweet. There are letters from people with whom he once served, from former members of regiments of which he is Colonel-in-Chief, and from journalists and authors. Each of these is read, and a reply indicated. As Mrs Smith remembered, he "sees it all"—a time-consuming task which nonetheless is an indication of his concern to do his job properly.

Prince Philip receives an annual allowance of £135,000 from the Civil List. Some people imagine that this is some sort of salary for him; in fact, all this money is spent in the work that we have been considering. The salaries of his staff take about half his allowance—in spite of Mrs Smith's belief that she was less well paid at the Palace than she ought to have been. He also has to pay the rents and rates on the flats or homes of his more important staff. He wants to have them to hand, therefore they have to live within a few minutes' walk of the Palace so that they won't be affected by a strike or some untoward incident on railway line or road. He also has to pay towards the cost of the upkeep of the two royal cars which he uses; he must also pay the two chauffeurs as well as making a contribution to the cost of their uniforms.

Although he lives 'all found' at the Palace and at other royal households, he has to pay for the cost of entertaining members of his family whenever they come from Germany on a private visit to the Palace. The ministry or department concerned delves away at the Palace expenditure until it comes up with the difference made by having his relatives stay there. His treasurer has similar arguments with the Department of the Environment which pays for the office equipment—typewriters, copying machines and the like—but, strangely, does not pay for desks, chairs and the like. This led to one of those 'other world' arguments so beloved of the bureaucrats over the matter of filing cabinets. Were these to be listed with machines (as the Prince's office argued) or were they similar to other cabinets made of wood and so to be listed with desks, chairs and so on? The victory went to Philip's treasurer so that the Prince's allowance has to pay only for desks, chairs and other 'made by carpenters' items.

There is no doubt, however, about who has to pay for the hundreds of gifts which he is expected to hand out each year during his British visits. He has to pay for the wallets, photographs, cuff-links and similar gifts which the recipient treasures. Until 1971 he was also expected to pay the cost of foreign engagements undertaken without the Queen, and even today he has to pay for items which the Foreign and Commonwealth Office chooses to regard as 'out of the ordinary'. Thus, gifts to players in a polo game in Mexico had to be paid for by the Prince's treasurer as do the gifts which he makes to the crews of aircraft and the girls from the office who tour with him.

What is he like to work for? How does he strike people who have worked with him? We know a good deal about the impression he makes on newspaper reporters who also report the impression he makes on people who do not like him. David Leitch, for example, a *Sunday Times* reporter, spoke of "members of a Yacht Club in the Bahamas [who] assured me that he had all the social graces of a pig."[3] It has to be said, in fairness to Leitch, that he describes himself as "a sceptic and callow cynic"[4] so that we ought not to expect a great depth of understanding or much sympathy from his account of his meeting with the Prince in Rabat in December 1966.[5] But it has to be noted that it is just such reports and accounts which the majority of us have to read and from which many people may draw their opinion of the Royal Family in general and the Prince in particular.

It may be that Mrs Smith presents a fairer, rounder picture of her former employer, and it is all the more objective because she was forced to leave the Palace staff on her engagement. One might think that this could have made her somewhat more critical of the organization which until recently treated girls in this out-of-date way.

She remembers with admiration his ability to assimilate a great deal of knowledge, quickly and on a wide variety of subjects. This enabled him to talk intelligently to many of the people he met during his visits and tours. He himself is deprecating about this, saying that he is "a fund of useless information".[6] But if it is, it is a very useful trick to be able to know something about everything and to be able to use the information intelligently. He seems always to know enough to ask intelligent questions at factories or mines, workshops or boardrooms, research laboratories or meetings of athletes. This pleases the people he is meeting—and that cannot be a bad thing.

Mrs Smith also saw him as a man with driving energy, with the wish to do everything he tackles as well as he possibly can. This comes as no surprise to people who have considered the lives of earlier Mountbattens—Prince Louis and the late Earl.

Mrs Smith also saw him as someone who desperately wanted to put things to right. This fits in with the views of others who wrote to me. One thought that he would have made a great Prime Minister. In September 1969 the *Daily Telegraph* invited readers to say who would make a good dictator and who might make the best dictator. Prince Philip came top of both polls, ahead of Enoch Powell, Harold Wilson, Edward Heath and, almost at the bottom of the poll, the Queen. In 1968 he had also topped the list of an *Observer* poll on who would make the best British President.[7]

This driving obsession with getting things done and putting things right is one major cause of his prickly relations with the Press and with British expatriates in such havens as the Bahamas, for if he makes a criticism of something it is so easily and often interpreted as arrogance.

His own will to work long hours at what proves to be a thankless task—indeed one which often gets him a bad Press—helps to explain his attitude towards his own staff. Mrs Smith told me of a foreign tour during which she sat in the royal Andover aircraft "typing for a solid eight hours". I asked whether the Prince showed any appreciation of such work. "No, he would just expect the work to be done if it was there to be done." Some people might put this down as a black mark, a sign of rudeness, but those who worked with him are not among that critical minority. It was the reaction of a hard-working boss who expected no thanks for the work he did and gave none when people did what he saw as their duty. Mrs Smith was quick to add as an afterthought, "Mind you, he cooked breakfast for all of us on board the Andover." The way to a woman's heart . . .

Finally, would Mrs Smith like to change her present well-paid job in a London office for her old job at the Palace? There wasn't a hesitation—"Oh, yes." And this in spite of the overwork, the untoward hours, the absence of a private life and the unthanking 'boss'. Maybe it was the glamour of those foreign tours? "No, I can say that I have gone three times around the world and visited dozens of countries. But we always had so much work to do that I never had a chance to see much of most of the places we visited." Maybe it was the pleasure of going through the door of the Palace or staying at Balmoral? No; and even at Balmoral the work went on. "He has a most efficient system for getting letters from London to wherever he is. Abroad the stuff came out and no one in London was allowed to make a decision on his behalf. And the work flowed to Balmoral throughout the summer as you will have seen if you've watched the Cawson TV film." So, if it wasn't foreign travel, the glamour of Palace life, and it certainly wasn't pay, why would Mrs Smith go back if she had the chance? "Well, I like things to be done properly and I have never found an office which worked so well as Prince Philip's." Perhaps that's the answer for people such as David Leitch who writes of the "misleading myth that Royals work like dogs . . . their programmes are rarely taxing . . .".[8] I find that all the more amusing since I am writing this during a strike of journalists for more money for their less than eight-hour day.

Part IX

THE PRINCE AND CRITICISM

40

Prince Philip—Politics and Politicians

IT IS HARDLY SURPRISING THAT Prince Philip is naturally distrustful of most, if not all, politicians and sceptical of their grandiose promises to put their world to rights. Even the briefest glimpse of the careers of his grandfather and father must have led him to see that the biblical advice—"Put not your trust in princes"—might be rephrased to princely advantage. And the treatment he received from the British politicians between 1947 and 1952 was sufficient to have burnt the iron of distrust and scepticism deep into his soul.

We have seen that he has taken great care to divorce himself from the political side of the Queen's life, but like other intelligent men he has political views. At Gordonstoun and Dartmouth he revealed an above-average ability and intelligence, which led Prime Minister Attlee to think that he would have made a name for himself if he had been given the chance. One of his former secretaries, a mature and experienced business woman when I interviewed her in 1979, thought that if he had been born Bill Bloggs he would have reached the top in whatever job he had chosen. So it is hardly surprising that he has fairly well-defined political views—and that these have made him even more distrusted by some politicians, who are surprised that 'a royal' should think in political terms.

Lord Louis Mountbatten was known to have socialist views. Philip himself wrote of "the concept of social justice [which] began in the universities some forty years ago in the depression of the 1930s."[1] One may want to pre-date the concern for social justice. There can be little doubt that in the 1930s many people—and not only from universities—first became aware of the failure of the existing system to provide an adequate quality of life for millions of people. Lord Mountbatten may well have been one such 'convert' to moderate socialism. I only discovered Mountbatten's socialism when I began my research into the lives of various members of the Royal Family. Others have known about this for a very long time. I have a letter which tells of a wartime drinking session in an east-coast pub. Among the group was Lieutenant-Commander

Frederick E. C. Davies, who had been with Scott on the ill-starred Polar expedition. My correspondent writes:

> . . . and the talk got around to the popularity of Lord Louis and this young Philip; and I well remember one skipper (you couldn't tell rank as most kept their blue raincoats on) seriously opined, "Well, don't you know. All the Mountbattens are Socialists."[2]

The skipper was certainly right in his judgement of Lord Louis's political views, but equally wrong about Philip's. His views are much further to the right. Indeed, in Brazil in 1968 he "startled one Government official by saying that there wasn't much wrong with representational government, a system in which only certain people are allowed to vote, because there was no guarantee the majority were always correct. Perhaps he was right about Brazil."[3] In Paraguay he told the dictator, Alfredo Stroessner, that it "was a pleasant change to be in a country that isn't ruled by its people."[4]

These off-the-cuff remarks may be taken as unfortunate utterances by the "royal bull in the democratic china shop".[5] But in October 1977 he spoke on Radio Clyde in a series of programmes entitled 'Platform: Towards 2000'. In 1978 this talk was published as part of a symposium called *The Coming Confrontation*. In this essay Prince Philip analysed the political system as it had developed, was developing and, as he saw it, would develop. In so doing he gave a number of hostages to fortune because, inevitably, he revealed his own political opinions.

Before examining these in some detail it ought to be noted that the other contributors to the symposium were six professors, of history, economics, economic history and sociology, and three MPs, one Labour, one Conservative and one Liberal. That his work sits well with the work of such a high-powered team is a tribute to his intelligence, grasp of ideas and ability to express them clearly. It would be well if all his politician-critics showed the same clarity of thought and experience.

Prince Philip's views will be the better understood after a brief summary of the views of some of the other contributors to the symposium. Professor Challoner, Professor of Economic History at the University of Manchester, wrote of the differences between the peaceful Glorious English Revolution of 1688–1689 and the more bloody French Revolution of 1789. The former had sought to establish a democratic form of government which limited the Monarch's power so that people might go freely about their business. The French Revolution, on the other hand, with its slogans of liberty, equality and fraternity, had led to the great Massacres of the Terror, the rise of Napoleon and a long period of European War. "The pursuit of 'equality' is a will-o'-the-wisp . . . widespread among children and immature adults—while 'fraternity', if not based on the family or the close association of the voluntary society or club, is nebulous nonsense."[6]

But, goes on Challoner, modern British intellectuals view the British Revolution with suspicion while they laud the French Revolution and its violence which justifies their sympathy with "revolutionary violence and judicial murder"; 'you can't make omelettes without breaking eggs'.[7] The English Revolution is now criticized by radicals for being concerned mainly with "the doctrine of possessive individualism" which runs counter to the opinions of the modern collectivists with their doctrine of statism and egalitarianism. This, says Challoner, explains their reluctance to support the movement for a new Bill of Rights which would serve as a guarantee of British freedom.

Professor Gash, Professor of History, examined the growth of the state in our economic, social and cultural lives. He saw this as "the steady progress towards a form of corporate state incompatible with [the] basic principles of personal liberty . . .".[8] This theme was also taken up by Professor Hayek, winner of the Nobel Prize for Economic Science in 1974. He argued that ". . . an Almighty Parliament means the death of the freedom of the individual" if it means ". . . a licence to the majority in Parliament to act as it pleases."[9]

Professor Gould, Professor of Sociology at the University of Nottingham wrote of the way in which the modern radicals have re-interpreted 'equality'. When the demand for social justice began "forty years ago" there was a demand for "equality of opportunity". But the view of modern radicals is expressed in the Open University book of sociological readings, *Schooling and Capitalism*: "The idea of equality of opportunity, the drive to establish a meritocracy based upon ability, while compensating those deprived of opportunity to participate in the movement towards upward social mobility, are shown neither to threaten nor to replace the essential structures of society."[10] And the radical left use this failure and the need to "threaten [or] replace" as an excuse to organize violence in pursuit of their "will-o'-the-wisp".

The disappointment which follows the failure of the reformers to bring about the promised equality drives the governing bureaucracies to make even more extravagant promises—realizable, they declare, on condition that they play an even greater part in our lives. And when this, in turn, fails, the politicians resort to what an American professor described as "organized, institutionalized lying in government".[11] Those of us who have watched the development of events in Britain will have our own examples of this "falsehood explosion". There was "the social contract which was not a contract; or cease fires in which terrorism continues, or the lies of politicians on the extent of inflation."[12] Other powerful organizations have imitated their political masters; drug companies deny responsibility for the proven damages done by their products; trade unions protest that they want to narrow the gap between the lower and higher paid—but also want to maintain the differentials paid to skilled men.

This is only a brief summary of some of the points made by the 'professional' contributors to the symposium. When Prince Philip made his broadcast in October 1977 he did not have access to these contributions which did not appear until late in 1978, but his earlier broadcast dealt with most of the trends which the 'professionals' were to write about. He refers knowledgeably and pertinently to a variety of sources, showing that he has lost none of that ability to extract the relevant from what he reads. He admits that he has a biased view of things. "If you have grown up with or acquired a certain set of principles, they will inevitably colour your selection of historical factors and the emphasis you give to the conclusions you draw from them."[13] It would be a good thing if all his critics had an equal honesty. It is regrettable that "unscrupulous prophets find it easier to start with the conclusion they wish to reach and then simply search around for the appropriate cases to prove it."[14]

The "Utopian salesmen"[15] such as the Marxists have imagined a state in which everything is ideal and seek to devise the means of reaching that desirable end. But, as the history of Lenin's Russia showed in 1918 and 1919, the consequences are "never exactly what was originally intended". But convinced that their laudable ends justify whatever means they choose to employ, the Utopians assume that organized violence and terror should be employed. This means that "the community has to suffer the means while the Utopian end is never likely to be achieved."[16] Prince Philip's fear that violence would become part of the political scene was echoed, as we have seen, by Professor Challoner.[17]

Prince Philip argued that "the most frightful horrors are condoned because they are justified by the greatness of the idea. Such are the Inquisition, revolutionary terrorism and the Gulag Archipelago."[18] But in spite of the evidence from the past the radical left still insists that it is possible to attain equality if only . . . and then set off with propositions which often contain the seeds of a repetition of the "frightful horrors" of the past.

In his talk he showed that he was able to take a wide view of the economy. "Governments . . . tend to be concerned . . . with . . . unemployment. Employers are concerned with wealth-creating for the benefit of . . . investors, managers and the work force . . . Trade unions . . . see automation . . . as a threat to existing jobs."[19] The group, and the individuals in each group, view development from their own selfish standpoint. This self-interest has been modified, until recently, by the "Christian ethic". Prince Philip thought that "if we abandon the Christian doctrine of loving our neighbour . . . we shall most certainly revert to a state of jungle warfare."[20] He showed that it was the decline in moral convictions linked to the Utopian promises of Hitler's propaganda which were responsible for the concentration camps and gas chambers . . . "not in line with the normal behaviour of the German people and quite beyond the range of expectation."[21] At a lower level the British people witnessed an outbreak of jungle warfare during the winter of 1978–1979 when the demands for inflationary wage increases saw London being deprived of an ambulance service, sewage flowing into the water supplies in the Liverpool area and cancer patients not receiving their drugs because of a picket at hospital gates. When an ambulance driver was asked how he would feel if someone died on the streets of London because of the absence of ambulances, he replied, "So be it." The history of France (1790s), Germany (1930s) and Russia (1917–19) shows that the veneer of civilization is thin. There is no reason to suppose that it is any thicker in this country than in other European countries.

As 1978–1979 proves, there is a real danger that this country could witness the development of anarchy, where organized trade unions defy governments, members of unions defy the instructions of their leaders and there has been a decline of "individual restraint and good sense".[22] Each group seeks to impose its will on the community at large. This might well lead to a ruling group forcing its views on the rest of the people—in what Hayek called the "Almighty Parliament". Prince Philip shared Hayek's fears, ". . . the national interest must include the interests of the individual and not be limited to the self-interest of the ruling group or any other organization exercising power on behalf of a sectional interest."[23]

In introducing his talk Prince Philip had been at pains to explain that he was "going to be concerned only with what I think may happen. What I would like to see happen is an entirely different story."[24] Having reviewed the way in which things had developed in Britain during the last forty years or so, he concluded with a set of predictions. It will come as no surprise that he was gloomy—for so are many others in all the main political parties. He sees "an increasing bureaucratic involvement in every aspect of the lives of individual citizens [which] will mean a gradual reduction in the freedom . . . of individual responsibility."[25] Here he was expressing the fears which had led a former Labour Minister, Roy Jenkins, to declare that "democracy was in danger when the Government and its bureaucratic agents dispose of more than fifty per cent of the gross national product of any State."[26] He sees "wages and salaries [becoming] less important as all the major necessities [are] provided . . . out of taxation and also because fringe benefits associated with employment and trade unions will increase. This . . . will ensure a very high degree of job discipline . . . Slavery is no more than a system of directed labour and fringe benefits."[27] In this Prince Philip was expressing the fears which the socialist novelist George Orwell had developed in his famous novels, *Animal Farm* and *1984*. He concluded his talk with a warning; "Some of the things I have said may seem unthinkable in this country with its tradition of freedom and tolerance. There were people in many other countries who felt the same way, but the unthinkable happened to them. The Russian dissident Alexander Solzhenitsyn said: 'It is not how the Soviet Union will find a way out of totalitarianism, but how the West will be able to avoid the same fate.' "[28]

A number of people who wrote with their personal memoirs of Prince Philip concluded with a note that HRH Prince Philip would make a superb Prime Minister.[29] We have seen that this opinion was supported by the findings of a Gallup poll. In other chapters we have seen evidence of his impatience, arrogance, tendency to bully and the like. These may not seem to be the best qualities to look for in a Prime Minister—although Attlee did think that a good Prime Minister had to be a ruthless "butcher" of Ministers who had failed. But there can be little doubt that the intelligent, widely-read and clear-minded Consort has shown a greater political awareness than many of his shallow critics. It is not surprising that they, and the radical left, seek to present him in an unfavourable light.

41

Prince Philip's Relations with the Press

IN THE SPRING OF 1944 Prince Philip was in Newcastle-upon-Tyne waiting for the destroyer *Whelp* to be commissioned. It was here that he gave his first interview to a newspaper reporter, Olga Franklin, then working for the *Newcastle Journal*. She spoke glowingly of the "tall, ash-blond first lieutenant, RN".[1] This was Prince Philip's introduction to the British Press which, since 1947, has written about him in much less flattering terms and has almost invited his antipathy towards the Press in general and towards Press photographers in particular.

This hostility has been well publicized and reported. In 1951, for example, during the royal tour of Canada, he quickly came to resent the way in which photographers tried to push onlookers around so that they could get a better picture of Princess Elizabeth and himself. In Toronto he found that the crush of photographers obstructed the view of a crowd of school-children. He stood in his car and angrily waved the photographers aside so that the children could see the royal procession. And at Niagara Falls he growled, "What are they belly-aching about now?" after he and Lilibet had posed for pictures . . . and the cameramen wanted still more.[2]

Some reports of his antipathy to Press photographers have been very exaggerated, others are simply untrue. There is the almost legendary report of his having doused photographers with water at the Chelsea

Flower Show. The *Daily Mail* reported, "Prince Philip sprayed water from an electronic garden spray over two photographers when he visited the Chelsea Flower Show yesterday." The truth was very different. An official showing him around the Show pointed out that if he pressed a certain button he could soak the cameramen. "Not likely", said the Prince. So the official pressed it.[3] But every newspaper imitated the *Daily Mail* and blamed the Prince.

Some reports of his hostility are true—and so are reports of his apologies. When he was surrounded by reporters and cameramen when visiting the monkey enclosure in Gibraltar, he did say caustically, "Which are the monkeys and which are the reporters?" His subsequent apology did little to soothe the ruffled feelings of the pressmen—and received much less publicity than the original remark.

Some of his criticisms have been aimed specifically at individual newspapers. Speaking to American journalists at a luncheon in London in November 1962 he condemned the *Daily Mirror* for being "not quite respectable" and *The Times* for being "too stodgy". But he reserved his most severe criticism for the *Daily Express* which he accused of being "far too savage" in its attacks on the Royal Family. Earlier in 1962 in Rio de Janeiro he had described the *Daily Express* as a "bloody awful newspaper". This is hardly surprising. The hostility of the Beaverbrook Press towards Lord Louis—and by proxy towards Prince Philip—seems to have its origins in the ill-fated Dieppe raid of 1942.[4] Beaverbrook himself wrote about the heavy casualties and the useless sacrifice of Canadian lives. Writing of himself in the third person he went on: "He allowed his bitterness to outrun his discretion to the extent of launching an ill-tempered attack on the chief of combined operations, Lord Louis Mountbatten. The occasion was a private gathering at which Lord Louis was present. Beaverbrook accused him in unmeasured terms of faulty planning leading to the needless sacrifice of human lives. Lord Louis replied that the plans were his, but that in execution they were not carried out. The general sympathy of the gathering was certainly with the defence." Beaverbrook's biographer, A. J. P. Taylor commented: "It is said that from this moment Beaverbrook pursued a vendetta against Mountbatten. That is an exaggeration."[5] But in another part of the biography Taylor quotes from a letter which Beaverbrook wrote to his son, Max Aitken, on the 20th April 1958: "Print these statements, simple statements. Don't Trust Mountbatten in Any Public Capacity. Together with a further quotation from Mountbatten's speech in Canada where he said he took full responsibility for Dieppe. Four thousand men set forth and three thousand did not come back."[6] Taylor comments: "It is difficult not to feel that more lay behind. None of Beaverbrook's friends could discover what it was. Something about Mountbatten touched Beaverbrook on a raw nerve. However, the troubled story had a happy ending. In 1962 Macmillan brought the two men together, and they were reconciled."[7]

But by 1963 the newspapers of the *Express* chain had spent some sixteen years attacking "Phil the Greek" and had helped create that mutual antipathy between the Pess and Prince Philip, and that hostility did not cease with the ending of the Beaverbrook feud against Lord Louis. During the Caribbean tour in 1966 Prince Philip was told by a matron of a hospital, "We have a lot of trouble with mosquitoes." "I know what you mean," he replied. "You have mosquitoes, I have the Press."[8] Angry reporters demanded—and received—an apology, but the underlying and joint antipathy remained. Ten years later, in July 1973, Prince Philip was in Glasgow for the graduation ceremony at Paisley College of Technology. Before going to that ceremony he spoke at a Newspaper Press Fund Lunch and told the assembled pressmen that he knew his reputation with the Press was "not all that good". In fact, the American magazine *Time* had said he was "no friend of the Press". He went on: "That's the trouble with reputations—they cling much more tenaciously than the truth. I know your reputation, don't try to confuse me with the facts—that reflects an attitude that is not altogether unknown. Incidentally, if anyone can offer me advice about how I can improve this reputation or even offer any reason why I have this reputation, I shall be more than grateful. Perhaps I made the mistake of saying what I think, but surely any good journalist is expected to do that every working day."[9]

In what some may see as a battle with the Press Prince Philip is at a substantial disadvantage. It is, after all, the Press which dictates the terms of the clash; it alone decides what should be reported and how. Thus we have untrue reports about incidents such as the mythical soaking of the photographers at Chelsea. But the Press has a more important advantage in its ability to use adjectives, adverbs and verbs in a particularly insidious way. When the Press wishes to support someone or some movement it employs such adjectives as 'forceful', 'efficient' and 'well-known' with the adverbs 'dramatically' and 'forcefully' jostling alongside 'convincingly'. But when the newspapers wish to downgrade someone or something then it employs 'unimaginative', 'uncaring' and 'illiberal' as adjectives and 'pedantically', 'dully' and 'boringly' as adverbs. The favoured person is said to 'maintain' or 'assert' while the unfortunate person under attack merely 'claims'. So it was that the British and American Press created the 'image' of a "charismatic" and "dynamic" John F. Kennedy. In this almost subliminal way too did the British Press first build up Harold Wilson in 1963–1964, only to employ its language-assassination on him after 1970.

Prince Philip has suffered from this sort of insidious attack against which it is almost impossible to defend oneself. During the Jubilee celebrations in 1977 the *New Statesman* published a long article on the Duke of Edinburgh subtitled 'Neither Dignified nor Efficient'.[10] In this anonymous article the author described him as "a survivor from Europe's most discredited Royal House", failing to say whether this was a reference to his father's or his mother's ancestry. It referred to his "many years" as "a part of the high-born rabble which drifted around the continent" and to the "moderate distinction with which he served in the wartime Royal Navy, the astute manner of his naturalization, his acquisition of British titles . . ." all of which are half-truths ignoring his ability as a naval officer and Attlee's belief that he might have gone as far as did Lord Louis, his own wish not to be given a British title when he became a naturalized Britisher, and the reasons for that naturalization. Prince Philip's comments on industry, science, medicine, health education and the like are dismissed as "braying platitudes" while "the collective memory of his activities is almost entirely composed of clichés". The World Wildlife Fund is described as "a good staple for cartoonists"; the Award Scheme is "celebrated by news editors for the easy copy it offers at slow Bank Holiday weekends when pinched and hungry schoolboys can be found huddled around a freezing cairn in Snowdonia after being lost by their baggy-shorted housemaster or wardens."

It is hardly surprising that the Duke of Edinburgh resents this form of criticism with its curt dismissal and trivialization of so much valuable work. Sometimes he has reacted and become the first member of the Royal Family to reply to criticism in public. When one newspaper criticized the royals as being "under-employed thumb-twiddlers" the busy Duke responded when he spoke to an audience in Birmingham: "You know what I am doing?" he asked them. "I'm twiddling my thumbs . . ." He has had to meet criticism for what he does ("the Duke plays polo on Sunday" thunders the Sunday Observance League) or what he does not do; for what he says ("Prince attacks British management" complains a trade paper) and for what he does not say. He has had to come to terms with the fact that the London-based Press is generally hostile although he can take comfort from the knowledge that even *The Times* believes that "the world of Westminster, Whitehall, the West End clubs and even Fleet Street is curiously remote from what goes on in the rest of the country."[11]

For the rest of the country Prince Philip continues to be as popular a figure as he was when a poll was conducted by the *Observer* in 1968 in which he was chosen as the best candidate for a proposed post of President of the Republic of Great Britain. In September 1969 the *Daily Telegraph* conducted a poll asking who would be a good dictator and who the best dictator. Prince Philip topped both these polls leaving politicians such as Harold Wilson, Enoch Powell, Edward Heath and Barbara Castle far behind although ahead of the Queen. But when he looks at the provincial Press the Prince finds small comfort, for while this large section of the newspaper industry does not often echo the savage criticisms of Fleet Street, it suffers from a tendency to concentrate its attention on royal tittle-tattle. *The Scotsman*, for example, wishes that biographers of members of the Royal Family would provide readers with 'human stories' and information such as "the corgis didn't sleep in dog baskets but in real beds with blankets and pillows. And by the side of the Queen Mother's bed were stone angels with gold haloes and staffs." This, *The Scotsman* claimed, "throws new light on the Queen Mother".[12] It is small wonder that the real work of the Royal Family goes unreported or misunderstood.

Perhaps the main reason for the Duke's antipathy to the London Press lies in his anger at the way in which it intrudes into the privacy of royal lives. In this matter the British Press is less offensive than, for example, the American Press with its gory detailing of President Johnson's stomach operation. Nor does the British Press have the inventiveness of the French Press which has carried almost as many reports of the Queen's imminent abdication, as of her forthcoming divorce from Prince Philip—although as early as February 1957 the British Press carried a spate of rumours about the private life of the Queen and Prince Philip which was not ended by an announcement from Buckingham Palace which stated: "It is quite untrue that there is any rift between the Queen and the Duke of Edinburgh." Prince Philip later spoke about the significance of rumour and reputation and the way in which people—and the Press—ignored or misconstrued "facts". One fact of the case in February 1957 was that the Prince had been away from England for four months. He had gone to open the Melbourne Olympics and then had undertaken the tour of the Antarctic.[13] Another fact was that the marriage of his secretary, Michael Parker, was being ended in the divorce court. A third fact was that in February 1957 the Queen and Prince Philip were due to make a state visit to Portugal. It had been arranged that Prince Philip would sail to Gibraltar in *Britannia* and join the Queen when she flew from London to Lisbon. A fourth fact was that *Britannia* arrived in Gibraltar some eight days before the Queen was due in Lisbon.

Prince Philip might have flown home from Gibraltar and then flown back again with the Queen to Lisbon—and, no doubt, would have been criticized for needless extravagance. He let it be known that he felt that it would be "deserting ship" if he, alone, was allowed to fly home while the rest of the crew of *Britannia* had to stay aboard in Gibraltar. But some reporters preferred to believe that he stayed aboard as a sign of rebellion against the enforced resignation of his secretary. Others carried speculations many stages further. Some extrapolated the break up of Parker's marriage into a "report of the Royal marriage". A reporter for the *Baltimore Sun* sent in an account which began, "The whisper started last summer . . ." of a break up of the marriage. There was the frustration of a bored Prince imprisoned in 'the cage', his attendance at the all-male lunches at the meetings of the Thursday Club which met above Wheeler's Restaurant in Compton Street and the alleged anger of the Queen at her husband's patronage of these and similar stag parties. Indeed, said some reporters, the Prince's long absence in the Antarctic had been a royal ploy to get the Prince out of the country with time "to cool off". Newspapers in Canada, Australia and Europe built up the story, some alleging that the retired Prime Minister, Churchill, was being brought back from the Riviera to help sort things out. At first British newspapers exercised a self-imposed censorship and did not carry any of these reports. But the

Press Association sought Buckingham Palace comment on the rumours. It would have been best if the Palace had refused to make any comment—although it is likely that even that would have been used as a hook on which to hang the story. In the event the Queen's Private Secretary issued the official denial of any rift. This was used as the excuse needed by the British newspapers to carry a flood of reports—each hypocritically denied by the newspapers which nonetheless continued to carry them.

It is not surprising that the Prince was deeply hurt by these rumours, stories and reports which had no basis in fact and which deliberately misconstrued the facts of the case as well as taking attention away from the hard work which had been undertaken during the previous four months. In 1961 while on a tour of India with the Queen he watched a Pakistani photographer fall from a tree where he had been trying to get a different angle for a royal photograph. "I hope to God that he breaks his bloody neck," said Prince Philip.[14] In that off-the-cuff and heartfelt remark he summarized his view of reporters and photographers in general—few objective onlookers can blame him for his attitude.

42

Prince Philip and Royal Finances

IN NOVEMBER 1969 PRINCE PHILIP WAS interviewed on American television. He was asked about the stories that the Royal Family were spending more than the £475,000 annual allowance made by the government. His reply started off a controversy that has not yet died down:

> We go into the red next year, which is not bad housekeeping if you come to think of it. We've in fact kept the thing going on a budget which was based on costs of eighteen years ago. So there have been very considerable corners that have had to be cut, and it's beginning to have its effects.
>
> There's no question of we just get a lump sum and we can do what we like with it. The thing is that it's allocated for particular purposes. Now, inevitably, if nothing happens we shall either have to—I don't know, we may have to move into smaller premises, who knows?
>
> We've closed down—well, for instance, we had a small yacht which we've

had to sell, and I shall probably have to give up polo fairly soon, things like that. I'm on a different allowance anyhow, but I've also been on it for the last eighteen years.[1]

Buckingham Palace tried to get the tapes cut before the interview went out on British television, but British journalists had been present at the original interview and to have doctored the interview would have been very unwise. So the interview was replayed on British television—and there was widespread comment under headings such as "In the Red". This was reminiscent of the furore that had broken out in 1845 when Queen Victoria had asked Peel that Parliament should grant her £150,000 to put Buckingham Palace in order. *Punch* printed a cartoon showing the Prince Consort, cap in hand and surrounded by his family, addressing the ragged poor of London:

Good people, pray take compassion on us. It is now nearly seven years since either of us have known the blessing of a comfortable residence. If you do not believe it, good people, come and see where we live at Buckingham Palace and you will be satisfied that there is no deception in our story. Such is our distress, that we should be truly grateful for the blessing of a comfortable two-pair back, with commonly decent sleeping rooms for our children and domestics. With our slender means, and our increasing family, we declare to you that we do not know what to do. The sum of one hundred and fifty thousand pounds will be all that will be required to make the needful alterations to our dwelling. Do, good people, bestow your charity to this little amount, and may you never live to feel the want of so small a trifle.

In 1969 comment was less forthright, but eventually it forced Prime Minister Harold Wilson to announce that a Select Committee would be set up during the next Parliament to examine the whole question of the Civil List.

The first Civil List Act was passed in 1697 when William III reigned and ruled. Parliament voted the annual sum of £600,000 to enable them to run the civil government. In 1727 the new King, George II, persuaded Parliament that he would need £800,000. On the accession of George III in 1760 a new arrangement was made. The Crown handed over to the Treasury some of the Crown Lands and in return the government took over the entire cost of running the government of the country. An annual sum, fixed at the start of each reign, was to be given to the Monarch for running the Royal Family's part in the process of government. In 1777 this allowance was increased to £900,000 a year but Queen Victoria's Civil List was set at £385,000 a year. This was sufficiently large for the economy-minded Albert to be able to save £200,000 to buy Osborne on the Isle of Wight and £300,000 to pay for the Sandringham and Balmoral estates.

Edward VII's Civil List was fixed at £470,000 a year, of which his Privy Purse, or private salary, was £110,000. It remained at this figure until 1936 when it was reduced to £410,000 as the Monarch's contribution to the government policy of cutting public expenditure during the Depression. In 1952 Parliament voted the new Queen's Civil List. This was fixed at

£475,000 allocated, as Prince Philip said in his interview, "for particular purposes":

		£ per annum
Class I	: Her Majesty's Privy Purse	60,000
Class II	: Salaries of Her Majesty's Household	185,000
Class III	: Expenses of Her Majesty's Household	121,800
Class IV	: Royal bounty, alms and special services	13,200
Class V	: Supplementary provision	95,000
		£475,000

The Privy Purse is the historic name for the private spending by the Monarch. In fact the Queen used this money for both 'private' and 'public' expenses. Some of it was spent on her private affairs—such as the estates at Balmoral and Sandringham. Some of it has been used to set up pension funds for employees not already covered. Some of it has been given to pay the official or public expenses of members of the Royal Family who do not get an allowance from the government.

In addition to the Queen's allowance of £475,000 a year, there were also provisions for other members of the Royal Family. Prince Philip, as we have seen, received £40,000 a year; the Queen Mother £70,000; the Duke of Gloucester £35,000 and Princess Margaret £15,000. There were also provisions for the Queen's children. Princesses would receive £6,000 a year until they were twenty-one and £15,000 a year after marriage. Princes, other than Prince Charles, would receive £10,000 a year until they were twenty-one and £25,000 a year after marriage.

Other 'working' members of the Royal Family—the younger members of the Gloucester and Kent families—had to rely on the money which the Queen could afford from her Class V provision. It was agreed in 1952 that £25,000 of that allowance should be spent on paying the expenses of members of the family not otherwise provided for. The remaining £70,000 was to be set aside to build up a fund which, it was hoped, would build up to provide against post-war inflation.

Until 1962 there was no problem; the allowance was always more than the expenditure and by 1962 the 'inflation fund' had built up to over £700,000. In 1962 for the first time spending was greater than £475,000—due largely to inflation and increases in salaries of Household Staff.

Each year after 1962 the family had to draw on the 'inflation fund'. In 1970, as Prince Philip knew when he spoke on American television, the total spending was £1,235,000—or £760,000 more than the money provided by the Civil List. And, to meet this massive deficit, there was now only £30,000 left in the 'inflation fund'. Hence Prince Philip's claim of being in the red.

The Conservatives won the election in the summer of 1970 and it was the Heath government which had to fulfil Wilson's promise of setting up a Select Committee. On the 19th May 1971 the Queen sent a "most Gracious Message" to the Commons asking for an increase in the Civil List because of the "developments in the intervening years" since 1952. A Select Committee was set up after a Commons' Debate which showed that MPs, like the majority of the British people, knew very little about royal finances. And, as we shall see, the proceedings of the Select Committee were only the start of a public debate on the subject which still concerns an increasing number of people. The Committee met six times between the 21st January and the 27th July 1971 and made a thorough investigation of the official royal finances.

One of the few solid facts which emerged from the work of that Select Committee was that the money allocated in the Civil List is only a small fraction of the money spent on or by the Royal Family. There is what Robert Lacey called "a hidden subsidy" amounting to about three million pounds a year. The Department of the Environment maintains the Royal Palaces. In 1971–1972 the Treasury set aside £385,887 for maintaining Buckingham Palace—paying for the fuel, gas, electricity and water; for maintaining the furniture and refurbishing the fabric of the building. The total cost for Windsor Castle was £377,584 with another £265,766 going on Hampton Court; £197,802 for St James's Palace and £101,104 on Holyroodhouse in Edinburgh. Here there was a total spending of over £900,000 a year.

The Ministry of Defence paid for the maintenance of the royal yacht *Britannia*, which first entered service in 1954 at a final cost to the taxpayer of £2.25 million. By 1974 the yacht had been refitted ten times. The refit of June 1974 cost £1.75 million—almost as much as she had cost in the first place. The annual running cost of the yacht had risen from £29,000 in 1953–1954 to over £75,000 in 1970–1971.

The Ministry of Defence also pays for the upkeep of the Queen's Flight. This Flight consists of three light planes and two helicopters which are also used by Cabinet Ministers when necessary. In 1973 the cost of the Flight was £800,000.

British Rail pays for the maintenance of the royal train and meets other costs of royal travel by rail—at a cost of about £36,000 a year. Other government departments make similar payments; the Post Office provides postal and telecommunication services estimated to be worth £52,000 a year, while the Treasury repays taxes paid on any goods bought for state or ceremonial purposes.

All in all, there is a hidden subsidy which the Select Committee of 1971 estimated to come to £2,932,000. Leading politicians seemed unaware of this in 1971. Jeremy Thorpe, for example, then Leader of the Liberal Party, reckoned that the Commons was discussing "fiddling little sums of money! The annual cost of the Monarchy is the same as that of the British Embassy in Paris."[2] This ignorance—shared by politicians and public alike—also extended to the income received from the Duchies of Lancaster and Cornwall.

George III handed over only a portion of the Crown lands to the Treasury in 1760. He held on to those lands which he owned as Duke of Lancaster. This was a title which Henry VI had retained after his Accession in 1399 and since then all monarchs—male and female—have been Dukes of Lancaster. The Lancaster estates consist of coal-mines, all of Lancashire's foreshore, agricultural and moorland, property in Pickering, the Strand in London and the City, in Aldershot, Bedford, Bristol and other cities and towns as well as residential property scattered throughout twelve counties.

This property is administered by a Cabinet Minister—the Chancellor of the Duchy of Lancaster. He spends less than a day a week on the work of supervising Duchy affairs so that the Cabinet post is normally given by the Prime Minister to a colleague whom he wishes to have available to look after special duties. The income from the Duchy, however, is far from negligible. Between 1952 and 1974 the Queen, as Duke of Lancaster, received three million pounds—and this income, like all her income was tax free.

Her tax position was only revealed by the work of the Select Committee. In 1969 Norman St John Stevas contributed to *The Monarchy and Its Future* and asserted, "It is sometimes thought that the Queen is not liable to pay income tax, but this is not the case."[3] In the same year the Central Office of Information published a pamphlet, *The Monarchy in Britain*, which stated that the Queen pays income tax on her income from her private estates. But the Treasury informed the Select Committee that "the Queen is not liable to income tax or surtax and is entitled to claim repayment of any income tax suffered at source (e.g. on company dividends). She is not liable to capital gains tax."[4]

Until 1970 she had not had to draw on any of her private income for private or public purposes. It was only when the 'inflation fund' had almost run out that there was a danger that the Queen would have to spend some of her own money. And, as we have seen, at that point Prince Philip claimed that "we go into the red" while the Queen and her Prime Minister, Harold Wilson, agreed to the setting up of the Select Committee with a view to increasing the allocations under the Civil List.

The Queen is the untaxed Duke of Lancaster. Her eldest son, as heir to the throne was, from the moment of birth, the Duke of Cornwall. The Duchy of Cornwall owns estates in the Scilly Isles, shops, offices and houses in Kennington—including the Oval Cricket ground. The net income from these various properties amounts, in 1968, to £220,000 a year. This means that by the time he was twenty-one (1969) Prince Charles had received something like half a million pounds from the Duchy—the total income from the Duchy over the same period amounting to about ten million pounds.

Like his mother, Prince Charles, as heir to the throne, was not liable to income tax. In 1969 he decided that he would pay fifty per cent of his Duchy of Cornwall income to the Treasury and also agreed that because of the remaining income from the Duchy he would not need any provision from the Civil List. This led him to pay over about £110,000 as income tax—leaving him an after-tax income of £110,000. Since this was a voluntary decision he could, presumably, make a decision not to pay tax—and so increase his income from £110,000 to something over £220,000. And even the decision to pay fifty per cent in tax made Prince Charles the most fortunate of taxpayers. If, in fact, he were treated as an ordinary taxpayer he would have to earn about £2,500,000 to have an after-tax income of £220,000. If on the other hand he paid the normal rates of tax on his Duchy income of £220,000 he would retain a little more than £22,000.

The Queen and Prince Charles are not subject to income tax. Nor does the Queen pay capital gains tax or the capital transfer taxes which have now replaced the former death duties. Balmoral was bought and rebuilt by Prince Albert from money saved out of Queen Victoria's Civil List. Sandringham was bought and improved from incomes received from the Duchies of Lancaster and Cornwall. Together they amount to about 47,000 acres—handed on intact from Victoria to Edward VII and so on to our present Queen. If the Sovereign had to pay the same death duties or, now, capital transfer taxes, these estates could never have been handed on.

In September 1978 I took part in a number of 'phone-in programmes in connection with my recently published *Our Future King.* In this short study of the life of Prince Charles I had made a brief reference to his income and his tax position. This was the only point which some reviewers picked out of the text. It was also the point which most participants in the radio programmes wished to talk about. One defender of the Queen's tax-free position argued that if she had to pay death duties then we would, today, see Windsor, Buckingham Palace and other palaces 'Open for Viewing' as are other stately homes. In fact, as we have seen, these royal homes are maintained by the Department of the Environment as part of that "hidden subsidy". Balmoral and Sandringham are the estates which would have suffered if the Sovereign had had to pay the same taxes as the rest of the people. And these estates are the family's private property. To have them broken up by death duties would not lead to a diminution of the public face of the Monarchy—as represented by the royal palaces—but it would lead to a change in the private life of the family.

Prince Albert had been able to buy Balmoral and Sandringham from Victoria's income and that of her son as Duke of Cornwall. What investments have succeeding monarchs made with that income? The simple answer is that no one outside the immediate family knows. The Select Committee pressed this question on the Queen's representative, Lord Cobbold, the Lord Chamberlain. He pleaded ignorance. "The Officers of the Household, including myself, do not handle Her Majesty's private funds and are not conversant with the details of such funds. Her

Majesty handles these matters herself, as did the late King and earlier Sovereigns."[5]

This allowed wild speculation as to the size of the Queen's private fortune. A former palace spokesman, Sir Richard Colville, suggested in a letter to *The Times* that the true figure was probably about two million pounds. Others suggested that the figure must be nearer a hundred million pounds. Lord Cobbold would merely state that the Queen wished it to be known that such suggestions were wildly exaggerated. This satisfied few of the members of the Select Committee. Roy Jenkins, a former Chancellor of the Exchequer, and a leader of the right-wing group inside the Labour Party argued:

> . . . what we are concerned about is not the information given to us but the case we are going to be able to present to the House as a whole and to the public . . . I wonder whether by going as far as that and by not being a little more precise there is not a possible danger of getting the worst of both worlds and approaching precision without really achieving it.[6]

The staid *Financial Times* examined the work of the Committee and then claimed, ". . . the central question is, *how much is the Queen's PRIVATE income?*"[7] On Sunday 5th December, the *Observer* took a similarly critical line while the *Guardian* argued that "to say that the Queen's private income is irrelevant is altogether too deferential. There is a need for more openness and clarity. A constitutional monarchy needs to be democratic in form as well as in good intent."[8]

But the furore died down and the Civil List was more than doubled to £980,000 a year. This took account of the need to set aside further provisions against inflation. There were also additional and separate increases in the allowances paid to the Queen Mother (£95,000 a year), Prince Philip (£65,000), Princess Margaret (£35,000), the Duke of Gloucester (£45,000) and Princess Anne (£15,000 to be increased to £35,000 after marriage).

But the runaway inflation which set in around 1973 made even these generous provisions meaningless. By 1975 the Civil List needed at least another half a million pounds if it was to stay out of the red. In February 1975 the House of Commons discussed yet again the question of royal finances, and once again it was obvious that the question was being discussed 'in the dark'. This time the unease was best expressed by Michael Stewart, a former Foreign Secretary and, like Roy Jenkins, a leading member of the right-wing section of the Labour Party. On the 26th February he said:

> The difficulty in discussing this question is that we do not know how much tax is being forgone [by] the nation.
>
> We are now living in a community where we are always exhorting each other to show respect for the law, to have some sense of national unity and to have a fair sharing of burdens . . . The example of a Head of State who is immune from that part of the law that requires us to pay taxes is unfortunate . . .

> I am not talking about the size of the bill. I am saying that immunity from tax exposes the Monarchy to unnecessary criticism. I am saying that this way of paying for the Monarchy by granting an inadequate Civil List, because the Queen does not have to pay income tax, is slovenly and an undignified way of going about the matter.[9]

Parliament voted the necessary increase, and there, at the time of writing, the matter rests. But this may be only a temporary respite. There seems little doubt that there will be a renewed attack on this tax-free aspect of the Monarch's wealth whenever the Civil List comes up for consideration in the future, and the complexity of the issue of royal finance will then be seen to be far removed from the simple "in the red" which Prince Philip described in 1969.

An Interim Summing Up

AT DIFFERENT TIMES THROUGHOUT HIS LIFE various people have made reports on Prince Philip. In writing this biography I have drawn on the reports made by his Parisian schoolteachers, Kurt Hahn, the Captain at the Royal Naval College at Dartmouth and his naval superiors. Other people have given less official estimates of the Prince and in this biography I have drawn on the judgement of members of his family such as ex-Queen Alexandra as well as of people who have worked with him in different capacities.

The picture which emerges from these many sources is a complex one. There is, for example, plenty of evidence that he has retained that energetic drive and will to succeed which was a feature of earlier reports and that, as he has grown older, he has channelled these into projects which will have a lasting effect on British life, such as the Medical Commission, the Award Scheme and the World Wildlife Fund.

There is also evidence that Hahn was right to make a caveat in his last report in which he pointed out that if the Prince were not given something worthwhile to do he might find life difficult. He has, indeed, found it hard to follow royal protocol and has often shown that he can be tetchy,[1] and too easily bored[2] with a good deal of the royal round. But on this royal round he has also shown himself to be "the devoted husband, doing his utmost to support his wife in the prodigious, complex and well-nigh impossible task for which she seemed so ill-prepared. Where the Queen went, he went too, discreet and attentive, always ready to fly to her rescue with work or gesture."[3]

It is generally agreed that as he has grown older he has mellowed. Maybe this is because the Queen herself has grown more confident with her years of experience so that he does not have to be so much on guard to protect and help her. This in turn has given him an opportunity to play the role of "the emancipated husband. He is still there to bear the brunt, but he is no longer the Sovereign's faithful shadow. He has on occasion taken the leading role, and does not hesitate, if the opportunity arises, to take a bold initiative, even if it runs contrary to royal protocol . . . This is no Prince Charming, but a mature man, thinking for himself and living his own life. Some people would go so far as to say that it is he who is King."[4]

Since he is not a fairy-tale "Prince Charming" it is hardly surprising that critics have been able to find flaws in the man—his occasional rudeness, his impatience with the less than efficient whom he sometimes has to meet, and his anger with, for example, the Press. But few people can have known him as well as did Uffa Fox with whom Prince Philip spent many hours sailing. Anyone who has read Fox's biography by June Dixon will know that he was no respecter of persons or rank. This gives all the greater force to Fox's summing up of Prince Philip: "You could put your heart in his hand and know it would be cared for."[5] That is an admirable summing up of the character of the man whom, perhaps, the British people may honour in a special way during his sixtieth year. In 1969 A. P. Herbert asked, "Why on earth is he not Prince Consort?"[6] It might be a fitting way to honour his sixtieth birthday by the award of this title.

THE GREEK AND DANISH ROYAL FAMILIES

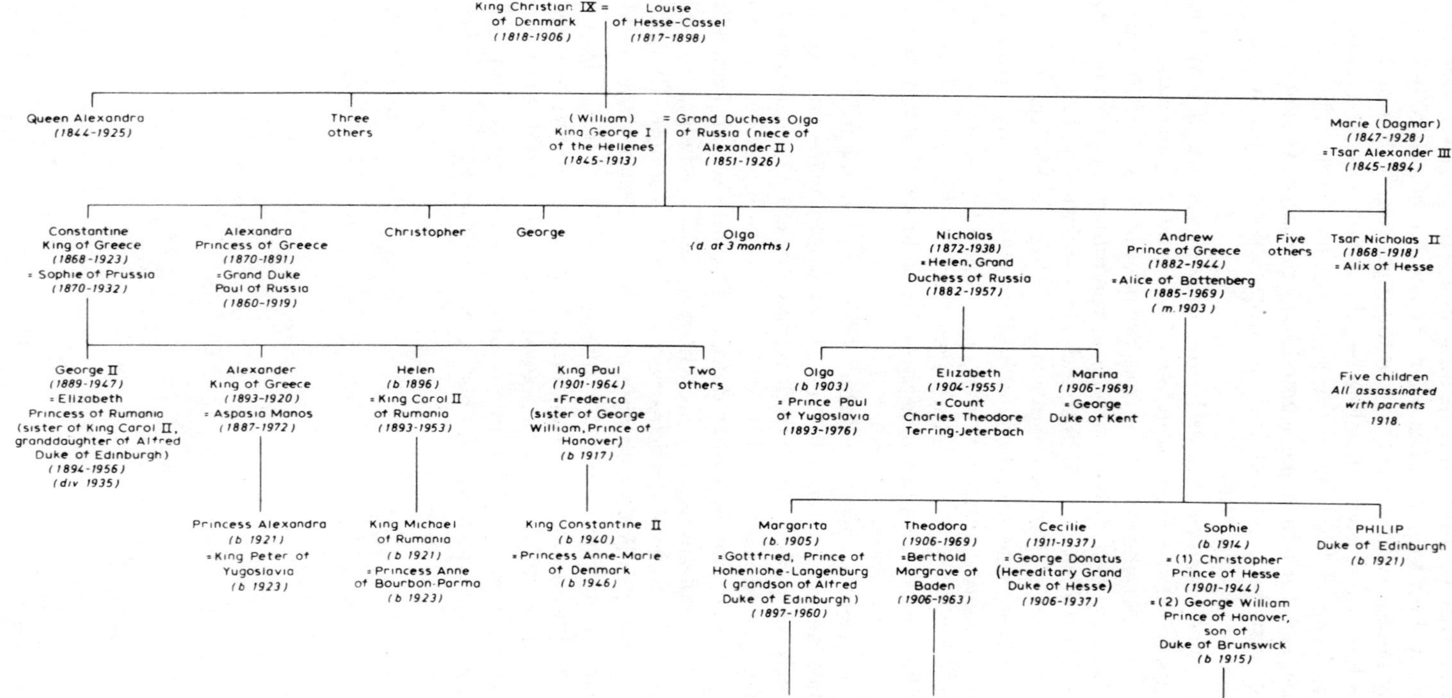

THE MOUNTBATTENS

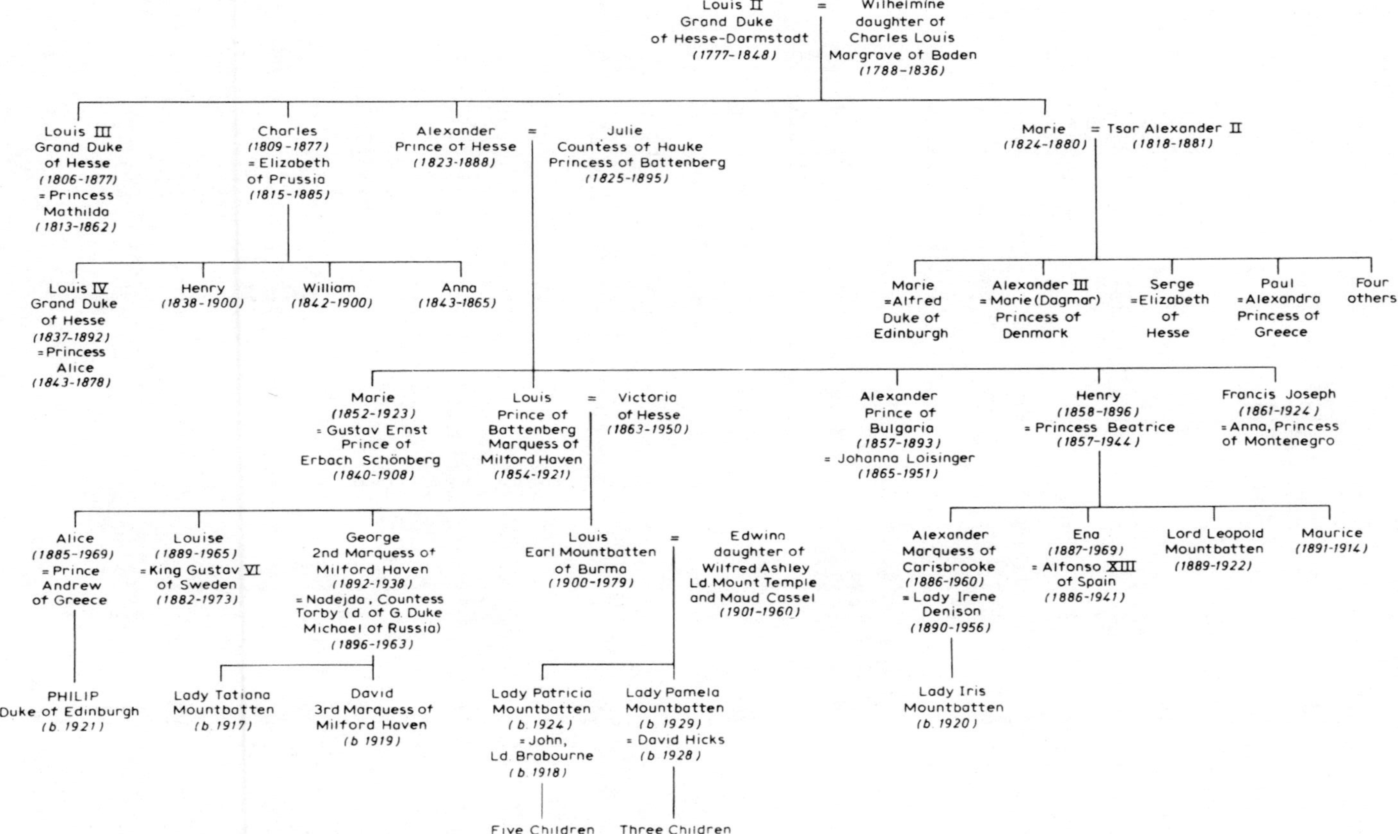

THE BRITISH ROYAL FAMILY

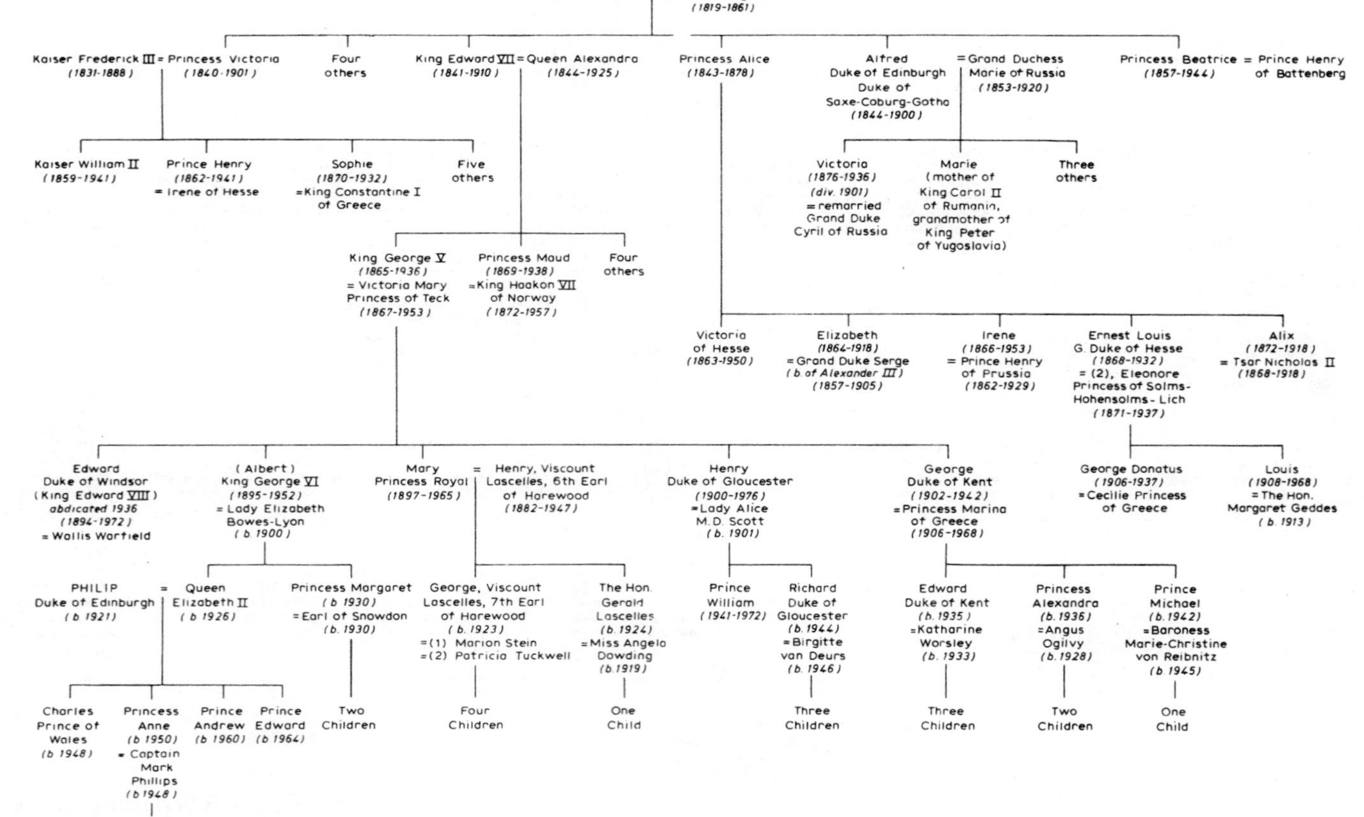

1. Prince George of Denmark
2. Princess George of Greece
3. King Peter of Yugoslavia
4. Queen Alexandra of Yugoslavia
5. Lord Mountbatten of Burma
6. Count of Barcelona
7. Prince Bernhard of the Netherlands
8. King of Norway
9. Prince Charles of Belgium
10. Prince George of Greece
11. Prince René of Bourbon-Parma
12. King of Denmark
13. King of Rumania
14. Prince Michael of Bourbon-Parma
15. Duchess of Aosta
16. Hereditary Prince of Luxemburg
17. Princess Eugénie of Greece
18. Lady Milford Haven
19. Princess Andrew of Greece
20. Lady Mountbatten of Burma
21. Duchess of Kent
22. Princess Juliana of the Netherlands
23. Queen of Greece
24. Queen Mary
25. Queen Victoria Eugénie
26. Queen of Denmark
27. Crown Princess of Sweden
28. Princess Margaret
29. Lord Milford Haven
30. Princess Elizabeth
31. Duke of Edinburgh
32. Princess Alexandra of Kent
33. The King

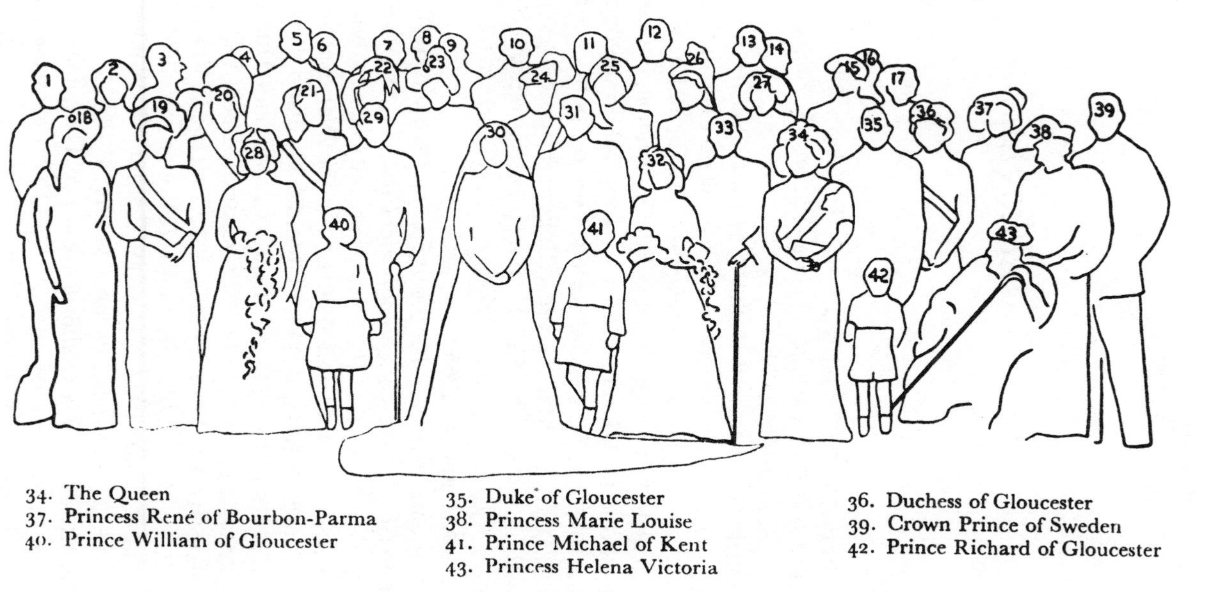

34. The Queen
35. Duke of Gloucester
36. Duchess of Gloucester
37. Princess René of Bourbon-Parma
38. Princess Marie Louise
39. Crown Prince of Sweden
40. Prince William of Gloucester
41. Prince Michael of Kent
42. Prince Richard of Gloucester
43. Princess Helena Victoria

Key to illustration No. 26

Bibliography

AIRLIE, MABELL, COUNTESS OF, *Thatched with Gold*, Hutchinson, 1962
ALEXANDRA, QUEEN, *Prince Philip: A Family Portrait*, Hodder & Stoughton, 1959
ANDREW, PRINCE OF GREECE, *Towards Disaster*, John Murray, 1930
ANSON, W. E., *The Law and Custom of the Constitution*, 1886
ATTLEE, CLEMENT, *As It Happened*, Heinemann, 1954
BAGEHOT, WALTER, *The English Constitution*, Fontana, 1963
BARKER, B., *When the Queen was Crowned*, Routledge & Kegan Paul, 1976
BARNETT, C., *The Sword Bearers*, Eyre & Spottiswoode, 1963
BOLITHO, H., *King Edward VIII*, Eyre & Spottiswoode, 1937
BOOTHROYD, J. B., *Philip: An Informal Biography*, Longman, 1971
BUTLER, D. E., and KING, A., *The British General Election of 1964*, Macmillan, 1965
CARSON, RACHEL, *The Silent Spring*, Penguin, 1970
CATHCART, H., *The Queen in Her Circle*, W. H. Allen, 1977
CHANDOS, LORD, *The Memoirs of Lord Chandos*, Bodley Head, 1962
CHANNON, SIR HENRY ('CHIPS'), *The Diaries of Sir Henry Channon, MP*, (ed. R. R. James) Weidenfeld & Nicolson, 1967
CHRISTOPHER, PRINCE OF GREECE, *Memoirs*, Hurst & Blackett, 1938
CRAWFORD, M., *The Little Princesses*, Cassell, 1950
DEAN, J., *HRH Prince Philip: A Portrait by His Valet*, Robert Hale
DIXON, JUNE, *Uffa Fox*, Angus & Robertson, 1978
DONALDSON, LADY FRANCES, *Edward VIII*, Weidenfeld & Nicolson, 1974
DUFF, D., *Albert and Victoria*, Muller, 1972
DUNCAN, A., *The Reality of Monarchy*, Heinemann, 1970
EDINBURGH, THE DUKE OF, *The Environmental Revolution*, André Deutsch, 1978
ERNST, J., *The Germans and Their Modern History*, Columbia, 1966
EVANS, JOAN, *The Victorians*, Cambridge University Press, 1966
EYCK, F., *The Prince Consort*, Chatto & Windus, 1959
FREDERICA, QUEEN, *A Measure of Understanding*, Macmillan, 1970

FRERE, J. A., *The British Monarchy at Home*, Gibbs & Phillips, 1963
FISHER, G. and H., *The Crown and The Ring*, Robert Hale, 1972
FRISCHAUER, WILLI, *Margaret, Princess Without a Cause*, Michael Joseph, 1977
GAVIN, C., *The House of War*, Hodder & Stoughton, 1970
GILBERT, M., *A Recent History Atlas, 1860–1960*, Weidenfeld & Nicolson, 1970
GILBERT, M., *Sir Horace Rumbold, Portrait of a Diplomat*, Heinemann, 1973
GORE, JOHN, *King George V, A Personal Memoir*, John Murray, 1941
GREY, SIR C., *The Early Years of the Prince Consort, annotated by Queen Victoria*, William Kimber, 1967
HAMILTON, W., *My Queen and I*, Quartet Books, 1975
HATCH, A., *The Mountbattens*, W. H. Allen, 1966
HOME, LORD, *The Way the Wind Blows*, Collins, 1976
HOUGH, R., *Louis and Victoria*, Hutchinson, 1974
IRVING, D., *Hitler's War*, Hodder & Stoughton, 1977
JAMES, R. R., *Ambitions and Realities: British Politics, 1964–1970*, Weidenfeld & Nicolson, 1972
JENKINS, R., *Asquith*, Collins, 1965 (3rd ed.)
JONES, T., *Whitehall Diary, Vol. I, 1918–1925*, Oxford University Press, 1969
JONES, T., *A Diary with Letters, 1931–1950*, Oxford University Press, 1969
JORDAN, R., *Princess Margaret and Her Family*, Robert Hale, 1974
KERR, M., *Prince Louis, Admiral of the Fleet*, Longman, 1934
KING, CECIL, *The Cecil King Diary, 1965–1970*, Jonathan Cape, 1972
LACEY, R., *Majesty*, Hutchinson, 1977
LAIRD, D., *Queen Elizabeth, The Queen Mother*, Hodder & Stoughton, 1966
LANE, P., *Europe*, Batsford, 1978
LANE, P., *Our Future King*, Andrew Barker, 1978
LANE, P., *The Queen Mother*, Robert Hale, 1979
LEE, SIR ARTHUR S. GOULD, *The Royal House of Greece*, Ward Lock, 1948
LEE, SIR SIDNEY, *Queen Victoria*, Smith & Elder, 1902
LEE OF FAREHAM, VISCOUNT, *A Good Innings*, John Murray, 1974
LEITCH, D., *God Stand Up for Bastards*, André Deutsch, 1973
LIVERSIDGE, D., *Prince Philip*, Andrew Barker, 1976
LONGFORD, LADY ELIZABETH, *Victoria, R.I.*, Weidenfeld & Nicolson, 1964
MACMILLAN, H., *The Blast of War*, Macmillan, 1967
MACMILLAN, H., *The Tides of Fortune 1945–1955*, Macmillan, 1969
MACMILLAN, H., *Pointing the Way*, Macmillan, 1972
MAGNUS, SIR PHILIP, *King Edward the Seventh*, John Murray, 1964
MANSON, M., *Edwina, The Biography of the Countess of Burma*, Robert Hale, 1958
MARDER, ARTHUR J., *From the Dreadnought to Scapa Flow*, Oxford University Press, 1961
MARQUAND, D., *Ramsay MacDonald*, Jonathan Cape, 1977

MARTIN, K., *The Crown and the Establishment*, Hutchinson, 1962

MOOREHEAD, A., *Gallipoli*, Hamish Hamilton, 1956

MOORHOUSE, G., *The Other England*, Penguin, 1964

MORGAN, K., *The Age of Lloyd George*, Allen & Unwin, 1971

MORGAN, K. O., (ed.), *Lloyd George: Family Letters, 1885–1936*, Oxford University Press, 1973

MORRAH, D., *The Royal Family in Africa*, Hutchinson, 1947

MORRAH, D., *Princess Elizabeth, Duchess of Edinburgh*, Odhams, 1950

MORRAH, D., *The Work of the Queen*, William Kimber, 1958

MURRAY-BROWN, J., (ed.), *The Monarchy and its Future*, Allen & Unwin, 1969

NABARRO, SIR G., *NAB 1*, Pergammon, 1969

NICOLSON, H., *King George V*, Constable, 1953

NICOLSON, H., *Diaries and Letters, 1930–1939*, Collins, 1966

NICOLSON, H., *Diaries and Letters, 1945–1962*, Collins, 1968

PEACOCK, H. L., *Europe and Beyond*, Heinemann, 1974

PETRIE, SIR C., *Monarchy in the Twentieth Century*, Eyre & Spottiswoode, 1952

POPE-HENNESSY, SIR JAMES, *Queen Mary*, Allen & Unwin, 1959

POUND, ADMIRAL REGINALD, *Biography of Prince Albert*, Michael Joseph, 1973

PURCELL, W., *Fisher of Lambeth*, Hodder & Stoughton, 1969

REES, G., *A Chapter of Accidents*, Chatto & Windus, 1971

RIDLEY, J., *Lord Palmerston*, Constable, 1970

RUMBOLD, SIR H., *Recollections of a Diplomatist, Vol. 2*, Arnold, 1902

SAMPSON, A., *The Arms Bazaar*, Hodder & Stoughton, 1977

SELDON, A. and HARRIS, R., *The Coming Confrontation*, Institute of Economic Affairs, 1978

TAYLOR, A. J. P., (ed.), *Churchill: Four Faces and the Man*, Dial Press, 1969

TAYLOR, A. J. P., *English History 1914–1945*, Oxford University Press, 1965

TAYLOR, A. J. P., *Beaverbrook*, Hamish Hamilton, 1972

TERRAINE, J., (ed.), *The Life and Times of Lord Mountbatten*, Hutchinson, 1969

TERRAINE, J., *Haig: The Educated Soldier*, Hutchinson, 1963

THOMAS, SIR MILES, *Out on a Wing*, Michael Joseph, 1964

THOMPSON, A., *The Day Before Yesterday*, Panther, 1971

TOWNSEND, P., *The Last Emperor: The Decline & Fall of the British Empire*, Weidenfeld & Nicolson, 1976

TOWNSEND, P., *Time and Chance*, Collins, 1978

WAKEFORD, G., *The Heir Apparent*, Robert Hale, 1967

WHEELER-BENNETT, SIR JOHN, *King George VI*, Macmillan, 1958

WILSHER, P., *The Pound in Your Pocket, 1870–1970*, Cassell, 1970

WINDSOR, THE DUCHESS OF, *The Heart has its Reasons*, Michael Joseph, 1956

WINDSOR, THE DUKE OF, *A King's Story*, Cassell, 1951

WOOLTON, LORD, *Memoirs*, Cassell, 1954

Notes on Sources

INTRODUCTION
1 Crawford, p. 59.

PART I
CHAPTER 1
1 Quoted in Boothroyd, p. 82.
2 *Christian Science Monitor*, 27th November 1947.
3 Quoted in Boothroyd, p. 38.
4 Ibid., p. 17.
5 *See* pp. 330–2.
6 Quoted in Boothroyd, p. 19.
7 Rumbold, Vol. 2, p. 25.
8 Christopher, p. 46.
9 Ibid.
10 Alexandra, p. 26.
11 Ibid.
12 Ibid.
13 Royal Marriages Act, 1772.
14 Alexandra, p. 27.
15 Alexandra, p. 27.
16 Kerr, 1934, p. 170.
17 Kerr, pp. 171–172.
18 Hatch, p. 75.
19 Alexandra, p. 28.

CHAPTER 2
1 Alexandra, p. 25.
2 Alexandra, p. 24.
3 Alexandra, p. 25.
4 Quoted Boothroyd, p. 116.
5 Alexandra, p. 28, *see also* p. 20. (Chapter 1).
6 Christopher, p. 46, and *passim*.
7 Nicolson, 1953, p. 29.
8 Nicolson, pp. 29–30.
9 Nicolson, pp. 39–40.
10 Christopher, p. 33.

CHAPTER 3
1 Moorehead, p. 338.
2 Nicolson, 1953, p. 286.
3 Nicolson, p. 282.
4 Nicolson, p. 283–284.
5 Alexandra, pp. 28–29.
6 Alexandra, p. 29.
7 Christopher, p. 147.
8 Quoted in Liversidge, pp. 13–14.
9 Andrew, p. 11.
10 Jones, 1969, p. 248.
11 Andrew, p. 78.
12 Andrew, pp. 297–298.
13 Morgan, p. 197.

CHAPTER 4
1 Boothroyd, p. 77.
2 Quoted in Duncan, p. 113.
3 Hatch, p. 209.
4 Chapter 1, p. 21.
5 *Home Notes*, September 1908, quoted in Boothroyd, p. 77.
6 Alexandra, pp. 21–23.
7 Wakeford, pp. 121–122.
8 Alexandra, p. 22.
9 Liversidge, p. 1.
10 Alexandra, p. 32.

11 Mrs Blower, quoted in Liversidge, p. 2.

CHAPTER 5

1 Alexandra, p. 34.
2 Christopher, pp. 174–175.
3 Christopher, p. 175.
4 Quoted in Boothroyd, p. 74.
5 Quoted in Boothroyd, p. 63.
6 *See* Lacey, pp. 170–171 for a fuller account.
7 Quoted in Boothroyd, p. 63.
8 Nicolson, 1953, p. 372.
9 Quoted in Ridley, p. 524.
10 Boothroyd, pp. 74–75.
11 Quoted in Liversidge, p. 16.
12 Quoted in Liversidge, p. 17 and Boothroyd, p. 76.
13 Hatch, p. 392.
14 Quoted in Boothroyd, pp. 80–81.

CHAPTER 6

1 Quoted in Boothroyd, p. 54.
2 Alexandra, p. 37.
3 *See* p. 21.
4 Alexandra, p. 38.
5 *See* p. 237.
6 Alexandra, p. 40.
7 Quoted in Boothroyd, p. 109.
8 Boothroyd, p. 109.
9 Quoted in Boothroyd, p. 108.
10 Quoted in Liversidge, p. 18.
11 Quoted in Liversidge, p. 19.
12 Hatch, p. 393.
13 *Christian Science Monitor*, 27th November 1947
14 Ibid.
15 Miss C. M. Pegg, cousin to Mrs Levitsky in a letter to the author.
Subsequent history of Catherine Pegg Levitsky: at the outbreak of war (1939) the school was moved to Hossepor in S. W. France but the pupils were soon dispersed. When France fell she was put into a concentration camp as she was a British subject—Nika, her husband, being a stateless person. She suffered great privation. She came to England after the end of the war to see her friends, but on returning to France became seriously ill. Her late employer, Mr MacJannet, arranged for her to convalesce in the USA. She never came back to Europe. She could not get Nika into the USA but later she was able to join him in Ottawa where she died in 1949.
16 *Christian Science Monitor*, 27th November 1947.
17 *Christian Science Monitor*, 27th November 1947.
18 Alexandra, p. 43.
19 Boothroyd, p. 113.
20 Quoted in Liversidge, p. 22.
21 *See* p. 37.
22 Gould Lee, p. 273.
23 Alexandra, p. 24.
24 Alexandra, p. 25.
25 Alexandra, p. 25.
26 *See* p. 98.
27 Frederica, p. 22.
28 Alexandra, p. 22.
29 Macmillan, 1967, pp. 589–590.
30 *See* p. 43.
31 Boothroyd, p. 83.

PART II

CHAPTER 7

1 Masson, p. 62, quoted in Wakeford, p. 187.
2 Quoted in Liversidge, p. 96.
3 Quoted in Hatch, p. 3.
4 Hatch, p. 14.
5 Hatch, pp. 1–102, and Hough.
6 Hatch, p. 72.
7 Hatch, p. 21.
8 Hatch, p. 63.
9 Fisher quoted in Hatch, p. 63.
10 Quoted in Hatch, p. 93.
11 Quoted in Hatch, p. 101.
12 Quoted in Hatch, p. 119.
13 Quoted in Hatch, p. 119.
14 Hatch, p. 120.
15 Quoted in Hatch, p. 121.
16 Quoted in Hatch, p. 123.
17 Quoted in Hatch, p. 129.
18 Nicolson, 1953, p. 247.
19 Rupert Brooke: *The Treasure*, I. 'Peace'.
20 Hatch, p. 142.
21 Lee of Fareham, pp. 135–136.
22 Ed. Taylor, p. 72.
23 Quoted in Hatch, p. 143.
24 Quoted in Hatch, pp. 143–144.
25 Jenkins, p. 333.
26 Jenkins, p. 372 f.n.
27 Jenkins, p. 339; *see also* Hatch, p. 144.
28 Quoted in Hatch, p. 145.

29 Quoted in Hatch, p. 145.
30 Quoted in Thompson, p. 189.
31 Quoted in Hatch, p. 146.
32 Quoted in Hatch, pp. 146–147.
33 Nicolson, 1953, p. 231.
34 Lee of Fareham, p. 136.
35 Quoted in Hatch, p. 148.
36 *See* Hatch, p. 148.
37 Lee of Fareham quoted in Hatch, p. 161.
38 Lee of Fareham quoted in Hatch, p. 161.
39 Boothroyd, p. 40.

CHAPTER 8

1 Quoted in Nicolson, 1953, p. 250.
2 Quoted in Nicolson, 1953, p. 250.
3 *See* H. Hamilton Fyfe, *Northcliffe: An Intimate Biography*, Chapter 4.
4 Quoted in Nicolson, 1953, p. 250.
5 Quoted in Masson, p. 54.
6 *See* Masson, pp. 242–243.
7 Quoted in Nicolson, 1953, pp. 307–308.
8 Quoted in Hatch, p. 157.
9 Edward Iwi writing in *The Law Journal*, 18th March 1960.
10 Quoted in Nicolson, 1953, p. 310.
11 Quoted in Hatch, p. 157.
12 Quoted in Hatch, p. 158.
13 Quoted in Nicolson, 1953, p. 310.

CHAPTER 9

1 Attlee on p. 58.
2 Hatch, p. 168.
3 Liversidge, p. 29.
4 Ibid., p. 29.
5 Masson, p. 65.
6 Hatch, p. 171.
7 Quoted in Hatch, p. 102.
8 Hatch, p. 168.
9 Quoted in Hatch, p. 155.
10 Quoted in Hatch, p. 395 f.n., and Liversidge, p. 30.
11 Alexandra, p. 37.
12 Quoted in Boothroyd, p. 116, and Liversidge, pp. 29–30.
13 Alexandra, p. 64.
14 Quoted in Terraine, 1969, pp. 66–67.

CHAPTER 10

1 *See* p. 74.
2 Hatch, p. 167.
3 Terraine, p. 15.
4 Gould Lee, p. 273.
5 Terraine, p. 23.
6 *See* p. 68.
7 Masson, *passim*.
8 Ibid., *passim*.
(*9 to 40 are taken from Terraine as follows:*)
9 p. 39.
10 p. 42.
11 p. 43.
12 p. 49.
13 p. 53.
14 p. 55.
15 p. 79.
16 p. 82.
17 p. 83.
18 p. 85.
19 p. 87.
20 p. 87.
21 p. 84.
22 p. 84.
23 pp. 88–89.
24 p. 90.
25 p. 96.
26 p. 96.
27 p. 98.
28 p. 98.
29 p. 99.
30 Conversations with former soldiers.
31 p. 107.
32 p. 109.
33 p. 120.
34 p. 121.
35 p. 126.
36 p. 142.
37 p. 146.
38 p. 172.
39 p. 173.
40 p. 180
41 Lord Zuckerman writing in the *Observer*, 2nd September 1979.
42 John Grigg, writing in the *Observer*, 2nd September 1979.

PART III

CHAPTER 11

1 p. 47.
2 Chapter 16.
3 Wakeford, p. 68 and Liversidge, p. 28.
4 Wakeford, p. 79 and Liversidge pp. 28–29.
5 Wakeford, p. 81.
6 Wakeford, p. 80.
7 Alexandra, p. 47.
8 Alexandra, p. 49.

9 Alexandra, p. 49.
10 Alexandra, p. 49.

CHAPTER 12

1 Quoted in Terraine, 1963, p. 433.
2 *See* Barnett, pp. 274–354.
3 Ernst, quoted in Lane, 1978, p. 30.
4 Boothroyd, p. 118.
5 The Margrave of Baden quoted in Boothroyd, p. 118.
6 Quoted in Wakeford, p. 136.
7 Quoted in Boothroyd, p. 119.
8 Quoted in Boothroyd, p. 119.
9 Quoted in Boothroyd, p. 119.
10 Liversidge, p. 32.
11 Quoted in Alexandra, p. 49.
12 Gilbert, 1973, p. 374.
13 Quoted in Liversidge, p. 33, and Boothroyd, p. 128.
14 Alexandra, p. 50.

CHAPTER 13

1 Magnus, pp. 222–228.
2 Marquand, p. 188 and *passim*.
3 Alexandra, p. 51.
4 Alexandra, p. 52.
5 Letters to the author from Robert L. Mackie.
6 Quoted in Liversidge, p. 36.
7 Quoted in Liversidge, p. 36.
8 p. 49.
9 Letters to the author from Robert L. Mackie.
10 Liversidge, p. 37.
11 Quoted in Boothroyd, p. 119.
12 Wakeford, pp. 155–157.
13 Quoted in Alexandra, p. 52, and Liversidge, p. 35.
14 Letter from Robert L. Mackie.
15 Quoted in Alexandra, p. 53.
16 Letter from a former nurse.
17 Alexandra, pp. 52–53.
18 Alexandra, p. 52.
19 Alexandra, p. 54.
20 Alexandra, p. 55.
21 Quoted in Hatch, p. 399, and Liversidge, p. 44.

CHAPTER 14

1 Wheeler-Bennett, p. 354.
2 Churchill in House of Commons, (339 House of Commons Debates, 5a. 359–373).
3 Wheeler-Bennett, p. 357.
4 Wheeler-Bennett, p. 364.
5 Wheeler-Bennett, p. 364.
6 Speech in House of Commons, 31st March 1939.
7 Wheeler-Bennett, pp. 395–396.
8 Alexandra, p. 64.
9 Liversidge, p. 45.
10 Quoted in Alexandra, p. 64.
11 Hatch, p. 402.
12 Wheeler-Bennett, pp. 396–397.
13 Alexandra, p. 65.
14 Airlie, p. 227.
15 Alexandra, p. 65.
16 Alexandra, p. 65.
17 Crawford, p. 59.
18 Crawford, p. 59.
19 Alexandra, p. 65.
20 Crawford, p. 59.
21 Crawford, p. 60.
22 Hatch, p. 401.
23 Hatch, p. 401.
24 Alexandra, p. 66.
25 Crawford, p. 60.
26 Alexandra, p. 66.
27 Hatch, p. 401.
28 Liversidge, p. 46.
29 Boothroyd, p. 24.
30 Wheeler-Bennett, p. *v*.
31 Wheeler-Bennett, p. 749.
32 Alexandra, p. 67.

PART IV

CHAPTER 15

1 Irene Huggett in a letter to the author.
2 Quoted in Boothroyd, p. 86.
3 Quoted in Boothroyd, p. 87.
4 Alexandra, p. 68.
5 Boothroyd, p. 92.
6 Boothroyd, p. 92.
7 Ex-Leading Signalman Wm. Beattie in a letter to the author.
8 Alexandra, p. 68.
9 George Lovell, ex-MAA in a letter to the author.
10 Quoted in Boothroyd, pp. 76–77 and Liversidge, pp. 50–51.
11 Channon, pp. 283 and 286–287.
12 Quoted in Boothroyd, p. 90.
13 Fisher, p. 112.
14 G. A. Hancock in a letter to the author.
15 Thomas H. Spence in a letter.
16 Quoted in Liversidge, p. 56.
17 Quoted in Liversidge, pp. 57–58.
18 Frederica, pp. 43–45.

19 Alexandra, pp. 70–71.
20 Hatch, p. 405.
21 Alexandra, pp. 71–72.
22 Alexandra, p. 72.
23 John Elliott in a letter to the author.
24 Michael Joyce in a letter to the author.
25 Eric Oates, ex-AB in a letter to the author.
26 Eric Oates, ex-AB in a letter to the author.
27 Eric Oates, ex-AB in a letter to the author.
28 Michael Joyce in a letter to the author.
29 Eric Oates, ex-AB in a letter to the author.
30 Michael Joyce in a letter to the author.
31 Eric Oates, ex-AB in a letter to the author.
32 Eric Oates, ex-AB in a letter to the author.
33 Michael Joyce in a letter to the author.
34 Eric Oates, ex-AB in a letter to the author.
35 Eric Bailey, ex-CWS.
36 Princess Alice quoted in Liversidge, p. 53.
37 Alexandra, p. 71.
38 Alexandra, p. 81.
39 W. A. Magill in a letter to the author.
40 Eric Bailey in a letter to the author.
41 L. G. Coombe, ex-POW, in a letter to the author.
42 Alexandra, p. 80.
43 Hatch, p. 409.

CHAPTER 16

1 Hatch, p. 409.
2 Wheeler-Bennett, p. 749.
3 Macmillan, 1967, p. 570.
4 Macmillan, 1967, p. 563.
5 Macmillan, 1967, p. 570.
6 Macmillan, 1967, p. 572.
7 Macmillan, 1967, p. 602.
8 Wheeler-Bennett, p. 750.
9 Alexandra, pp. 80–81.
10 Hatch, p. 414.
11 Terraine, pp. 141–142.
12 Quoted in Liversidge, p. 67.
13 Quoted in Liversidge, p. 31; *see also* Lacey, pp. 160–161 f.n.
14 Nabarro, p. 249.

CHAPTER 17

1 *The Law Journal*, 18th March 1960.
2 p. 114.
3 Hatch, p. 402.
4 p. 17.
5 Alexandra, p. 87; Fisher, p. 127, and Boothroyd, p. 39.
6 Lacey, p. 160.
7 Liversidge, p. 68.
8 Liversidge, p. 68.
9 *The Law Journal*, 18th March 1960.
10 Hatch, p. 417.
11 Quoted in Liversidge, p. 73.
12 Boothroyd, p. 54.
13 Quoted in Liversidge, p. 74, and Boothroyd, p. 39.
14 Wheeler-Bennett, p. 751, and Alexandra, p. 87.
15 Dean, pp. 32–34.
16 *The Law Journal*, 18th March 1960.

CHAPTER 18

1 p. 58.
2 Alexandra, p. 62.
3 Alexandra, pp. 77–78.
4 p. 109.
5 Quoted in Lacey, p. 144.
6 p. 118.
7 Alexandra, p. 72.
8 p. 116.
9 Channon, pp. 286–287.
10 Boothroyd, p. 12.
11 Hatch, p. 407.
12 Quoted in Lacey, p. 147; Liversidge, p. 61, and Hatch, p. 408.
13 Alexandra, p. 75.
14 Liversidge, p. 61.
15 Alexandra, p. 76.
16 Channon, p. 386.
17 Liversidge, p. 64.
18 Wheeler-Bennett, p. 749.
19 Airlie, p. 225.
20 Airlie, p. 224.
21 Quoted in Lacey, p. 153.
22 Fisher, p. 119.
23 Wheeler-Bennett, p. 626.
24 Alexandra, p. 80.
25 Airlie, pp. 227–228.
26 Quoted in Boothby, p. 22.
27 Alexandra, p. 83.
28 Alexandra, p. 84.
29 Quoted in Hatch, p. 414.
30 Alexandra, p. 85.

CHAPTER 19

1 Quoted in Fisher, p. 127.
2 Dean, p. 38, and Masson, p. 165.
3 Dean, p. 38.
4 Airlie, pp. 225–226.
5 Alexandra, p. 88.
6 Quoted in Wheeler-Bennett, p. 691.
7 Alexandra, p. 89.
8 Wheeler-Bennett, p. 751.
9 Alexandra, p. 89.
10 Fisher, p. 129.
11 Alexandra, p. 90.
12 Ibid.
13 Alexandra, pp. 90–91, and Liversidge, p. 71.
14 Alexandra, p. 91.
15 Wheeler-Bennett, p. 751.
16 Pope-Hennessy, p. 615.
17 Wheeler-Bennett, p. 752.
18 Alexandra, p. 92.
19 Nicolson, 1968, p. 102.
20 Alexandra, p. 92.

CHAPTER 20

1 Liversidge, p. 77.
2 Alexandra, p. 95.
3 Alexandra, pp. 107–108.
4 Quoted in Boothroyd, p. 34.
5 Purcell, p. 170.
6 Alexandra, p. 97.
7 Alexandra, pp. 97–98.
8 Alexandra, pp. 95–96.
9 Hatch, p. 419, and Liversidge, p. 73.
10 Wheeler-Bennett, p. 753.
11 Channon, p. 418.
12 Channon, pp. 418–419.
13 Wheeler-Bennett, p. 753.
14 Hatch, p. 421.
15 Dean, p. 56.
16 Airlie, pp. 229–230.
17 Alexandra, p. 96.
18 Channon, p. 418.
19 Airlie, p. 230.
20 Purcell, p. 128.
21 Channon, p. 418.
22 Quoted in Purcell, p. 172.
23 Quoted in Wheeler-Bennett, p. 754.
24 Hatch, p. 424.
25 Terraine, p. 163.
26 Hatch, p. 426 and Alexandra, p. 101.
27 Wheeler-Bennett, pp. 754–755.
28 Channon, p. 420.

PART V

CHAPTER 21

1 A letter from B. Smith to the author.
2 Quoted in Alexandra, p. 88.
3 A letter from R. H. Lilley to the author.
4 Quoted in Alexandra, p. 89.
5 Dean, p. 45.
6 Quoted in Dean, pp. 43–44.
7 Dean, pp. 36 and 47.
8 Alexandra, p. 140.
9 Alexandra, p. 105.
10 Ibid.
11 Boothroyd, p. 142.
12 Wheeler-Bennett, p. 736.
13 Liversidge, p. 77.
14 Private information.
15 Dean, p. 63.
16 Dean, p. 119.
17 Hatch, p. 429.
18 Terraine, p. 168.
19 Boothroyd, p. 105.
20 Alexandra, p. 120.
21 Alexandra, p. 123.
22 Boothroyd, p. 144.
23 Boothroyd, p. 146.

CHAPTER 22

1 Quoted in Alexandra, p. 107.
2 Terraine, p. 163.
3 Dean, p. 104.
4 Quoted in Liversidge, p. 77.
5 Quoted in Liversidge, p. 77.
6 Airlie, pp. 219–220.
7 Airlie, p. 225.
8 Fisher, pp. 139–140.
9 Fisher, p. 140.
10 Alexandra, p. 114.
11 Dixon, p. 136.
12 Ibid., p. 137.
13 Ibid., p. 175.
14 Channon, p. 425.
15 Alexandra, p. 111.
16 Dean, p. 83.
17 Alexandra, p. 111.
18 Dean, pp. 77–78.
19 Quoted in Alexandra, p. 112.
20 Alexandra, p. 116.
21 Dean, p. 81.
22 Alexandra, pp. 112–113.
23 Alexandra, p. 113.
24 Pope-Hennessy, p. 616.
25 Lane, 1978, p. 12.
26 Dean, pp. 113–115.

CHAPTER 23
1 Lane, 1979, Chapter 23.
2 Quoted in Wheeler-Bennett, p. 762.
3 Lane, 1979, Chapter 8.
4 Wheeler-Bennett, pp. 764–765.
5 Wheeler-Bennett, pp. 786–787.
6 Wheeler-Bennett, p. 787.
7 Alexandra, pp. 128–129.
8 Dean, p. 138.
9 Alexandra, p. 129.
10 Ibid.
11 Dean, pp. 132–133.
12 Alexandra, p. 130.
13 Ibid.
14 Alexandra, p. 130.
15 Lane, 1979, Chapter 19.
16 Quoted in Dean, p. 139.
17 Quoted in Alexandra, p. 131.
18 Quoted in Wheeler-Bennett, p. 799.
19 Wheeler-Bennett, p. 799.
20 Quoted in Wheeler-Bennett, p. 799.
21 Lane, 1979, Chapter 19.
22 Wheeler-Bennett, p. 800.
23 Wheeler-Bennett, p. 801.
24 Dean, p. 140.

CHAPTER 24
1 Fisher, p. 151.
2 Alexandra, p. 134.
3 Alexandra, p. 135.
4 Channon, p. 463.
5 Dean, p. 144.
6 Thomas, pp. 306–307.
7 Chandos, p. 425.
8 Channon, p. 462.
9 Dean, p. 147.
10 Ibid.
11 Ibid.
12 Dean, pp. 147–148.
13 Quoted in Boothroyd, p. 104.
14 Dean, p. 148.
15 Quoted in Hatch, p. 437.
16 Dean, pp. 148–149.
17 Dean, p. 150.
18 Ibid.
19 Hatch, p. 438.
20 Dean, p. 150.
21 Channon, pp. 464–465.
22 Hatch, p. 439.
For accounts of King George VI's funeral *see* Channon, p. 465 and Airlie, p. 235.

PART VI
CHAPTER 25
1 *The Times*, 22nd October 1955.
2 Woolton, pp. 381–382.
3 Macmillan, 1969, p. 372.
4 Greville Memoirs.
5 Quoted in Lacey, p. 194.
6 Lane, 1979, pp. 81–82.
7 Private information.
8 Macmillan, 1969, p. 373.
9 Woolton, p. 382.
10 Quoted in Cathcart, 1977, p. 130.
11 Woolton, p. 382.
12 Quoted in Woolton, p. 382.
13 Chandos, p. 425.
14 Ibid.
15 *London Gazette*, 30th September 1952.
16 and 17 Private information.

CHAPTER 26
1 Quoted in Lacey, p. 195.
2 Channon, pp. 466–467.
3 Lacey, p. 196.
4 Ibid.
5 Boothroyd, pp. 47–48.
6 *The Times* quoted in Wakeford, p. 187.
7 Lacey, p. 188.
8 Chandos, p. 425.
9 Boothroyd, pp. 49–50.
10 Lacey, p. 196.
11 Lacey, p. 288.
12 Liversidge, p. 84.
13 Hatch, p. 441.
14 Quoted in Fisher, p. 37.
15 *Debrett*, 1961.
16 p. 69.
17 Quoted in Fisher, p. 37.
18 *London Gazette*, 9th April 1962.
19 Quoted in Hatch, p. 440.
20 *The Law Journal*, March 1960.
21 Quoted in Hatch, p. 440.
22 Lane, 1971, p. 71.
23 Quoted in Liversidge, p. 99.
24 Quoted in Liversidge, p. 99.
25 Quoted in Liversidge, pp. 99–100.
26 Quoted in Liversidge, p. 100.
27 Ibid.

CHAPTER 27
1 Edward Walpole, cited by R. Nevill in *Life and Letters of Lady Dorothy Nevill* (1919) and quoted in Evans, p. 7.
2 Quoted in Boothroyd, p. 40.
3 Duff, p. 23.
4 Lee, p. 119.

5 Dean, p. 133.
6 Lane, 1978, p. 11.
7 Ivor Spencer, President of the Guild of Toastmasters, in a letter to the author.
8 Duff, p. 238.
9 Longford, p. 190.
10 Bolitho, *Prince Consort*, p. 53 quoted in Duff, p. 179.
11 Longford, p. 190, and Duff, p. 179.
12 Longford, p. 190.
13 Liversidge, p. 96.
14 Dean, pp. 157 and 159.
15 Channon, pp. 470–471.

CHAPTER 28

1 Quoted in Alexandra, p. 140.
2 Dean, p. 182.
3 Clement Attlee, quoted in Hatch, p. 3.
4 Airlie, p. 235.
5 Airlie, p. 236.
6 Channon, p. 473.
7 Alexandra, p. 147.
8 Channon, p. 474.
9 Alexandra, p. 144.
10 Alexandra, p. 142.
11 Alexandra, p. 143.
12 Barker, p. 116.
13 Barker, p. 116.
14 Hatch, p. 444.
15 Quoted in Barker, p. 131.
16 Wheeler-Bennett, p. 691.
17 Quoted in Barker, p. 25.
18 Quoted in Lacey, p. 190.
19 Quoted in Lacey, p. 190.

PART VII

CHAPTER 29

1 Barker, p. 191.
2 Frischauer, p. 88.
3 *The People*, 11th June 1953.
4 Frischauer, p. 34.
5 Quoted in Frischauer, p. 37.
6 Quoted in Duff, p. 319.
7 A personal interview.
8 Airlie, p. 225.
9 Channon, p. 439.
10 Dean, p. 105.
11 Royal Marriages Act, 1772.
12 Alexandra, p. 149.
13 Frischauer, p. 99.
14 Lane, 1979, Chapter 27.

CHAPTER 30

1 Purcell, p. 242.
2 Purcell, pp. 242–245.
3 Purcell, pp. 247–248.
4 Frischauer, p. 114.
5 Hatch, p. 449.
6 Frischauer, p. 177.
7 Frischauer, p. 177.
8 Frischauer, p. 175.
9 Quoted in Frischauer, p. 179.
10 *Daily Express*, quoted in Frischauer, p. 125.
11 Frischauer, p. 133.
12 Frere, p. 154.
13 Quoted in Frischauer, p. 170.

CHAPTER 31

1 Quoted in Churchill, *Lord Derby*.
2 *See also* Wheeler-Bennett, p. 16.
3 Lane, 1979, Chapters 1 and 2.
4 Lane, 1979, Chapters 6 and 8.
5 Lacey, p. 282.
6 Fisher, p. 84.
7 Alexandra, p. 173.
8 Alexandra, p. 175.
9 Wakeford, pp. 229–231.
10 Quoted in Fisher, p. 75.

PART VIII

CHAPTER 32

1 Lacey, p. 170.
2 Dean, p. 99.
3 Fisher, p. 184.
4 Alexandra, p. 110.
5 Alexandra, p. 140.
6 Longford, p. 170.
7 Eyck, p. 41; *London Gazette*, 20th September 1952, and C 27.1.
8 Quoted in Hatch, p. 441.
9 Pound, pp. 88–89, 116, 262.
10 Quoted in Alexandra, p. 140.
11 Quoted in Alexandra, pp. 140–141.
12 Quoted in Boothroyd, p. 51.
13 Boothroyd, pp. 51–52.
14 Quoted in Hatch, pp. 441–442.
15 Hatch, p. 442.
16 Sampson, pp. 122–123.
17 Alexandra, p. 131.
18 Longford, p. 229.
19 Duncan, pp. 106, 111.
20 Lane, 1978, pp. 130–131.
21 Lacey, p. 279.

CHAPTER 33

1 Ed. Murray-Brown, p. 189.

2 Alexandra, p. 171.
3 Ivor Spencer, President of the Guild of Toastmasters, in a letter to the author.
4 From a correspondent who wishes to remain anonymous.
5 From a correspondent who wishes to remain anonymous.
6 Ed. Murray-Brown, p. 190.
7 Information provided by the Incorporated Liverpool School of Tropical Medicine.
8 Information provided by the Institution of Public Health Engineers.
9 Alexandra, p. 112.
10 Information provided by the Council for National Academic Awards.
11 Information provided by the Council for National Academic Awards.
12 Thomas, pp. 355–356.
13 Ed. Murray-Brown, p. 82.

CHAPTER 34

1 *The People*, 19th July 1959.
2 Duncan, p. 14.
3 Duncan, p. 14.
4 Alexandra, p. 181.
5 Alexandra, pp. 150–151.
6 Alexandra, p. 151.
7 Alexandra, p. 152.
8 Alexandra, p. 153.
9 Alexandra, p. 153.
10 Alexandra, p. 153.
11 Alexandra, p. 153.
12 Alexandra, p. 155.
13 Alexandra, p. 157.
14 Duncan, p. 23.
15 Alexandra, p. 154.
16 Lacey, p. 330.
17 Duncan, p. 39.
18 Alexandra, p. 182.
19 Duncan, p. 72.
20 King, p. 20.
21 In Alexandra, pp. 196–197.
22 In Alexandra, p. 206.
23 In Lacey, p. 214.
24 Macmillan, 1972, pp. 459 ff.
25 In Alexandra, p. 197.
26 Ed. Murray-Brown, p. 143.
27 Ed. Murray-Brown, pp. 91–92.

CHAPTER 35

1 Dean, pp. 162–163.
2 Duncan, p. 116.
3 Dean, p. 162.
4 Alexandra, p. 109.
5 Wheeler-Bennett, p. 115.
6 Wheeler-Bennett, p. 116.
7 Quoted in Boothroyd, p. 167.
8 Alexandra, p. 109.
9 Alexandra, p. 110.
10 Alexandra, p. 110.
11 Alexandra, p. 111.
12 Quoted in Fisher, p. 145.
13 From an explanatory booklet published by the Variety Club of Great Britain.
14 *The British Barker*, November/December 1978.

CHAPTER 36

In preparing this chapter I drew on a number of reports and other publications issued by the London office of the Award Scheme. I am particularly grateful for the help provided by James Monahan of the London Headquarters.

1 Duncan, p. 116.
2 Duncan, pp. 116–117.
3 A letter from Mrs Cully to the author.
4 A letter from a former Lord Mayor of Bradford.
5 *The Award Journal*, No. 28, Issue 9, 1979.
6 A letter from Mrs Lily Caldecatt to the author.
7 A letter from Moira Kaye Madden to the author.

CHAPTER 37

I am grateful to James Orr, CVO, Secretary of the Medical Commission on Accident Prevention for allowing me to use several of the Reports of the Commission.

1 Windsor, 1951, p. 267.
2 Working Party on Accident Prevention and Life-Saving, 1961–63, p. 15.
3 Ibid., p. 15.
4 Ibid., p. 15.
5 Quoted in Duncan, p. 114.
6 Working Party, 1961–63, pp. 17–19.
7 A private conversation.

8 Working Party, 1961–63, pp. 3–6.
9 Ibid., p. 63.
10 Ibid., p. 5.
11 Preliminary Report of a Conference held at Ditchley Park, pp. 17–19.
12 Annual Report of the Medical Commission, May 1967, p. 16.
13 A speech made on 5th July 1968.

CHAPTER 38

1 Ed. Murray-Brown, p. 100.
2 Ibid., p. 101.
3 Diamond Jubilee dinner of the Wildfowlers Association, 9th July 1968.
4 In *New Scientist*, 18th January 1979.
5 Duncan, p. 109.
6 *The Environmental Revolution* quoted in the *New Scientist*, 18th January 1979.
7 Ibid.
8 Ibid.
9 Duncan, p. 109.

CHAPTER 39

1 Cathcart, 1973, pp. 149–150.
2 Boothroyd, p. 3.
3 Leitch, p. 141.
4 Leitch, p. 44.
5 Leitch, pp. 141–154.
6 Boothroyd, p. 45.
7 Lacey, p. 283 f.n.
8 Leitch, p. 137.

PART IX

CHAPTER 40

1 Seldon, p. 214.
2 Letter from Jon Ellison to the author, 8th January 1979.
3 Duncan, p. 40.
4 *Look*, 4th July 1964, quoted in Lacey, p. 283.
5 Hamilton, p. 11.
6 Seldon, p. 34.
7 Seldon, p. 34.
8 Seldon, p. 54.
9 Seldon, p. 70.
10 Quoted in Seldon, p. 79.
11 Seldon, p. 83.
12 Seldon, p. 87.
13–25 Appear in Seldon, pp. 204–216.
26 The *Daily Telegraph*, 25th January 1979.
27 Seldon, pp. 217–218.
28 Seldon, p. 218.
29 Letter from the President of the Guild of Toastmasters, 6th January 1979.

CHAPTER 41

1 In Boothroyd, p. 13.
2 Alexandra, p. 130.
3 Boothroyd, p. 197.
4 *See* p. 83.
5 Taylor, p. 690.
6 In Taylor, p. 815.
7 Ibid.
8 In Duncan, p. 42.
9 *Birmingham Post*, 11th July 1973.
10 *New Statesman*, 3rd June 1977.
11 *The Times* quoted in G. Moorhouse, *The Other England*, Penguin, 1964.
12 *The Scotsman*, 18th October 1979.
13 *See* p. 293.
14 *Time*, 2nd March 1961.

CHAPTER 42

1 Quoted in Duncan, pp. 171–172.
2 Quoted in Hamilton, p. 50.
3 Quoted in Hamilton, p. 67.
4 Quoted in Hamilton, p. 67.
5 Quoted in Lacey, p. 309.
6 Quoted in Hamilton, p. 45.
7 *Financial Times*, 3rd December 1971.
8 The *Guardian*, 11th December 1971.
9 *Hansard*, quoted in Lacey, p. 313.

AN INTERIM SUMMING UP

1 Duncan, xiii.
2 Ibid., p. 278.
3 Ed. Murray-Brown, pp. 91–92.
4 Ibid., p. 92.
5 Dixon, p. 196.
6 Ed. Murray-Brown, p. 82.

Index